SHORT STORY/SHORT FILM

SHORT STORY/
SHORT FILM

Fred H. Marcus

California State University, Los Angeles

PRENTICE-HALL, INC., *Englewood Cliffs, New Jersey* 07632

Library of Congress Cataloging in Publication Data

Marcus, Fred Harold, 1921–
  Short story/short film.

  Bibliography: p.
  1. Film adaptations. 2. Moving-pictures and
literature. I. Title.
PN1997.85.M27   791.43'7   76–28801
ISBN 0–13–809558–2

Printed in the United States of America

10 9 8 7 6 5 4 3 2 1

PRENTICE-HALL INTERNATIONAL, INC., *London*
PRENTICE-HALL OF AUSTRALIA PTY. LIMITED, *Sydney*
PRENTICE-HALL OF CANADA, LTD., *Toronto*
PRENTICE-HALL OF INDIA PRIVATE LIMITED, *New Delhi*
PRENTICE-HALL OF JAPAN, INC., *Tokyo*
PRENTICE-HALL OF SOUTHEAST ASIA PTE. LTD., *Singapore*
WHITEHALL BOOKS LIMITED, WELLINGTON, *New Zealand*

To Edie

Contents

Preface

Short Story/Short Film reflects a phenomenon of the past decade. For many years, the motion picture industry ransacked literary storehouses seeking sources for feature films. Only during the last ten years, however, have short films adapted from short stories become numerous enough and attained the quality necessary to merit serious academic study. Of the fifteen films represented by stories in this volume, seven were produced in the 1970s, five in the late 1960s, and only three more than ten years ago.

Most of these adaptations are quite short. None runs over thirty minutes. Eight run under twenty minutes. They fit comfortably into conventional classroom modules. The shorter films, particularly, lend themselves to a useful pedagogic process: they can be shown, analyzed, and reshown within a single period. Short films are also economical for schools to purchase and rent. These films range in cost from $100 to $375. Most rent for $25 or less. (A complete survey of all fifteen films appears on p. 431.)

Why conjoin film and fiction? Fiction is a form of artistically structured language designed to produce reader involvement. Fiction allows readers to augment their own experiences; it offers vicarious experience otherwise unattainable. The detailed study of short fiction helps a reader to identify the key concepts and crucial incidents in a story. It gives him greater insight into the ways in which a writer can organize and express the complexities of human behavior. The close textual study of fiction strengthens a student's ability to recognize important aspects of a writer's technique.

In essence, the study of film yields similar perceptual skills. For some contemporary students, watching a film may be more congenial than reading a story. Too often, however, viewing tends to be a passive activity. Learning *how* a film means may well be as original an experience as learning how to cope with fictional diversity. While students may float naturally and comfortably in the cinematic milieu, it does not follow that their aquatic thrashing has either fluidity or direction. But their usual willingness to shift from merely testing the waters to a purposeful charting of the stream augurs well.

Statistics published annually by the American Film Institute testify to the phenomenal growth of film courses and programs in colleges and universities. Nor is it surprising that English teachers increasingly link films to language and literature. Similarities between film and fiction as storytelling modes are apparent. Ironically, however, it is in the study of differences between the two media that students are most likely to learn more about how each medium works. Just as close textual study of a story is crucial to sharpening a student's literary perception, so close cinematic scrutiny is necessary to develop a student's sensitivity to the strategies and techniques of a filmmaker. The organization of *Short Story/Short Film* deliberately emphasizes and encourages close cinematic scrutiny.

The book is divided into six chapters. Chapter 1, "Film, Fiction, and Criticism," stresses some of the similarities of film and fiction as narrative modes. In addition, it examines the application of terms of literary criticism to the discussion of films. Chapter 2, "Film and Fiction: Contrasts in Media," analyzes significant differences between the two media. One part of this section focuses on how film and fiction express the passing of time. In Chapter 3, "Point of View and Tone in Film and Fiction," additional differences are discussed. In Chapter 4, "The Art of Animation," several short animated films illustrate key points. Chapter 5 contains five short stories but no film materials. The purpose here is to give the teacher and student greater flexibility. After the discipline of the earlier sections, the students may wish to develop their own film materials, using these stories as a basis. The final chapter, a series of appendices, adds information about the films studied in the book. One appendix lists awards received by the films; another lists the film distributors with their addresses. Still another suggests additional short films adapted from fiction. The final chapter is followed by a film glossary and a selective bibliography.

The first four chapters present ten short stories together with materials related to their film adaptations. There are six screenplays, four film continuities, two shot analyses, one storyboard, and two film treatments. Moreover, each of the ten story-film combinations is followed by questions and written exercises. The questions are intended to foster critical assessment of story and film details. They often focus on contrast-in-media examples and concepts, thus reinforcing the theoretical discussions that open each section. Suggestions for papers follow the questions for critical analysis. The writing calls for both critical and creative papers.

One major function of the first four chapters is to clarify the creative evolution of a film adapted from a short story. For example, Chapter 1 opens with Hawthorne's short story, *Young Goodman Brown*. This is followed by two screenplays written by the film director prior to shooting the film. After reading the screenplays, the student should view the film. Finally, there is a series of questions and suggestions for papers followed by a sample critique. There are five such sample contrast-in-media critiques; they not only shed light on the creative and critical processes of adaptation but also illustrate the kinds of writing expected of students. All but one of the critiques were written by students taking a contrast-in-media film/fiction course.

The creative process is viewed from another perspective in Chapter 2 which opens with *The Upturned Face* by Stephen Crane. After seeing the film, the student can refresh his memory of its details and sequences by referring to the shot analysis, a detailed description of the individual shots and dialogue of the film. Finally, the student reads an unproduced screenplay. He can then compare the film adaptation with the original story and assess the relative merits of the actual film with a proposed film which was never produced. Finally, there are again questions for critical evaluation and suggestions for papers. In Chapter 3, two sequential screenplays preceding the making of *The Open Window* allow students to see the director's mental processes *en route* to the filming. In Chapter 4, students read *The Legend of Sleepy Hollow*, examine two very different treatments proposed for the film, study an early storyboard, and then see the film itself. Once again, there are questions, suggestions for papers, and a sample of a student critique.

As indicated in the paragraph above, screenplays, treatments, and storyboards precede the making of a film. Film continuities and shot analyses are prepared after the film is complete. A film continuity describes the sequences of the finished film and includes the dialogue. A shot analysis is even more detailed; it describes each individual shot of the film. Both film continuities and shot analyses are very helpful in recalling a film to the mind's eye. They are verbal representations of the film. Because a motion picture moves so rapidly, it would probably be impossible for even a practiced viewer to reproduce its shots in exact sequential order. A shot analysis allows us to read a description of the skeleton of a film and to recall specific details. Film continuities and shot analyses serve another function. While a screenplay is a blueprint for a director, actual shooting of a film frequently results in changes from the screenplay. Therefore, a screenplay approximates the final picture; a shot analysis is usually a more accurate final description of the film itself.

The first four chapters all begin with discussions of theory and then present two or three short stories supplemented by film-related materials. Chapter 1 also contains three critiques of live-action films while Chapter 4 contains two contrast-in-media critiques of animated films. The discussions which begin each of the chapters are illustrated by many specific examples of film adaptations of fiction; most of these examples are drawn from the fifteen film and story combinations represented in this book. While *Short Story/Short Film* reproduces the fiction from which the film adaptations stem, it is important to recognize that the motion pictures themselves, if they are effective works of art, must necessarily be able to stand entirely on their own. It is, therefore, interesting to note that most of the films—ten out of fifteen—are multiple prize-winners, earning film festival acclaim both here and abroad. Two have won Academy Awards in the category of best live-action short films.

Throughout the book, the aim has been to engage the student's creative and critical powers to the end of discovering how films and fiction function as storytelling modes. To further assist the student, each story/film unit is prefaced by brief editorial comments on the story and the specific film adaptation linked to it. Thus, while more than one filmmaker has adapted Washington Irving's *The Legend of Sleepy Hollow* or Herman Melville's *Bartleby*, the materials in those units relate specifically to the 1972 Bosustow/Pyramid version of the Irving story and the 1969 adaptation of Melville's story by Encyclopaedia Britannica.

The heterogeneous materials gathered in this volume might have been assembled under an alternative title, *From Story to Screen: The Art of Adaptation*, to reflect one significant text function: the gathering together of materials that begin with a short story and culminate in a short film. Since many young filmmakers lose interest in the prefatory materials once the film exists, some desirable items could not be located. For example, it was not possible to obtain a screenplay for *The Upturned Face*; it would have been interesting to compare the screenplay of this film with the unproduced screenplay by Jim Stinson. In addition, limitations of space forced other deletions. In lieu of screenplays for *Bartleby* and *The Lady or the Tiger*, it was more expedient to substitute film continuities, which are appreciably shorter.

Finally, no collection of materials such as this ever comes into existence without owing a great deal to those who have cooperated in various ways. My greatest obligation must be to David Adams of Pyramid Films; his concern for quality films is revealed by the awards his films have garnered at film festivals everywhere. I also owe a substantial debt to Larry Yust whose adaptations and productions for Encyclopaedia Britannica launched their "Short Story Showcase" in 1969 and precipitated a major breakthrough for short films adapted from short stories. To my students, whose infectious enthusiasm never waned, I owe thanks, particularly since they were the first to sharpen their critical faculties on these contrast-in-media materials. Six of them are represented here. Four wrote contrast-in-media critiques, and two others, Bernadette Kornfeld and Patsy Sirrine, were largely responsible for the shot analyses and one of the film continuities. I am also indebted to Steve Bosustow, as fine a producer as one can find in the specialized field of film animation. For her encouragement and confidence, I am grateful to Marilyn Brauer. I also want to thank Fred Bernardi and Cynthia Miller for their highly professional editing of the manuscript. Finally, I owe a debt of gratitude to those critics who read the manuscript so scrupulously and whose suggestions proved so valuable. They will find evidences of their insights throughout the book.

Pasadena, California

F.H.M.

chapter 1

Film, Fiction, and Criticism

Fiction precedes film. This assertion is valid in two senses. First, fiction is a considerably older art form. Second, the very notion of adaptation necessarily presupposes the existence of a story. Despite fiction's greater maturity and more established role in the cultural mainstream of our society, studies reveal the primacy of pictures over print when both are measured quantitatively. The average American high school graduate has seen more than fifteen thousand hours of television and over five hundred films. He has spent less than twelve thousand hours in class.[1] How many books has a high school graduate read?

Given our image-oriented society, it is important that film be accorded a place with fiction as a serious art form. Fortunately, the two lend themselves to a study in tandem. Filmmakers consistently seek out literary sources for film adaptation. Film critics delight in comparing movies with their literary predecessors. Despite many significant differences between motion pictures and fiction as story-telling modes, their similarities deserve attention.

[1]John M. Culkin, "Film Study in the High School," *Catholic High School Quarterly Bulletin*, Vol. xxii, No. 3 (October, 1965), p. 1.

1

Film and Fiction: A Look at Likeness

The similarities of film and fiction far surpass those of film and drama. Unlike the fixed vantage point of a playgoer, the reader and filmgoer have views ranging from panoramic vistas to close-ups of exquisitely detailed particulars. The cameraman can focus on a leaf; the writer can describe its veining. But a playwright must resort to having an actor describe the leaf to the audience. In the film adaptation of "The Lottery," the camera focuses on the crowd from above and then zeroes in on a close-up of a tightly clenched fist gripping a piece of paper. Both writer and film director can alter our angles of vision or change the distances and perspectives from which we perceive the action.

Even the play's structural units, the scene and act, are substantially larger building blocks than the filmmaker's shots and sequences or the writer's sentences and paragraphs. Film and fiction can change locales more rapidly and more frequently than can a play. The stage curtain is a more cumbersome method of shifting scenes. While the stage director can increase flexibility by using separate areas of the stage as different "settings," he cannot risk confusing his viewers with too many rapid changes. His medium is subject to conventions which are different from those of film or fiction. In the manipulation of space, both film and fiction have greater flexibility. Film and fiction can also depict physical events in a way unavailable to the play. In "An Occurrence at Owl Creek Bridge," Ambrose Bierce describes Peyton Farquhar freeing himself underwater. The film adaptation graphically shows us the underwater sequence.

Neither the filmmaker nor the writer is limited by real space or real time. When a stage actor must cross from left to right, he is bound by physical laws of space and time. In "The Lottery" by Shirley Jackson, a single sentence whisks the reader through changes in space and time without the slightest discomfort:

> The night before the lottery, Mr. Summers and Mr. Graves made up the slips of paper and put them in the box, and it was then taken to the safe of Mr. Summer's coal company and locked up until Mr. Summers was ready to take it to the square next morning.

This sentence contains three different locales and several different points in time. Its context is also revealing; it occurs in the story immediately *after* the description of Mr. Summers stirring the papers inside the box on the morning of the lottery. In cinematic terms, the writer has given us a flashback.

A filmmaker has similar flexibility. In one shot, we see the actor board an airplane; the subsequent shot shows him exiting from his plane at some distant airport. Only within a single shot is the actor bound to real time and place. Through the editing process, time can be compressed or expanded. In *An Occurrence at Owl Creek Bridge*, we have shots of Peyton Farquhar swept over a waterfall, we see him emerging as a tiny speck on the screen further downstream, and we see him within easy reach of land in what seems to be a shallow bywater of the river. The cinematic time consumed by the sequence can be measured in seconds; real time for the events would be appreciably greater.

The units of a film are frame, shot, scene, and sequence; the elements of fiction are word, sentence, paragraph, and chapter (for the novel). Both the filmmaker's shot and the writer's sentence take on additional meaning from their contexts. In *The Late George Apley*, one sentence reads,

> I called on your Uncle William yesterday, who is very poorly; he asked after you particularly, and surprised me by saying that he liked you.

The full irony stems from the following sentence.

> His mind has been wandering a good deal of late.

Humor by judicious juxtaposition of shots is also available to the filmmaker. In *Modern Times*, Chaplin's opening shot shows a flock of sheep rushing across the screen. In the following shots, groups of workmen hectically run past the camera. The juxtaposition makes an analogy which is pointedly humorous.

Because film depends primarily on images and fiction depends on words, the two modes handle the concept of connotation differently, but both make extensive use of connotative techniques for shaping an audience's responses. In Ambrose Bierce's short story, "An Occurrence at Owl Creek Bridge," Peyton Farquhar is described as assenting to "the frankly villainous dictum that all is fair in love and war." The tonal quality of "frankly villainous" is negative. But it is the voice of the story's narrator, an omniscient voice undoubtedly reflecting Bierce's bias, that makes the judgment. By using this pejorative tone, Bierce has diluted any sympathy his readers might have for the protagonist. In film, techniques of lighting and angles of shooting serve similar editorial functions. Thus, in the screen adaptation of "The Unicorn in the

Garden," the wife is always shown in the dark while her husband always appears in the light; this is consistent with the filmmaker's attitudes toward the two characters.

Film and Fiction: The Language of Literary Criticism

Probably the most important similarity between film and fiction is the fact that both are storytelling modes. As a result, the language of literary criticism is readily adapted to the discussion of motion pictures. While the inherent limitations of a solely literary analysis of films must be avoided, the benefits of an existing and useful critical language cannot be ignored. In the following five paragraphs, you will find specific critical observations of short stories and films adapted from those stories. Common literary terms are italicized to show how easily such terms lend themselves to film criticism.

1. In the film adaptation of *The Masque of the Red Death,* many changes in *plot* occur. While Poe devotes only a single paragraph to a description of the Red Death's impact upon the lower classes before turning to Prince Prospero and the nobility, the filmmaker devotes a substantial segment of his film to lower-class victims. We see the plague ravaging the countryside; it destroys farm workers, craftsmen, and members of the clergy before sweeping on to the castle. Probably the most dramatic *plot* change occurs in the personification of Death as a woman. Despite the *plot* alterations, both story and film contain common *themes*. In each, we learn that death is no respecter of rank, and we note the inexorable march of time. While the short story utilizes the *symbol* of an ebony clock as the harbinger of death, the filmmaker uses the *symbol* of a pendulum for the same purpose.

2. In the film adaptation of *Bartleby,* the story's first-person *point of view* changes to a primarily third-person, omniscient camera *point of view*. The greater subjectivity of the story shifts to a more objective *point of view*. As a result, the *characterization* of Melville's lawyer-narrator is modified. It becomes easier for a film viewer to sympathize with the lawyer's difficulty in coping with Bartleby. Both film and short story make use of *symbols* to suggest Bartleby's isolation and alienation. However, the filmmaker neglects a

Bartleby (1969) "... the story's first person point of view changes to a primarily third person omniscient camera point of view." The face of the actor becomes the playing surface for characterization. *Still shot reproduced courtesy of Encyclopaedia Britannica Educational Corporation.*

crucial *structural* detail in his adaptation, Bartleby's alleged
employment in the Dead Letter Office in Washington, D.C.,
a detail strategically located at the very end of the story.
With this omission, the filmmaker makes Bartleby's highly
idiosyncratic behavior seem even more erratic. In the story,
the lawyer finally arrives at a rationalization which soothes
his conscience: Bartleby is "a man by nature and misfortune
prone to a pallid hopelessness." The implied predestination
frees the lawyer from his Christian obligation to be his
brother's keeper; the fault is in Bartleby, not in himself. An
additional inference flows from the Dead Letter Office detail:
both private employment and government employment tend
to be repetitive and destructive. Thus, one of Melville's
themes is a criticism of an age where mechanistic values tend
to take precedence over aesthetic ones. This view gains even
more strength if Bartleby, the scrivener, *symbolizes* Melville,
the writer.

3. In *Young Goodman Brown*, the filmmaker changes one *set-
    ting* of the story from the village of Salem to a sun-drenched
    hilltop. However, the contrast of *symbolic* locales so impor-
    tant in Hawthorne is maintained in the motion picture. The
    forest remains the *setting* for evil. One film limitation occurs
    in *characterization* of Young Goodman Brown. In the story,
    he intends to keep his appointment with the devil in the
    forest and still follow Faith to Heaven. He is guilty of *hubris*,
    that overweening pride that makes him feel secure in dallying
    with evil. His feeling of superiority is apparent in the way
    he behaves with Faith: he is condescending and self-confi-
    dent. At the end of the story, Young Goodman Brown's self-
    pride leads him to assume that he is competent to judge his
    fellow Puritans. For him, the ambiguity of the "dream" is
    no ambiguity. Thus, Hawthorne *ironically* parallels Young
    Goodman Brown's initial behavior with his later actions. In
    changing the *characterization* of Young Goodman Brown the
    filmmaker misses an important *theme*. Both film and story
    use the same basic *structure*. Both begin with a specific
    setting, move on to the forest sequences, and return to the
    original *setting*.

4. "The Lottery," by Shirley Jackson, achieves its effect in
    several ways. The central conflict in the story reveals the
    difficulty individuals face in confronting the conformist pat-

terns of a culture. Irrational traditions are maintained even
when those traditions have ceased to have meaning. While
this *theme* is not unusual in fiction—or film—the enormity
of stoning a woman to death looms as a monstrous contradiction in an apparently civilized society. The story *rhythm*
or *pace* also plays a crucial role in its impact on readers. It
begins quietly on a lovely summer day. Flowers are "blossoming profusely," and the grass is "richly green." Within this
idyllic *setting*, a horrible ritual unfolds. At midstory, the
pace begins to quicken and continues to increase to the very
end of the story. The physical paragraphing of the story
intensifies its *rhythm*. The opening paragraphs are long and
detailed; the closing paragraphs are short and staccato. The
film adaptation alters this *rhythm*. The movie opens with
a series of quick cuts and shots that immediately generate
tremors of apprehension in the audience. Because film unreels
at a fixed rate, an audience has less time for pondering the
implications of what is unfolding; instead, its uneasiness
increases as the film continues at a hectic *pace*. The film's
short length, eighteen minutes, contributes to maintaining
a high level of tension. In the film, the lottery's black box,
a fatal *symbol*, does not carry the same force as its literary
predecessor. The repetition of the words "black box" in the
story focuses the reader's attention on the adjective "black"
and its dire connotations. In the film, a close-up could achieve
a similar effect, but the director uses other methods to create
feelings of foreboding. In the film, the juxtaposition of a
contemporary *setting* with a primitive ritual shocks viewers
unfamiliar with the *plot* of the narrative. The story, with its
reference to "tractors," is also contemporary in time, but
the reader is less aware of its implication when the time-
signalling word occurs early in the *plot*.

5. In Ambrose Bierce's story, "An Occurrence at Owl Creek
    Bridge," the author's descriptive *style* plays a key role. At
    several points in the story, the descriptive language is par-
    ticularly poetic. Then, a harshly realistic statement undercuts
    the illusion created by the poetic language. Two specific
    examples illustrate this *stylistic* technique. A paragraph begins,

> He closed his eyes in order to fix his last thoughts upon
> his wife and children. The water, touched to gold by
> the early sun, the brooding mists . . . all had distracted

him. And now he became conscious of a new disturbance. Striking through the thought of his dear ones was
a sound which he could neither ignore nor understand,
a sharp, distinct, metallic percussion like the stroke of
a blacksmith's hammer upon the anvil; it had the same
ringing quality. . . . Its recurrence was regular, but as
slow as the tolling of a death knell.

The closing sentence of the paragraph returns us to reality:

What he heard was the ticking of his watch.

A second example occurs when Farquhar has apparently
escaped from his captors and been swept over the waterfall.

He dug his fingers into the sand. . . . It looked like
diamonds, rubies, emeralds; he could think of nothing
beautiful which it did not resemble. The trees upon
the bark were giant garden plants; he noted a definite
order in their arrangement, inhaled the fragrance of
their blooms. A strange, roseate light shone through
the spaces among their trunks and the wind made in
their branches the music of Aeolian harps. He had no
wish to perfect his escape—was content to remain in
that enchanting spot until retaken.

The next sentence destroys the mood:

A whiz and rattle of grapeshot among the branches
high above his head roused him from his dream.

These two examples parallel the pattern of the entire story.
What seems to be actual turns out to be illusory. Peyton
Farquhar's apparent escape is belied by the closing line of
the story. In the film adaptation, Robert Enrico uses a similar
stylistic structure. When Peyton Farquhar initially dreams
of his wife, a harsh voice saying, "Take his watch," disrupts
his escapist reverie. When Farquhar swims safely ashore, his
ecstasy is abruptly terminated with the explosion of a cannon
shot. At the end of the movie, as Farquhar and his wife reach
out to embrace, a final jolting sequence demolishes any illusion of escape. Because filmmakers often use slow motion
photography to suggest a poetic *tone,* it is not surprising to
find Enrico using slow motion in two of the above sequences.
In retrospect, slow motion becomes the *symbolic* equivalent
of illusionary events.

YOUNG GOODMAN BROWN

Nathaniel Hawthorne

Described by critics as a psychological realist who anticipated twentieth-century ideas Hawthorne wrote "Young Goodman Brown" in 1835. As in so many of his stories and novels, a preoccupation with Puritanism and its geographical locales leads him to probe human nature deeply. At least one story clue points to Hawthorne's feeling of guilt as a descendant of the infamous Judge Hathorne, a principal in the Salem witch trials.

"Young Goodman Brown" poses a particularly cinematic problem for the filmmaker: using a reality-oriented medium to capture the deliberate ambiguities of the writer.

The film was released in 1973 and has won a number of film festival awards. Directed by Don Fox, a young filmmaker working at the American Film Institute, it was shot in the redwoods of northern California. Two quite different screenplays show the changes that occurred from the time of Fox's original conception to the final form of the film. The changes between the second screenplay and the film merit particular critical attention.

Young Goodman Brown came forth at sunset into the street at Salem village; but put his head back, after crossing the threshold, to exchange a parting kiss with his young wife. And Faith, as the wife was aptly named, thrust her own pretty head into the street, letting the wind play with the pink ribbons of her cap while she called to Goodman Brown.

"Dearest heart," whispered she, softly and rather sadly, when her lips were close to his ear, "prithee put off your journey until sunrise and sleep in your own bed to-night. A lone woman is troubled with such thoughts that she's afeared of herself sometimes. Pray tarry with me this night, dear husband, of all nights in the year."

"My love and my Faith," replied young Goodman Brown, "of all nights in the year, this one night must I tarry away from thee. My journey, as thou callest it, forth and back again, must needs be done 'twixt now and sunrise. What, my sweet, pretty wife, dost thou doubt me already, and we but three months married?"

"Then God bless you!" said Faith, with the pink ribbons; "and may you find all well when you come back."

"Amen!" cried Goodman Brown. "Say thy prayers, dear Faith, and go to bed at dusk, and no harm will come to thee."

So they parted; and the young man pursued his way until, being about to turn the corner by the meeting-house, he looked back and saw the head of Faith still peeping after him with a melancholy air, in spite of her pink ribbons.

"Poor little Faith!" thought he, for his heart smote him. "What a wretch am I to leave her on such an errand! She talks of dreams, too. Methought as she spoke there was trouble in her face, as if a dream had warned her what work is to be done to-night. But no, no; 't would kill her to think it. Well, she's a blessed angel on earth; and after this one night I'll cling to her skirts and follow her to heaven."

With this excellent resolve for the future, Goodman Brown felt himself justified in making more haste on his present evil purpose. He had taken a dreary road, darkened by all the gloomiest trees of the forest, which barely stood aside to let the narrow path creep through, and closed immediately behind. It was all as lonely as could be; and there is this peculiarity in such a solitude, that the traveller knows not who may be concealed by the innumerable trunks and the thick boughs overhead; so that with lonely footsteps he may yet be passing through an unseen multitude.

"There may be a devilish Indian behind every tree," said Goodman Brown to himself; and he glanced fearfully behind him as he added, "What if the devil himself should be at my very elbow!"

His head being turned back, he passed a crook of the road, and, looking forward again, beheld the figure of a man, in grave and decent attire, seated at the foot of an old tree. He arose at Goodman Brown's approach and walked onward side by side with him.

"You are late, Goodman Brown," said he. "The clock of the Old South was striking as I came through Boston, and that is full fifteen minutes agone."

"Faith kept me back a while," replied the young man, with a tremor in his voice, caused by the sudden appearance of his companion, though not wholly unexpected.

It was now deep dusk in the forest; and deepest in that part of it where these two were journeying. As nearly as could be discerned, the second traveller was about fifty years old, apparently in the same rank of life as Goodman Brown, and bearing a considerable resemblance to him, though perhaps more in expression than features. Still they might have been taken for father and son. And yet, though the elder person was as simply clad as the younger, and as simple in manner too, he had an indescribable air of one who knew the world, and who would not have felt abashed at the governor's dinner table or in King William's court, were it possible that his affairs should call him thither. But the only thing about him that could be fixed upon as remarkable was his staff, which bore the likeness of a great black snake, so curiously wrought that it might almost be seen to twist and wriggle itself like a living serpent. This, of course, must have been an ocular deception, assisted by the uncertain light.

"Come, Goodman Brown," cried his fellow-traveller, "this is a dull pace for the beginning of a journey. Take my staff, if you are so soon weary."

"Friend," said the other, exchanging his slow pace for a full stop, "having kept covenant by meeting thee here, it is my purpose now to return whence I came. I have scruples touching the matter thou wot'st of."

"Sayest thou so?" replied he of the serpent, smiling apart. "Let us walk on, nevertheless, reasoning as we go; and if I convince thee not thou shalt turn back. We are but a little way in the forest yet."

"Too far! too far!" exclaimed the goodman, unconsciously resuming his walk. "My father never went into the woods on such an errand, nor his father before him. We have been a race of honest men and good Christians since the days of the martyrs; and shall I be the first of the name of Brown that ever took this path and kept—"

"Such company, thou wouldst say," observed the elder person, interpreting his pause. "Well said, Goodman Brown! I have been as well acquainted with your family as with ever a one among the Puritans; and that's no trifle to say. I helped your grandfather, the constable, when he lashed the Quaker woman so smartly through the streets of Salem; and it was I that brought your father a pitch-pine knot, kindled at my own hearth, to set fire to an Indian village, in King Philip's war. They were my good friends, both; and many a pleasant walk have we had along this path, and returned merrily after midnight. I would fain be friends with you for their sake."

"If it be as thou sayest," replied Goodman Brown, "I marvel they never spoke of these matters; or, verily, I marvel not, seeing that the least rumor of the sort would have driven them from New England. We are a people of prayer, and good works to boot, and abide no such wickedness."

"Wickedness or not," said the traveller with the twisted staff, "I have a very general acquaintance here in New England. The deacons of many a church have drunk the communion wine with me; the select-men of divers towns make me their chairman; and a majority of the Great and General Court are firm supporters of my interest. The governor and I, too—But these are state secrets."

"Can this be so?" cried Goodman Brown, with a stare of amazement at his undisturbed companion. "Howbeit, I have nothing to do with the governor and council; they have their own ways, and are no rule for a simple husbandman like me. But, were I to go on with thee, how should I meet the eye of that good old man, our minister, at Salem village? Oh, his voice would make me tremble both Sabbath day and lecture day."

Thus far the elder traveller had listened with due gravity; but now burst into a fit of irrepressible mirth, shaking himself so violently that his snakelike staff actually seemed to wriggle in sympathy.

"Ha! ha! ha!" shouted he again and again; then composing himself, "Well, go on, Goodman Brown, go on; but, prithee, don't kill me with laughing."

"Well, then, to end the matter at once," said Goodman Brown, considerably nettled, "there is my wife, Faith. It would break her dear little heart; and I'd rather break my own."

"Nay, if that be the case," answered the other, "e'en go thy ways, Goodman Brown. I would not for twenty old women like the one hobbling before us that Faith should come to any harm."

As he spoke he pointed his staff at a female figure on the path, in whom Goodman Brown recognized a very pious and exemplary dame, who had taught him his catechism in youth, and was still his moral and spiritual adviser, jointly with the minister and Deacon Gookin.

"A marvel, truly, that Goody Cloyse should be so far in the wilderness at nightfall," said he. "But with your leave, friend, I shall take a cut through the woods until we have left this Christian woman behind. Being a stranger to you, she might ask whom I was consorting with and whither I was going."

"Be it so," said his fellow-traveller. "Betake you the woods, and let me keep the path."

Accordingly the young man turned aside, but took care to watch his companion, who advanced softly along the road until he had come within a staff's length of the old dame. She, meanwhile, was making the best of her way, with singular speed for so aged a woman, and mumbling some indistinct words—a prayer, doubtless—as she went. The traveller put forth his staff and touched her withered neck with what seemed the serpent's tail.

"The devil!" screamed the pious old lady.

"Then Goody Cloyse knows her old friend?" observed the traveller, confronting her and leaning on his writhing stick.

"Ah, forsooth, and is it your worship indeed?" cried the good dame. "Yea, truly is it, and in the very image of my old gossip, Goodman Brown, the grandfather of the silly fellow that now is. But—would your worship believe it?—my broomstick hath strangely disappeared, stolen, as I suspect, by that unhanged witch, Goody Cory, and that, too, when I was all anointed with the juice of smallage, and cinquefoil, and wolf's bane—"

"Mingled with fine wheat and the fat of a new-born babe," said the shape of old Goodman Brown.

"Ah, your worship knows the recipe," cried the old lady, cackling aloud. "So, as I was saying, being all ready for the meeting, and no horse to ride on, I made up my mind to foot it; for they tell me there is a nice young man to be taken into communion to-night. But now your good worship will lend me your arm, and we shall be there in a twinkling.

"That can hardly be," answered her friend. "I may not spare you my arm, Goody Cloyse; but here is my staff, if you will."

So saying, he threw it down at her feet, where, perhaps, it assumed life, being one of the rods which its owner had formerly lent to the Egyptian magi. Of this fact, however, Goodman Brown could not take cognizance. He had cast up his eyes in astonishment, and, looking down again, beheld neither Goody Cloyse nor the serpentine staff, but his fellow-traveller alone, who waited for him as calmly as if nothing had happened.

"That old woman taught me my catechism," said the young man; and there was a world of meaning in this simple comment.

They continued to walk onward, while the elder traveller exhorted his companion to make good speed and persevere in the path, discoursing so aptly that his arguments seemed rather to spring up in the bosom of his auditor than to be suggested by himself. As they went, he plucked a branch of maple to serve for a walking stick, and began to strip it of the twigs and little boughs, which were wet with evening dew. The moment his fingers touched them they became strangely withered and dried up as with a week's sunshine. Thus the pair proceeded, at a good free pace, until suddenly, in a gloomy hollow of the road, Goodman Brown sat himself down on the stump of a tree and refused to go any farther.

"Friend," said he, stubbornly, "my mind is made up. Not another step will I budge on this errand. What if a wretched old woman do choose to go to the devil when I thought she was going to heaven: is that any reason why I should quit my dear Faith and go after her?"

"You will think better of this by and by," said his acquaintance, composedly. "Sit here and rest yourself a while; and when you feel like moving again, there is my staff to help you along."

Without more words, he threw his companion the maple stick, and was as speedily out of sight as if he had vanished into the deepening gloom. The young man sat a few moments by the roadside, applauding himself greatly, and thinking with how clear a conscience he should meet the minister in his morning walk, nor shrink from the eye of good old Deacon Gookin. And what calm sleep would be his that very night, which was to have been spent so wickedly, but so purely and sweetly now, in the arms of Faith! Amidst these pleasant and praiseworthy meditations, Goodman Brown heard the tramp of horses along the road, and deemed it advisable to conceal himself within the verge of the forest, conscious of the guilty purpose that had brought him thither, though now so happily turned from it.

On came the hoof tramps and the voices of the riders, two grave old voices, conversing soberly as they drew near. These mingled sounds appeared to pass along the road, within a few yards of the young man's hiding-place; but, owing doubtless to the depth of the gloom at that particular spot, neither the travellers nor their steeds were visible. Though their figures brushed the small boughs by the wayside, it could not be seen that they intercepted, even for a moment, the faint gleam from the strip of bright sky athwart which they must have passed. Goodman Brown alternately crouched and stood on tiptoe, pulling aside the branches and thrusting forth his head as far as he durst without discerning so much as a shadow. It vexed him the more, because he could have sworn, were such a thing possible, that he recognized the voices of the minister and Deacon Gookin, jogging along quietly, as they were wont to do, when bound to some ordination or ecclesiastical council. While yet within hearing, one of the riders stopped to pluck a switch.

"Of the two, reverend sir," said the voice like the deacon's, "I had rather miss an ordination dinner than to-night's meeting. They tell me that some of our community are to be here from Falmouth and beyond, and others from Connecticut and Rhode Island, besides several of the Indian powwows, who, after their fashion, know almost as much deviltry as the best of us. Moreover, there is a goodly young woman to be taken into communion."

"Mighty well, Deacon Gookin!" replied the solemn old tones of the minister. "Spur up, or we shall be late. Nothing can be done, you know, until I get on the ground."

The hoofs clattered again; and the voices, talking so strangely in the empty air, passed on through the forest, where no church had ever been gathered or solitary Christian prayed. Whither, then, could these holy men be journeying so deep into the heathen wilderness? Young Goodman Brown caught hold of a tree for support, being ready to sink down on the ground, faint and overburdened with the heavy sickness of his heart. He looked up to the sky, doubting whether there really was a heaven above him. Yet there was the blue arch, and the stars brightening in it.

"With heaven above and Faith below, I will yet stand firm against the devil!" cried Goodman Brown.

While he still gazed upward into the deep arch of the firmament and had lifted his hands to pray, a cloud, though no wind was stirring, hurried across the zenith and hid the brightening stars. The blue sky was still visible, except directly overhead, where this black mass of cloud was sweeping swiftly northward. Aloft in the air, as if from the depths of the cloud, came a confused and doubtful sound of voices. Once the listener fancied that he could distinguish the accents of townspeople of his own, men and women, both pious and ungodly, many of whom he had met at the communion table, and had seen others rioting at the tavern. The next moment, so indistinct were the sounds, he doubted whether he had heard aught but the murmur of the old forest, whispering without a wind. Then came a stronger swell of those familiar tones, heard daily in the sunshine at Salem village, but never until now from a cloud of night. There was one voice, of a young woman, uttering lamentations, yet with an uncertain sorrow, and entreating for some favor, which, perhaps, it would grieve her to obtain; and all the unseen multitude, both saints and sinners, seemed to encourage her onward.

"Faith!" shouted Goodman Brown, in a voice of agony and desperation; and the echoes of the forest mocked him, crying, "Faith! Faith!" as if bewildered wretches were seeking her all through the wilderness.

The cry of grief, rage, and terror was yet piercing the night, when the unhappy husband held his breath for a response. There was a scream, drowned immediately in a louder murmur of voices, fading into far-off laughter, as the dark cloud swept away, leaving the clear and silent sky above Goodman Brown. But something fluttered lightly down through the air and caught on the branch of a tree. The young man seized it, and beheld a pink ribbon.

"My Faith is gone!" cried he, after one stupefied moment. "There is no good on earth; and sin is but a name. Come, devil; for to thee is this world given."

And, maddened with despair, so that he laughed loud and long, did Goodman Brown grasp his staff and set forth again, at such a rate that he seemed to fly along the forest path rather than to walk or run. The road grew wilder and drearier and more faintly traced, and vanished at length, leaving him in the heart of the dark wilderness, still rushing onward with the instinct that guides mortal man to evil. The whole forest was peopled with frightful sounds—the creaking of the trees, the howling of wild beasts, and the yell of Indians; while sometimes the wind tolled like a distant church bell, and sometimes gave a broad roar around the traveller, as if all Nature were laughing him to scorn. But he was himself the chief horror of the scene, and shrank not from its other horrors.

"Ha! ha! ha!" roared Goodman Brown when the wind laughed at him. "Let us hear which will laugh loudest. Think not to frighten me with your deviltry. Come witch, come wizard, come Indian powwow, come devil himself, and here comes Goodman Brown. You may as well fear him as he fear you."

In truth, all through the haunted forest there could be nothing more frightful than the figure of Goodman Brown. On he flew among the black pines, brandishing his staff with frenzied gestures, now giving vent to an inspiration of horrid blasphemy, and now shouting forth such laughter as set all the echoes of the forest laughing like demons around him. The fiend in his own shape is less hideous than when he rages in the breast of man. Thus sped the demoniac on his course, until, quivering among the trees, he saw a red light before him, as when the felled trunks and branches of a clearing have been set on fire, and throw up their lurid blaze against the sky, at the hour of midnight. He paused, in a lull of the tempest that had driven him onward, and heard the swell of what seemed a hymn, rolling solemnly from a distance with the weight of many voices. He knew the tune; it was a familiar one in the choir of the village meeting-house. The verse died heavily away, and was lengthened by a chorus, not of human voices, but of all the sounds of the benighted wilderness pealing in awful harmony together. Goodman Brown cried out, and his cry was lost to his own ear by its unison with the cry of the desert.

In the interval of silence he stole forward until the light glared full upon his eyes. At one extremity of an open space, hemmed in by the dark wall of the forest, arose a rock, bearing some rude, natural resemblance either to an altar or a pulpit, and surrounded by four blazing pines, their tops aflame, their stems untouched, like candles at an evening meeting. The mass of foliage that had overgrown the summit of the rock was all on fire, blazing high into the night and fitfully illuminating the whole field. Each pendent twig and leafy festoon was in a blaze. As the red light arose and fell, a numerous congregation alternately shone forth, then disappeared in shadow, and again grew, as it were, out of the darkness, peopling the heart of the solitary woods at once.

"A grave and dark-clad company," quoth Goodman Brown.

In truth they were such. Among them, quivering to and fro between gloom and splendor, appeared faces that would be seen next day at the council board of the province, and others which, Sabbath after Sabbath, looked devoutly heavenward, and benignantly over the crowded pews, from the holiest pulpits in the land. Some affirm that the lady of the governor was there. At least there were high dames well known to her, and wives of honored husbands, and widows, a great multitude, and ancient maidens, all of excellent repute, and fair young girls, who trembled lest their mothers should espy them. Either the sudden gleams of light flashing over the obscure field bedazzled Goodman Brown, or he recognized a score of the church members of Salem village famous for their especial sanctity. Good old Deacon Gookin had arrived, and waited at the skirts of that venerable saint, his revered pastor. But, irreverently consorting with these grave, reputable, and pious people, these elders of the church, these chaste dames and dewy virgins, there were men of dissolute lives and women of spotted fame, wretches given over to all mean and filthy vice, and suspected even of horrid crimes. It was strange to see that the good shrank not from the wicked, nor were the sinners abashed by the saints. Scattered also among their pale-faced enemies were the Indian priests, or powwows, who had often scared their native forest with more hideous incantations than any known to English witchcraft.

"But where is Faith?" thought Goodman Brown; and, as hope came into his heart, he trembled.

Another verse of the hymn arose, a slow and mournful strain, such as the pious love, but joined to words which expressed all that our nature can conceive of sin, and darkly hinted at far more. Unfathomable to mere mortals is the lore of fiends. Verse after verse was sung; and still the chorus of the desert swelled between like the deepest tone of a mighty organ; and with the final peal of that dreadful anthem there came a sound, as if the roaring wind, the rushing streams, the howling beasts, and every other voice of the unconcerted wilderness were mingling and according with the voice of guilty man in homage to the prince of all. The four blazing pines threw up a loftier flame, and obscurely discovered shapes and visages of horror on the smoke wreaths above the impious assembly. At the same moment the fire on the rock shot redly forth and formed a glowing arch above its base, where now appeared a figure. With reverence be it spoken, the figure bore no slight similitude, both in garb and manner, to some grave divine of the New England churches.

"Bring forth the converts!" cried a voice that echoed through the field and rolled into the forest.

At the word, Goodman Brown stepped forth from the shadow of the trees and approached the congregation, with whom he felt a loathful brotherhood by the sympathy of all that was wicked in his heart. He could have well-nigh sworn that the shape of his own dead father beckoned him to advance, looking downward from a smoke wreath, while a woman, with dim features of despair, threw out her hand to warn him back. Was it his mother? But he had no power to retreat one step, nor to resist, even in thought, when the minister and good old Deacon Gookin seized his arms and led him to the blazing rock. Thither came also the slender form of a veiled female, led between Goody Cloyse, that pious teacher of the catechism, and Martha Carrier, who had received the devil's promise to be queen of hell. A rampant hag was she. And there stood the proselytes beneath the canopy of fire.

"Welcome, my children," said the dark figure, "to the communion of your race. Ye have found thus young your nature and your destiny. My children, look behind you!"

They turned; and flashing forth, as it were, in a sheet of flame, the fiend worshippers were seen; the smile of welcome gleamed darkly on every visage.

"There," resumed the sable form, "are all whom ye have reverenced from youth. Ye deemed them holier than yourselves, and shrank from your own sin, contrasting it with their lives of righteousness and prayerful aspirations heavenward. Yet here are they all in my worshipping assembly. This night it shall be granted you to know their secret deeds: how hoary-bearded elders of the church have whispered wanton words to the young maids of their households; how many a woman, eager for widows' weeds, has given her husband a drink at bedtime and let him sleep his last sleep in her bosom; how beardless youths have made haste to inherit their fathers' wealth; and how fair damsels —blush not, sweet ones—have dug little graves in the garden, and bidden me, the sole guest, to an infant's funeral. By the sympathy of your human hearts for sin ye shall scent out all the places—whether in church, bed-chamber, street, field, or forest—where crime has been committed, and shall exult to behold the whole earth one stain of guilt, one mighty blood spot. Far more than this. It shall be yours to penetrate, in every bosom, the deep mystery of sin, the fountain of all wicked arts, and which inexhaustibly supplies more evil impulses than human power—than my power at its utmost—can make manifest in deeds. And now, my children, look upon each other."

They did so; and, by the blaze of the hell-kindled torches, the wretched man beheld his Faith, and the wife her husband, trembling before that unhallowed altar.

"Lo, there ye stand, my children," said the figure, in a deep and solemn tone, almost sad with its despairing awfulness, as if his once angelic nature could yet mourn for our miserable race. "Depending upon one another's hearts, ye had still hoped that virtue were not all a dream.

Now are ye undeceived. Evil is the nature of mankind. Evil must be your only happiness. Welcome again, my children, to the communion of your race."

"Welcome," repeated the fiend worshippers, in one cry of despair and triumph.

And there they stood, the only pair, as it seemed, who were yet hesitating on the verge of wickedness in this dark world. A basin was hollowed, naturally, in the rock. Did it contain water, reddened by the lurid light? or was it blood? or, perchance, a liquid flame? Herein did the shape of evil dip his hand and prepare to lay the mark of baptism upon their foreheads, that they might be partakers of the mystery of sin, more conscious of the secret guilt of others, both in deed and thought, than they could now be of their own. The husband cast one look at his pale wife, and Faith at him. What polluted wretches would the next glance show them to each other, shuddering alike at what they disclosed and what they saw!

"Faith! Faith!" cried the husband, "look up to heaven, and resist the wicked one."

Whether Faith obeyed he knew not. Hardly had he spoken when he found himself amid calm night and solitude, listening to a roar of the wind which died heavily away through the forest. He staggered against the rock, and felt it chill and damp; while a hanging twig, that had been all on fire, besprinkled his cheek with the coldest dew.

The next morning young Goodman Brown came slowly into the street of Salem village, staring around him like a bewildered man. The good old minister was taking a walk along the graveyard to get an appetite for breakfast and meditate his sermon, and bestowed a blessing, as he passed, on Goodman Brown. He shrank from the venerable saint as if to avoid an anathema. Old Deacon Gookin was at domestic worship, and the holy words of his prayer were heard through the open window. "What God doth the wizard pray to?" quoth Goodman Brown. Goody Cloyse, that excellent old Christian, stood in the early sunshine at her own lattice, catechizing a little girl who had brought her a pint of morning's milk. Goodman Brown snatched away the child as from the grasp of the fiend himself. Turning the corner by the meeting-house, he spied the head of Faith, with the pink ribbons, gazing anxiously forth, and bursting into such joy at sight of him that she skipped along the street and almost kissed her husband before the whole village. But Goodman Brown looked sternly and sadly into her face, and passed on without a greeting.

Had Goodman Brown fallen asleep in the forest and only dreamed a wild dream of a witch-meeting?

Be it so if you will; but, alas! it was a dream of evil omen for

young Goodman Brown. A stern, a sad, a darkly meditative, a distrustful, if not a desperate man did he become from the night of that
fearful dream. On the Sabbath day, when the congregation were singing
a holy psalm, he could not listen because an anthem of sin rushed loudly
upon his ear and drowned all the blessed strain. When the minister
spoke from the pulpit with power and fervid eloquence, and, with his
hand on the open Bible, of the sacred truths of our religion, and of
saint-like lives and triumphant deaths, and of future bliss or misery
unutterable, then did Goodman Brown turn pale, dreading lest the roof
should thunder down upon the gray blasphemer and his hearers. Often,
awaking suddenly at midnight, he shrank from the bosom of Faith; and
at morning or eventide, when the family knelt down at prayer, he
scowled and muttered to himself, and gazed sternly at his wife, and
turned away. And when he had lived long, and was borne to his grave
a hoary corpse, followed by Faith, an aged woman, and children and
grandchildren, a goodly procession, besides neighbors not a few, they
carved no hopeful verse upon his tombstone, for his dying hour was
gloom.

screenplay
YOUNG GOODMAN BROWN
Donald Fox

FADE IN:
EXTERIOR, VILLAGE; DAY.
In the quiet stillness of the late afternoon, crows can be heard cawing
far away. In the distance is the village of Salem as it existed in the late
17th century. One small house is seen among the others. The door
opens and Goodman Brown steps out. But then he puts his head back
to give his young wife, Faith, a parting kiss. As he turns to go, she puts
her head out of the doorway and calls to him.

FAITH
Dear, put off your journey until sunrise and stay in your own
bed tonight. A lone woman is troubled with such dreams and

thoughts that she's afraid of herself sometimes. Stay with me
this night of all nights.

GOODMAN

Sweet love, of all nights in the year, this one night must I
stay away. My journey must be done between now and
sunrise.

She grabs hold of him, fearing that something terrible might happen.

GOODMAN

What my young wife, do you doubt me already, and we but
three months married?

FAITH

Then God bless you! And may you find all well when you
come back.

GOODMAN

Amen! Say your prayers, dear Faith, and go to bed at dusk,
and no harm will come to you.

So they part, and Goodman goes his own way until he is about to
turn the corner by the meeting house. There he turns back and sees the
head of Faith still peeping after him. Seeing her, he quickly turns and
walks down the street towards the forest.

HILLS AND FIELDS; SUNSET.

Goodman is seen walking across the bleak landscape as the sky grows
darker.

FOREST; SUNSET.

Goodman is now walking across a large field which lies near a large,
dense forest. His pace increases as he nears it. For a moment he is
afraid, but he plunges into the gloom and walks on.

At this time, the forest is bathed in a dim and diffused light; the massive
trees, dense foliage, and narrow path give the place a foreboding appearance. Goodman looks around as he walks, as if half-expecting someone
or something to jump out of the bushes at him. Every little sound makes
him more uneasy. He is passing a particularly gloomy hollow when he
hears a screech from above and looks up. Seeing nothing, he looks back
down and discovers a man standing before him. The sudden appearance
of the man makes Goodman very nervous.

MAN

You are late, Goodman Brown. The clock of the Old South
Church was striking as I came through Boston, and that is
a full fifteen minutes ago.

GOODMAN

Faith kept me back a while.

As they go, Goodman looks at the man. The man is about fifty years
old and is dressed in an older style of clothing than Goodman. The
man carries a crooked staff that looks something like a large black
snake. He points it around as he talks. Goodman immediately takes an
interest in it.

At this time of day, the forest is lighted very faintly by the light of
deep dusk. The two travelers are tiny specks as they walk among the
giant pines of the forest. The man continues to be very friendly and
cheerful, in spite of the dreary quality of the journey. It is almost as
if he is putting on an act to make Goodman more at ease. Goodman is
aware that something about the man makes him uneasy but thinks no
further about it.

As they walk on, Goodman continues to keep to himself, glancing at
the staff or the man's face and then suddenly back to the path ahead.
The sounds, the gloomy appearance of the forest as it grows wilder and
more sinister, and the presence of the old man become overpower-
ingly oppressive. He is uncomfortable; he wishes he could go back.
As they continue, he becomes more uneasy, and his pace begins to
slow until he is behind. The man, who has not been taking much notice
of him, does not notice that Goodman has fallen behind him. Then, as
he turns to Goodman, he sees that he is not at his side.

MAN

Come, Goodman Brown, this is a slow pace and we have only
started. Take my staff, if you are so soon weary.

GOODMAN

Old man, I have kept my promise by meeting you here. I
wish to turn back.

MAN

You do? (pause) Tell me, why?

GOODMAN

I have scruples touching this matter.

The man seems amused by Goodman's remarks and puts his hand on Goodman's shoulder and leads him onward.

MAN

Let us walk on, nevertheless, reasoning as we go; and if I convince you not you shall turn back. We are but a little way in the forest yet.

Goodman becomes alarmed at this remark but absentmindedly continues walking along.

GOODMAN

Too far! too far! My father never went into the woods on such an errand, nor his father before him. We have been a race of honest men and good Christians since the days of the martyrs; and shall I be the first of the name of Brown that ever took this path and kept—

The man takes the staff in both his hands and points it at himself.

MAN

Such company, you would say. Well said, Goodman Brown! I have been as well acquainted with your family as ever a one among the Puritans; and that's no trifle to say. I helped your grandfather, the constable, when he lashed the Quaker woman so smartly through the streets of Salem; and it was I that brought your father a pitch-pine knot, kindled at my own hearth, to set fire to an Indian village, in King Philip's war. They were my good friends, both; and many a pleasant walk have we had along this path, and returned merrily after midnight. I would fain be friends with you for their sake.

Goodman is now becoming more intrigued by the man. The man draws him on. He quickens his pace and Goodman follows. But Goodman is still a bit suspicious as he thinks over what the man has just said.

GOODMAN

I marvel they never spoke of these matters. We are a people of prayer, and good works to boot, and abide no such wickedness.

MAN

Wickedness or not, I have a very general acquaintance here in New England. The deacons of many a church have drunk the communion wine with me; and the selectment of divers

towns make me their chairman; and a majority of the Great
and General Court are firm supporters of my interest. And
as for the Governor—

Goodman almost stops when he hears this; he is awed by the man.

GOODMAN

Is this true? How could you know them?

MAN

Do not worry; you shall meet them soon enough.

Amazed, Goodman continues staring for a moment, but then he looks
away, saddened, as if something troubling him has just come to mind.
The man looks concerned for the first time.

MAN

What is it?

Goodman is too embarrassed to answer.

MAN

What is wrong?

GOODMAN

It is the reverend. If I went on with you, how should I ever
look him in the face?

All of this time the man has been fairly serious, with perhaps a smile
or two on his face, but now he breaks out in hysterics, and his pace
slows down to a mere crawl.

MAN

What? Our Reverend Henderson? Well, go on, Goodman
Brown, go on; but don't kill me with laughing.

Goodman is now really embarrassed, and does not know what to say.
For a moment there is complete silence.

GOODMAN

Well, there is my wife to think of. It would break her heart
if she knew I were here.

The man stops laughing and becomes serious.

MAN

If that be the case, then go your own way, Goodman Brown.
I would not for twenty old women like the one hobbling
before us that Faith should come to any harm.

The man points his staff down the path towards Goody Cloyse, who is hobbling quickly away from them at a short distance. Realizing who she is, Goodman becomes troubled.

GOODMAN

A marvel, truly, that Goody Cloyse should be so far in the wilderness at nightfall. It's best she not see me here.

MAN

Be it so.

Goodman hides behind the bushes along the path and follows the man as he walks towards the old woman. She is moving down the path at a much faster rate than an old person normally walks. She is mumbling something to herself as she goes. When the man gets close enough, he raises his staff and pokes her on the back of the neck with it. She screams.

GOODY

The devil!

MAN

Then Goody Cloyse knows her old friend?

She turns around, relieved at the man's sight.

GOODY

Ah, forsooth, and is it your worship indeed? Yea, truly is it, and in the very image of my old friend, Goodman Brown, the grandfather of the silly fellow that now is.

The man stands, leaning on his staff, smiling to himself at her animated character and listening to her talk.

GOODY

But would your worship believe it—my stick hath strangely disappeared, stolen, as I suspect, by that unhanged witch, Goody Cory, and that, too, when I was all anointed with the juice of smallage, cinquefoil, and wolfsbane—

The man smiles at her.

MAN

Mingled with fine wheat and the fat of a new-born babe—

GOODY

Ah, your worship knows the recipe! So, as I was saying, being already for the meeting, and no horse to ride on, I

made up my mind to foot it; for they tell me there is a nice
young man to be taken into communion tonight.

She takes his arm as they begin walking down the path.

GOODY

But now your good worship will lend me your arm, and we
shall be there in a twinkling.

The man takes his arm away from hers.

MAN

That can hardly be. I may not spare you my arm, Goody
Closye; but here is my staff, if you will.

He throws the staff at her feet. Goodman looks on, hearing a strange
sound of shifting leaves, as if the staff were moving like a snake. When
he looks up to the man, he finds Goody gone with the staff. Goodman
stares for a moment, and then comes slowly out of the bushes, looking
as glum as ever.

GOODMAN

That old woman taught me my catechism.

They continue to walk along. Once in a while they exchange glances,
but mostly they keep to themselves. The man stops after a time to pick
a maple branch. When his hand touches the branch, the branch turns
black and the leaves curl up and fall off. As they walk, he strips off
the little twigs. Goodman looks over after a time. He is surprised to
see that the man has now produced a new staff, looking exactly like
the one he had earlier.

All this time, Goodman continues to mull over what has happened. He
looks depressed, and once more his pace begins to slow. Not wanting
him to fall back again, the man turns to him.

MAN

What's the matter?

Goodman stops and sits down on a tree stump in the gloomy hollow.

GOODMAN

Old man, my mind is made up. Not another step will I budge
on this errand.

The man does not seem to be troubled by this remark.

MAN

You will think better of this by and by. Sit here and rest

yourself a while; and when you feel like moving again, there is my staff to help you along.

Without saying more, he hands Goodman the staff and walks quickly out of sight. Goodman is relieved that the man is gone. He sits there for a moment, thinking how nice it will be to go back to the village. Then suddenly he hears the tramp of horses moving down the path. Alarmed, he hides behind some bushes.

EXTERIOR, FOREST; NIGHT.

Soon the tramping becomes louder, and Goodman crouches lower so as not to be seen. Then he hears someone speaking. He is startled when he recognizes the two people speaking as the reverend and the deacon. He looks up and sees both of them on horseback, and he becomes quite disturbed. He looks on as they talk.

DEACON

Of the two, my Reverend Henderson, I had rather miss an ordination dinner than tonight's meeting. They tell me that some of our community are going to be here from Falmouth and beyond, besides several of the Indian priests, who, after their fashion, know almost as much deviltry as the best of us. Moreover, there is a goodly young woman to be taken into communion.

REVEREND

Mighty well, Deacon Gookin! Spur up, or we shall be late. Nothing can be done, you know, until I get on the ground.

The horses' hoofs clatter on until their sound disappears into the gloom. Goodman is again by himself and is utterly shattered by what those two pious old men said. About to collapse, he catches hold of a tree for support; he hears a strange sound and looks up into the sky, which is bright with stars and a full moon.

As he looks up, he sees a dark cloud pass in front of the moon and stars. Although there is no wind, the cloud continues to move across the dark blue sky, which is still visible, except directly overhead where the black mass is sweeping swiftly northward.

High overhead, as if from the depths of the cloud, comes the sound of far off voices, combined with a strange kind of chanting sound. At first these sounds are indistinct; but as the sky grows darker, they become louder. Soon a strange, ethereal choral music grows out of the other sounds.

Goodman is at first surprised to hear sounds that seem to be voices distorted in a strange way. Then he becomes uneasy. It seems that the voices are those of his fellow villagers, but he is not sure. The sounds begin to die away and then grow louder.

One sound becomes predominant: it is a woman crying and laughing hysterically. The other voices seem to be encouraging her on to some unknown fate.

FAITH

Please, oh God, no!

When Goodman realizes that it is his Faith who is crying out, he becomes upset and shouts out.

GOODMAN

Faith!

His cry reverberates throughout the forest and gradually dies out in the distance. He looks up with an expression of utter disillusionment as he hears Faith scream. Her scream is immediately muffled in a drone of laughter that follows. Then the laughter begins to fade as the cloud starts passing from overhead and moving away.

Goodman is completely numbed. Then something flutters down from the sky and rests lightly on a branch near him. He quickly grabs the pink ribbon that his wife had worn earlier in the day and cries hysterically.

GOODMAN

My Faith is gone!

Maddened with despair, he grabs the staff and runs off down the path in the direction that the man took earlier.

He runs as fast as he can, holding out the staff. In the distance is heard the sound of mournful bells pealing, as if tolling for a funeral. As he runs, the forest suddenly changes color from the dull, dark green to a red color that shines in all the foliage. He looks around him, bewildered. The sounds of the forest, the howls of animals, screams of birds, rustle of leaves, and the sound of the wind merge into a strange reverberating sound that comes from all around him. On he runs, until he suddenly sees a red light glowing in the distance through the trees.

Suddenly the color of the forest darkens and returns to its normal hue. Goodman stops and looks into the distance where he can see the red glow of a fire burning. He walks slowly on towards the light. As he goes, he hears a hymn, rolling solemnly from the distance with the weight of many voices. It is a familiar tune. The hymn dies away and is followed by a chorus, not of human voices, but of all the sounds of the forest pealing together. The sound is so terrifying that Goodman cries out, but his cry is drowned out by the sounds.

Finally, in an interval of silence, he comes forward until the red light is full upon his face. He is standing at the edge of a clearing in the forest. At the other end of the clearing stands a large rock which resembles a crude altar or pulpit. Surrounding the rock are four pine trees with their tops on fire, like candles. The summit of the rock is also on fire, and its light illuminates the whole field.

To Goodman's surprise, there are people standing out on the field. As the light rises and falls, he can make out his fellow villagers. He sees those whom he has known to be very pious, as well as individuals who are known to be evil and ungodly. He sees the deacon standing, talking with Goody Cloyse. He looks around again but does not see Faith.

Then all of a sudden, the rock shoots up a higher flame and a rumbling sound can be heard coming from the bowels of the earth. Goodman is terrified. As the rumbling becomes louder, a light appears at the top of the rock. The disk of light begins rising over the top of the rock. Goodman looks up, feeling as if the end of the world were upon him. At the top, a figure can be seen growing larger as the disk of light rises higher. Finally the figure is silhouetted against the light. Over the top, high in the sky, a light burns.

In a stern and powerful reverberating voice that sounds like thunder from the sky, the figure speaks to his followers.

FIGURE
Bring forth the converts!

Trembling with fear, Goodman steps forward out of the shadow of a tree and approaches the congregation. Suddenly, the deacon and the constable grab him by the arms and lead him to the rock. As he is being led out, he sees a veiled woman also being taken out to the rock. He recognizes Faith. She is led by Goody Cloyse and another old woman. Beneath the roaring fire, they stand.

FIGURE
Welcome, my children to the communion of your race. Ye have found thus young your nature and your destiny. My children, look behind you!

Goodman and Faith both turn around. Through sheets of flame, they see their fellow villagers. A dark, welcoming smile is on each face.

FIGURE

There are all whom ye have reverenced from your youth. Ye
deemed them holier than yourselves, and shrank from your
own sin. Yet here are they all in my worshipping assembly.
This night it shall be granted you to know their secret deeds;

Goodman and Faith have turned back toward the figure. Goodman is
utterly terrified. But Faith is completely hypnotized by the figure and
his speech. She looks at him in awe. The figure wears a hood to protect
his face from the light. Nothing of his face can be seen in the shadow
of the hood.

FIGURE (cont'd)

how elders of the church have whispered words to the maids
of their households, and how many a woman, eager for widows' weeds, has given her husband a drink at bedtime and let
him sleep his last sleep. By the sympathy of your human
hearts for sin ye shall scent out all places where crime has
been committed, and shall exult to behold the whole earth
one stain of guilt, one spot of blood. Far more than this. It
shall be yours to penetrate, in every soul, the deep mystery of
sin. And now, my children, look upon each other.

Goodman and Faith look at each other.

FIGURE

Lo, there ye stand, my children. Depending upon one another's hearts, ye had still hoped that virtue were not all a
dream. Now are ye undeceived. Evil is the nature of mankind.
Evil must be your only happiness. Welcome again, my children, to the communion of your race.

CHORUS

Welcome!

After the chorus cries out, the figure dips its hands into a basin in the
rock which is filled with a liquid flame. Then he descends from the rock
and towards the pair. As he approaches to lay the mark of baptism on
their foreheads, Goodman tries to get Faith's attention by shaking her,
but she is hopelessly entranced by the figure. Goodman is now completely petrified as the figure is almost before him. The fire in the sky
burns all around them as the figure stretches out his hand to lay the
mark on Goodman's forehead. Suddenly Goodman jumps over and
tears the hood away, revealing the reverend under it. Goodman screams
out.

GOODMAN

Faith! Faith! Look up to heaven, and resist the wicked one.

The fire flashes up around him, and everything explodes into light.

EXTERIOR, FOREST; DAY.

Over the top of a hill, the sun rises into the sky in a gigantic ball of fire. The forest is very quiet as the sun rises higher into the sky. Goodman is sitting by a small stream in the forest. He is in a trance, staring at the sun which is reflected in the water. The water sparkles and dances in glittering patterns of light. Coming around, he looks over to the sun shining through the leaves of the trees. Mist is drifting through the forest. Seeing it, he gets up and walks away.

EXTERIOR, VILLAGE; DAY.

Goodman is seen walking into the village. He looks around him like a bewildered man. The reverend is taking a morning's walk by the cemetery, and bestows a blessing on Goodman as he passes. Goodman walks quickly on, without saying a word, staring at the reverend oddly. The reverend is puzzled by this strange behavior. As he passes the church, Goodman hears the deacon at domestic worship. He hurries past this area and towards his house. He sees Goody Cloyse digging in her yard, and she is happy to see Goodman.

GOODY

Good morning, Goodman Brown.

Goodman rushes on by without saying anything. Goody is also puzzled. Finally Goodman turns the corner by the meeting house and sees Faith, who is anxiously looking for him. Seeing him, she bursts into cries of joy and runs to him. Unaware of his angry mood, she embraces him, but he pushes her aside and walks on without saying so much as a word. She stands there for a moment and then turns to follow him.

END

screenplay

YOUNG GOODMAN BROWN

Donald Fox and William Phelps

FADE IN:

EXTERIOR, FOREST; DAY.

Late afternoon; the sun, just above some distant hills, shines faintly through thick clouds. It is a damp and dark day and a coastal fog hangs in thin, still layers above the ground. A slight breeze breaks this calm and blows the mist away from a barren hilltop, revealing a group of people silhouetted against the evening sky. They are gathered about a lone tree.

Roped to a small, gnarled oak is a wild-looking woman in her late twenties. Her face has a haunted, terrified look; her peasant dress is in tatters. Mud and bramble scratches cover her legs and arms. She watches a man dressed in drab, Puritan work clothes and a greying, unruly wig shovel out a small hole in the earth before her. Her eyes shift to another man shaving the bark off a five-foot log with a long knife. She looks again to two or three men chopping and gathering up wood in a large pile. All these people are dressed in the clothes of 17th century New England. They are all devout, simple Puritans, members of the community of Salem. Busily engaged in their tasks, they pay no attention to the young woman's suffering.

The young woman looks further down the hill. Some of the townsfolk are leaving, but others stay. Her attention is attracted to a handsome young couple standing off in the distance. They are conversing with a matronly older woman, Goody Cloyse.

The man is Young Goodman Brown, a lean, quiet farmer in his mid-twenties. His pretty, hardy wife is Faith. They listen politely, but nervously, to the older woman speak. She gestures to the woman tied to the tree.

CLOYSE

They chased her through the woods and found her deep within a clearing. She was dancing wildly about, as if she

Young Goodman Brown (1973) "... devout, simple Puritans ... they pay no attention to the young woman's suffering." What the writer tells the film-maker must show. *Still shot reproduced courtesy of Pyramid films.*

was possessed. Strange music played, coming from the trees themselves, so the Constable tells me. Proof enough, I say. (She stops, and looks them both over with a smile.) My but you two are looking nice together. (Pause) Well, good day.

FAITH

Good day, Goody Cloyse.

The older woman turns and leaves. She has made Brown and his wife ill at ease. After a moment, Brown picks up his leather satchel, as if he is also leaving. Faith is disturbed.

FAITH

So soon?

BROWN

Yes.

He turns from her to go and she follows him down the path that leads from the hill. Further down the path the deacon is approaching them. Brown does not want to meet him, but he cannot avoid it.

DEACON

Good evening, Goodman Brown.

BROWN

Good evening.

DEACON

It shall be a blessing to see that witch go to the flames in the morning. (Pause) You will be here for that?

BROWN

It is expected. (Pause) Come Faith.

Brown and Faith turn away from the Deacon and walk down the path. When they are finally away from the execution area, Brown stops and gives Faith a parting kiss. He then turns to go, but she becomes more melancholy and calls after him.

FAITH

Please—

Brown turns around to face her.

FAITH

Put off your journey until sunrise and stay with me tonight.

I've been troubled with such dreams and thoughts that I'm afraid to be alone.

BROWN

Faith, of all nights in the year, I must stay away tonight. My journey must be done between now and sunrise.

FAITH

Please stay!

BROWN

You can't keep me back—it's already been decided. I cannot turn away now!

FAITH

But what if the devil himself should be in those woods! Pray give this up and sleep with me tonight.

BROWN

I can't. I must go or I'll be late.

FAITH

Please—

Faith grabs Brown. He is more on edge now, trying to get away. Then she turns towards the witch on the hill. He looks in the same direction.

FAITH

They found her in the forest. (Pause) They say there's something in those woods, something dark—black as the pit itself!

Brown gives her a strange, dark smile.

BROWN

Then I hope I find it!

FAITH

Don't say such things. Don't go.

He blows up.

BROWN

Woman I've had enough! Do you doubt me so soon, and we but three months married?

Faith looks away saddened, almost in tears. Her pink ribbons flutter in the wind. Brown becomes a bit embarrassed by this and is about to turn away.

FAITH

Then God bless you, Goodman Brown! And may you find all
well when you come back.

BROWN

Amen! Say your prayers and go to bed at dusk and no harm
will come to you. Have the reverend take you home. You will
be safe with him.

Brown turns and walks quickly down the path towards the forest in
the distance. As he walks, he passes the constable walking toward the
execution grounds. The constable greets Brown with a dark, gloomy
expression, and Brown hurries by. As he is about to descend the hill,
he looks back and sees Faith still looking at him with a sad expression
on her face. Seeing this, he turns quickly around and walks on down
the hill.

HILLS AND FIELDS; SUNSET.

Brown is seen walking across the bleak landscape as the sky grows
darker.

FOREST; LATE AFTERNOON.

Brown is walking through a treeless field covered with a growth of high
grass. At the end of the field is a wall of trees, marking the beginning
of a forest.

He enters through an opening in the trees. The trees have massive
trunks, and at this point are spaced fairly far apart. Late afternoon
light slants through at a low angle, and shadows of the redwood boughs
are cast on the forest floor. Goodman Brown begins to relax, enjoying
the beauty of the forest. Doves call to each other from their perches.
Suddenly a low voice calls to him from behind.

MAN (Voice-Over)

You are late, Goodman Brown.

Goodman Brown turns around and is surprised to see a Man leaning
against a thick redwood trunk. He holds a birch staff in his hand.
The Man pushes himself away from the tree and slowly walks toward
Brown.

MAN

The clock of the Old South Church was striking as I came
through Boston, and that is a full fifteen minutes ago.

The Man puts his arm around Brown's shoulder, guiding him forward.

BROWN

Faith kept me back a while.

Brown looks at the staff, strangely wrought and black; it looks like a snake. They walk on a ways until the path takes a turn.

At the turn, the broad footpath becomes a narrow rut, with dense shrubbery making the passage difficult. The forest thickens, the leafy boughs blocking out more of the remaining sunlight. Instead of doves, a pair of crows caw. Brown slows his pace and looks uncertainly at the path ahead.

MAN

Come, Goodman Brown, this is a slow pace and we have only started.

The Man resumes his pace. After a couple of steps he looks over his shoulder. Brown has fallen back again.

MAN

Take my staff, if you are so soon weary.

He turns and offers his staff, but Brown refuses.

BROWN

I have kept my promise by meeting you here. I wish to turn back!

MAN (amused)

You do? (Pause) Tell me, why?

Brown does not move. He lowers his eyes, unable to meet the Man's piercing stare.

BROWN

I—I—have scruples—concerning these matters.

The Man smiles comfortingly. He walks back toward Brown and puts his hand on his shoulder.

MAN

Is that so?

He guides him forward again.

MAN

Let us walk on, nevertheless, reasoning as we go.

The Man slashes away at some overhanging vines with his staff.

MAN

And if I don't convince you, why then, you shall turn back.
We are but a little way in the forest yet.

Any semblance of the path disappears. They are totally in shade.

BROWN

Too far!

The Man does not pay attention, but continues hacking through the
brush.

BROWN

My father never went into the woods for such a purpose,
nor his father before him. We have been a race of honest
men and good Christians—

The Man stops slashing, but still keeps his back to Brown.

BROWN

—and shall I be the first to break this tradition by keeping—

The Man turns around and looks Brown coolly in the eye.

MAN

Such company, you would say.

The brush has been cleared away, and the passage is free. The Man
walks back, dropping behind Brown. He now stands directly behind him.

MAN

Well said, Goodman Brown. But I have known your family
for quite some time now.

He pushes him forward through the cleared section. The path widens
and is free of brush. The sun breaks through the trees and the doves
are heard again.

MAN

When your father and grandfather were in need I helped
them both.

He looks at Brown, his face smug and knowing. Brown is fascinated.

MAN

They were my good friends; and many a pleasant walk did
we have along this path—returning merrily after midnight.
For their sake—

The Man smiles.

MAN

I would like to be your friend.

They walk on. The sky is red, the sun nearly down.

BROWN

I marvel they never spoke of these matters. But we are a people of prayer and goodworks. We do not abide such wickedness.

MAN

Wickedness or not, I'm well liked here in New England. The very best members of the church have drunk communion wine with me, and so have the judges of the General Court. And as for the governor—

The Man stops, cautioning himself.

MAN

—oh, but these are state secrets.

The Man resumes walking. The forest thickens once more, and the sky darkens. The sun is setting.

BROWN (afraid)

Is this true? How could you know them?

MAN

Don't worry, Goodman Brown; you shall meet them soon enough.

Brown stops, adamantly refusing to move forward.

BROWN

If I go, how could I look the reverend in the face?

The Man explodes with mocking laughter.

MAN

What? Our Reverend Henderson? Well, go on, Goodman Brown, go on; but please don't kill me with laughing.

They both stand, facing each other.

BROWN (strongly)

Then there is my wife to think of. It would break her heart if she knew . . .

The Man is serious and full of false compassion.

MAN

If that be the case, then go your own way, Goodman Brown.
I would not want Faith to come to any harm.

Goodman Brown nods, then turns away to leave. Down the path he
sees an old woman hobbling forward. The woman's eyes are on the
ground and she does not see Brown.

BROWN

That old woman may know me. It's best she not see me here.

He looks to the Man for confirmation.

MAN

So be it.

Brown disappears into the bushes. The Man stands by the path's side.
The old woman is perturbed, mumbling angrily to herself. She is
looking at the ground and does not see the Man. She walks a few
steps past him. The Man creeps up behind and touches her on the
shoulder.

CLOYSE

The devil!

She spins around, surprised.

MAN

Then Goody Cloyse knows her old friend?

She sits down on a low stump, relieved. She takes a moment to catch
her breath.

CLOYSE

And is it your worship indeed?

She sees that it is.

CLOYSE

Yes it is. And in the very image of my old friend, Goodman
Brown, the grandfather of the silly young fellow.

The Man folds his hands over the head of his staff, amused by the
old woman's babble.

CLOYSE

But would your worship believe it? My stick hath strangely

disappeared, stolen, as I suspect, by that unhanged witch, Goody Cory, and that too, when I was all anointed with the juice of smallage, cinquefoil, and wolfsbane—

MAN

Mingled with fine wheat and the fat of a new-born babe—

She screeches with laughter. Goodman Brown peers out from behind a bush, amazed.

CLOYSE

Ah, your worship knows the recipe! So, as I was saying, being all ready for the meeting, and no horse to ride on, I made up my mind to foot it; for they tell me there is a nice young man to be taken into communion tonight.

She stands up, now rested, and takes the Man's arm.

CLOYSE

But now your good worship will lend me your arm, and we shall be there in a twinkling.

The Man pulls his arm away from her, still smiling.

MAN

I'm sorry, Goody Cloyse, that cannot be. I may not spare you my arm, but here is my staff, if you will.

He gives her the staff. She beams her appreciation.

CLOYSE

Ah, your worship is too kind to an old woman.

Grabbing the stick, she walks down the path.

When Goodman Brown emerges from his hiding place, she is gone. Brown is amazed that she is out of sight so quickly.

The Man is breaking a sturdy young branch off a tree.

Brown walks up to the Man. The Man has finished tearing loose the branch, and Goodman Brown is surprised to see that the branch is already dried and withered.

MAN (explaining)

I do not like to be without a staff. There may be some need for one.

BROWN

Goody Cloyse is already gone.

The Man laughs.

> MAN
>
> So she is!

He starts moving forward.

> MAN
>
> But come, we must hurry. There is a great company to be met.

The forest becomes nearly impenetrable. Using the new staff, the Man flays away at the twisted growth.

> MAN
>
> In our communion, the great and small join together as one. They are alike and equal. (Pause) You should appreciate this, Goodman Brown.

Animals wail in wild confusion. The walk is uphill, over rocky terrain. The growth is dense and they walk in near darkness.

Concerned, Brown falls back. The Man looks around.

> MAN
>
> What's the matter?

Goodman Brown stops and stares at him for a moment. Gaining courage, he turns around and walks away.

> MAN (shouting)
>
> Don't turn back now!

Brown shouts back, his voice filled with conviction. He has turned to face the Man.

> BROWN
>
> I've made up my mind. I'm going back.

But the Man freezes him with his stare. Abject, Brown sinks to his knees. The Man moves downhill towards him.

> BROWN
>
> Please—let me be.

> MAN (gently)
>
> Don't worry. You will think better of this—soon enough.
>
> Sit here and rest yourself awhile.

Brown squats back on his heels, his face turned to the earth.

MAN

And when you feel like moving again, here is my staff to help you along.

He thrusts the staff into the ground before Brown. The staff quivers from the violent force. Upon impact, all forest sounds die. The silence is deafening.

Goodman Brown looks up, but there is no one there. Then a strange thing happens. The staff slowly falls forward, until its head is but a foot above the ground. It beckons him.

Brown stands up, and moves toward the magic stick. He takes it in his hands, uncertain of what to do. He is fascinated by it. As he ponders the stick, he hears the tramp of horses moving up the rocky path towards him. Becoming frightened, he rushes towards the bush by the side of the path and hides out of sight.

Soon the peculiar laugh of Deacon Gookin is heard piercing through the forest. Brown looks puzzled once more as he hears two old men talking to one another. Cautiously looking over the bushes he sees the Deacon and the Reverend riding down the path on horseback.

REVEREND

It is not my custom to speculate, sir, especially on the choices you have offered.

DEACON (laughs again)

Well, of the two, reverend sir, if I had to choose, I'd rather miss an ordination dinner than tonight's meeting.

REVEREND

They tell me that some of our community are to be here from Falmouth and beyond.

DEACON

I heard, too, that there is a goodly young woman to be taken into communion.

REVEREND

That's good, Deacon Gookin. Let's hurry or we shall be late. Nothing can be done, you know, until I get on the ground.

DEACON

Yes, reverend sir.

They pass on out of sight as Brown looks on, completely shaken by the experience. He does not know what to think after seeing those pious old men talking about the meeting. Finally the sounds of the horses and their laughter disappear into the gloom, and Brown is again by himself. He is about to collapse but catches hold of a tree for support; he hears a strange sound from above and looks up into the sky, which is bright with stars and a full moon.

As he looks up, he sees a dark cloud pass in front of the moon and stars. Although there is no wind, the cloud continues to move across the dark blue sky, which is still visible, except directly overhead where the black mass is sweeping swiftly northward.

High in the air, as if from the depths of the cloud, comes the sound of far-off voices, combined with a strange kind of chanting sound. At first these sounds are indistinct; but as the sky grows darker, they become louder. Soon a strange, ethereal choral music grows out of the other sounds.

Brown is at first surprised to hear sounds that seem to be voices, but distorted in a strange way. He becomes uneasy at hearing these sounds. It seems to him that the voices are those of his fellow villagers, but he is not sure. The sounds begin to die away and then become louder.

Out of these sounds comes another: it is a woman crying and laughing hysterically. The other voices seem to be encouraging her on to some unknown fate.

VOICES

Be not afraid—we will help—Come with us—Come—come —have no fear—we will help—come with us—

FAITH

Please, oh God, no!

VOICES

Come with us—no fear—come—

When Brown realizes that it is his Faith who is crying out, he becomes crazed and shouts out.

BROWN

Faith!

His cry reverberates throughout the forest and gradually dies out in the distance. He looks up with an expression of utter disillusionment as he hears Faith scream. Her scream is immediately muffled in a drone of laughter that follows. Then the laughter begins to fade as the cloud passes from overhead.

Goodman is completely numbed. Then something flutters down from the sky and rests lightly on a branch near him. He quickly grabs the pink ribbon that his wife had worn earlier in the day and cries out hysterically. He puts the ribbon in his pocket.

BROWN

My Faith is gone!

Maddened with despair, he grabs the staff and runs off down the path in the direction of the cloud.

He runs as fast as he can, holding out the staff. In the distance is heard the sound of mournful bells pealing. As he runs, the forest suddenly changes color from dull, dark green to brilliant red. He looks around, bewildered. The sounds of the forest, the howls of animals, screams of birds, rustle of leaves, and the sound of the wind, merge into a strange reverberating sound that comes from all around him. On he rushes, using the staff to slash through the brush.

Suddenly the sounds of the forest fade away, and the faint sound of singing is heard. The hymn-like melody sung by many voices rises in intensity and then falls away as Brown stops running and walks slowly on toward the source of this song. The red color of the forest has also faded away. A fire is burning in the forest, somewhere in the distance. He walks towards the fire. It begins to fade away into the darkness of the forest as he continues on. As he walks, he hears the singing get louder again. Finally he comes to a clearing in the forest.

CLEARING; NIGHT.

The clearing is lighted in the deep blue light of the moon. Brown can see a number of people standing at the other end, holding torches. Looking more closely, Brown can make out many of the people he saw on the hill earlier in the day. He can see Goody Cloyse, the deacon, and the constable there. There are rich-looking people mixing with people who seem like beggars. Above and behind a huge rock rises some one hundred feet into the air. Below the rock stands a smaller outcropping that looks something like a pulpit. Brown cannot make out exactly what is going on at the rock's base, but there seems to be some kind of activity. Several robed figures are performing a ceremony as the people chant incantations.

Brown becomes a bit uneasy at what he sees. All of a sudden he hears several voices shout out.

VOICES

He's ready!

Then a loud rumbling sound is heard coming from the very bowels of the earth. Brown is completely terrified of the sound and begins stepping back from the clearing. As he turns around, he sees four robed and hooded figures standing in front of him. He does not know what to do. He stands there almost paralyzed. They approach him, take hold of his arms, and lead him out into the clearing. As they walk, Brown looks up and sees the rock looming awesomely above him.

As he watches, a dim light begins slowly moving up behind the rock. Out in the clearing, the four men give Brown over to the deacon and the constable. They hold him as he watches the light at the top of the rock grow brighter. At first he sees light rays emerging from behind the rock. They are terribly bright. Then a disk of light begins rising over the top of the rock. Brown continues looking up, feeling as if the end of the world were upon him. At the top, a figure can be seen growing larger as the disk of light rises higher. Finally the figure is silhouetted against the light. Over the top, high in the sky, a fire burns. In a stern and powerfully reverberating voice that sounds like thunder from the sky, the figure speaks to his followers.

FIGURE

Bring forth the converts!

Trembling with fear, Brown is conducted forward by the deacon and the constable. He sees Faith being led by Goody Cloyse and another woman. Finally they all arrive beneath the rock. The figure has now descended the higher rock and is standing on a smaller one, not far from them.

FIGURE

Who sponsoreth this man into our unholy baptism?

DEACON AND CONSTABLE

We do.

They both step away from Brown. The figure turns to the three women on the other side.

FIGURE

Who sponsoreth this woman into our unholy baptism?

CLOYSE AND WOMAN

We do.

They step back from Faith. Only Brown and Faith remain before the rocky pulpit.

FIGURE

Welcome, my children to the communion of your race. You have now found your nature and your destiny. My children, look behind you!

Brown and Faith both turn around. Through sheets of flame, they see their fellow villagers. There is a dark, welcoming smile on each of their faces.

FIGURE

They are all whom you have reverenced from your youth. You thought them holier than yourselves, and shrank from your own sins. Yet here are they all in my worshipping assembly. This night it shall be granted you to know their secret deeds.

Brown is utterly terrified of the figure. But Faith is completely hypnotized by him and his speech. She looks at him in awe. The figure wears a hood to protect his face from the light. Nothing of his face can be seen in the shadow of the hood.

FIGURE

By the sympathy of your human hearts for sin you shall scent out all places where crime has been committed, and shall exult to behold the whole earth one stain of guilt, one spot of blood. Far more than this. It shall be yours to penetrate, in every soul, the deep mystery of sin. And now, my children, look upon each other.

Brown and Faith look at each other. The figure's tone of speech changes to one of solemnity, almost despairingly sad.

FIGURE

Lo, there you stand, my children. You depended upon one another's heart, hoping that virtue were not all a dream. Now you are undeceived. Evil is the nature of mankind. Evil must be your only happiness. Welcome again, my children, to the communion of your race.

CHORUS

Welcome!

After the chorus cries out, the figure dips its hands into the basin in the rock which is filled with a liquid flame. Then he descends from the rock and approaches the pair. As he approaches to lay the mark of baptism on their foreheads, Brown tries to get Faith's attention by shaking her, but she is hopelessly entranced by the figure. Brown is now completely petrified, and the figure is almost before him. The fire in the sky burns all around them as the figure stretches out his burning hand to lay the mark on Brown's forehead. Suddenly Brown jumps over and tears the hood away, revealing the reverend under it. Brown screams to Faith.

BROWN
Faith! Look to heaven and resist the evil one!

The fire flashes up around him, and everything explodes into light.

EXTERIOR, FOREST; DAY.

Over the top of a hill, the sun rises into the sky in a gigantic ball of fire. Brown is seated on the bank of a small stream. The image of the sun reflected in the brook's shallow water fascinates him. He dips his hand in the water and touches the spot where the sun's light glints. Its iciness revives him, and he rises to his feet.

FIELD; DAY.

Brown leaves the edge of the forest and enters the field. He walks quickly. In the distance he sees the hill where the witch is being burnt. His pace quickens.

HILL; DAY.

With a sense of urgency, Brown climbs the hillside. When he gets a full view of the scene he stops, stunned. The fire is almost out, but the embers still glow brilliantly. Smoke swirls up from the damp wood. Standing before the fire, the Reverend leads a small group in incantations. The dull chanting of their voices is barely heard. The Constable stands at the rear of the group, closest to Brown. Sensing Brown's presence, he turns as Brown approaches.

CONSTABLE
A pity you are late, Goodman Brown.

Brown does not acknowledge the Constable and moves on by. He sees Faith on the other side of the hill, beyond the burning. From behind him as he walks, the Deacon approaches.

DEACON
Justice has been done, my friend.

But Brown does not stop or look at the Deacon. His eyes are fixed on Faith. She is looking at the fire, unaware of his approach.

Brown continues toward his young wife. It is a long walk. He passes Goody Cloyse.

CLOYSE
We missed you, Goodman Brown.

Brown moves by, as if he has not heard her. He steps up to Faith, who now sees him. She looks at him demurely, an unreadable expression on her face. His attention is attracted by the pink ribbon, perfectly set in her hair. His hand reaches out, almost touching the ribbon.

But he halts. He shifts his gaze to his belt, to the place where he hung the pink ribbon he found the night before. It is not there.

At that moment, the chanting of Christian verses subtly changes into the chants he heard at the devil's sabbath the night before.

He looks back up at his wife. Her sad eyes are fixed on him. The chants of the sabbath change back to the Christian verse. Puzzled, he looks from Faith to the fire again.

Through the smoke, he sees the charred bones and seared flesh of the burnt witch. The Reverend continues his chant in a dull, monotonous tone.

Bewildered, but trying to contain his fright, he looks back to his wife. But she is looking at the fire.

He walks away.

Faith remains in the foreground, looking at the fire. The Reverend continues leading the others in chanting the litany for the witch's soul.

THE END

YOUNG GOODMAN BROWN
QUESTIONS

1. One approach to Hawthorne's "Young Goodman Brown" focuses on the *hubris* of the protagonist. What evidence in the story supports this approach? To what extent has the filmmaker based his adaptation on this approach?

2. Compare and contrast the dominant point of vieiw in the story with the point of view employed by the filmmaker.

3. In what significant way is the incident of Goody Cloyse in the

forest treated differently by Nathaniel Hawthorne and the film-maker?

4. Two conflicting interpretations of Nathaniel Hawthorne's story center on the reality or unreality of Young Goodman Brown's experience in the forest. What story evidence implies dream? What evidence refutes dream? What film evidence supports or denies the belief that Young Goodman Brown had a dream while in the forest?

5. The film was shot in the redwoods of California. Does this locale affect the viewer's reaction to the film? Explain.

6. Much of Hawthorne's symbolism depends on color imagery. Give several examples of color imagery in the story; then, analyze the filmmaker's use of color symbolism.

7. Settings play a significant part in Hawthorne's story. In a film the landscape often has a major role. In the film version of *Young Goodman Brown*, the two most significant locations are the forest where the devil's communion occurs and the hilltop where the woman has been burned. Compare the way the filmmaker shoots his scenes at these sites.

8. Filmmakers must create concrete visuals to communicate abstract ideas. How well does Don Fox communicate the ambiguity of Hawthorne's words, "Had Goodman Brown fallen asleep in the forest and only dreamed a wild dream of a witch meeting?"

9. How much sexual imagery do you find in Hawthorne's short story? How much emphasis has the filmmaker put on sexual imagery?

10. Compare and contrast Young Goodman Brown's meeting with the man in the woods as portrayed in the story, the two screenplays, and the film. Explain the aim of each treatment. Assess the film-maker's final handling of the scene in the movie.

YOUNG GOODMAN BROWN
SUGGESTIONS FOR PAPERS

1. In the light of the story, assess the filmmaker's invention of the witch-burning sequences at the beginning and end of the film.

Support your generalizations with relevant details from the story and film.

2. Compare and contrast the settings used by Hawthorne in the short story and by Don Fox in the film adaptation.

3. Describe and explain your reactions to the special effects in the film version of *Young Goodman Brown*.

4. If you had the opportunity, what changes would you make in the closing sequences of the film, beginning when young Goodman Brown emerges from the forest? Explain the reasons for your proposed revisions.

5. Identify another Hawthorne short story that you think would lend itself to effective adaptation. Explain your selection by discussing specific details in the story in terms of their cinematic possibilities.

FILM, FICTION, AND FAITH

Judith A. Rambeau

Three subjects generally (and jokingly) considered taboo as topics of conversation at social gatherings are sex, politics, and religion. One reason for the taboo is that irrational and emotional exchanges often ensue when these subjects are raised. Since we cannot discuss them reasonably, we try not to discuss them at all. But, given the human tendency to rebel against even self-imposed restraint (the vigorously prohibited becoming the ardently desired), one or more of these subjects inevitably finds a voice in most "earnest" conversations. And furthermore, these three "unmentionables" are often the primary subject matter, or at least subordinate elements, in film, a medium in which emotional response governs intellectual attitudes and judgments. During a film, we (the audience) undergo an emotional experience which, if the film is successful, leads to a cerebral experience. When we say that a certain film is "thought provoking," we mean that it has stirred our emotions and readied us for an exercise in understanding.

The film adaptation of Nathaniel Hawthorne's short story "Young Goodman Brown" successfully deals with many taboo subjects, including black magic, devil worship, and witch-hunting. More questions than answers grow out of the film experience, and this seems appropriate to the subject matter because unanswerable questions are the backbone of faith, be that faith Christian *or* satanic. Inherent in religious faith is the idea of belief without need of proof.

Divine visions are spiritual phenomena which cannot be verified but in which the "faithful" firmly believe. Young Goodman Brown experiences what could be called a "dark vision," and in the film we experience it with him. We are caught up in the illusory world of film; we *see* the events in the forest and therefore believe, together with Goodman, that they are real. We are swept by the filmmaker into Hawthorne's world of the diabolic. Instead of a light, glorious, heavenly vision, we see a dark, evil, hellish picture. The film skillfully displays what Hawthorne has described. We see what Goodman Brown sees; yet, when the vision has passed, we wonder with him if it really happened. In the short story we read, "Had Goodman Brown fallen

Used by permission.

asleep in the forest and only dreamed a wild dream of a witch-meeting?" In the film we "read" the same question on Goodman's face and in his actions toward his wife and the other townspeople. Is our questioning of reality of what we have *seen* in the film a tribute to our rationality and our ability to see through illusion? Or is it a sign of our inability to accept phenomena which clash with our beliefs? Goodman's experience and questions become *our* experience and questions, too, more through the film than through the story. In this way the art of film adds a new dimension to the literary work.

The power of fiction emanates from the word—the verbalization of events, ideas, attitudes, behavior. Hawthorne describes the mysterious and supernatural elements in "Young Goodman Brown" in the following ways:

> . . . all through the haunted forest there could be nothing more frightful than the figure of Goodman Brown.
>
> . . . the fire on the rock shot redly forth and formed a glowing arch above its base, where now appeared a figure.
>
> A basin was hollowed, naturally, in the rock. Did it contain water, reddened by the lurid light? or was it blood? or, perchance, a liquid flame?

The film communicates similar images through visual means. The "fiend raging in the breast" of Goodman as he plunges through the forest is vividly depicted. Goodman becomes a distorted figure seen through a convex lens. The forest colors at first change from warm, lush greens and browns to cold, shadowy blues, whites, and light greens. Finally, the foliage becomes bright purple and blue; Goodman's flesh is green. This is accomplished by omitting certain color transparencies when developing the frames. Unnatural colors and effects become associated with the deep forest of evil.

The special effects are very successful. They begin with a star-studded sky filled with wispy clouds from which the pink ribbon drifts down and culminate in red and yellow explosions behind the granite "throne." A violent eruption brings forth a faceless figure, outlined with flashes of light and gesturing with green hands. Nearby is the fiery-hot, molten lava in the basin. All these special effects are deliberately "unrealistic." The lack of realism is appropriate to the subject matter whether the viewer sees the events of the film as dream-like or supernatural. Dreams usually contain elements of both the real and the "unreal" (slow-motion falling, inanimate objects coming to life), and the supernatural can be anything! There is no formula for the unknown. And as for twentieth-century special effects being used to interpret a seventeenth-century story, I can only say that the ideas of the story and film are alive and well today in an age in which the occult exists side by side with other forms of religious belief. And the story invites—almost demands—the use of the most powerful special effects available.

Film, though, is not limited to visual means of expression. It makes use of dialogue, music, and sound effects as well. Many of the subtle (and some not-so-subtle) ironies and double entendres in the story are present in the film. We appreciate the double meaning in phrases such as "Faith kept me back awhile" and "My Faith is gone!" and the demonic irony of the statement, "I would not want Faith to come to any harm." Sounds, which comprise much of Hawthorne's description in the narrative, come to life in the film aided appropriately by dissonant music (not the harmony so loved in the seventeenth century).

The forest or wood of evil is the main setting of both story and film and is one of many images used by Hawthorne to create an atmosphere of diabolism. The wood of evil is traditionally the site of a religious test (as in Milton's *Comus*). There one meets evil and either resists it or succumbs to it. In "Young Goodman Brown," the Salem Puritans seem to have embraced evil in the wood rather than turning from it. "Evil is the nature of mankind." The "communion of the race" is not celebrated by partaking of Christ's flesh and blood (also a somewhat ghoulish rite in the literal sense), but by baptism with some "liquid flame." In the eye of the evil one (rather than God) "the great and small . . . are alike and equal." The rock and staff (symbols of God) are here equated with Satan. All the members of the religious hierarchy of the village hold positions in the "dark world."

Where the film-maker has changed certain episodes in the story, he has retained the tone. For instance, the staff is not shown as a writhing snake; but, a feeling that black magic is at work is conveyed when the branch cut by the man takes on a carved and polished appearance similar to the original staff loaned to Goody Cloyse. In the story Goodman suddenly finds himself alone at the site of the witch-meeting, his cheek sprinkled with dew from a branch. In the film he is sitting by a stream from which he draws water to pat on his face. This could be both an attempt to purify himself and clarify his thoughts. Here the filmmaker focuses on reflections in the water, pointing out that what looks tangible there disappears upon contact (just as the evil figure disappeared when Goodman touched it at the meeting).

Since the film-maker chose to omit the closing details of Hawthorne's story dealing with the rest of Goodman Brown's life in capsule form, he had to substitute something to help the audience see the effect of the night in the forest on Goodman. For this reason he changed the opening scene also. Instead of framing the forest sequence with the village scenes, he begins the film on a hilltop where preparations for a witch burning are being made and, at the end, returns to the same hilltop after the burning has taken place. We are told by Hawthorne that Goodman Brown became "a stern, a sad, a darkly meditative, a distrustful, if not a desperate man" after his "dream." In the film, Goodman's facial expression shows his reactions to the burning of the condemned witch by the witches of his dream. We see him shrink from his wife and fellow villagers, no longer merely a trusting, "simple husbandman." The invented film scenes help establish a foreboding mood, and also provide a means to show the change that has taken place inside Goodman Brown.

The similar effect of both story and film is attained partly by the technique of never telling the reader or audience anything *positively*. We don't know for sure that "the man in the woods" is the devil. He evidently has some magic powers; he is dressed, unlike the Puritans, in a long black cape; he was "friendly" with Goodman Brown's grandfather, yet looks little older than Goodman himself. Goody Cloyse *seems* to say he is the devil—but her sequence of statements actually contributes to the ambiguity. We are reminded in both story and film that Goodman's vision may be a dream, but we are not led definitely to that conclusion. Faith speaks of dreams, the devil figure in the film says, "You depended upon one another's heart, hoping that virtue were not all a dream" (another skewing of Christian ideals). And, of course, Hawthorne says that if we think it all a dream, we should know that it was a very effective "dream of evil omen" that molded Goodman's life from that night forward. The film-maker conspires with Hawthorne in the achievement of ambiguity by fade-outs at strategic points in the film (just as Goodman enters the woods and just after he pulls off the hood of the faceless figure). That climactic moment when Goodman shouts, "Look to heaven and resist the evil one!" is like the moment when a dreamer awakens himself with a shout, but it is also the way spells are broken.

Donald Fox obviously felt that Hawthorne's story lent itself to a film adaptation because of the opportunity to combine dissimilar cinematic techniques and perhaps also to show that the basic questions about good and evil, illusion and reality haven't changed much in three hundred years. I think Nathaniel Hawthorne, if he could see *Young Goodman Brown*, would agree that in tone and visual-aural expression of themes the film is "faithful" to his story but can successfully stand as a work of art in its own right.

THE LOTTERY

Shirley Jackson

When "The Lottery" initially appeared in the June 27, 1948, issue of The New Yorker *magazine, it produced a barrage of criticism, mostly unfavorable. Since then, it has become one of the most widely anthologized short stories of our time.*

As part of the Encyclopaedia Britannica "Short Story Showcase" films released in 1969, the Larry Yust production was designed to be a faithful adaptation of the original story. The movie retains much of the story dialogue word for word.

The shock impact of both story and film has inevitably led to censorship problems. Anticipating possible difficulty, Encyclopaedia Britannica opened the film with the sentence, "The following is fiction" printed across the bottom of the screen.

The morning of June 27th was clear and sunny, with the fresh warmth of a full-summer day; the flowers were blossoming profusely and the grass was richly green. The people of the village began to gather in the square, between the post office and the bank, around ten o'clock; in some towns there were so many people that the lottery took two days and had to be started on June 26th, but in this village, where there were only about three hundred people, the whole lottery took less than two hours, so it could begin at ten o'clock in the morning and still be through in time to allow the villagers to get home for noon dinner.

The children assembled first, of course. School was recently over for the summer, and the feeling of liberty sat uneasily on most of them; they tended to gather together quietly for a while before they broke into boisterous play, and their talk was still of the classroom and the teacher, of books and reprimands. Bobby Martin had already stuffed his pockets full of stones, and the other boys soon followed his example, selecting the smoothest and roundest stones; Bobby and Harry Jones and Dickie Delacroix—the villagers pronounced this name "Dellacroy"—eventually made a great pile of stones in one corner of the square and guarded it against the raids of the other boys. The girls stood aside, talking among themselves, looking over their shoulders at the boys, and the very small children rolled in the dust or clung to the hands of their older brothers or sisters.

Soon the men began to gather, surveying their own children, speaking of planting and rain, tractors and taxes. They stood together, away from the pile of stones in the corner, and their jokes were quiet and they smiled rather than laughed. The women, wearing faded house dresses and sweaters, came shortly after their menfolk. They greeted one another and exchanged bits of gossip as they went to join their husbands. Soon the women, standing by their husbands, began to call to their children, and the children came reluctantly, having to be called four or five times. Bobby Martin ducked under his mother's grasping hand and ran, laughing, back to the pile of stones. His father spoke up sharply, and Bobby came quickly and took his place between his father and his oldest brother.

The lottery was conducted—as were the square dances, the teenage club, the Halloween program—by Mr. Summers, who had time and energy to devote to civic activities. He was a round-faced, jovial man and he ran the coal business, and people were sorry for him, because he had no children and his wife was a scold. When he arrived in the square, carrying the black wooden box, there was a murmur of conversation among the villagers, and he waved and called, "Little late today, folks." The postmaster, Mr. Graves, followed him, carrying a three-legged stool, and the stool was put in the center of the square and Mr. Summers set the black box down on it. The villagers kept their distance, leaving a space between themselves and the stool, and when Mr. Summers said, "Some of you fellows want to give me a hand?" there was a hesitation before two men, Mr. Martin and his oldest son, Baxter, came forward to hold the box steady on the stool while Mr. Summers stirred up the papers inside it.

The original paraphernalia for the lottery had been lost long ago, and the black box now resting on the stool had been put into use even before Old Man Warner, the oldest man in town, was born. Mr. Summers spoke frequently to the villagers about making a new box, but no one liked to upset even as much tradition as was represented by the black box. There was a story that the present box had been made with some pieces of the box that had preceded it, the one that had been constructed when the first people settled down to make a village here. Every year, after the lottery, Mr. Summers began talking again about a new box, but every year the subject was allowed to fade off without anything's being done. The black box grew shabbier each year; by now it was no longer completely black but splintered badly along one side to show the original wood color, and in some places faded or stained.

Mr. Martin and his oldest son, Baxter, held the black box securely on the stool until Mr. Summers had stirred the papers thoroughly with his hand. Because so much of the ritual had been forgotten or discarded, Mr. Summers had been successful in having slips of paper substituted for the chips of wood that had been used for generations. Chips of wood, Mr. Summers had argued, had been all very well when the village was tiny, but now that the population was more than three hundred and likely to keep on growing, it was necessary to use something that would fit more easily into the black box. The night before the lottery, Mr. Summers and Mr. Graves made up the slips of paper and.put them in the box, and it was then taken to the safe of Mr. Summers' coal company and locked up until Mr. Summers was ready to take it to the square next morning. The rest of the year, the box was put away, sometimes one place, sometimes another; it had spent one year in Mr. Graves's barn and another year underfoot in the post office, and sometimes it was set on a shelf in the Martin grocery and left there.

There was a great deal of fussing to be done before Mr. Summers declared the lottery open. There were the lists to make up—of heads of families, heads of households in each family, members of each household in each family. There was the proper swearing-in of Mr. Summers by the postmaster, as the official of the lottery; at one time, some people remembered, there had been a recital of some sort, performed by the official of the lottery, a perfunctory, tuneless chant that had been rattled off duly each year; some people believed that the official of the lottery used to stand just so when he said or sang it, others believed that he was supposed to walk among the people, but years and years ago this part of the ritual had been allowed to lapse. There had been, also, a ritual salute, which the official of the lottery had had to use in addressing each person who came up to draw from the box, but this also had changed with time, until now it was felt necessary only for the official to speak to each person approaching. Mr. Summers was very good at all this; in his clean white shirt and blue jeans, with one hand resting carelessly on the black box, he seemed very proper and important as he talked interminably to Mr. Graves and the Martins.

Just as Mr. Summers finally left off talking and turned to the assembled villagers, Mrs. Hutchinson came hurriedly along the path to the square, her sweater thrown over her shoulders, and slid into place in the back of the crowd. "Clean forgot what day it was," she said to Mrs. Delacroix, who stood next to her, and they both laughed softly. "Thought my old man was out back stacking wood," Mrs. Hutchinson went on, "and then I looked out the window and the kids was gone,

and then I remembered it was the twenty-seventh and came a-running."
She dried her hands on her apron, and Mrs. Delacroix said, "You're in
time, though. They're still talking away up there."

Mrs. Hutchinson craned her neck to see through the crowd and
found her husband and children standing near the front. She tapped
Mrs. Delacroix on the arm as a farewell and began to make her way
through the crowd. The people separated good-humoredly to let her
through; two or three people said, in voices just loud enough to be
heard across the crowd, "Here comes your Missus, Hutchinson," and
"Bill, she made it after all." Mrs. Hutchinson reached her husband,
and Mr. Summers, who had been waiting, said cheerfully, "Thought
we were going to have to get on without you, Tessie." Mrs. Hutchinson
said, grinning, "Wouldn't have me leave m'dishes in the sink, now,
would you, Joe?," and soft laughter ran through the crowd as the
people stirred back into position after Mrs. Hutchinson's arrival.

"Well, now," Mr. Summers said soberly, "guess we better get
started, get this over with, so's we can go back to work. Anybody
ain't here?"

"Dunbar," several people said. "Dunbar, Dunbar."

Mr. Summers consulted his list. "Clyde Dunbar," he said. "That's
right. He's broke his leg, hasn't he? Who's drawing for him?"

"Me, I guess," a young woman said, and Mr. Summers turned to
look at her. "Wife draws for her husband," Mr. Summers said. "Don't
you have a grown boy to do it for you, Janey?" Although Mr. Summers
and everyone else in the village knew the answer perfectly well, it
was the business of the official of the lottery to ask such questions
formally. Mr. Summers waited with an expression of polite interest
while Mrs. Dunbar answered.

"Horace's not but sixteen yet," Mrs. Dunbar said regretfully.
"Guess I gotta fill in for the old man this year."

"Right," Mr. Summers said. He made a note on the list he was
holding. Then he asked, "Watson boy drawing this year?"

A tall boy in the crowd raised his hand. "Here," he said. "I'm
drawing for m'mother and me." He blinked his eyes nervously and
ducked his head as several voices in the crowd said things like "Good
fellow, Jack," and "Glad to see your mother's got a man to do it."

"Well," Mr. Summers said, "guess that's everyone. Old Man
Warner make it?"

"Here," a voice said, and Mr. Summers nodded.

A sudden hush fell on the crowd as Mr. Summers cleared his
throat and looked at the list. "All ready?" he called. "Now, I'll read
the names—heads of families first—and the men come up and take a
paper out of the box. Keep the paper folded in your hand without

looking at it until everyone has had a turn. Everything clear?"

The people had done it so many times that they only half listened to the directions; most of them were quiet, wetting their lips, not looking around. Then Mr. Summers raised one hand high and said, "Adams." A man disengaged himself from the crowd and came forward. "Hi, Steve," Mr. Summers said, and Mr. Adams said, "Hi, Joe." They grinned at one another humorlessly and nervously. Then Mr. Adams reached into the black box and took out a folded paper. He held it firmly by one corner as he turned and went hastily back to his place in the crowd, where he stood a little apart from his family, not looking down at his hand.

"Allen," Mr. Summers said. "Anderson. . . . Bentham."

"Seems like there's no time at all between lotteries any more," Mrs. Delacroix said to Mrs. Graves in the back row. "Seems like we got through with the last one only last week."

"Time sure goes fast," Mrs. Graves said.

"Clark. . . . Delacroix."

"There goes my old man," Mrs. Delacroix said. She held her breath while her husband went forward.

"Dunbar," Mr. Summers said, and Mrs. Dunbar went steadily to the box while one of the women said, "Go on, Janey," and another said, "There she goes."

"We're next," Mrs. Graves said. She watched while Mr. Graves came around from the side of the box, greeted Mr. Summers gravely, and selected a slip of paper from the box. By now, all through the crowd there were men holding the small folded papers in their large hands, turning them over and over nervously. Mrs. Dunbar and her two sons stood together, Mrs. Dunbar holding the slip of paper.

"Harburt. . . . Hutchinson."

"Get up there, Bill," Mrs. Hutchinson said, and the people near her laughed.

"Jones."

"They do say," Mr. Adams said to Old Man Warner, who stood next to him, "that over in the north village they're talking of giving up the lottery."

Old Man Warner snorted. "Pack of crazy fools," he said. "Listening to the young folks, nothing's good enough for *them*. Next thing you know, they'll be wanting to go back to living in caves, nobody work any more, live *that* way for a while. Used to be a saying about 'Lottery in June, corn be heavy soon.' First thing you know, we'd all be eating stewed chickweed and acorns. There's *always* been a lottery," he added petulantly. "Bad enough to see young Joe Summers up there joking with everybody."

"Some places have already quit lotteries," Mrs. Adams said.

"Nothing but trouble in *that*," Old Man Warner said stoutly. "Pack of young fools."

"Martin." And Bobby Martin watched his father go forward. "Overdyke. . . . Percy."

"I wish they'd hurry," Mrs. Dunbar said to her older son. "I wish they'd hurry."

"They're almost through," her son said.

"You get ready to run tell Dad," Mrs. Dunbar said.

Mr. Summers called his own name and then stepped forward precisely and selected a slip from the box. Then he called, "Warner."

"Seventy-seventh year I been in the lottery," Old Man Warner said as he went through the crowd. "Seventy-seventh time."

"Watson." The tall boy came awkwardly through the crowd. Someone said, "Don't be nervous, Jack," and Mr. Summers said, "Take your time, son."

"Zanini."

After that, there was a long pause, a breathless pause, until Mr. Summers, holding his slip of paper in the air, said, "All right, fellows." For a minute, no one moved, and then all the slips of paper were opened. Suddenly, all the women began to speak at once, saying, "Who is it?," "Who's got it?," "Is it the Dunbars?," "Is it the Watsons?" Then the voices began to say, "It's Hutchinson. It's Bill," "Bill Hutchinson's got it."

"Go tell your father," Mrs. Dunbar said to her older son.

People began to look around to see the Hutchinsons. Bill Hutchinson was standing quiet staring down at the paper in his hand. Suddenly, Tessie Hutchinson shouted to Mr. Summers, "You didn't give him time enough to take any paper he wanted. I saw you. It wasn't fair."

"Be a good sport, Tessie," Mrs. Delacroix called, and Mrs. Graves said, "All of us took the same chance."

"Shut up, Tessie," Bill Hutchinson said.

"Well, everyone," Mr. Summers said, "that was done pretty fast, and now we've got to be hurrying a little more to get done in time." He consulted his next list. "Bill," he said, "you draw for the Hutchinson family. You got any other households in the Hutchinsons?"

"There's Don and Eva," Mrs. Hutchinson yelled. "Make *them* take their chance!"

"Daughters draw with their husbands' families, Tessie," Mr. Summers said gently. "You know that as well as anyone else."

"It wasn't *fair*," Tessie said.

"I guess not, Joe," Bill Hutchinson said regretfully. "My daughter draws with her husband's family, that's only fair. And I've got no other family except the kids."

"Then, as far as drawing for families is concerned, it's you," Mr. Summers said in explanation, "and as far as drawing for households is concerned, that's you, too. Right?"

"Right," Bill Hutchinson said.

"How many kids, Bill?" Mr. Summers asked formally.

"Three," Bill Hutchinson said. "There's Bill, Jr., and Nancy, and little Dave. And Tessie and me."

"All right, then," Mr. Summers said. "Harry, you got their tickets back?"

Mr. Graves nodded and held up the slips of paper. "Put them in the box, then," Mr. Summers directed. "Take Bill's and put it in."

"I think we ought to start over," Mrs. Hutchinson said, as quietly as she could. "I tell you it wasn't *fair*. You didn't give him time enough to choose. *Everybody* saw that."

Mr. Graves had selected the five slips and put them in the box, and he dropped all the papers but those onto the ground, where the breeze caught them and lifted them off.

"Listen, everybody," Mrs. Hutchinson was saying to the people around her.

"Ready, Bill?" Mr. Summers asked, and Bill Hutchinson, with one quick glance around at his wife and children, nodded.

"Remember," Mr. Summers said, "take the slips and keep them folded until each person has taken one. Harry, you help little Dave." Mr. Graves took the hand of the little boy, who came willingly with him up to the box. "Take a paper out of the box, Davy," Mr. Summers said. Davy put his hand into the box and laughed. "Take just *one* paper," Mr. Summers said. "Harry, you hold it for him." Mr. Graves took the child's hand and removed the folded paper from the tight fist and held it while little Dave stood next to him and looked up at him wonderingly.

"Nancy next," Mr. Summers said. Nancy was twelve, and her school friends breathed heavily as she went forward, switching her skirt, and took a slip daintily from the box. "Bill, Jr.," Mr. Summers said, and Billy, his face red and his feet over-large, nearly knocked the box over as he got a paper out. "Tessie," Mr. Summers said. She hesitated for a minute, looking around defiantly, and then set her lips and went up to the box. She snatched a paper out and held it behind her.

"Bill," Mr. Summers said, and Bill Hutchinson reached into the box and felt around, bringing his hand out at last with the slip of paper in it.

The crowd was quiet. A girl whispered, "I hope it's not Nancy," and the sound of the whisper reached the edges of the crowd.

"It's not the way it used to be," Old Man Warner said clearly. "People ain't the way they used to be."

"All right," Mr. Summers said. "Open the papers. Harry, you open little Dave's."

Mr. Graves opened the slip of paper and there was a general sigh through the crowd as he held it up and everyone could see that it was blank. Nancy and Bill, Jr., opened theirs at the same time, and both beamed and laughed, turning around to the crowd and holding their slips of paper above their heads.

"Tessie," Mr. Summers said. There was a pause, and then Mr. Summers looked at Bill Hutchinson, and Bill unfolded his paper and showed it. It was blank.

"It's Tessie," Mr. Summers said, and his voice was hushed. "Show us her paper, Bill."

Bill Hutchinson went over to his wife and forced the slip of paper out of her hand. It had a black spot on it, the black spot Mr. Summers had made the night before with the heavy pencil in the coal-company office. Bill Hutchinson held it up, and there was a stir in the crowd.

"All right, folks," Mr. Summers said. "Let's finish quickly."

Although the villagers had forgotten the ritual and lost the original black box, they still remembered to use stones. The pile of stones the boys had made earlier was ready; there were stones on the ground with the blowing scraps of paper that had come out of the box. Mrs. Delacroix selected a stone so large she had to pick it up with both hands and turned to Mrs. Dunbar. "Come on," she said. "Hurry up."

Mrs. Dunbar had small stones in both hands, and she said, gasping for breath, "I can't run at all. You'll have to go ahead and I'll catch up with you."

The children had stones already, and someone gave little Davy Hutchinson a few pebbles.

Tessie Hutchinson was in the center of a cleared space by now, and she held her hands out desperately as the villagers moved in on her. "It isn't fair," she said. A stone hit her on the side of the head.

Old Man Warner was saying, "Come on, come on, everyone." Steve Adams was in the front of the crowd of villagers, with Mrs. Graves beside him.

"It isn't fair, it isn't right," Mrs. Hutchinson screamed, and then they were upon her.

film continuity

THE LOTTERY

1. Montage: children playing in square of small town; truck approaching; two men, two women, shopkeeper, little girls—

BOBBY: Hey, there's lots over here!

ADA ADAMS: Steve hates to eat those TV dinners. I don't blame him.

NANCY: Dick Delacroix's a pest.

PHYLLIS: I think he's cute.

SALLY: I like Miz Spangler better'n I did that second-grade teacher.

2. Montage: men walking toward square; boys playing; people forming family groups

ZANINI: Get your new roof up?

ANDERSON: Finished yesterday.

BOBBY: Come on, Harry. Put it back!

OVERDYKE: You ever hear of taxes going down?

JEAN DELACROIX: Then I'm going to finish it off with some lace around the sleeves.

NANCY JONES: Harry, you come here now.

ADA: Sally, come here.

ALTA MARTIN: Bobby Martin!

MARTIN: You, Bob! Come here! Now!

3. Sequence: people in square; two men carrying black box; Joe Summers stirring contents of box

SUMMERS: Little late today, folks. Guess this'll do it, Harry. Some of you fellows want to give me a hand?

MARTIN: Come on, Baxter.

SUMMERS: Thank you, Phil. How're you, Baxter? Think that should do it.

4. Sequence: Tessie Hutchinson hurrying into square, moving through crowd, approaching man in center of square

TESSIE: I clean forgot what day it was. I looked out the window and

64

the kids was gone, and I remembered it was the twenty-seventh. I came a-runnin'.

JEAN: You're in time. They're still gettin' ready.

GRAVES: Do you solemnly swear that you will perform without prejudice or favoritism those duties prescribed by custom and dictated by law?

SUMMERS: I do.

TESSIE: Bill's up front. I'll see you later.

GRAVES: As postmaster of this community, by the authority of my office, I appoint you master of the lottery.

MAN: Here comes Tessie, Bill.

SUMMERS: Thought we were going to have to get on without you, Tessie.

TESSIE: You wouldn't have me leave my dishes in the sink, would you, Joe?

5. Sequence: Summers addressing crowd; people answering

SUMMERS: Well, now, guess we better get started, get this over with so's we can go back to work. Anybody else ain't here?

WOMAN: Dunbar.

MAN: Clyde Dunbar ain't here.

SUMMERS: Clyde Dunbar? That's right, he's broke his leg, hasn't he? Who's drawin' for him this year?

JANEY DUNBAR: Me, I guess.

SUMMERS: Janey, ain't you got a grown boy to do it for you?

JANEY: Well, Horace ain't but sixteen yet. I guess I'll have to do it myself this year.

SUMMERS: Watson boy drawin' this year?

WATSON: Here. I'm drawin' for me and my ma.

VOICE: Good boy, Jack. Glad to see your mother's got a man to do it.

SUMMERS: Well, I guess that's everyone. Old Man Warner make it?

WARNER: Here.

6. Sequence: crowd; people drawing slips of paper out of box, one by one

SUMMERS: All ready? I'll read the names, then—heads of families first—the men come up and draw a paper out of the box. Now, keep the paper folded in your hand without lookin' at it until everyone's had a turn. Everything clear? Adams.

ADAMS: Hi, Joe.

SUMMERS: Hi, Steve. Anderson . . . Bentham.

7. Sequence: people talking among themselves, going up for slips from box

JEAN: Seems like there's no time at all between lotteries any more. Seems like only last week we got through with the last one.

MRS. GRAVES: Yeah, time sure does go fast.

SUMMERS: Clark . . . Morning, Andy.

CLARK: Morning, Joe.

SUMMERS: Delacroix . . . Hi, Stan.

DELACROIX: Hi, Joe.

SUMMERS: Dunbar.

TESSIE: There she goes.

MRS. GRAVES: We're next.

SUMMERS: Graves . . . Harburt . . . Hutchinson.

TESSIE: Get up there, Bill.

VOICE: That a girl, Tessie.

SUMMERS: Jones.

ADAMS: They say over in Warren County they're talking about giving up the lottery.

8. Sequence: close-up of faces; Old Man Warner talking angrily

WARNER: Pack of crazy fools, listening to the young folks. Nothing's good enough for them.

SUMMERS: Judd.

WARNER: First thing you know everybody'll be wantin' to go back to livin' in caves, nobody work any more, live *that* way for a while.

SUMMERS: Klepfer.

WARNER: Used to be a saying, "Lottery in June, corn heavy soon." Next thing we'd know, we'd all be eating stewed chickweed and acorns.

SUMMERS: Langley.

WARNER: There's always been a lottery.

SUMMERS: Hi, Mitch.

LANGLEY: Hi, Joe.

WARNER: Bad enough to see young Joe Summers out there joking with everybody.

SUMMERS: Martin.

MRS. ADAMS: Some places have already quit lotteries.

WARNER: Nothing but trouble in that. Pack of young fools!

SUMMERS: Overdyke.

JANEY: I wish they'd hurry.

9. Sequence: men drawing slips; Warner going up for slip; young man going up nervously; close-up of expectant faces

SUMMERS: Percy . . . Robinson . . . Summers . . . Warner.

WARNER: Seventy-seventh year I've been in the lottery, seventy-seventh time.

SUMMERS: Watson.

VOICE: Don't be nervous, Jack.

SUMMERS: Take your time, son . . . Zanini . . . Hi, George.

10. Sequence: everyone opening his slip of paper; Tessie rushing forward

SUMMERS: All right, fellows.

VOICE: Bill Hutchinson's got it.

TESSIE: You didn't give him time enough to pick the one he wanted. I saw you. You didn't give him time. It wasn't fair!

JEAN: Be a good sport, Tessie.

JANEY: We all took the same chance.

HUTCHINSON: Shut up, Tessie.

11. Sequence: Summers addressing crowd, putting slips into box

SUMMERS: Well, everybody, that went pretty fast. Now we're going to have to be hurryin' a little more to get done in time. Bill, you drew for the Hutchinson family. You got any other households in the Hutchinsons? Any in-laws? Grandchildren?

TESSIE: There's Don and Eva. Make *them* take their chance!

SUMMERS: Daughters draw with their husbands' families. You know that as well as anyone else, Tessie.

TESSIE: It isn't fair!

HUTCHINSON: I guess not, Joe. My married daughter draws with her husband's family. It's only fair. I got no other family except the kids.

SUMMERS: How many kids, Bill?

HUTCHINSON: Three—Nancy, Bill Junior, Davy—and Tessie and me.

SUMMERS: All right, Harry, you got four tickets ready?

HARRY: Yeah.

SUMMERS: Drop them in the box. Take Bill's and put it in.

12. Sequence: Tessie shouting to crowd; children drawing slips out of box; Tessie drawing

SUMMERS: Ready, Bill?

TESSIE: I think we should start over. It wasn't fair. They didn't give him time enough to choose. Everybody saw that. Well, you all *saw* that! Please listen to me. Joe didn't give Bill enough time.

SUMMERS: You ready, Bill? Remember, take a slip and keep it folded until each person's taken one. Harry, you help little Davy. Take a paper out of the box, Davy. Just take one. Harry, you hold it for him. Nancy . . . Bill Junior . . . Tessie . . . Bill.

13. Sequence: Hutchinson drawing; close-up of Warner; papers being opened and shown to crowd

PHYLLIS: I hope it's not Nancy

WARNER: It ain't the way it used to be. People ain't the way they used to be.

SUMMERS: All right, open the papers. Harry, you open up Davy's . . . Nancy . . . Bill Junior . . . Tessie . . . Bill . . . It's Tessie. Show us her paper, Bill.

14. Sequence: people gathering rocks, running toward Tessie, throwing rocks; close-up of Tessie being stoned; view of square; crowd moving in on Tessie

SUMMERS: All right, folks. Let's finish quickly.

JEAN: Come on! Hurry up!

JANEY: I can't run. You go ahead, I'll catch up with you.

MRS. GRAVES: Here, Davy.

TESSIE: It isn't fair! It isn't fair! It isn't right!

THE LOTTERY
QUESTIONS

1. Study the opening half-dozen paragraphs of the story and the concluding half-dozen. How does the length of the paragraphs affect the rhythm or pace of the story? How does the author's choice of words contribute to the pace of each section? Has the filmmaker been influenced by the story's rhythm?

2. Shirley Jackson's story makes use of some name symbolism. It is ironic that Mr. Summers is responsible for the deadly lottery, and appropriate that someone named Graves assists him. Old Man Warner warns people about what will happen if the lottery is discontinued. Ms. Jackson emphasizes the Anglicized pronunciation of the name Delacroix. Has the filmmaker made use of the name symbolism? How do you explain his decision?

3. At the conclusion of the film, the audience sees evidence of a sudden rainstorm. In addition, thunder can be heard during the course of the film. Since these represent departures from the literal story line, what function do they serve in the film? Evaluate the effectiveness of these additions.

4. Compare and contrast the role of the "black box" in the short story and film versions of *The Lottery*.

5. In the exchange between Old Man Warner and Mrs. Adams, the cameraman points his camera at Mrs. Adams to reveal her *reaction* to Old Man Warner's snarl, "Pack of young fools." How is this shot particularly cinematic?

6. Why does Old Man Warner say "Lottery in June, corn be heavy soon"? Why does the author transpose the idea of an ancient fertility rite to modern times?

7. In the story, the Watson boy blinks nervously and ducks his head as he acknowledges his readiness to draw a lottery slip. How do you explain his nervousness? Why does the filmmaker visualize *both* the Watson boy and his mother? What inferences might be drawn from the actions of his mother?

8. When Davy Hutchinson is given a rock by Mrs. Graves, the camera shot is taken from the height of a small child. How does this affect the force of the shot? How does the visual appearance of Mrs. Graves affect the impact of the sequence?

9. In the short story, Shirley Jackson uses the term "ritual" several times. What problems does this term pose for the film director? How does he solve the problems? Assess his solution.

10. The closing line of the opening paragraph states that the lottery could begin at ten in the morning and ". . . still be through in time for noon dinner." In the context of the entire story, explicate the line. How has the film director handled this line?

11. The filmmaker sets his film in a contemporary time and small

town setting. In the light of the story, how appropriate are his
choices of time and place?

THE LOTTERY
SUGGESTIONS FOR PAPERS

1. Before the film begins, the statement, "The following is fiction,"
   appears at the bottom of the screen. In the light of the distinctions
   between film and fiction as narrative modes, assess the statement.

2. Compare and contrast the roles of Mr. and Mrs. Adams in the
   short story and film. On the basis of your observations, what
   inferences can you draw?

3. To what extent does the film's rhythm parallel or deviate from
   the pace of the short story? What conclusions follow from your
   observations. Explain.

4. Describe your reactions to Tessie Hutchinson at the beginning,
   middle, and end of the film version of *The Lottery*. How do you
   account for your responses?

5. If you were preparing a screen adaptation of Shirley Jackson's
   short story, what significant changes—if any—would you make
   from the film as produced? Explain the reasons for any modifications you propose.

TWO LOTTERIES:
THE VERBAL AND THE VISUAL

As a medium, film derives some of its forcefulness from purely cine-matic devices unavailable to any other art form. Movies have been described as a medium not of action, but of *reaction*. In *The Lottery*, for example, we not only see Tessie's response to "winning" the lottery, but we see and hear others react to her responses. When Mrs. Adams says, almost plaintively, "Some places have already quit lotteries," and Old Man Warner snarls, "Pack of young fools," the cameraman points his camera at Mrs. Adams, capturing her anguished reaction to his harsh response. Film's simultaneity allows us to see and hear immedi-ately, not linearly and sequentially as we must experience language.

As a further example, study the Watson boy incident in the story. He blinks nervously and ducks his head as he acknowledges his readi-ness to draw a lottery slip. He is described as a "tall *boy*" [italics mine], so we may assume that he is not older than eighteen or so. At this relatively young age he is the man of the house, and we might wonder what happened to his father. Shirley Jackson does not say, but in a community like this, the father may well have been a previous lottery "winner". This would go far toward explaining the boy's blink-ing eyes and nervousness. The film director shoots this scene with young Watson speaking the story's dialogue. But the filmmaker shows both Jack Watson *and his mother*. Her eyes are cast down, her head bowed in pain. A subtle detail in the story becomes more vivid in the film because we can see both Jack and his mother and at the same time hear Jack's words, "I'm drawing for m'mother and me." The simul-taneity of words and images creates an immediacy of experience.

The filmmaker gives an effective interpretation of the horrifying moment in the story when ". . . someone gave little Davy Hutchinson a few pebbles." The "someone" is particularized in Mrs. Graves, a very kindly-looking, motherly lady. She bends down to give Davy a stone; the camera shot is taken from the height of a small boy. We experience his confusion as we see the lower halves of people streaming past. The camera then cuts directly to the protesting Tessie striving ineffectually to ward off the crowd closing in on her. But this does not diminish the power of the previous shot. On the contrary, it is the juxtaposing of the two shots that gives each its maximum effect.

Fiction has advantages as a medium too. For example, the concept

The Lottery (1969) "A subtle story inference becomes more stark in the film because we can see both characters simultaneously." *Still shot reproduced courtesy of Encyclopaedia Britannica Educational Corporation.*

of "ritual" recurs in the story: "much of the ritual had been forgotten," "the ritual had been allowed to lapse," "a ritual salute." Ritual is a relatively abstract term that conjures up ideas but cannot easily be visualized. Moreover, references to lapsed or forgotten rituals adds the further difficulty of picturing what once was but no longer is. The flexibility of language in referring to earlier points in time has no purely cinematic counterpart. While the filmmaker might consider showing former lotteries, the shorthand of verbal allusion is unavailable to film except through dialogue. The director of *The Lottery* alludes to the past through dialogue. Mrs. Delacroix says, "Seems like there's no time at all between lotteries any more." Old Man Warner boasts, "Seventy-seventh year I been in the lottery." But these statements are less connotative than Shirley Jackson's reiteration of the term, "ritual."

In re-reading the story, some details take on more sinister meanings. For example, the closing line of the opening paragraph states that the lottery could begin at ten in the morning and ". . . still be through in time for noon dinner." Later, Mr. Summers starts the lottery formalities by observing, ". . . guess we better get started, get this over with,

The Lottery (1969) ". . . camera shot taken from the height of the small confused boy. . . . The metaphorical lowness is appropriate." *Still shot reproduced
courtesy of Encyclopaedia Britannica Educational Corporation.*

so's we can go back to work." In the context of the lottery, both statements are dreadful. However, the "noon dinner" allusion is more hideous. In the film adaptation, Larry Yust chooses to be faithful to the
dialogue and quotes Mr. Summers. In the process, he misses a superb
opportunity to substitute the earlier reference. In this instance, literal
fidelity to the dialogue is less true to Shirley Jackson's larger theme.
"The Lottery" is a terrifying story of whose horror the reader is not
fully aware until he has absorbed all its details.

How, precisely, does the story make its impact? The title prepares
the reader for a benign tale. A lottery connotes the winning of a
worthwhile prize. The opening sentence reveals a morning that is
"clear and sunny"; flowers are "blossoming profusely," and the grass
is "richly green." A misleading aura of benevolence has been established, thereby creating a substantial gulf between initial expectations
and ultimate reality. Early clues do suggest an underlying malignancy:
boys gather stones; men tell "quiet" jokes, and smile rather than laugh.
But these clues are overshadowed by the initial tone. Even the introduction of the black wooden box is not a threatening sign because it

is mentioned in conjunction with square dances, the Halloween program, and the teenage club. And Tessie's playful humor imparts a light-hearted touch to the scene.

As the lottery proceeds, a conversation between Mr. and Mrs. Adams and Old Man Warner stirs only a ripple of unrest until Tessie's anguished, "It wasn't fair," jolts the reader. Something is clearly out of joint. However, the mechanics of the lottery blunt a clear perception of the enormity to come. The pace of the story accelerates greatly in the closing paragraphs. Mr. Summers says, "Let's finish quickly." Mrs. Delacroix adds, "Hurry up." Mrs. Dunbar, gasping for breath, says, "You'll have to go ahead and I'll catch up with you." Old Man Warner says, "Come on, come on, everyone." And the story closes, ". . . then they were upon her." The crescendo of horror grips the reader.

Structurally, the story lends itself to a simple diagram, as follows:

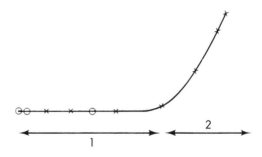

```
O - the benign        1 - the pace is relatively tranquil
× - the malignant     2 - the mounting horror
```

Along the base of the diagram is the quiet, even misleading, story line. Despite clues, the larger bulk of the early narrative raises few tremors. Then, the upsurge of fear begins numbing a reader's potential recognition of evil. Suddenly, the terrible *dénouement* arrives. The story ends, but its horrible implications continue to reverberate. Remembered details take on a gruesome significance: Mr. Adams, who mentions the idea of giving up the lottery, ends up in the front line of stone-throwing villagers; Nancy and Bill, Jr. beam and laugh, but their escape assures the imminent death of a parent; little Davy is given some pebbles, which indicates that the mores of the tribe are learned early, prior to the age of reason. Something is terribly rotten in this ritual-bound community, but Shirley Jackson gives us no medieval Denmark. Indeed, her "tractors and taxes" and Anglicized names make very explicit the contemporaneity of the story.

One final structural and rhythmic pattern remains to be discussed. A study of the first seven paragraphs of the story reveals the average length of those paragraphs to be about fourteen lines. The last seven paragraphs have an average length of less than three lines. With that structure, Shirley Jackson catapults her readers into horror.

What are the cinematic implications of this structural and rhythmic analysis? If the filmmaker is to go beyond literal plot fidelity to tonal fidelity, he must employ patterns structurally analogous to those of the story. Instead, the film begins with a series of short, jolting shots filled with movement, in a very rapid pattern of alternation. In lieu of a "misleading," placid pace, the rhythm of the film is hectic, almost frenzied. The great difference between initial expectations and final reality which makes the story so effective is minimized in the film, and this lessens the film's impact.

In an effort to maintain fidelity, the film version retains characters, dialogue, and plot. Three examples of modification merit attention. The film begins with a curious addition. The printed message, "The following is fiction," appears across the base of the screen. Obviously, the producers recognized and hoped to forestall the dangers of censorship. One can sympathize with their problem and recognize the validity of their concern. However powerful Shirley Jackson's story—and the history of its publication in The *New Yorker* and the reaction to it demonstrates its verbal potency—a film's potential force may be equally threatening. Ironically, the great thrust of film stems from its *not* being fiction, from the apparent reality of its images. To suggest that the images are "fiction" is to diminish their force. Strategically, the producers may have placed their warning at the beginning of the film to protect themselves while simultaneously expecting the "warning" to go unheeded as the visuals of the picture took hold. Since the film medium does not "tell" but "shows," and since "seeing is believing," one can assume that the initial injunction plays a minor role in the viewers' final reactions. At the very least, one can hope that movie viewers would not suspend their belief—despite the words.

A second modification of the story takes the form of omission, an omission that negates a subtle psychological realism. Mr. Adams, who seems to consider the possibility of giving up the lottery, appears, at the end of the story, "in the front of the crowd of villagers. . . ." The one small hope that decency and humanity might prevail is shattered. The worst takes place: people still remember to use stones even though they have forgotten other parts of the ritual, and any feelings of compassion in Steve Adams are obliterated in a kind of mass blood lust. The filmmaker, however, neglects this psychologically telling detail and

Steve Adams does not appear at the head of the stone-throwing villagers.

The third modification is the most dramatic. At the very moment that Tessie's winning of the lottery heralds her impending destruction, the sound of thunder is heard. In the final shots of the film, when the villagers are stoning Tessie, we see puddles left by a rainstorm. While the sound of thunder may be an appropriate symbol for dread events to come, the story is very different. Shirley Jackson prefers irony to cliché. The stoning occurs in the context of a lovely, sunny day in late June. Thus, we have a potent contrast: benign nature vs. malignant man.

Clearly the filmmakers intended to create a film faithful to the original story. To do so, they retained the story's plot and characters; they followed the original dialogue. What they missed was more subtle! They ignored the artistry reflected in the rhythm and pace of the story and in the juxtaposition of nature's bounty with man's most evil and primitive traditions. In missing the tone of the story, their film is flawed.

BARTLEBY: A STORY OF WALL STREET

Herman Melville

In 1853, Melville published "Bartleby," regarded today as one of the greatest stories ever written. At this point in his life, Melville was in despair; despite the publication of Moby Dick in 1851, his literary reputation was minimal. Many critics read "Bartleby" as a bitter denunciation of a materialistic society unattuned to the needs of the artist.

In 1969, Encyclopaedia Britannica released its "Short Story Showcase," a group of five films adapted from short stories. Larry Yust wrote all of the screenplays and directed the five films. He regards Bartleby as the best film in the Showcase. A film continuity of Bartleby follows the short story.

Unlike a screenplay which verbally presents the plan of an adaptation prior to actual shooting, a film continuity is a verbal resume of the movie based on its actual footage. In addition, the film continuity reproduces the actual dialogue of the motion picture. A film continuity is useful in refreshing the memory of a viewer who has seen the movie. Much as a reader can return to the story, a film continuity allows a viewer to "return" to the movie.

I am a rather elderly man. The nature of my avocations, for the last thirty years, has brought me into more than ordinary contact with what would seem an interesting and somewhat singular set of men, of whom, as yet, nothing, that I know of, has ever been written—I mean, the law-copyists, or scriveners. I have known very many of them, professionally and privately, and, if I pleased, could relate divers histories, at which good-natured gentlemen might smile, and sentimental souls might weep. But I waive the biographies of all other scriveners, for a few passages in the life of Bartleby, who was a scrivener, the strangest I ever saw, or heard of. While, of other law-copyists, I might write the complete life, of Bartleby nothing of that sort can be done. I believe that no materials exist, for a full and satisfactory biography of this man. It is an irreparable loss to literature. Bartleby was one of those beings of whom nothing is ascertainable, except from the original sources, and, in his case, those are very small. What my own astonished eyes saw of Bartleby, *that* is all I know of him, except, indeed, one vague report, which will appear in the sequel.

Ere introducing the scrivener, as he first appeared to me, it is fit

I make some mention of myself, my employés, my business, my chambers, and general surroundings; because some such description is indispensable to an adequate understanding of the chief character about to be presented. Imprimis: I am a man who, from his youth upward, has been filled with a profound conviction that the easiest way of life is the best. Hence, though I belong to a profession proverbially energetic and nervous, even to turbulence, at times, yet nothing of that sort have I ever suffered to invade my peace. I am one of those unambitious lawyers who never addresses a jury, or in any way draws down public applause; but, in the cool tranquillity of a snug retreat, do a snug business among rich men's bonds, and mortgages, and title-deeds. All who know me, consider me an eminently *safe* man. The late John Jacob Astor, a personage little given to poetic enthusiasm, had no hesitation in pronouncing my first grand point to be prudence; my next, method. I do not speak it in vanity, but simply record the fact, that I was not unemployed in my profession by the late John Jacob Astor; a name which, I admit, I love to repeat; for it hath a rounded and orbicular sound to it, and rings like unto bullion. I will freely add, that I was not insensible to the late John Jacob Astor's good opinion.

Some time prior to the period at which this little history begins, my avocations had been largely increased. The good old office, now extinct in the State of New York, of a Master in Chancery, had been conferred upon me. It was not a very arduous office, but very pleasantly remunerative. I seldom lose my temper; much more seldom indulge in dangerous indignation at wrongs and outrages; but, I must be permitted to be rash here, and declare, that I consider the sudden and violent abrogation of the office of Master in Chancery, by the new Constitution, as a—premature act; inasmuch as I had counted upon a life-lease of the profits, whereas I only received those of a few short years. But this is by the way.

My chambers were upstairs, at No. — Wall Street. At one end, they looked upon the white wall of the interior of a spacious skylight shaft, penetrating the building from top to bottom.

This view might have been considered rather tame than otherwise, deficient in what landscape painters call 'life.' But, if so, the view from the other end of my chambers offered, at least, a contrast, if nothing more. In that direction, my windows commanded an unobstructed view of a lofty brick wall, black by age and everlasting shade; which wall required no spy-glass to bring out its lurking beauties, but, for the benefit of all near-sighted spectators, was pushed up to within ten feet of my window panes. Owing to the great height of the surrounding buildings, and my chambers being on the second floor, the interval between this wall and mine not a little resembled a huge square cistern. At the period just preceding the advent of Bartleby, I had two persons as copyists in my employment, and a promising lad as an office-boy. First, Turkey; second, Nippers; third, Ginger Nut. These may seem names, the like of which are not usually found in the Directory. In truth, they were nicknames, mutually conferred upon each other by my three clerks, and were deemed expressive of their respective persons or characters. Turkey was a short, pursy Englishman, of about my own age—that is, somewhere not far from sixty. In the morning, one might say, his face was of a fine florid hue, but after twelve o'clock, meridian—his dinner hour—it blazed like a grate full of Christmas coals; and continued blazing—but, as it were, with a gradual wane—till six o'clock, P.M., or thereabouts; after which, I saw no more of the proprietor of the face, which, gaining its meridian with the sun, seemed to set with it, to rise, culminate, and decline the following day, with the like regularity and undiminished glory. There are many singular coincidences I have known in the course of my life, not the least among which was the fact, that, exactly when Turkey displayed his fullest beams from his red and radiant countenance, just then, too, at that critical moment, began the daily period when I considered his business capacities as seriously disturbed for the remainder of the twenty-four hours. Not that he was absolutely idle, or averse to business, then; far from it. The difficulty was, he was apt to be altogether too energetic. There was a strange, inflamed, flurried, flighty recklessness of activity about him. He would be incautious in dipping his pen into his inkstand. All his blots upon my documents were dropped there after twelve o'clock, meridian. Indeed, not only would he be reckless, and sadly given to making blots in the afternoon, but, some days, he went further, and was rather noisy. At such times, too, his face flamed with augmented blazonry, as if cannel coal had been heaped on anthracite. He made an unpleasant racket with his chair; spilled his sand-box; in mending his pens, impatiently split them all to pieces, and threw them on the floor in a sudden passion; stood up, and leaned over his table, boxing his papers about in a most indecorous manner, very sad to behold in an elderly man like him. Nevertheless, as he was in many ways a most valuable person to me, and all the time before twelve o'clock, meridian, was the quickest, steadiest creature, too, accomplishing a great deal of work in a style not easily to be matched—for these reasons, I was willing to overlook his eccentricities, though, indeed, occasionally, I remonstrated with him. I did this very gently, however, because, though the civilest, nay, the blandest and most reverential of men in the morning, yet, in the afternoon, he was disposed, upon provocation, to be slightly rash with his tongue—in fact, insolent. Now, valuing his morning services as I did, and resolved not to lose them—yet, at the same time, made uncomfortable by his inflamed ways after twelve o'clock—and being a man of peace, unwilling by my admonitions to call forth unseemly retorts from him, I took upon me, one Saturday noon (he was always worse on Saturdays) to hint to him, very kindly, that, perhaps, now that he was growing old, it might be well to abridge his labours; in short, he need not come to my chambers after twelve o'clock, but, dinner over, had best go home to his lodgings, and rest himself till tea-time. But no; he insisted upon his afternoon devotions. His countenance became intolerably fervid, as he oratorically assured me—gesticulating with a long ruler at the other end of the room— that if his services in the morning were useful, how indispensable, then, in the afternoon?

'With submission, sir,' said Turkey, on this occasion, 'I consider myself your right-hand man. In the morning I but marshal and deploy my columns; but in the afternoon I put myself at their head, and gallantly charge the foe, thus'—and he made a violent thrust with the ruler.

'But the blots, Turkey,' intimated I.

'True; but, with submission, sir, behold these hairs! I am getting old. Surely, sir, a blot or two of a warm afternoon is not to be severely urged against gray hairs. Old age—even if it blot the page—is honourable. With submission, sir, we *both* are getting old.'

This appeal to my fellow-feeling was hardly to be resisted. At all events, I saw that go he would not. So, I made up my mind to let him stay, resolving, nevertheless, to see to it that, during the afternoon, he had to do with my less important papers.

Nippers, the second on my list, was a whiskered, sallow, and, upon the whole, rather piratical-looking young man, of about five-and-twenty. I always deemed him the victim of two evil powers—ambition and indigestion. The ambition was evinced by a certain impatience of the duties of a mere copyist, an unwarrantable usurpation of strictly professional affairs, such as the original drawing up of legal documents. The indigestion seemed betokened in an occasional nervous testiness and grinning irritability, causing the teeth to audibly grind together over mistakes committed in copying; unnecessary maledictions, hissed, rather than spoken, in the heat of business; and especially by a continual discontent with the height of the table where he worked. Though of a very ingenious mechanical turn, Nippers could never get this table to suit him. He put chips under it, blocks of various sorts, bits of pasteboard, and at last went so far as to attempt an exquisite adjustment, by final pieces of folded blotting-paper. But no invention would answer. If, for the sake of easing his back, he brought the table lid at a sharp angle well up toward his chin, and wrote there like a man using the steep roof of a Dutch house for his desk, then he declared that it stopped the circulation in his arms. If now he lowered the table to his waistbands, and stooped over it in writing, then there was a sore aching in his back. In short, the truth of the matter was, Nippers knew not what he wanted. Or, if he wanted anything, it was to be rid of a scrivener's table altogether. Among the manifestations of his diseased ambition was a fondness he had for receiving visits from certain ambiguous-looking fellows in seedy coats, whom he called his clients. Indeed, I was aware that not only was he, at times, considerable of a ward-politician, but he occasionally did a little business at the Justices' courts, and was not unknown on the steps of the Tombs. I have good reason to believe, however, that one individual who called upon him at my chambers, and who, with a grand air, he insisted was his client, was no other than a dun, and the alleged title-deed, a bill. But, with all his failings, and the annoyances he caused me, Nippers, like his compatriot Turkey, was a very useful man to me; wrote a neat, swift hand; and, when he chose, was not deficient in a gentlemanly sort of deportment. Added to this, he always dressed in a gentlemanly sort of way; and so, incidentally, reflected credit upon my chambers. Whereas, with respect to Turkey, I had much ado to keep him from being a reproach to me. His clothes were apt to look oily, and smell of eating-houses. He wore his pantaloons very loose and baggy in summer. His coats were execrable; his hat not to be handled. But while the hat was a thing of indifference to me, inasmuch as his natural civility and deference, as a dependent Englishman, always led him to doff it the moment he entered the room, yet his coat was another matter. Concerning his coats, I reasoned with him; but with no effect. The truth was, I suppose, that a man with so small an income could not afford to sport such a lustrous face and a lustrous coat at one and the same time. As Nippers once observed, Turkey's money went chiefly for red ink. One winter day, I presented Turkey with a highly respectable-looking coat of my own—a padded gray coat, of a most comfortable warmth, and which buttoned straight up from the knee to the neck. I thought Turkey would appreciate the favour, and abate his rashness and obstreperousness of afternoons. But no; I verily believe that buttoning himself up in so downy and blanket-like a coat had a pernicious effect upon him—upon the same principle that too much oats are bad for horses. In fact, precisely as a rash, restive horse is said to feel his oats, so Turkey felt his coat. It made him insolent. He was a man whom prosperity harmed.

Though, concerning the self-indulgent habits of Turkey, I had
my own private surmises, yet, touching Nippers, I was well persuaded
that, whatever might be his faults in other respects, he was, at least,
a temperate young man. But, indeed, nature herself seemed to have
been his vintner, and, at his birth, charged him so thoroughly with an
irritable, brandy-like disposition, that all subsequent potations were
needless. When I consider how, amid the stillness of my chambers,
Nippers would sometimes impatiently rise from his seat, and stooping
over his table, spread his arms wide apart, seize the whole desk, and
move it, and jerk it, with a grim, grinding motion on the floor, as if the
table were a perverse voluntary agent, intent on thwarting and vexing
him, I plainly perceive that, for Nippers, brandy-and-water were altogether superfluous.

It was fortunate for me that, owing to its peculiar cause—indigestion—the irritability and consequent nervousness of Nippers were
mainly observable in the morning, while in the afternoon he was com-
paratively mild. So that, Turkey's paroxysms only coming on about
twelve o'clock, I never had to do with their eccentricities at one time.
Their fits relieved each other, like guards. When Nippers's was on,
Turkey's was off; and *vice versa*. This was a good natural arrangement,
under the circumstances.

Ginger Nut, the third on my list, was a lad, some twelve years
old. His father was a carman, ambitious of seeing his son on the bench
instead of a cart, before he died. So he sent him to my office, as student
at law, errand-boy, cleaner and sweeper, at the rate of one dollar a
week. He had a little desk to himself, but he did not use it much. Upon
inspection, the drawer exhibited a great array of the shells of various
sorts of nuts. Indeed, to this quick-witted youth, the whole noble science of the law was contained in a nutshell. Not the least among the
employments of Ginger Nut, as well as one which he discharged with
the most alacrity, was his duty as cake and apple purveyor for Turkey
and Nippers. Copying law-papers being proverbially a dry, husky sort
of business, my two scriveners were fain to moisten their mouths very
often with Spitzenbergs, to be had at the numerous stalls nigh the
Custom House and Post Office. Also, they sent Ginger Nut very
frequently for that peculiar cake—small, flat, round, and very spicy—
after which he had been named by them. Of a cold morning, when
business was but dull, Turkey would gobble up scores of these cakes,
as if they were mere wafers—indeed, they sell them at the rate of six
or eight for a penny—the scrape of his pen blending with the crunching
of the crisp particles in his mouth. Of all the fiery afternoon blunders
and flurried rashnesses of Turkey, was his once moistening a ginger-

cake between his lips, and clapping it on to a mortgage, for a seal. I came within an ace of dismissing him then. But he mollified me by making an oriental bow, and saying—'With submission, sir, it was generous of me to find you in stationery on my own account.'

Now my original business—that of a conveyancer and title-hunter, and drawer-up of recondite documents of all sorts—was considerably increased by receiving the master's office. There was now great work for scriveners. Not only must I push the clerks already with me, but I must have additional help.

In answer to my advertisement, a motionless young man one morning stood upon my office threshold, the door being open, for it was summer. I can see that figure now—pallidly neat, pitiably respectable, incurably forlorn! It was Bartleby.

After a few words touching his qualifications, I engaged him, glad to have among my corps of copyists a man of so singularly sedate an aspect, which I thought might operate beneficially upon the flighty temper of Turkey, and the fiery one of Nippers.

I should have stated before that ground-glass folding doors divided my premises into two parts, one of which was occupied by my scriveners, the other by myself. According to my humour, I threw open these doors, or closed them. I resolved to assign Bartleby a corner by the folding-doors, but on my side of them, so as to have this quiet man within easy call, in case any trifling thing was to be done. I placed his desk close up to a small side-window in that part of the room, a window which originally had afforded a lateral view of certain grimy back-yards and bricks, but which, owing to subsequent erections, commanded at present no view at all, though it gave some light. Within three feet of the panes was a wall, and the light came down from far above, between two lofty buildings, as from a very small opening in a dome. Still further to a satisfactory arrangement, I procured a high green folding-screen, which might entirely isolate Bartleby from my sight, though not remove him from my voice. And thus, in a manner, privacy and society were conjoined.

At first, Bartleby did an extraordinary quantity of writing. As if long famishing for something to copy, he seemed to gorge himself on my documents. There was no pause for digestion. He ran a day and night line, copying by sun-light and by candle-light. I should have been quite delighted with his application, had he been cheerfully industrious. But he wrote on silently, palely, mechanically.

It is, of course, an indispensable part of a scrivener's business to verify the accuracy of his copy, word by word. Where there are two or more scriveners in an office, they assist each other in this exami-

Bartleby (1969) "... copying by sunlight and by candlelight ... he wrote on silently, palely, mechanically." *Still shot reproduced courtesy of Encyclopaedia Britannica Educational Corporation.*

nation, one reading from the copy, the other holding the original. It is a very dull, wearisome, and lethargic affair. I can readily imagine that, to some sanguine temperaments, it would be altogether intolerable. For example, I cannot credit that the mettlesome poet, Byron, would have contentedly sat down with Bartleby to examine a law document, of say, five hundred pages, closely written in a crimpy hand.

Now and then, in the haste of business, it had been my habit to assist in comparing some brief document myself, calling Turkey or Nippers for this purpose. One object I had, in placing Bartleby so handy to me behind the screen, was, to avail myself of his services on such trivial occasions. It was on the third day, I think, of his being with me, and before any necessity had arisen for having his own writing examined, that, being much hurried to complete a small affair I had in hand, I abruptly called to Bartleby. In my haste and natural expectancy of instant compliance, I sat with my head bent over the original on my desk, and my right hand sideways, and somewhat nervously extended with the copy, so that, immediately upon emerging from his retreat, Bartleby might snatch it and proceed to business without the least delay.

In this very attitude did I sit when I called to him, rapidly stating what it was I wanted him to do—namely, to examine a small paper with me. Imagine my surprise, nay, my consternation, when, without moving from his privacy, Bartleby, in a singularly mild, firm voice, replied, 'I would prefer not to.'

I sat a while in perfect silence, rallying my stunned faculties. Immediately it occurred to me that my ears had deceived me, or Bartleby had entirely misunderstood my meaning. I repeated my request in the clearest tone I could assume; but in quite as clear a one came the previous reply, 'I would prefer not to.'

'Prefer not to,' echoed I, rising in high excitement, and crossing the room with a stride. 'What do you mean? Are you moon-struck? I want you to help me compare this sheet here—take it,' and I thrust it toward him.

'I would prefer not to,' said he.

I looked at him steadfastly. His face was leanly composed; his gray eye dimly calm. Not a wrinkle of agitation rippled him. Had there been the least uneasiness, anger, impatience, or impertinence in his manner; in other words, had there been anything ordinarily human about him, doubtless I should have violently dismissed him from the premises. But as it was, I should have as soon thought of turning my pale plaster-of-paris bust of Cicero out of doors. I stood gazing at him a while, as he went on with his own writing, and then reseated myself at my desk. This is very strange, thought I. What had one best do? But my business hurried me. I concluded to forget the matter for the present, reserving it for my future leisure. So calling Nippers from the other room, the paper was speedily examined.

A few days after this, Bartleby concluded four lengthy documents, being quadruplicates of a week's testimony taken before me in my High Court of Chancery. It became necessary to examine them. It was an important suit, and great accuracy was imperative. Having all things arranged, I called Turkey, Nippers, and Ginger Nut, from the next room, meaning to place the four copies in the hands of my four clerks, while I should read from the original. Accordingly, Turkey, Nippers, and Ginger Nut had taken their seats in a row, each with his document in his hand, when I called to Bartleby to join this interesting group.

'Bartleby! quick, I am waiting.'

I heard a slow scrape of his chair legs on the uncarpeted floor, and soon he appeared standing at the entrance of his hermitage.

'What is wanted?' said he mildly.

'The copies, the copies,' said I hurriedly. 'We are going to examine them. There'—and I held toward him the fourth quadruplicate.

'I would prefer not to,' he said, and gently disappeared behind the screen.

For a few moments I was turned into a pillar of salt, standing at the head of my seated column of clerks. Recovering myself, I advanced toward the screen, and demanded the reason for such extraordinary conduct.

'*Why* do you refuse?'

'I would prefer not to.'

With any other man I should have flown outright into a dreadful passion, scorned all further words, and thrust him ignominiously from my presence. But there was something about Bartleby that not only strangely disarmed me, but, in a wonderful manner, touched and disconcerted me. I began to reason with him.

'These are your own copies we are about to examine. It is labour saving to you, because one examination will answer for your four papers. It is common usage. Every copyist is bound to help examine his copy. Is it not so? Will you not speak? Answer!'

'I prefer not to,' he replied in a flute-like tone. It seemed to me that, while I had been addressing him, he carefully revolved every statement that I made; fully comprehended the meaning; could not gainsay the irresistible conclusion; but, at the same time, some paramount consideration prevailed with him to reply as he did.

'You are decided, then, not to comply with my request—a request made according to common usage and common sense?'

He briefly gave me to understand, that on that point my judgment was sound. Yes: his decision was irreversible.

It is not seldom the case that, when a man is browbeaten in some unprecedented and violently unreasonable way, he begins to stagger in his own plainest faith. He begins, as it were, vaguely to surmise that, wonderful as it may be, all the justice and all the reason is on the other side. Accordingly, if any disinterested persons are present, he turns to them for some reinforcement for his own faltering mind.

'Turkey,' said I, 'what do you think of this? Am I not right?'

'With submission, sir,' said Turkey, in his blandest tone, 'I think you are.'

'Nippers,' said I, 'what do *you* think of it?'

'I think I should kick him out of the office.'

(The reader, of nice perceptions, will here perceive that, it being morning, Turkey's answer is couched in polite and tranquil terms, but

Nippers replies in ill-tempered ones. Or, to repeat a previous sentence, Nippers's ugly mood was on duty, and Turkey's off.)

'Ginger Nut,' said I, willing to enlist the smallest suffrage in my behalf, 'what do *you* think of it?'

'I think, sir, he's a little *luny*,' replied Ginger Nut, with a grin.

'You hear what they say,' said I, turning toward the screen, 'come forth and do your duty.'

But he vouchsafed no reply. I pondered a moment in sore perplexity. But once more business hurried me. I determined again to postpone the consideration of this dilemma to my future leisure. With a little trouble we made out to examine the papers without Bartleby, though at every page or two Turkey deferentially dropped his opinion, that this proceeding was quite out of the common; while Nippers, twitching in his chair with a dyspeptic nervousness, ground out, between his set teeth, occasional hissing maledictions against the stubborn oaf behind the screen. And for his (Nippers's) part, this was the first and the last time he would do another man's business without pay.

Meanwhile Bartleby sat in his hermitage, oblivious to everything but his own peculiar business there.

Some days passed, the scrivener being employed upon another lengthy work. His late remarkable conduct led me to regard his ways narrowly. I observed that he never went to dinner; indeed, that he never went anywhere. As yet I had never, of my personal knowledge, known him to be outside of my office. He was a perpetual sentry in the corner. At about eleven o'clock though, in the morning, I noticed that Ginger Nut would advance toward the opening in Bartleby's screen, as if silently beckoned thither by a gesture invisible to me where I sat. The boy would then leave the office, jingling a few pence, and reappear with a handful of ginger-nuts, which he delivered in the hermitage, receiving two of the cakes for his trouble.

He lives, then, on ginger-nuts, thought I; never eats a dinner, properly speaking; he must be a vegetarian, then; but no; he never eats even vegetables, he eats nothing but ginger-nuts. My mind then ran on in reveries concerning the probable effects upon the human constitution of living entirely on ginger-nuts. Ginger-nuts are so called, because they contain ginger as one of their peculiar constituents, and the final flavouring one. Now, what was ginger? A hot, spicy thing. Was Bartleby hot and spicy? Not at all. Ginger, then, had no effect upon Bartleby. Probably he preferred it should have none.

Nothing so aggravates an earnest person as a passive resistance. If the individual so resisted be of a not inhumane temper, and the resisting one perfectly harmless in his passivity, then, in the better moods of the former, he will endeavour charitably to construe to his imagination what proves impossible to be solved by his judgment. Even so, for the most part, I regarded Bartleby and his ways. Poor fellow! thought I, he means no mischief; it is plain he intends no insolence; his aspect sufficiently evinces that his eccentricities are involuntary. He is useful to me. I can get along with him. If I turn him away, the chances are he will fall in with some less-indulgent employer, and then he will be rudely treated, and perhaps driven forth miserably to starve. Yes. Here I can cheaply purchase a delicious self-approval. To befriend Bartleby; to humour him in his strange wilfulness, will cost me little or nothing, while I lay up in my soul what will eventually prove a sweet morsel for my conscience. But this mood was not invariable with me. The passiveness of Bartleby sometimes irritated me. I felt strangely goaded on to encounter him in new opposition—to elicit some angry spark from him answerable to my own. But, indeed, I might as well have essayed to strike fire with my knuckles against a bit of Windsor soap. But one afternoon the evil impulse in me mastered me, and the following little scene ensued:—

'Bartleby,' said I, 'when those papers are all copied, I will compare them with you.'

'I would prefer not to.'

'How? Surely you do not mean to persist in that mulish vagary?'

No answer.

I threw open the folding-doors near by, and, turning upon Turkey and Nippers, exclaimed:

'Bartleby a second time says, he won't examine his papers. What do you think of it, Turkey?'

It was afternoon, be it remembered. Turkey sat glowing like a brass boiler; his bald head steaming; his hands reeling among his blotted papers.

'Think of it?' roared Turkey; 'I think I'll just step behind his screen, and black his eyes for him!'

So saying, Turkey rose to his feet and threw his arms into a pugilistic position. He was hurrying away to make good his promise, when I detained him, alarmed at the effect of incautiously rousing Turkey's combativeness after dinner.

'Sit down, Turkey,' said I, 'and hear what Nippers has to say. What do you think of it, Nippers? Would I not be justified in immediately dismissing Bartleby?'

'Excuse me, that is for you to decide, sir. I think his conduct quite unusual, and, indeed, unjust, as regards Turkey and myself. But it may only be a passing whim.'

'Ah,' exclaimed I, 'you have strangely changed your mind, then—you speak very gently of him now.'

'All beer,' cried Turkey; 'gentleness is effects of beer—Nippers and I dined together to-day. You see how gentle *I* am, sir. Shall I go and black his eyes?'

'You refer to Bartleby, I suppose. No, not to-day, Turkey,' I replied; 'pray, put up your fists.'

I closed the doors, and again advanced toward Bartleby. I felt additional incentives tempting me to my fate. I burned to be rebelled against again. I remembered that Bartleby never left the office.

'Bartleby,' said I, 'Ginger Nut is away; just step around to the Post Office, won't you? (it was but a three minutes' walk), and see if there is anything for me.'

'I would prefer not to.'

'You *will* not?'

'I *prefer* not.'

I staggered to my desk, and sat there in a deep study. My blind inveteracy returned. Was there any other thing in which I could procure myself to be ignominiously repulsed by this lean, penniless wight?—my hired clerk? What added thing is there, perfectly reasonable, that he will be sure to refuse to do?

'Bartleby!'

No answer.

'Bartleby,' in a louder tone.

No answer.

'Bartleby,' I roared.

Like a very ghost, agreeably to the laws of magical invocation, at the third summons, he appeared at the entrance of his hermitage.

'Go to the next room, and tell Nippers to come to me.'

'I prefer not to,' he respectfully and slowly said, and mildly disappeared.

'Very good, Bartley,' said I, in a quiet sort of serenely-severe self-possessed tone, intimating the unalterable purpose of some terrible retribution very close at hand. At the moment I half intended something of the kind. But upon the whole, as it was drawing toward my dinner-hour, I thought it best to put on my hat and walk home for the day, suffering much from perplexity and distress of mind.

Shall I acknowledge it? The conclusion of this whole business was, that it soon became a fixed fact of my chambers, that a pale young scrivener, by the name of Bartleby, had a desk there; that he copied for me at the usual rate of four cents a folio (one hundred words); but he was permanently exempt from examining the work done by him, that duty being transferred to Turkey and Nippers, out of compliment, doubtless, to their superior acuteness; moreover, said Bartleby was never, on any account, to be dispatched on the most trivial errand of any sort; and that even if entreated to take upon him such a matter, it was generally understood that he would 'prefer not to'—in other words, that he would refuse point-blank.

As days passed on, I became considerably reconciled to Bartleby. His steadiness, his freedom from all dissipation, his incessant industry (except when he chose to throw himself into a standing revery behind his screen), his great stillness, his unalterableness of demeanour under all circumstances, made him a valuable acquisition. One prime thing was this—*he was always there*—first in the morning, continually through the day, and the last at night. I had a singular confidence in his honesty. I felt my most precious papers perfectly safe in his hands. Sometimes, to be sure, I could not, for the very soul of me, avoid falling into sudden spasmodic passions with him. For it was exceeding difficult to bear in mind all the time those strange peculiarities, privileges, and unheard-of exemptions, forming the tacit stipulations on Bartleby's part under which he remained in my office. Now and then, in the eagerness of dispatching pressing business, I would inadvertently summon Bartleby, in a short, rapid tone, to put his finger, say, on the incipient tie of a bit of red tape with which I was about compressing some papers. Of course, from behind the screen the usual answer, 'I prefer not to,' was sure to come; and then, how could a human creature, with the common infirmities of our nature, refrain from bitterly ex- claiming upon such perverseness—such unreasonableness. However, every added repulse of this sort which I received only tended to lessen the probability of my repeating the inadvertence.

Here it must be said, that according to the custom of most legal gentlemen occupying chambers in densely populated law-buildings, there were several keys to my door. One was kept by a woman residing in the attic, which person weekly scrubbed and daily swept and dusted my apartments. Another was kept by Turkey for convenience sake. The third I sometimes carried in my own pocket. The fourth I knew not who had.

Now, one Sunday morning I happened to go to Trinity Church, to hear a celebrated preacher, and finding myself rather early on the ground I thought I would walk round to my chambers for a while. Luckily I had my key with me; but upon applying it to the lock, I found it resisted by something inserted from the inside. Quite surprised, I called out; when to my consternation a key was turned from within; and thrusting his lean visage at me, and holding the door ajar, the apparition of Bartleby appeared, in his shirt-sleeves, and otherwise in a strangely tattered dishabille, saying quietly that he was sorry, but he was deeply engaged just then, and—preferred not admitting me at present. In a brief word or two, he moreover added, that perhaps I had better walk round the block two or three times, and by that time he would probably have concluded his affairs.

Now, the utterly unsurmised appearance of Bartleby, tenanting my law-chambers of a Sunday morning, with his cadaverously gentlemanly nonchalance, yet withal firm and self-possessed, had such a strange effect upon me, that incontinently I slunk away from my own door, and did as desired. But not without sundry twinges of impotent rebellion against the mild effrontery of this unaccountable scrivener. Indeed, it was his wonderful mildness chiefly, which not only disarmed me, but unmanned me as it were. For I consider that one, for the time, is a sort of unmanned when he tranquilly permits his hired clerk to dictate to him, and order him away from his own premises. Furthermore, I was full of uneasiness as to what Bartleby could possibly be doing in my office in his shirtsleeves, and in an otherwise dismantled condition of a Sunday morning. Was anything amiss going on? Nay, that was out of the question. It was not to be thought of for a moment that Bartleby was an immoral person. But what could he be doing there?—copying? Nay again, whatever might be his eccentricities, Bartleby was an eminently decorous person. He would be the last man to sit down to his desk in any state approaching to nudity. Besides, it was Sunday; and there was something about Bartleby that forbade the supposition that he would by any secular occupation violate the proprieties of the day.

Nevertheless, my mind was not pacified; and full of a restless curiosity, at last I returned to the door. Without hindrance I inserted my key, opened it, and entered. Bartleby was not to be seen. I looked round anxiously, peeped behind his screen; but it was very plain that he was gone. Upon more closely examining the place, I surmised that for an indefinite period Bartleby must have ate, dressed, and slept in my office, and that, too, without plate, mirror, or bed. The cushioned seat of a rickety old sofa in one corner bore the faint impress of a lean, reclining form. Rolled away under his desk, I found a blanket; under the empty grate, a tin basin, with soap and a ragged towel; in a newspaper a few crumbs of ginger-nuts and a morsel of cheese. Yes, thought I, it is evident enough that Bartleby has been making his home here, keeping bachelor's hall all by himself. Immediately then the thought came sweeping across me, what miserable friendlessness and loneliness are here revealed! His poverty is great; but his solitude, how horrible!

Think of it. Of a Sunday, Wall Street is deserted as Petra; and every night of every day it is an emptiness. This building, too, which of weekdays hums with industry and life, at nightfall echoes with sheer vacancy, and all through Sunday is forlorn. And here Bartleby makes his home; sole spectator of a solitude which he has seen all-populous—a sort of innocent and transformed Marius brooding among the ruins of Carthage!

For the first time in my life a feeling of overpowering stinging melancholy seized me. Before I had never experienced aught but a not unpleasing sadness. The bond of a common humanity now drew me irresistibly to gloom. A fraternal melancholy! For both I and Bartleby were sons of Adam. I remembered the bright silks and sparkling faces I had seen that day, in gala trim, swan-like sailing down the Mississippi of Broadway; and I contrasted them with the pallid copyist, and thought to myself, Ah, happiness courts the light, so we deem the world is gay; but misery hides aloof, so we deem that misery there is none. These sad fancyings—chimeras, doubtless, of a sick and silly brain—led on to other and more special thoughts, concerning the eccentricities of Bartleby. Presentiments of strange discoveries hovered round me. The scrivener's pale form appeared to me laid out, among uncaring strangers, in its shivering winding-sheet.

Suddenly I was attracted by Bartleby's closed desk, the key in open sight left in the lock.

I mean no mischief, seek the gratification of no heartless curiosity, thought I; besides, the desk is mine, and its contents, too, so I will make bold to look within. Everything was methodically arranged, the papers smoothly placed. The pigeonholes were deep, and removing the files of documents, I groped into their recesses. Presently I felt something there, and dragged it out. It was an old bandanna handkerchief, heavy and knotted. I opened it, and saw it was a savings-bank.

I now recalled all the quiet mysteries which I had noted in the man. I remembered that he never spoke but to answer; that, though at intervals he had considerable time to himself, yet I had never seen him reading—no, not even a newspaper; that for long periods he would stand looking out, at his pale window behind the screen, upon the dead brick wall; I was quite sure he never visited any refectory or eating-house; while his pale face clearly indicated that he never drank beer like Turkey, or tea and coffee even, like other men; that he never went anywhere in particular that I could learn; never went out for a walk, unless, indeed, that was the case at present; that he had declined telling who he was, or whence he came, or whether he had any relatives in the world; that though so thin and pale, he never complained of ill health. And more than all, I remembered a certain unconscious air of pallid—how shall I call it?—of pallid haughtiness, say, or rather an austere reserve about him, which had positively awed me into my tame compliance with his eccentricities, when I had feared to ask him to do the slightest incidental thing for me, even though I might know, from his long-continued motionlessness, that behind his screen he must be standing in one of those dead-wall reveries of his.

Revolving all these things, and coupling them with the recently discovered fact, that he made my office his constant abiding-place and home, and not forgetful of his morbid moodiness; revolving all these things, a prudential feeling began to steal over me. My first emotions had been those of pure melancholy and sincerest pity; but just in proportion as the forlornness of Bartleby grew and grew to my imagination, did that same melancholy merge into fear, that pity into repulsion. So true it is, and so terrible, too, that up to a certain point the thought or sigh of misery enlists our best affections; but, in certain special cases, beyond that point it does not. They err who would assert that invariably this is owing to the inherent selfishness of the human heart. It rather proceeds from a certain hopelessness of remedying excessive and organic ill. To a sensitive being, pity is not seldom pain. And when at last it is perceived that such pity cannot lead to effectual succour, commonsense bids the soul be rid of it. What I saw that morning persuaded me that the scrivener was the victim of innate and incurable disorder. I might give alms to his body; but his body did not pain him; it was his soul that suffered, and his soul I could not reach.

I did not accomplish the purpose of going to Trinity Church that morning. Somehow, the things I had seen disqualified me for the time from church-going. I walked homeward, thinking what I would do with Bartleby. Finally, I resolved upon this—I would put certain calm questions to him the next morning, touching his history, etc., and if he declined to answer them openly and unreservedly (and I supposed he would prefer not), then to give him a twenty-dollar bill over and above whatever I might owe him, and tell him his services were no longer required; but that if in any other way I could assist him, I would be happy to do so, especially if he desired to return to his native place, wherever that might be, I would willingly help to defray the expenses. Moreover, if, after reaching home, he found himself at any time in want of aid, a letter from him would be sure of a reply.

The next morning came.

'Bartleby,' said I, gently calling to him behind his screen.

No reply.

'Bartleby,' said I, in a still gentler tone, 'come here; I am not going to ask you to do anything you would prefer not to do—I simply wish to speak to you.'

Upon this he noiselessly slid into view.

'Will you tell me, Bartleby, where you were born?'

'I would prefer not to.'

'Will you tell me *anything* about yourself?'

'I would prefer not to.'

'But what reasonable objection can you have to speak to me? I feel friendly toward you.'

He did not look at me while I spoke, but kept his glance fixed upon my bust of Cicero, which, as I then sat, was directly behind me, some six inches above my head.

'What is your answer, Bartleby?' said I, after waiting a considerable time for a reply, during which his countenance remained immovable, only there was the faintest conceivable tremor of the white attenuated mouth.

'At present I prefer to give no answer,' he said, and retired into his hermitage.

It was rather weak in me, I confess, but his manner, on this occasion, nettled me. Not only did there seem to lurk in it a certain calm disdain, but his perverseness seemed ungrateful, considering the undeniable good usage and indulgence he had received from me.

Again I sat ruminating what I should do. Mortified as I was at his behaviour, and resolved as I had been to dismiss him when I entered my office, nevertheless I strangely felt something superstitious knocking at my heart, and forbidding me to carry out my purpose, and denouncing me for a villain if I dared to breathe one bitter word against this forlornest of mankind. At last, familiarly drawing my chair behind his screen, I sat down and said: 'Bartleby, never mind, then, about revealing your history; but let me entreat you, as a friend, to comply as far as may be with the usages of this office. Say now, you will help to examine papers to-morrow or next day; in short, say now, that in a day or two you will begin to be a little reasonable:—say so, Bartleby.'

'At present I would prefer not to be a little reasonable," was his mildly cadaverous reply.

Just then the folding doors opened, and Nippers approached. He seemed suffering from an unusually bad night's rest, induced by severer indigestion than common. He overheard those final words of Bartleby.

'*Prefer not*, eh?' gritted Nippers—'I'd *prefer* him, if I were you, sir,' addressing me—'I'd *prefer* him; I'd give him preferences, the stubborn mule! What is it, sir, pray, that he *prefers* not to do now?'

Bartleby moved not a limb.

'Mr. Nippers,' said I, 'I'd prefer that you would withdraw for the present.'

Somehow, of late, I had got into the way of involuntarily using this word 'prefer' upon all sorts of not exactly suitable occasions. And I trembled to think that my contact with the scrivener had already and seriously affected me in a mental way. And what further and deeper aberration might it not yet produce? This apprehension had not been without efficacy in determining me to summary measures.

As Nippers, looking very sour and sulky, was departing, Turkey blandly and deferentially approached.

'With submission, sir,' said he, 'yesterday I was thinking about Bartleby here, and I think that if he would but prefer to take a quart of good ale every day, it would do much toward mending him, and enabling him to assist in examining his papers.'

'So you have got the word too,' said I, slightly excited.

'With submission, what word, sir,' asked Turkey, respectfully crowding himself into the contracted space behind the screen, and by so doing, making me jostle the scrivener. 'What word, sir?'

'I would prefer to be left alone here,' said Bartleby, as if offended at being mobbed in his privacy.

'*That's* the word, Turkey,' said I—'*that's* it.'

'Oh, *prefer?* oh yes—queer word. I never use it myself. But, sir, as I was saying, if he would but prefer——'

'Turkey,' interrupted I, 'you will please withdraw.'

'Oh certainly, sir, if you prefer that I should.'

As he opened the folding-door to retire, Nippers at his desk caught a glimpse of me, and asked whether I would prefer to have a certain paper copied on blue paper or white. He did not in the least roguishly accent the word prefer. It was plain that it involuntarily rolled from his tongue. I thought to myself, surely I must get rid of a demented man, who already has in some degree turned the tongues, if not the heads of myself and clerks. But I thought it prudent not to break the dismission at once.

The next day I noticed that Bartleby did nothing but stand at his window in his dead-wall revery. Upon asking him why he did not write, he said that he had decided upon doing no more writing.

'Why, how now? what next?' exclaimed I, 'do no more writing?'

'No more.'

'And what is the reason?'

'Do you not see the reason for yourself?' he indifferently replied.

I looked steadfastly at him, and perceived that his eyes looked dull and glazed. Instantly it occurred to me, that his unexampled diligence in copying by his dim window for the first few weeks of his stay with me might have temporarily impaired his vision.

I was touched. I said something in condolence with him. I hinted that of course he did wisely in abstaining from writing for a while; and urged him to embrace that opportunity of taking wholesome exercise in the open air. This, however, he did not do. A few days after this, my other clerks being absent, and being in a great hurry to dispatch certain letters by the mail, I thought that having nothing else earthly to do, Bartleby would surely be less inflexible than usual, and carry these letters to the Post Office. But he blankly declined. So, much to my inconvenience, I went myself.

Still added days went by. Whether Bartleby's eyes improved or not, I could not say. To all appearance, I thought they did. But when I asked him if they did, he vouchsafed no answer. At all events, he would do no copying. At last, in reply to my urgings, he informed me that he had permanently given up copying.

'What!' exclaimed I; 'suppose your eyes should get entirely well —better than ever before—would you not copy then?'

'I have given up copying,' he answered, and slid aside.

He remained as ever, a fixture in my chamber. Nay—if that were possible—he became still more of a fixture than before. What was to be done? He would do nothing in the office; why should he stay there? In plain fact, he had now become a millstone to me, not only useless as a necklace, but afflicted to bear. Yet I was sorry for him. I speak less than truth when I say that, on his own account, he occasioned me uneasiness. If he would but have named a single relative or friend, I would instantly have written, and urged their taking the poor fellow away to some convenient retreat. But he seemed alone, absolutely alone in the universe. A bit of wreck in the mid-Atlantic. At length, necessities connected with my business tyrannised over all other considerations. Decently as I could, I told Bartleby that in six days' time he must unconditionally leave the office. I warned him to take measures, in the interval, for procuring some other abode. I offered to assist him in this endeavour, if he himself would but take the first step toward a removal. 'And when you finally quit me, Bartleby,' added I, 'I shall see that you go not away entirely unprovided. Six days from this hour, remember.'

At the expiration of that period, I peeped behind the screen, and lo! Bartleby was there.

I buttoned up my coat, balanced myself; advanced slowly toward him, touched his shoulder, and said, 'The time has come; you must quit this place; I am sorry for you; here is money; but you must go.'

'I would prefer not,' he replied, with his back still toward me.

'You *must.*'

He remained silent.

Now I had an unbounded confidence in this man's common honesty. He had frequently restored to me sixpences and shillings carelessly dropped upon the floor, for I am apt to be very reckless in such shirt-button affairs. The proceeding, then, which followed will not be deemed extraordinary.

'Bartleby,' said I, 'I owe you twelve dollars on account; here are thirty-two; the odd twenty are yours—Will you take it?' and I handed the bills toward him.

But he made no motion.

'I will leave them here, then,' putting them under a weight on the table. Then taking my hat and cane and going to the door, I tranquilly turned and added—'After you have removed your things from these offices, Bartleby, you will of course lock the door—since everyone is now gone for the day but you—and if you please, slip your key underneath the mat, so that I may have it in the morning. I shall not see you again; so goodbye to you. If, hereafter, in your new place of abode, I can be of any service to you, do not fail to advise me by letter. Good-bye, Bartleby, and fare you well.'

But he answered not a word; like the last column of some ruined temple, he remained standing mute and solitary in the middle of the otherwise deserted room.

As I walked home in a pensive mood, my vanity got the better of my pity. I could not but highly plume myself on my masterly management in getting rid of Bartleby. Masterly I call it, and such it must appear to any dispassionate thinker. The beauty of my procedure seemed to consist in its perfect quietness. There was no vulgar bullying, no bravado of any sort, no choleric hectoring, and striding to and fro across the apartment, jerking out vehement commands for Bartleby to bundle himself off with his beggarly traps. Nothing of the kind. Without loudly bidding Bartleby depart—as an inferior genius might have done —I *assumed* the ground that depart he must; and upon that assumption built all I had to say. The more I thought over my procedure, the more I was charmed with it. Nevertheless, next morning, upon awakening, I had my doubts—I had somehow slept off the fumes of vanity. One of the coolest and wisest hours a man has, is just after he awakes in the morning. My procedure seemed as sagacious as ever—but only in theory. How it would prove in practice—there was the rub. It was truly a beautiful thought to have assumed Bartleby's departure; but, after all, that assumption was simply my own, and none of Bartleby's. The great point was, not whether I had assumed that he would quit me, but whether he would prefer so to do. He was more a man of preferences than assumptions.

After breakfast, I walked down town, arguing the probabilities *pro* and *con*. One moment I thought it would prove a miserable failure, and Bartleby would be found all alive at my office as usual; the next moment it seemed certain that I should find his chair empty. And so I kept veering about. At the corner of Broadway and Canal Street, I saw quite an excited group of people standing in earnest conversation.

'I'll take odds he doesn't,' said a voice as I passed.

'Doesn't go?—done!' said I; 'put up your money.'

I was instinctively putting my hand in my pocket to produce my own, when I remembered that this was an election day. The words I had overheard bore no reference to Bartleby, but to the success or non-success of some candidate for the mayoralty. In my intent frame of mind, I had, as it were, imagined that all Broadway shared in my excitement, and were debating the same question with me. I passed on, very thankful that the uproar of the street screened my momentary absent-mindedness.

As I had intended, I was earlier than usual at my office door. I stood listening for a moment. All was still. He must be gone. I tried the knob. The door was locked. Yes, my procedure had worked to a charm; he indeed must be vanished. Yet a certain melancholy mixed with this; I was almost sorry for my brilliant success. I was fumbling under the doormat for the key, which Bartleby was to have left there for me, when accidentally my knee knocked against a panel, producing a summoning sound, and in response a voice came to me from within— 'Not yet; I am occupied.'

It was Bartleby.

I was thunderstruck. For an instant I stood like the man who, pipe in mouth, was killed one cloudless afternoon long ago in Virginia, by summer lightning; at his own warm open window he was killed, and remained leaning out there upon the dreamy afternoon, till someone touched him, when he fell.

'Not gone!' I murmured at last. But again obeying that wondrous ascendency which the inscrutable scrivener had over me, and from which ascendency, for all my chafing, I could not completely escape, I slowly went downstairs and out into the street, and while walking round the block, considered what I should next do in this unheard-of perplexity. Turn the man out by an actual thrusting I could not; to drive him away by calling him hard names would not do; calling in the police was an unpleasant idea; and yet, permit him to enjoy his cadaverous triumph over me—this, too, I could not think of. What was to be done? or, if nothing could be done, was there anything further that I could *assume* in the matter? Yes, as before I had prospectively assumed that Bartleby would depart, so now I might retrospectively assume that departed he was. In the legitimate carrying out of this assumption, I might enter my office in a great hurry, and pretending not to see Bartleby at all, walk straight against him as if he were air. Such a proceeding would in a singular degree have the appearance of a home-thrust. It was hardly possible that Bartleby could withstand such an application of the doctrine of assumptions. But upon second thoughts the success of the plan seemed rather dubious. I resolved to argue the matter over with him again.

'Bartleby,' said I, entering the office, with a quietly severe expression, 'I am seriously displeased. I am pained, Bartleby. I had thought better of you. I had imagined you of such a gentlemanly organisation, that in any delicate dilemma a slight hint would suffice—in short, an assumption. But it appears I am deceived. Why,' I added, unaffectedly starting, 'you have not even touched that money yet,' pointing to it, just where I had left it the evening previous.

He answered nothing.

'Will you, or will you not, quit me?' I now demanded in a sudden passion, advancing close to him.

'I would prefer *not* to quit you,' he replied, gently emphasising the *not*.

'What earthly right have you to stay here? Do you pay any rent? Do you pay my taxes? Or is this property yours?'

He answered nothing.

'Are you ready to go on and write now? Are your eyes recovered? Could you copy a small paper for me this morning? or help examine a few lines? or step round to the Post Office? In a word, will you do anything at all, to give a colouring to your refusal to depart the premises?'

He silently retired into his hermitage.

I was now in such a state of nervous resentment that I thought it but prudent to check myself at present from further demonstrations. Bartleby and I were alone. I remembered the tragedy of the unfortunate Adams and the still more unfortunate Colt in the solitary office of the latter; and how poor Colt, being dreadfully incensed by Adams, and imprudently permitting himself to get wildly excited, was at unawares hurried into his fatal act—an act which certainly no man could possibly deplore more than the actor himself. Often it had occurred to me in my ponderings upon the subject, that had that altercation taken place in the public street, or at a private residence, it would not have terminated as it did. It was the circumstance of being alone in a solitary office, upstairs, of a building entirely unhallowed by humanising domestic associations—an uncarpeted office, doubtless, of a dusty, haggard sort of appearance—this it must have been, which greatly helped to enhance the irritable desperation of the hapless Colt.

But when this old Adam of resentment rose in me and tempted me concerning Bartleby, I grappled him and threw him. How? Why, simply be recalling the divine injunction: 'A new commandment give I unto you, that ye love one another.' Yes, this it was that saved me. Aside from higher considerations, charity often operates as a vastly wise and prudent principle—a great safeguard to its possessor. Men have committed murder for jealousy's sake, and anger's sake, and hatred's sake, and selfishness' sake, and spiritual pride's sake; but no man, that ever I heard of, ever committed a diabolical murder for sweet charity's sake. Mere self-interest, then, if no better motive can be enlisted, should, especially with high-tempered men, prompt all beings to charity and philanthropy. At any rate, upon the occasion in question, I strove to drown my exasperated feelings toward the scrivener by benevolently construing his conduct. Poor fellow, poor fellow! thought I, he don't mean anything; and besides, he has seen hard times, and ought to be indulged.

I endeavoured, also, immediately to occupy myself, and at the same time to comfort my despondency. I tried to fancy, that in the course of the morning, at such time as might prove agreeable to him, Bartleby, of his own free accord, would emerge from his hermitage and take up some decided line of march in the direction of the door. But no. Half-past twelve o'clock came; Turkey began to glow in the face, overturn his inkstand, and become generally obstreperous; Nippers abated down into quietude and courtesy; Ginger Nut munched his noon apple; and Bartleby remained standing at his window in one of his profoundest dead-wall reveries. Will it be credited? Ought I to acknowledge it? That afternoon I left the office without saying one further word to him.

Some days now passed, during which, at leisure intervals, I looked a little into 'Edwards on the Will,' and 'Priestley on Necessity.' Under the circumstances, those books induced a salutary feeling. Gradually I slid into the persuasion that these troubles of mine, touching the scrivener, had been all predestinated from eternity, and Bartleby was billeted upon me for some mysterious purpose of an all-wise Providence, which it was not for a mere mortal like me to fathom. Yes, Bartleby, stay there behind your screen, thought I; I shall persecute you no more; you are harmless and noiseless as any of these old chairs;

in short, I never feel so private as when I know you are here. At last I see it, I feel it; I penetrate to the predestinated purpose of my life. I am content. Others may have loftier parts to enact; but my mission in this world, Bartleby, is to furnish you with office-room for such period as you may see fit to remain.

I believe that this wise and blessed frame of mind would have continued with me, had it not been for the unsolicited and uncharitable remarks obtruded upon me by my professional friends who visited the rooms. But thus it often is, that the constant friction of illiberal minds wears out at last the best resolves of the more generous. Though to be sure, when I reflected upon it, it was not strange that people entering my office should be struck by the peculiar aspect of the unaccountable Bartleby, and so be tempted to throw out some sinister observations concerning him. Sometimes an attorney, having business with me, and calling at my office, and finding no one but the scrivener there, would undertake to obtain some sort of precise information from him touching my whereabouts; but without heeding his idle talk, Bartleby would remain standing immovable in the middle of the room. So after contemplating him in that position for a time, the attorney would depart, no wiser than he came.

Also, when a reference was going on, and the room full of lawyers and witnesses, and business driving fast, some deeply occupied legal gentleman present, seeing Bartleby wholly unemployed, would request him to run round to his (the legal gentleman's) office and fetch some papers for him. Thereupon, Bartleby would tranquilly decline, and yet remain idle as before. Then the lawyer would give a great stare, and turn to me. And what could I say? At last I was made aware that all through the circle of my professional acquaintance, a whisper of wonder was running round, having reference to the strange creature I kept at my office. This worried me very much. And as the idea came upon me of his possibly turning out a long-lived man, and keep occupying my chambers, and denying my authority; and perplexing my visitors; and scandalising my professional reputation; and casting a general gloom over the premises; keeping soul and body together to the last upon his savings (for doubtless he spent but half a dime a day), and in the end perhaps outlive me, and claim possession of my office by right of his perpetual occupancy: as all these dark anticipations crowded upon me more and more, and my friends continually intruded their relentless remarks upon the apparition in my room; a great change was wrought in me. I resolved to gather all my faculties together, and forever rid me of this intolerable incubus.

Ere revolving any complicated project, however, adapted to this end, I first simply suggested to Bartleby the propriety of his permanent departure. In a calm and serious tone, I commended the idea to his careful and mature consideration. But, having taken three days to meditate upon it, he apprised me, that his original determination remained the same; in short, that he still preferred to abide with me.

What shall I do? I now said to myself, buttoning up my coat to the last button. What shall I do? what ought I to do? what does conscience say I *should* do with this man, or, rather, ghost. Rid myself of him, I must; go, he shall. But how? You will not thrust him, the poor, pale, passive mortal—you will not thrust such a helpless creature out of your door? you will not dishonour yourself by such cruelty? No, I will not, I cannot do that. Rather would I let him live and die here, and then mason up his remains in the wall. What, then, will you do? For all your coaxing, he will not budge. Bribes he leaves under your own paperweight on your table; in short, it is quite plain that he prefers to cling to you.

Then something severe, something unusual must be done. What! surely you will not have him collared by a constable, and commit his innocent pallor to the common jail? And upon what ground could you procure such a thing to be done?—a vagrant, is he? What! he a vagrant, a wanderer, who refuses to budge? It is because he will *not* be a vagrant, then, that you seek to count him *as* a vagrant. That is too absurd. No visible means of support; there I have him. Wrong again: for indubitably he *does* support himself, and that is the only unanswerable proof that any man can show of his possessing the means so to do. No more, then. Since he will not quit me, I must quit him. I will change my offices; I will move elsewhere, and give him fair notice, that if I find him on my new premises I will then proceed against him as a common trespasser.

Acting accordingly, next day I thus addressed him: 'I find these chambers too far from the City Hall; the air is unwholesome. In a word, I propose to remove my offices next week, and shall no longer require your services. I tell you this now, in order that you may seek another place.'

He made no reply, and nothing more was said.

On the appointed day I engaged carts and men, proceeded to my chambers, and, having but little furniture, everything was removed in a few hours. Throughout, the scrivener remained standing behind the screen, which I directed to be removed the last thing. It was withdrawn; and, being folded up like a huge folio, left him the motionless occupant of a naked room. I stood in the entry watching him a moment, while something from within me upbraided me.

I re-entered, with my hand in my pocket—and—and my heart in my mouth.

'Good-bye, Bartleby; I am going—good-bye, and God some way bless you; and take that,' slipping something in his hand. But it dropped upon the floor, and then—strange to say—I tore myself from him whom I had so longed to be rid of.

Established in my new quarters, for a day or two I kept the door locked, and started at every footfall in the passages. When I returned to my rooms, after any little absence, I would pause at the threshold for an instant, and attentively listen ere applying my key. But these fears were needless. Bartleby never came nigh me.

I thought all was going well, when a perturbed-looking stranger visited me, inquiring whether I was the person who had recently occupied rooms at No. — Wall Street.

Full of forebodings, I replied that I was.

'Then, sir,' said the stranger, who proved a lawyer, 'you are responsible for the man you left there. He refuses to do any copying; he refuses to do anything; he says he prefers not to; and he refuses to quit the premises.'

'I am very sorry, sir,' said I, with assumed tranquillity, but an inward tremor, 'but, really, the man you allude to is nothing to me— he is no relation or apprentice of mine, that you should hold me responsible for him.'

'In mercy's name, who is he?'

'I certainly cannot inform you. I know nothing about him. Formerly I employed him as a copyist; but he has done nothing for me now for some time past.'

'I shall settle him, then—good morning, sir.'

Several days passed, and I heard nothing more; and, though I often felt a charitable prompting to call at the place and see poor Bartleby, yet a certain squeamishness, of I know not what, withheld me.

All is over with him, by this time, thought I at last, when, through another week, no further intelligence reached me. But, coming to my room the day after, I found several persons waiting at my door in a high state of nervous excitement.

'That's the man—here he comes,' cried the foremost one, whom I recognised as the lawyer who had previously called upon me alone.

'You must take him away, sir, at once,' cried a portly person among them, advancing upon me, and whom I knew to be the landlord of No. — Wall Street. 'These gentlemen, my tenants, cannot stand it any longer; Mr. B———,' pointing to the lawyer, 'has turned him out of his room, and he now persists in haunting the building generally, sitting upon the banisters of the stairs by day, and sleeping in the entry by night. Everybody is concerned; clients are leaving the offices; some fears are entertained of a mob; something you must do, and that without delay.'

Aghast at this torrent, I fell back before it, and would fain have locked myself in my new quarters. In vain I persisted that Bartleby was nothing to me—no more than to anyone else. In vain—I was the last person known to have anything to do with him, and they held me to the terrible account. Fearful, then, of being exposed in the papers (as one person present obscurely threatened), I considered the matter, and, at length, said, that if the lawyer would give me a confidential interview with the scrivener, in his (the lawyer's) own room, I would, that afternoon, strive my best to rid them of the nuisance they complained of.

Going upstairs to my old haunt, there was Bartleby silently sitting upon the banister at the landing.

'What are you doing here, Bartleby?' said I.

'Sitting upon the banister,' he mildly replied.

I motioned him into the lawyer's room, who then left us.

'Bartleby,' said I, 'are you aware that you are the cause of great tribulation to me, by persisting in occupying the entry after being dismissed from the office?'

No answer.

'Now one of two things must take place. Either you must do something, or something must be done to you. Now what sort of business would you like to engage in? Would you like to re-engage in copying for someone?'

'No; I would prefer not to make any change.'

'Would you like a clerkship in a dry-goods store?'

'There is too much confinement about that. No, I would not like a clerkship; but I am not particular.'

'Too much confinement,' I cried, 'why, you keep yourself confined all the time!'

'I would prefer not to take a clerkship,' he rejoined, as if to settle that little item at once.

'How would a bar-tender's business suit you? There is no trying of the eyesight in that.'

'I would not like it at all; though, as I said before, I am not particular.'

His unwonted wordiness inspirited me. I returned to the charge.

'Well, then, would you like to travel through the country collecting bills for the merchants? That would improve your health.'

'No, I would prefer to be doing something else.'

'How, then, would going as a companion to Europe, to entertain some young gentleman with your conversation—how would that suit you?'

'Not at all. It does not strike me that there is anything definite about that. I like to be stationary. But I am not particular.'

'Stationary you shall be, then,' I cried, now losing all patience, and, for the first time in all my exasperating connection with him, fairly flying into a passion. 'If you do not go away from these premises before night, I shall feel bound—indeed, I *am* bound—to—to quit the premises myself!' I rather absurdly concluded, knowing not with what possible threat to try to frighten his immobility into compliance. Despairing of all further efforts, I was precipitately leaving him, when a final thought occurred to me—one which had not been wholly unindulged before.

'Bartleby,' said I, in the kindest tone I could assume under such exciting circumstances, 'will you go home with me now—not to my office, but my dwelling—and remain there till we can conclude upon some convenient arrangement for you at our leisure? Come, let us start now, right away.'

'No; at present I would prefer not to make any change at all.'

I answered nothing; but, effectually dodging everyone by the suddenness and rapidity of my flight, rushed from the building, ran up Wall Street toward Broadway, and, jumping into the first omnibus, was soon removed from pursuit. As soon as tranquillity returned, I distinctly perceived that I had now done all that I possibly could, both in respect to the demands of the landlord and his tenants, and with regard to my own desire and sense of duty, to benefit Bartleby, and shield him from rude persecution. I now strove to be entirely carefree and quiescent; and my conscience justified me in the attempt; though, indeed, it was not so successful as I could have wished. So fearful was I of being again hunted out by the incensed landlord and his exasperated tenants, that, surrendering my business to Nippers, for a few days, I drove about the upper part of the town and through the suburbs, in my rockaway; crossed over to Jersey City and Hoboken, and paid fugitive visits to Manhattanville and Astoria. In fact, I almost lived in my rockaway for the time.

When again I entered my office, lo, a note from the landlord lay upon the desk. I opened it with trembling hands. It informed me that the writer had sent to the police, and had Bartleby removed to the Tombs as a vagrant. Moreover, since I knew more about him than anyone else, he wished me to appear at that place, and make a suitable statement of the facts. These tidings had a conflicting effect upon me. At first I was indignant; but at last, almost approved. The landlord's energetic summary disposition had led him to adopt a procedure which I do not think I would have decided upon myself; and yet, as a last resort, under such peculiar circumstances, it seemed the only plan.

As I afterward learned, the poor scrivener, when told that he must be conducted to the Tombs, offered not the slightest obstacle, but, in his pale, unmoving way, silently acquiesced.

Some of the compassionate and curious bystanders joined the party; and headed by one of the constables arm in arm with Bartleby, the silent procession filed its way through all the noise, and heat, and joy of the roaring thoroughfares at noon.

The same day I received the note, I went to the Tombs, or, to speak more properly, the Halls of Justice. Seeking the right officer, I stated the purpose of my call, and was informed that the individual I described was, indeed, within. I then assured the functionary that Bartleby was a perfectly honest man, and greatly to be compassionated, however unaccountably eccentric. I narrated all I knew, and closed by suggesting the idea of letting him remain in as indulgent confinement as possible, till something less harsh might be done—though, indeed, I hardly knew what. At all events, if nothing else could be decided upon, the alms-house must receive him. I then begged to have an interview.

Being under no disgraceful charge, and quite serene and harmless in all his ways, they had permitted him freely to wander about the prison, and, especially, in the enclosed grass-platted yards thereof. And so I found him there, standing all alone in the quietest of the yards, his face toward a high wall, while all around, from the narrow slits of the jail windows, I thought I saw peering out upon him the eyes of murderers and thieves.

'Bartleby!'

'I know you,' he said, without looking round—'and I want nothing to say to you.'

'It was not I that brought you here, Bartleby,' said I, keenly pained at his implied suspicion. 'And to you, this should not be so vile a place. Nothing reproachful attaches to you by being here. And see, it is not so sad a place as one might think. Look, there is the sky, and here is the grass.'

'I know where I am,' he replied, but would say nothing more, and so I left him.

As I entered the corridor again, a broad meat-like man, in an apron, accosted me, and, jerking his thumb over his shoulder, said, 'Is that your friend?'

'Yes.'

'Does he want to starve? If he does, let him live on the prison fare, that's all.'

'Who are you?' asked I, not knowing what to make of such an unofficially speaking person in such a place.

'I am the grub-man. Such gentlemen as have friends here, hire me to provide them with something good to eat.'

'Is this so?' said I, turning to the turnkey.

He said it was.

'Well, then,' said I, slipping some silver into the grub-man's hands (for so they called him), 'I want you to give particular attention to my friend there; let him have the best dinner you can get. And you must be as polite to him as possible.'

'Introduce me, will you?' said the grub-man, looking at me with an expression which seemed to say he was all impatience for an opportunity to give a specimen of his breeding.

Thinking it would prove of benefit to the scrivener, I acquiesced; and, asking the grub-man his name, went up with him to Bartleby.

'Bartleby, this is a friend; you will find him very useful to you.'

'Your sarvant, sir, your sarvant,' said the grub-man, making a low salutation behind his apron. 'Hope you find it pleasant here, sir; nice grounds—cool apartments—hope you'll stay with us some time— try to make it agreeable. What will you have for dinner to-day?'

'I prefer not to dine to-day,' said Bartleby, turning away. 'It would disagree with me; I am unused to dinners.' So saying, he slowly moved to the other side of the enclosure, and took up a position fronting the dead-wall.

'How's this?' said the grub-man, addressing me with a stare of astonishment. 'He's odd, ain't he?'

'I think he is a little deranged,' said I sadly.

'Deranged? deranged is it? Well, now, upon my word, I thought that friend of yourn was a gentleman forger; they are always pale and genteel-like, them forgers. I can't help pity 'em—can't help it, sir. Did you know Monroe Edwards?' he added touchingly, and paused. Then, laying his hand piteously on my shoulder, sighed, 'he died of consumption at Sing-Sing. So you weren't acquainted with Monroe?'

'No, I was never socially acquainted with any forgers. But I cannot stop longer. Look to my friend yonder. You will not lose by it. I will see you again.'

Some few days after this, I again obtained admission to the Tombs, and went through the corridors in quest of Bartleby; but without finding him.

'I saw him coming from his cell not long ago,' said a turnkey, 'maybe he's gone to loiter in the yards.'

So I went in that direction.

'Are you looking for the silent man?' said another turnkey, passing me. 'Yonder he lies—sleeping in the yard there. 'Tis not twenty minutes since I saw him lie down.'

The yard was entirely quiet. It was not accessible to the common prisoners. The surrounding walls, of amazing thickness, kept off all sounds behind them. The Egyptian character of the masonry weighed upon me with its gloom. But a safe imprisoned turf grew under foot. The heart of the eternal pyramids, it seemed, wherein, by some strange magic, through the clefts, grass-seed, dropped by birds, had sprung.

Strangely huddled at the base of the wall, his knees drawn up, and lying on his side, his head touching the cold stones, I saw the wasted Bartleby. But nothing stirred. I paused; then went close up to him; stooped over, and saw that his dim eyes were open; otherwise he seemed profoundly sleeping. Something prompted me to touch him. I felt his hand, when a tingling shiver ran up my arm and down my spine to my feet.

The round face of the grub-man peered upon me now. 'His dinner is ready. Won't he dine to-day, either? Or does he live without dining?'

'Lives without dining,' said I, and closed the eyes.

'Eh!—He's asleep, ain't he?'

'With kings and counsellors,' murmured I.

There would seem little need for proceeding further in this history. Imagination will readily supply the meagre recital of poor Bartleby's interment. But, ere parting with the reader, let me say, that if this little narrative has sufficiently interested him, to awaken curiosity as to who Bartleby was, and what manner of life he led prior to the present narrator's making his acquaintance, I can only reply, that in such curiosity I fully share, but am wholly unable to gratify it. Yet here I hardly know whether I should divulge one little item of rumour, which came to my ear a few months after the scrivener's decease. Upon what basis it rested I could never ascertain; and hence, how true it is I cannot now tell. But, inasmuch as this vague report has not been without a certain suggestive interest to me, however sad, it may prove the same with some others; and so I will briefly mention it. The report was this: that Bartleby had been a subordinate clerk in the Dead Letter Office at Washington, from which he had been suddenly removed by a change in the administration. When I think over this rumour, hardly can I express the emotions which seize me. Dead letters! does it not sound like dead men? Conceive a man by nature and misfortune prone to a pallid hopelessness, can any business seem more fitted to heighten it than that of continually handling these dead letters, and assorting them for the flames? For by the cartload they are annually burned. Sometimes from out the folded paper the pale clerk takes a ring—the finger it was meant for, perhaps, moulders in the grave; a bank-note sent in swiftest charity—he whom it would relieve, nor eats nor hungers any more; pardon for those who died despairing; hope for those who died unhoping; good tidings for those who died stifled by unrelieved calamities. On errands of life, these letters speed to death.

Ah, Bartleby! Ah, humanity!

film continuity

BARTLEBY: A STORY OF WALL STREET

Titles and credits superimposed over clerk at desk reading copy aloud

1. Sequence: lawyer sitting at desk; Bartleby standing in door, walking into office, sitting in chair

(Clerk reading in background.)

LAWYER: Yes?

BARTLEBY: I've come in answer to your advertisement.

LAWYER: Oh, yes, of course. Come in here, please. Sit down.

2. Sequence: close-up of lawyer and Bartleby; view of two men in office

LAWYER: Your name?

BARTLEBY: Bartleby.

LAWYER: Well, Bartleby, first I should explain to you that I've recently had the good fortune to be named a master in chancery. That's a very rewarding office, but it does add a great deal more work for my clerks. There are many additional documents to be copied now.

(Clerk reading in background.)

LAWYER: Are you an experienced law copyist?

BARTLEBY: I am.

LAWYER: I pay the usual rate—four cents per one hundred words. Would that be satisfactory to you?

BARTLEBY: That would be satisfactory.

LAWYER: When can you begin to work?

BARTLEBY: Immediately.

LAWYER: Well, Bartleby, work you shall have.

3. Sequence: close-up of Bartleby working; view of two clerks working; close-up of lawyer seated at desk

4. Sequence: close-up of lawyer; lawyer walking over to Bartleby; close-up of Bartleby

LAWYER: Bartleby, come here, please. I have some copy to examine.

BARTLEBY: I would prefer not to.

LAWYER: Bartleby? Did you misunderstand me? I have some copy to check against the original. Come in here and help me.

BARTLEBY: I would prefer not to.

LAWYER: Prefer not to! What do you mean, prefer not to? I want you to compare this sheet. Here, take it.

BARTLEBY: I would prefer not to.

5. Sequence: close-up of lawyer moving from Bartleby's office to his desk; clerk appearing, sitting down with lawyer; three men sitting at table; Bartleby coming from behind screen

LAWYER: Turkey!

TURKEY: Yes, sir?

LAWYER: Examine this with me.

TURKEY: Yes, sir.

LAWYER: To all persons to whom these presents shall come comma Edward Masters of the City and County of New York comma the State of New York sendeth greeting colon.

(Several days later.)

LAWYER: Bartleby. Bartleby, quick, I'm waiting!

BARTLEBY: What is wanted?

LAWYER: The copies you've made. We're going to examine them. Now, here.

BARTLEBY: I would prefer not to.

6. Sequence: three men sitting around table; lawyer approaching screen, holding document; close-up of lawyer and Bartleby

LAWYER: Bartleby, why do you refuse?

BARTLEBY: I would prefer not to.

LAWYER: These are your own copies we're going to examine. It'll save you work. We can check all four sets at once. It's common practice. Every copyist is expected to help examine his copy. Isn't that so? Can't you speak? Answer me!

BARTLEBY: I prefer not to.

7. Sequence: Bartleby and lawyer; close-ups of Turkey, lawyer, Nippers, Ginger Nut

LAWYER: You refuse to do what I ask, when you know it's common practice and common sense?

BARTLEBY: Yes, I prefer not to do as you ask.

LAWYER: Turkey, what do you think about this? Aren't I right in what I ask him?

TURKEY: With submission, sir, I think you are.

LAWYER: Nippers, what do you think about it?

NIPPERS: I think I should kick him out of the office.

LAWYER: Ginger Nut, what about you?

GINGER NUT: I think he's a little loony.

LAWYER: Bartleby, you hear what they say? Come out and do your duty. Bartleby! Very well, we'll do it without him.

8. Sequence: lawyer; Bartleby; lawyer sitting at desk

LAWYER: Bartleby. Bartleby! Bartleby! Go to the next room and tell Nippers to come in here.

BARTLEBY: I would prefer not to.

9. Sequence: lawyer climbing stairs, trying door, door opening, revealing Bartleby, Bartleby closing door; lawyer walking downstairs and around the block

BARTLEBY: I'm sorry, but I'm occupied at the moment. I prefer not to let you in just now. Perhaps it would be best for you to walk around the block once or twice and come back then.

10. Sequence: close-up of the lawyer walking, trying to open door; view of offices; lawyer going through desk drawers; view of offices

LAWYER: He's been living in my office; How lonely he must be.

11. Sequence: lawyer sitting at desk; Bartleby appearing; close-up of lawyer, Bartleby

LAWYER: Bartleby. Bartleby, I'm not going to ask you to do anything you'd prefer not to do. I simply want to speak with you. Will you tell me, Bartleby, where you were born?

BARTLEBY: I would prefer not to.

LAWYER: Have you any relatives living? Will you tell me *anything* about yourself?

BARTLEBY: I would prefer not to.

LAWYER: Bartleby, what possible reason can you have not to speak to me? I feel friendly toward you. Bartleby, what is your answer?

BARTLEBY: At present I prefer to give no answer.

12. Sequence: lawyer at his desk, watching Bartleby; lawyer going into Bartleby's cubicle, sitting down; view of lawyer and Bartleby

LAWYER: Bartleby, never mind, then, telling me about yourself, but let me urge you as a friend to try to adapt yourself to the procedures of this office. Tell me now that you'll help examine your copies—tomorrow or the next day. What I want is for you to say now that in the next day or two you'll begin to be a little reasonable. Say so, Bartleby.

BARTLEBY: At present I prefer not to be a little reasonable.

13. Sequence: Bartleby standing by window; lawyer stepping into cubicle, staring at Bartleby

LAWYER: Bartleby, why aren't you copying?

BARTLEBY: I've decided to do no more copying.

LAWYER: No more copying?

BARTLEBY: No more.

LAWYER: What is the reason for that?

BARTLEBY: Can't you see the reason for yourself?

LAWYER: Bartleby, your eyes. I'm sorry. You've been working too hard in this dim light. Of course you're right to stop work for a while.

14. Sequence: close-up of Bartleby; lawyer and Bartleby
(Clerk reading in background.)

LAWYER: Your eyes seem very much improved. Isn't that so? Don't you think you might try a little copying again?

BARTLEBY: I have given up copying.

15. Sequence: lawyer putting on coat, approaching cubicle, stopping; lawyer entering cubicle, offering money to Bartleby; Bartleby standing by window

LAWYER: Bartleby. I'm sorry to do this, but I must. I'm giving you six days notice. In six days you must be gone from this office.
(Six days later.)
LAWYER: The time has come, Bartleby. You must leave here. I'm sorry for you—here's money—but you must go.

BARTLEBY: I would prefer not.

LAWYER: You must. Bartleby, I owe you twelve dollars on account. Here are thirty-two. The odd twenty are for you. Will you take it? I'll leave it here, then.

16. Sequence: view of offices; lawyer putting on hat and leaving; close-ups of lawyer, Bartleby; lawyer closing door behind him

LAWYER: When you remove your things from these offices, Bartleby, you will of course lock the door, since everyone's gone for the day but you. And if you please, slip your key under the mat so that I may get it in the morning. Good-bye to you, Bartleby, and good luck.

17. Sequence: lawyer staring at closed door, looking for key under mat; lawyer walking; close-ups of lawyer, Bartleby; view of lawyer and Bartleby

BARTLEBY: Not yet. I'm occupied.

LAWYER: Not gone! What am I going to do? Will you or will you not leave me?

BARTLEBY: I would prefer not to leave you.

LAWYER: What earthly right have you got to stay here? Do you pay any rent? Do you pay my taxes? Do you own this property? Will you go back to work? Are your eyes recovered? Will you copy one small paper for me this morning? Will you do *anything* to give some excuse for staying here?

18. Sequence: close-up of lawyer's eyes; lawyer hurrying out of cubicle, into office, and sitting at desk

LAWYER: "And this new commandment I give unto you, that ye shall love one another." Well, it's better than murder. Besides, poor fellow, he doesn't mean anything by it.

19. Sequence: lawyer seated at his desk; view of the two offices; lawyer rising

LAWYER: All right, Bartleby, stay there behind your screen. I shall persecute you no more. At last I can see the purpose of my life, Bartleby, and I'm content. Others may have more important roles to play, but my mission in this world, Bartleby, is to provide you with office space for as long as you may choose to remain.

20. Sequence: view of offices; lawyer's empty desk; attorney entering, talking to Bartleby

ATTORNEY: 'Morning. Anyone here? Is Mr. Wyckoff in? Of course. Foolish question. I can see he isn't. Can you tell me where he is? Can you tell me when he'll be back? Can you tell me anything at all?

21. Sequence: view of conference in lawyer's office; close-up of an attorney whispering to Bartleby; close-ups of Bartleby, attorney, lawyer (Witness talking in background.)

ATTORNEY: Psst. Run around to my office and ask my secretary for the papers on Peabody versus Fenton. Run along and fetch them back quick. My office is just next door, number fourteen. Hurry!
BARTLEBY: I would prefer not to.

22. Close-up of lawyer walking along the street

LAWYER: I can't have him thrown bodily out the door—such a poor, helpless creature. I can't dishonor myself with such cruelty. When I give him money, he doesn't even touch it. Bribes are useless. No, I can't have him sent to jail. After all, what harm has he committed? . . . Of course!

23. Sequence: close-ups of lawyer, Bartleby; men moving office equipment

LAWYER: Bartleby, I've decided these offices are too far from City Hall. I'm going to move next week. I'm telling you now so you may look for another place. . . . Wait! Leave that till last.

24. Sequence: view of empty offices, lawyer near door; Bartleby standing by window; men carrying screen; lawyer walking toward Bartleby, putting money in his hand; money falls to floor

LAWYER: Good-bye, Bartleby. I'm leaving. Good-bye, and may God some way bless you. And take this.

25. Sequence: lawyer sitting in office; Ginger Nut showing men into office; lawyer talking to men; close-up of lawyer and man

MAN: Are you the gentleman who recently kept offices at number sixteen Wall Street?

LAWYER: Yes.

MAN: Then you're responsible for the man you left there. He refuses to do any work—he says he prefers not to—and he refuses to leave my offices.

LAWYER: I'm very sorry, sir, but really the man you speak of is nothing to me. I am not responsible for him.

MAN: In mercy's name, then, who is he?

LAWYER: I can't tell you that. I know nothing about him.

MAN: I shall settle him, then. Good morning, sir.

26. Sequence: close-up of lawyer opening door, stepping into offices; view of five men waiting; close-ups of lawyer and man; view of five men; close-up of lawyer

MAN: That's the man!

ANOTHER MAN: There he is!

LANDLORD: You must take him away, sir, at once. These gentlemen are my tenants and they can't stand it any longer. Mr. Atlee forced your man out of the office, and now he haunts the rest of the building. In the daytime he perches on the stairs. At night he sleeps in the hall. He's disrupting everything. Clients are leaving the offices. You must do something immediately!

LAWYER: But he is nothing to me. I've no more to do with him than anyone else.

MAN: You were the last person known to have anything to do with him. You're responsible for him.

LAWYER: No. . . . Very well, I'll do what I can.

27. Sequence: lawyer entering building with five men; lawyer going upstairs; Bartleby perched on banister; lawyer leading Bartleby into office, closing door; lawyer talking with Bartleby

LAWYER: Bartleby, what are you doing there?

BARTLEBY: Sitting on the banister.

LAWYER: Come with me, Bartleby. Leave us alone, please. Now, Bartleby, do you realize that you are causing me a great deal of trouble by refusing to leave this place? Now, one of two things must happen. Either you must do something or something must be done to you.

28. Sequence: lawyer leaning against desk; Bartleby; close-up of lawyer; view of the two men

LAWYER: Now, what sort of business would you like to engage in? Would you like to go back to copying—for somebody else?

BARTLEBY: No, I'd prefer not to make any change at all.

LAWYER: Would you like to be a salesclerk in a clothing store?

BARTLEBY: There's too much confinement about that.

LAWYER: Too much confinement? Why, you keep yourself confined all the time.

BARTLEBY: I prefer not to be a salesclerk. But I'm not particular.

LAWYER: Would you like to be a bartender? You wouldn't have to strain your eyes at that.

BARTLEBY: I wouldn't like it at all. But as I said before, I'm not particular.

LAWYER: Then how about going as a companion to Europe to entertain some rich young gentleman with your sparkling conversation? How would that suit you?

BARTLEBY: Not at all. There doesn't seem to be anything definite about that. I like to be stationary.

29. Sequence: close-up of lawyer as he moves around room; lawyer opening door and leaving; view of five men around closed door

LAWYER: Stationary you shall be, then! If you do not leave this building before dark, I shall feel forced, indeed I shall be forced, to— to leave it myself. Bartleby, will you go home with me now? Not to my office, my home. You can stay there until we can make some convenient arrangement for you. Come with me now, Bartleby . . . Bartleby.

BARTLEBY: At present I would prefer not to make any change at all.

30. Sequence: lawyer standing at desk, reading letter; Bartleby standing in prison yard; lawyer walking toward Bartleby, talking to him, turning, walking away

LAWYER: They've sent him to prison. . . . Bartleby?

BARTLEBY: I know you, and I have nothing to say to you.

LAWYER: I didn't bring you here, Bartleby. And you musn't feel any shame at being here. It's not your fault. For you this shouldn't be so bad a place—the sky, the earth.

BARTLEBY: I know where I am.

LAWYER: Bartleby, isn't there anything I can do to help you?

31. Sequence: lawyer walking away from Bartleby, grub man stopping him; turnkey approaching; lawyer leading grub man toward Bartleby

GRUB MAN: That's your friend?

LAWYER: Yes.

GRUB MAN: Does he want to starve? If he does, let him live on prison food, that's all.

LAWYER: Who are you?

GRUB MAN: I'm the grub man. Such gentlemen as has friends here hire me to give them something good to eat.

LAWYER: Is that true?

TURNKEY: Yes, sir.

LAWYER: Yes, yes, then pay particular attention to my friend. Give him the best dinner you can get. And be sure to be as polite to him as possible. Bartleby. Bartleby, this is a friend. You'll find his services very useful.

GRUB MAN: Your servant, sir, your servant. And what can I get you for dinner today?

BARTLEBY: I prefer not to have any dinner today.

32. Sequence: lawyer and grub man; lawyer walking away, wandering through prison yard; turnkey walking with him, pointing to Bartleby; view of Bartleby lying on his side; lawyer hurrying to him

GRUB MAN: What's that? He's odd, ain't he?

LAWYER: Take care of him. You'll not lose by it. I must go now. I'll see you again.

(A few days later.)

TURNKEY: Hey, hey, are you looking for the silent man? There he is —sleeping in the yard. Saw him lie down there about twenty minutes ago.

LAWYER: Bartleby.

33. Sequence: lawyer kneeling down, touching Bartleby's hand; grub man leaning down, looking at Bartleby; lawyer kneeling at Bartleby's side

GRUB MAN: His dinner's ready. Won't he eat today either? Or does he live without eating?

LAWYER: He lives without eating.

Bartleby (1969)   "Lawyer: Give him the best dinner you can get. . . .
Grub-man: And what can I get you for dinner today?
Bartleby: I prefer not to have any dinner today."
The film continuity reproduces the actual dialogue of the motion picture.
Still shot courtesy of Encyclopaedia Britannica Educational Corporation.

GRUB MAN: Eh? He's asleep, ain't he?
LAWYER: With kings and counsellors.

BARTLEBY: A STORY OF WALL STREET
QUESTIONS

1. Perhaps the most apparent omission in the film adaptation of
    "Bartleby" is the lawyer's reference to Bartleby's rumored clerk-
    ship in the "Dead Letter Office at Washington." In your judg-
    ment, what is the function of this concluding section of the story?
    To what extent does its omission flaw the film?

2. Analyze the opening two paragraphs of the short story. What

elements from these paragraphs have been incorporated into the film? Which have not? Assess the filmmaker's decisions.

3. Turkey, Nippers, and Ginger Nut are nicknames "mutually conferred upon each other" by the three employees of the lawyer. Melville gives considerable space to their eccentricities and the lawyer's reactions to them. Why?

4. What is the role of fatalism in story and film?

5. What symbolism do you find in the story's subtitle, "A Story of Wall Street"? To what extent has the filmmaker used "wall" symbolism in the film?

6. A film critic suggests that in fiction feeling is a precipitate of thought while in film thought is a precipitate of feeling. To what extent is Melville's story primarily an appeal to intellect? Explain. To what extent is the film an appeal to emotion? Explain.

7. Evaluate the use of color in the film adaptation. To what extent has the filmmaker utilized colors suggested by the story?

8. Why does Bartleby's reiterated statement, "I would prefer not to," pose so great a difficutly for the lawyer?

9. What examples of humor do you find in story and film?

10. The lawyer's attitude towards Bartleby is complex. It contains components of compassion, anger, incomprehensibility, surprise, sympathy, and resentment. Which of these do you find most persistent? Why?

11. The lawyer's story is told in the past tense; the technique is similar to a cinematic flashback. However, the film is necessarily in the present tense; the filmmaker does not use a flashback technique. Assess the filmmaker's decisions.

12. Compare and contrast religious themes in the short story and film.

13. While Melville refers to Bartleby's copying, he does not specify actual details copied. In the film, we hear the actual words of contracts as they are read aloud by clerks. The filmmaker invented these details. What functions do they serve in the film? Are they consistent with the tone and themes of the story?

BARTLEBY: A STORY OF WALL STREET
SUGGESTIONS FOR PAPERS

1. Describe the differences in point of view in the film and story. How do you account for the filmmaker's choice of point of view?

2. To what extent, if any, does the lawyer shift from detachment to involvement in the story and film? Support your generalizations.

3. One critical interpretation of Melville's short story focuses on Bartleby's passive resistance as symbolic of the author's objection to a dehumanized and sterile society that is excessively materialistic. Evaluate this interpretation.

4. If you found the lawyer a sympathetic character in the film version of Bartleby, describe those incidents responsible for your feelings.

5. A student critic, writing about the film, says, "The long shot of the prison analogizes it with the Roman Coliseum where the Christians were persecuted." Describe your reactions to this observation and explain the reasons for your responses.

6. The film version of Bartleby largely omits the introductory pages of the story that describe the characters of Turkey and Nippers. Write the opening sequences of a screenplay that attempts to capture the lawyer's relationship with his two scriveners.

A DARK COMEDY: A CONTRAST OF THE FILM *BARTLEBY* AND THE STORY "BARTLEBY, THE SCRIVENER: A STORY OF WALL STREET"

Valarie Tolmasov

Both the film *Bartleby* and Herman Melville's story, "Bartleby, the Scrivener: A Story of Wall Street," create a dark comedy that reveals the absurdity of the human condition. Herman Melville's comic tone is "bittersweet." The tone brings laughter tinged with tears. In "The Storied World," George W. Linden writes:

> One thing we can conclude is that a director can change the plot of a novel, he can eliminate certain characters and scenes, and he can include scenes not included in the novel without violating it. But he cannot seriously violate the theme of a novel, and the one thing he must be able to translate into his new medium is its tone.[1]

In essence, the filmmaker must maintain a story's tone to intensify thematic concerns. The main theme of "Bartleby" is the problem of the outsider, the alienated, isolated individual. How does society handle the "outsider?" Ultimately, the film and the story reveal a destructive separation among men, symbolized by the deep separation between Bartleby and the lawyer, and between Bartleby and all men. This motif fosters a dark, pathetic tone, which emerges from the painful yet comical absurdity of the lawyer's situation. Both the story and film effectively present the theme of man's isolation from man through point of view, setting, characters, what might be called pace or "punctuation," and finally through symbols.

In "Tone and Point of View," Roy Huss and Norman Silverstein discuss the use of point of view in fiction:

> The writer of fiction immediately assumes a stance from which to see and judge the persons and events of his story. He may allow both himself and the reader the "aesthetic distance" af-

Used by permission.

[1]George W. Linden, "The Storied World," in *Film and Literature: Contrasts in Media*, ed. Fred H. Marcus (Scranton: Intext Educational Publishers, 1971), page 163.

forded by the third-person narration—that is, the point of view
of the omniscient author; or he may try to get the reader to
identify more closely with what is going on by using the first-
person narration—that is having a character recount the events.[2]

Herman Melville's story, "Bartleby, the Scrivener: A Story of Wall
Street" uses the first-person narration. The story is told from the
lawyer's point of view. The lawyer recalls his past experiences with
Bartleby. In contrast, the film takes place in the present. According
to Balazs, film has no past tense or future tense because pictures can
only occur in the present. As a result, the events unfold before the
film audience, immediately and intensely, communicating the lawyer's
situation with Bartleby.

    Huss and Silverstein further define attitude and point of view
within film:

> Some definitions are in order. The attitudes expressed in film
> may be objective, as in newsreels; subjective, as when the audi-
> ence sees the world from the point of view of a character; or
> objective-subjective, as when the director intermixes objective
> and subjective shots in order to impose his own attitude on the
> film the audience is seeing. Point of view, therefore refers to
> whether the filmed material purports to be unmalleable reality
> (objective) or reality as seen by character (subjective).[3]

In the film of *Bartleby*, the point of view is both objective and subjective. For example, the film opens in the law office of Alexander
Wyckoff. The lawyer looks up (objective shot) and says, "Yes?" Next,
the camera captures a subjective or "eyeline" shot of Bartleby standing
"motionless on the threshold of the half-opened office door." This is
the lawyer's point of view. The screenplay describes what the lawyer
sees: "He [Bartleby] is a pallidly neat young man, pitiably respectable,
incurably forlorn." This description comes alive in the film's visual
image of the tall, emaciated figure of Bartleby. So, the film audience
sees what the lawyer sees as well as the objective, surface reality of
the office and the other characters.

    The short story traces the lawyer's effort to understand Bartleby's
behavior "which . . . reveals more about himself than about the object
of his search."[4] For instance, the lawyer proudly asserts, "All who

    [2]Roy Huss and Norman Silverstein, "Tone and Point of View," in *Film and
Literature*, page 54.
    [3]*Ibid.*
    [4]John Seelye, *Melville: The Ironic Diagram* (Evanston: Northwestern Uni-
versity Press, 1970), page 97.

know me consider me an eminently safe man." In other words, the lawyer is a man that stays safely within social law, convention, and propriety. Throughout the story, the lawyer emphasizes the word "reason." His world is neatly compartmentalized and ordered, just as his office is neatly divided into an area for himself and an area for his workers. Nothing is out of order. Rules are upheld. Scriveners, for instance, help check each other's copies. This is why the lawyer is totally confused and perplexed by Bartleby. Bartleby doesn't follow the rules. He is outside and beyond social convention.

The film combines two points of view: there is a constant interplay between objective and subjective shots, allowing the audience to see the lawyer objectively as well as to see what the lawyer perceives subjectively. This blending of surface reality and psychological reality tells the audience much about the lawyer. For instance, the screenplay captures the lawyer's confusion when Bartleby fails to respond with the proper social politeness and decorum:

SIDE ANGLE CLOSE-UP of the LAWYER. He begins expansively.

LAWYER

Well, Bartleby, first I should explain to you that I've recently had the good fortune to be named a master in chancery.

The lawyer waits for a reaction to this news but gets none and continues.

LAWYER

That's a very rewarding office

CLOSE-UP OF BARTLEBY.

This early scene intensifies the lawyer's confusion and frustration with Bartleby. Even though he mentions that he has been appointed "master in chancery" the lawyer in the story does not tell Bartleby about this appointment in their initial meeting. This additional confrontation within the film poignantly magnifies the lawyer's social conventionalism and Bartleby's alien unconventionalism. The close-up of Bartleby in this scene also captures his total passive indifference through his unmoving, stone-like face. Bartleby appears to be a dead man.

The story delineates the lawyer's materialism: he is a "title hunter," and his private fear is that Bartleby may "perhaps outlive me, and claim possession of my office by right of his perpetual occupancy." The lawyer's materialism is demonstrated in the film by his attempts to buy off Bartleby, and by his repeated presentation of money to Bartleby. We recognize the lawyer's hypocrisy by his enraged, violent grip on an umbrella while he indignantly expounds on the

spiritual virtue of "loving one another." In the end, both the film and
the story employ particular points of view to characterize the lawyer
and vividly develop the struggle between reason (the lawyer) and un-
reason (Bartleby), materialism (the lawyer) and spirituality (Bartleby).

The setting created in both media becomes crucial in developing
tone and most importantly theme. In the short story, the lawyer describes the "claustrophobic" environment of his law office:

> My chambers were upstairs at No. — Wall Street. At one end
> they looked upon the white wall of the interior of a spacious
> skylight shaft, penetrating the building from top to bottom.
>
> This view might have been considered rather tame than otherwise,
> deficient in what landscape painters call "life." But, if so, the
> view from the other end of my chambers offered at least a con-
> trast, if nothing more in that direction, my windows commanded
> an unobstructed view of a lofty brick wall, black by age and ever-
> lasting shade, which wall required no spyglass to bring out its
> lurking beauties, but, for the benefit of all nearsighted spectators
> was pushed up to within ten feet of my windowpanes. Owing
> to the great height of the surrounding buildings and my cham-
> ber's being on the second floor, the interval between the wall
> and mine not a little resembled a huge square cistern.[5]

The lawyer and other characters are literally "walled in." Nature and
life, as a result, are walled out, and, most importantly, other men are
walled out. At the story's end, the lawyer discusses Bartleby's alleged
occupation in the Dead Letter Office, where "On errands of life, these
letters speed to death." In other words, the story explores the breakdown of communication and the walls men build to obstruct open
communication among themselves. In the film, this communication
breakdown is visually symbolized by the lawyer's divided office, Bartleby's isolated cubicule, and Bartleby's "dead-wall reveries," when he
faces the suffocatingly close brick wall without communicating with
the lawyer. The film also portrays the story's "landscape without life"
through the concentration of visual images on buildings, walls, and
the empty, dirt-filled prison yard. Even when the lawyer is seen outside
on the street, there is no evidence of nature's vital greenery. The
lawyer's world is a wasteland, a land devoid of life and freshness.
Society has forced man into tiny, dark offices, symbolized by Bartleby's
retreat into the darkness of his small, "hermetic" cubicule. In both
media, the environment consists literally of walls which obstruct
communication.

[5]*Herman Melville, "Bartleby: A Story of Wall Street,"* in *Short Story/Short
Film,* ed. Fred H. Marcus (unpublished manuscript), page 164.

Each medium examines character differently. The short story, for instance, spends a great deal of time discussing the "inflamed, flurried, flightly recklessness" of Turkey, "the ambition and indigestion of Nippers, and "the quick-witted" Ginger Nut. The development of Turkey's and Nippers's complementary characters also suggests the "divided and separated" world of the lawyer. In the film, Turkey, Nippers, and Ginger Nut are psychologically and visually in the background, just as they become less important in the story when Bartleby first enters the lawyer's office. The film focuses on Bartleby and the lawyer. They are the main characters and the central conflict takes place between them.

The story develops Bartleby's character through the repetition of certain words, such as "pallid," "forlorn," "motionless," "strange," "ghost," "cadaverous," and "apparition"; the film presents the visual image of a wan, pallid man wearing black clothes. The close-ups magnify Bartleby's wasted, bony face, a face of death. In the story, the lawyer states that Bartleby "wrote on silently, palely, mechanically." Bartleby's lifeless, mechanical nature is emphasized cinematically by the unceasing, monotonous sound of his pen, filtering endlessly through the green screen.

In the story, the lawyer's character clarifies his actions. "The novelist [or short story writer] tends to reveal what people do through what they are; the director, to reveal what they are through what they do."[6] The lawyer is a creature of reason and propriety; therefore, he constantly demands that Bartleby be "reasonable." Since Bartleby is outside of society, the lawyer cannot handle him. Consequently, the lawyer becomes indignant and frustrated. To the lawyer, life is orderly and "confined" by social laws, just as he buttons up his "coat to the last button." Bartleby, in contrast, doesn't follow accepted procedures and laws. He would "prefer not to." At first, the lawyer ignores Bartleby's eccentricities. Then, the lawyer makes rationalizations for Bartleby's behavior by claiming Bartleby is "absolutely alone in the universe. A bit of wreck in the mid-Atlantic." When Bartleby's behavior becomes more extreme and he refuses to copy, the lawyer thinks he can solve the problem by moving or escaping the situation. Throughout the story, the lawyer repeatedly expresses his ambivalence, confusion, and frustration:

> Turn the man [Bartleby] out by an actual thrusting I could not; to drive him away by calling him hard names would not do; calling in the police was an unpleasant idea; and yet, permit him

[6]Linden, page 158.

to enjoy his cadaverous triumph over me—this, too, I could not think of. What was to be done? or, if nothing could be done, was there anything that I could assume in the matter?[7]

To present the lawyer wavering between sympathy and violence, the filmmaker uses close-ups to reveal the lawyer's internal struggle. His face, for example, bears the grimace of apprehension and worry when he reluctantly mounts the stairs after he has given Bartleby his six-day notice. Since Bartleby refuses to leave, the lawyer's internal battle can hardly be contained. The filmmaker uses close-ups of the lawyer furiously enumerating his alternatives, while people on the street stare curiously at him. In "Tone and Point of View," Huss and Silverstein write, "Close shots, which peer at objects, create intensity; long shots, by their distance, imply detachment."[8] The close-ups of the lawyer's face convey the intensity of his frustration. After the lawyer moves away, the landlord and other tenants insists that it is the lawyer's responsibility to evict Bartleby. When Bartleby rejects the lawyer's job selections, while simultaneously insisting he is "not particular," the lawyer can no longer control his temper. A series of tight close-ups capture his sweat-drenched face, red with anger and frustration. The lawyer madly circles Bartleby, symbolically diagraming his confusion and psychological impasse. The screenplay reads, "Truck with the lawyer, keeping him in Extreme Close-Up, as he charges angrily about the room." This "Extreme Close-Up" moves the audience with the lawyer's meaningless circling. The lawyer can go nowhere visually or psychologically. His vision cannot penetrate the walls of reason and social convention.

In addition, the "punctuation" within the film and story enriches the tragi-comic tale of Bartleby. The *Dictionary of World Literature* defines punctuation as an aid to "intelligibility through pitch, stress, time and pause." In a sense, punctuation creates language's rhythm, flow, and logic. Punctuation articulates time. In the story, the reader experiences many long, convoluted sentences, filled with prepositional, adverbial, and other phrases. Since this is the lawyer's language, it suggests the logical and orderly patterns of the lawyer's thoughts. Also Bartleby's phrase "I would prefer not to" becomes a comical "refrain" and a "period" to the lawyer's intense questioning sentences. In the film, Bartleby's phrase ends most of the scenes. Language's punctuation serves to regulate the pauses, flow, and tempo of sentences, and the filmmaker uses certain optical effects to break the flow of scenes with pauses. In the film the optical effects telescope time. They consist of

[7]Melville, page 180.
[8]Huss and Silverstein, page 64.

art titles that reveal the place, year, or day. For example, the film opens with large white block letters, spelling "New York City." Next, the art titles give the year, "1840." Throughout the film, the art titles indicate the day on which the following scene will take place. These art titles regulate the flow of the action; their appearance indicates the end of one scene and the beginning of another.

Finally, specific symbols within the film and the short story powerfully convey the major isolation motif. Walls and the green screen are central symbols in both film and story. Walls enclose the office, the office is located on Wall Street, and Bartleby dies huddled near a wall. The wall becomes a vivid symbol of isolation and death. The story describes Bartleby's "dead-wall" reveries, while the film-maker gives the audience the vivid image of Bartleby facing the hard, cold, brick wall. In the story, the masonry of the prison wall has an "Egyptian character." This description suggests the transcendental or mystic qualities of the wall, which becomes a symbol of death, a wall that must be penetrated to understand the riddle of man's existence and to achieve communion with God and creation. In the film, the prison wall is not Egyptian in character. Instead, it is a plain, blank wall that symbolizes Bartleby's abnegation of life.

At the film's conclusion, Bartleby's lifeless body is curled in the fetal position. His hands are clasped together in the soft position of prayer. This prayer-like gesture seems to suggest a quest for harmony with the universe and God. Symbolically, Bartleby returns to the primal, fetal position, where man is in communion with the cosmos's unconscious consciousness.

The green screen in both film and story represents Bartleby's isolation from others and his denial of life. Green suggests life's fresh vibrancy. Bartleby is literally beyond feeling life's vitality. In the film, Bartleby remains unseen behind the green screen a great deal of the time. He is an outsider and alien to life. When Bartleby first enters the lawyer's office, the film audience hears the word "alien" from Turkey's background copy reading. Throughout the film, Bartleby is present primarily as a voice or as an unseen object of attention. Even when he is shown on the screen, Bartleby remains on the outside of the frame, just as he is outside of social convention.

Symbolically, both story and film move from the sealed office to the Tombs prison yard. This symbolic journey traces Bartleby's pathetic death. He has totally denied life. The filmmaker's addition of background copy reading enhances Bartleby's "living death." Nippers, for example, reads a will, while the film focuses on Bartleby staring blankly at the brick wall. Bartleby is spiritually dead.

The story's comedy is mainly the result of the lawyer's humorous thoughts, such as his contemplation of the effects of ginger-nut cake on Bartleby's constitution. In contrast, the comedy in the film arises from facial expressions or intonations of lines. The anxious looks of the landlord and his tenants, for instance, become comical in camera angles which make them appear as caricatures with enlarged heads and shrunken bodies. Also, Bartleby's reply, "Sitting on the banister," becomes comical in its playful intonation. Both the story and the film present a dark comedy that moves from the comical absurdity of the situation to Bartleby's pathetic, lonely death. The film adds to tragicomedy by moving from comic scenes and close-ups to the concluding long shots that exemplify Bartleby's isolation. Life is filled with walls: walls obstructing communication, walls of attitude and prejudice, walls of rigid psychological states, and most importantly the wall of death. Can these walls be broken down? Will man ever see beyond them? "Is the setting of "Bartleby" a Wall Street law office or the cosmic madhouse?"[9]

[9]Newton Arvin, *Herman Melville* (Toronto: William Sloane Associates, Inc., 1950), page 242.

chapter 2

Film and Fiction: Contrasts in Media

How does film fit into the spectrum of the arts? In the opening sentence of *Films and Feelings*, Raymond Durgnat describes film as "a *potpourri* of art forms."[1] His description is apt. The art of photography is an essential element of film. Because it makes use of actors, costumes, lighting, sets, and dialogue, film can also claim close kinship with the theater. The use of a soundtrack and the two-dimensional presentation of line, shape, and color link film to the arts of music and painting. Most importantly, film's propensity for narrative aligns it with fiction. In *Literature and Film*, Robert Richardson describes film as "a narrative medium and, like literature, . . . an art based on language."[2]

In what essential ways are the languages of film and fiction different? Most simply, film is visual; fiction is verbal. Short stories are created with words, films with images. As a result, fiction communicates indirectly with a reader through symbols which the reader transcribes into mental images and meanings. The viewer, on the other hand, receives screen images more directly. There is a danger that the film-goer may experience these images more or less passively, whereas the reader must actively use his imagination to interpret the verbal symbols.

[1]Raymond Durgnat, *Films and Feelings* (London: Faber and Faber, 1967), p. 19.
[2]Robert Richardson, *Literature and Film* (Bloomington: Indiana University, Press, 1969), p. 65.

This distinction prompted George W. Linden to comment: "In the novel, feeling is a precipitate of thought. In film, thought is a precipitate of feeling engendered by vision."[3] George Bluestone makes a related observation when he notes: "Where the moving image comes to us directly through perception, language must be filtered through the screen of conceptual apprehension."[4]

Most film theorists have observed that visual images are necessarily specific. In contrast, oral and written language tends to be more abstract. Durgnat observes that a film can show "a lame old black cat sitting on a worn grey mat" or "a playful tabby stretched out on a mat with a pattern of roses on it" but not the more general "the cat sat on the mat."[5] Film's ability to handle abstractions is limited. The implications for a director who elects to adapt a short story or novel are inescapable. The writer can *describe;* the filmmaker must *show.* Fiction's greater flexibility with abstractions can be easily exemplified. For instance, the opening sentence of *The Scarlet Letter* is:

> A throng of bearded men, in sad-colored garments and gray, steeple-crowned hats, intermixed with women, some wearing hoods and others bare-headed, was assembled in front of a wooden edifice, the door of which was heavily timbered with oak, and studded with iron spikes.

This sentence offers a vast array of cinematic alternatives. There are sufficient specific details to delight even a novice filmmaker. Turning, however, to the second sentence of Hawthorne's novel, we read:

> The founders of a new colony, whatever Utopia of human virtue and happiness they might originally project, have invariably recognized it among their earliest practical necessities to allot a portion of the virgin soil as a cemetery, and another portion as the site of a prison.

Hawthorne conjoins Utopia and prison, thereby creating a verbal irony of considerable magnitude; the task of a would-be adapter coping with this sentence would be prodigious. A literal representation of its specific elements would not suffice. Although the meaning of the sentence is clear, visual analogues do not come readily to mind. In the sentence, Hawthorne *describes;* what would a film director *show?*

---

[3]George W. Linden, *Reflections on the Screen* (Belmont: Wadsworth, 1970), p. 44.

[4]George Bluestone, *Novels Into Film* (Berkeley: University of California Press, 1971), p. 20.

[5]Durgnat, *Films and Feelings,* p. 19.

Fortunately for a filmmaker, the need to produce movement is easily met in several distinctive ways. For example, a man walks through the crowded lobby of a hotel; a cowboy races his horse toward a stampeding herd of cattle. These actions occur inside the film's frames. Moreover, the camera itself can move. In *The Open Window*, as Vera begins to explain to her family the reason for Framton Nuttel's hysterical dash from the house, none of the characters shifts position, but the camera dollies slowly toward Vera, easing the others out of the frame and focusing upon her. The camera movement parallels the meaning of the film; Vera is more important than the others, and the camera movement visually underlines her central position in the plot. Even when the camera itself does not actually move, the effect of rapid movement may be achieved by the use of a zoom lens. In *The Open Window*, when Nuttel whirls about to look at what he suspects may be ghosts approaching, the zoom lens flashes us to a close-up view of the on-coming figures.

The filmmaker also achieves movement through the editing process. He uses cuts, fades, and dissolves as a way of controlling cinematic rhythm and pace. In *The Lottery*, for example, the rapid cuts of the opening sequences heighten tension very early in the film. By contrast, the use of sub-titles in block letters to indicate the passage of time in *Bartleby* serves to slow its pace. The mid-nineteenth century setting arguably justifies the leisurely rhythm.

In fiction the pace and tone of an action depends in large part on the writer's choice of verbs, the elements of language most effective in producing charged mental images. For example, the sentence, "The boy walked across the park" changes dramatically in our mind's eye when it reads, "The boy scampered across the park" or "The boy hobbled across the park." It is the verbs which ignite and spark a writer's prose.

The film director also has language in the form of dialogue to further achieve movement in his films. He must, however, be wary. Motion pictures may suffer from excessive verbal pyrotechnics. This explains the great difficulty of adapting a Shakespearian or Shavian play to film. The richness of language makes its appeal to the mind through the ear, not the eye, and in film, the eye serves as the principal entry to the mind.

In adapting fiction to film, even relatively concrete details require greater film specificity. For example, in Ambrose Bierce's short story, "An Occurrence at Owl Creek Bridge," Peyton Farquhar's wife is ready to "embrace" him; he reaches out to "clasp" her. But there are embraces and embraces. Will her arms encircle his shoulders? Will she throw her arms around his waist? Will her fingers linger on the back of his head? In the film adaptation, the wife places her fingers at Peyton's throat, at the very place where, earlier, a hangman's noose had encircled his neck. Farquhar seems to slide through his wife's embrace to his death. Thus, the filmmaker creates a shocking irony. The leap from life and love to death is instantaneous. The distance between them, in cinematic time and space, is minuscule. An inventive director has particularized beyond the point at which the writer stopped, and the effect on the viewer is potent.

In "The Upturned Face," a short story by Stephen Crane, the two main characters, Lean and the adjutant, look at each other. At one point, Crane adds, ". . . they were always looking at each other." The line seems to pose no visual difficulties; what Crane tells his readers a film director could show his viewers. But the apparently simple statement contains a subtle and complex conception. Among the many pressures on the two officers—the harsh reality of death, the immediate danger of their situation, the anguish following a close

The Upturned Face (1974) ". . . they were always looking at each other . . . ." What Crane tells his readers a film director could show his viewers. *Still shot reproduced courtesy of Pyramid Films.*

friend's death, the military proprieties to be observed—not the least is each man's conscious concern for the role he has to play, and the impression he thereby makes on his fellow officer. Ironically, while self-preservation would seem to be the first priority, the psychological need to adopt a proper stance plays a more significant role. Yes, the filmmaker can easily show the men looking at each other. But can he also show, through images, the inner complexity of the abstract motives responsible for their eyeing each other?

"The Upturned Face" points to a related distinction between film and fiction. Stephen Crane does not provide details of the story's setting. Words like "hill," "turf," and "ridge" are the sole physical clues other than allusions to "Rostina" sharpshooters and "Spitzbergen" infantry. But a filmmaker must shoot his images against some specific background. In Edward Folger's film adaptation, the battle scenes take place in a setting of lush greenery. Death occurs in an idyllic locale. The irony of nature's bounty contrasted with man's destructiveness adds another dimension of meaning to the motion picture. The film setting lends itself to the naturalistic theme usually associated with Stephen Crane's fiction. It is the filmmaker's juxtaposition of discordant elements that creates cinematic irony.

While the preceding paragraphs demonstrate the greater specificity of motion pictures and the greater flexibility of fiction vis-à-vis abstractions, it does not follow that film is entirely incapable of using particulars to create generalized concepts. For example, what inferences can you draw from the following film sequences, each consuming a few seconds of screen time in film adaptations of well-known short stories?

Sequence 1

A small man sits in a breakfast nook, his scrambled eggs before him. He picks up a pepper mill. For several seconds, he turns a hand crank causing a steady stream of pepper to sift onto his eggs.

Sequence 2

A young man standing before a closed front door reaches tentatively for its substantial brass knocker. He taps very lightly. When there is no response, he timidly taps again. After a final feeble tap, a

The Unicorn in the Garden (1953) The husband's life is dull and desperately in need of additional spice. *Still shot reproduced courtesy of Learning Corporation of America.*

tiny smile flits across his face, and he begins to turn away from the door.

Sequence 3

A pallid young man sits before a window facing on a brick wall only inches away. He does not stir. A tall green screen behind him walls him off from the rest of the room.

Sequence 4

A spindly man striding along suddenly stops. He sniffs the aroma of a freshly baked pie cooling on a nearby window sill. Licking his lips in anticipation, he reaches for the pie; at that moment, it is withdrawn. Crestfallen, he stares in disbelief and disappointment.

Sequence 5

A man pictures himself married to a young heiress. He envisions himself seated like a king at one end of a table. His wife sits at the other

The Open Window (1972) "The contrast between the substantial brass knocker and the hesitant taps captures the essence of Framton Nuttel's timidity, his social incompetence, and his desire to avoid human confrontations." *Still shot reproduced courtesy of Pyramid Films.*

end. Tantalizing aromas are wafting from a huge platter of food in the center of the table.

Sequence 6

In an old study containing heavy furniture and ancient bookcases filled with old volumes, three young men and a young woman dance gaily. In a large mirror edged with cobwebs, they appear as four elderly people dancing ludicrously.

As noted earlier, these are descriptions of sequences from short films adapted from short stories. The images are highly specific; yet they lend themselves to the following more abstract inferences.

Sequence 1

The small man leads a dull life, a life desperately in need of additional spice. He is also more than a bit absent-minded, as befits a James Thurber protagonist. This sequence occurs early in an animated adaptation of James Thurber's fable, "The Unicorn in the Garden."

Sequence 2

The contrast between the substantial brass knocker and the hesitant taps captures the essence of Framton Nuttel's timidity, his social incompetence, and his desire to avoid human confrontations. His persistent uneasiness sets the tone for this tongue-in-cheek film adaptation of Saki's satirical short story, "The Open Window."

Sequence 3

The word "wall," as noun and verb, conveys what the visuals reveal, the isolation and alienation of Bartleby. In this screen adaptation of Herman Melville's story, the red brick wall and green folding screen have a common symbolic function. They represent human artifacts and testify to man's involvement in the alienating process.

Sequence 4

In a sequence invented for the animated adaptation of Washington Irving's short story, "The Legend of Sleepy Hollow," a few seconds of cinematic time demonstrate that Ichabod Crane loves food. His crestfallen disbelief when the pie is withdrawn suggests that his initial optimism was unrealistic. In a more abstract sense, this early film sequence establishes Ichabod as a "loser" and foreshadows events to come.

Sequence 5

In a later sequence, also from *The Legend of Sleepy Hollow*, Ichabod's values are revealed through spatial editing, a particularly cinematic device. Ichabod is distant from his wife, but appreciably closer to the food her father's wealth assures. Thus, Washington Irving's characterization of Ichabod as self-serving is captured in cinematic images.

Sequence 6

Hawthorne's short story, "Dr. Heidegger's Experiment," like many of his stories and novels, makes use of ambiguity. The writer tells us:

> by a strange deception . . . the tall mirror is said to have reflected the figure of the three old, gray, withered grandsires, ridiculously contending for the skinny ugliness of a shiveled grandam.

In depicting this scene, the filmmaker shows us both the real characters and their reflection in the mirror. The difference between the two calls into question the reliability of the water from the Fountain of Youth. A more abstract inference does emerge from the visuals. Young or old, these four remain essentially unchanged. The implication is that, like so many other people, they are unable to benefit or learn from prior experience. The images also foster ambiguity.

Film, Fiction, and Time

In Edgar Allan Poe's short story, "The Masque of the Red Death," a paragraph begins as follows:

> It was in this apartment, also, that there stood against the western wall, a gigantic clock of ebony. Its pendulum swung to and fro with a dull, heavy, monotonous clang; and when the minute-hand made the circuit of the face, and the hour was to be stricken, there came from the brazen lungs of the clock a sound which was clear and loud and deep and exceedingly musical, but of so peculiar a note and emphasis that, at each lapse of an hour, the musicians of the orchestra were constrained to pause, momentarily, in their performance, to hearken to the sound; and thus the waltzers perforce ceased their evolutions . . . .

What happens in a reader's imagination as he scans this passage? First, he envisions an ebony clock, then its pendulum; next, he hears its clanging sound. He notes that the minute hand is approaching the hour, and he imagines the sound of the "peculiar" note. Following this, he sees the musicians pause; finally, he sees the waltzers stop dancing. Clearly, a reader adds detail to detail in sequential fashion just as words are arranged in sequence. He does not discover, simultaneously, that there is a "peculiar" sound different from a clanging pendulum. No, the pendulum sound comes first; indeed the very fact of the pendulum's existence is learned prior to the nature of the pendulum's sound. For a reader, the process is one of accretion. He does not learn about the waltzers stopping until after he has read about the musicians pausing.

What happens, however, when a viewer encounters this scene in a hypothetical motion picture? It is possible for him to experience the ebony clock, its pendulum, the sound of its pendulum, and its minute hand about to strike the hour simultaneously. This is in the very nature of the film medium. When the bronze lungs of the clock sound their "peculiar" note, he hears the sound and observes the effect on the musicians simultaneously. Indeed, if the director elects to use a long shot, the viewer may see the dancers stop, the musicians pause, and hear the sound—all at once. Thus, we have a significant characteristic of film: simultaneous multi-sensory communication. This contrasts sharply with the linearity of fiction. A writer cannot present description, dialogue, and narrative at once, but the filmmaker can give his viewers such a simultaneous experience.

Film has been described as an immediate experience. The passage from Poe quoted above is in the past tense. A film adaptation of this passage would necessarily be in the present tense. All film happens now. Even in flashbacks, the events of the past occur in the present tense, thereby enhancing film's immediacy. While some fiction has been written in the present tense, most stories use the conventional past tense. Fiction, then, tends to move from the past toward the present. Film moves from the present toward the future.

Sometimes a writer may use the present tense to achieve a special effect. In "An Occurrence at Owl Creek Bridge," after consistently using the past tense through most of the story, the writer shifts to the present tense in the next-to-last paragraph, and this seems to hint at the unreality of the actions that are occurring. The last sentence, which returns to the past tense, abruptly and ruthlessly exposes the truth of the situation.

Film is an instantaneous medium with multiple messages being sent simultaneously, and it makes demands on its viewers because of their inability to regulate the rate or speed of those messages. A film unreels at a fixed rate. In contrast, a reader individually controls his reading. He may pause when he wishes; he can stop to look up a word or ponder a concept.

Technical develoments in film have made possible distortions of time unavailable to a writer of fiction. A filmmaker can create special effects by using a speed-up, slow motion, or a freeze. In the film version of *An Occurrence at Owl Creek Bridge*, Robert Enrico uses slow motion

An Occurrence at Owl Creek Bridge (1962) "When Peyton Farquhar thinks about his wife and family, his thoughts are visualized in slow motion. Then, harsh reality shatters the slow motion illusion." In Bierce's short story, poetic language signifies illusion while more mundane prose depicts reality. *Still shots reproduced courtesy of Contemporary/McGraw-Hill Films.*

for several purposes. When Peyton Farquhar thinks about his wife and family, his thoughts are visualized in slow motion. Then, the film returns to normal speed, and harsh reality shatters the illusion. His wife's actions near the end of the film are also in slow motion, and the director once again undercuts illusion by shifting to regular speed. In Bierce's story, the destruction of romantic illusion by harsh reality is achieved by alternating two tones of writing. Poetic language symbolizes the romantic and unreal. More mundane prose represents reality. For the filmmaker, time-distorted images create similar effects. In the film adaptation, *The Open Window,* Richard Patterson uses slow motion for ironic effect. When Framton Nuttel sees what he believes to be apparitions, he is galvanized into action. The use of slow motion to depict his reckless haste is ironic. Moreover, the irony extends back to Framton's words of a preceding scene, "My doctors agree in ordering me complete rest, an absence of mental excitement, and avoidance of anything in the nature of physical exercise." At the end of the film, the camera freezes on Vera; the film closes with the still. The freeze frame seems to have a greater significance than an ordinary shot. It is a means of emphasizing, a visual underlining. Tonally, it is the verbal equivalent of Saki's closing line, "Romance at short notice was her specialty."

Language has far greater flexibility than film in denoting the passing of time. Three examples illustrate both the differences between the media and the diversity of solutions film directors have chosen when confronted by the problem. In language, it is very easy to indicate a specific period of elapsed time. In "Bartleby," for example, Melville begins many paragraphs with simple phrases such as: "A few days after this . . . ," "Some days passed . . . ," "As days passed on . . . ," "The next morning . . . ," "After breakfast . . . ," "Acting accordingly, next day . . . ," "Several days passed . . . ," "The next day . . . ," and "Some few days after this . . . ." The director of the film version decided to indicate the passing of time by beginning each scene with titles like "THE SECOND DAY," "THE THIRD DAY," "SEVERAL DAYS LATER," "THE NEXT DAY," "THE FOLLOWING SUNDAY," "A WEEK LATER," etc. Thus, the filmmaker chose a verbal solution to a cinematic problem. On the other hand, the film takes place in the year 1840, and this may be a period sufficiently far removed in time to justify a somewhat old-fashioned technique.

In another short story, "The Bet," by Anton Chekhov, the author covers a fifteen-year period of self-imprisonment in five relatively short paragraphs; the paragraphs begin as follows: "In the first year . . . ," "In the second year . . . ," "In the second half of the sixth year . . . ,"

"Thereupon, after the tenth year . . . ," and "In the last two years . . . ." In the film adaptation, the passage of time is revealed in several ways. One method is the relatively trite technique of successive calendar shots. The second technique is more imaginative. We see significant physical changes in the protagonist. Initially, he is clean-shaven. Later, his beard is long and unkempt; still later, his beard is trimmed to a neat goatee. Finally, he is clean-shaven once more. Those differences in his physical appearance indicate the passage of time and, in addition, are related to important psychological changes which are taking place simultaneously.

In *The Legend of Sleepy Hollow,* a film adaptation of Washington Irving's short story, successive shots show Ichabod Crane striding along on what seems to be a fine spring or summer day. The next sequence begins on a wintry day in school. The filmmaker simply cuts to the new sequence and the altered landscape testifies to the passing of time. In addition, the voice-over reinforces the visual; we hear, "His schoolhouse, on a crisp winter day . . . ." Some sequences later, the cold winter scene is replaced by a cut to a seasonal shot of a late spring or summer day; we see farm animals and a rich orchard. Even the music becomes pastoral. No verbal clues are needed; we know that time has passed even if we do not know the specific number of days or months.

Both film and fiction have considerable flexibility in shifting back and forth in time. They can cover either short or long periods of time without difficulty. Thus, in *The Bet,* five years of time are condensed into twenty-four minutes of cinematic time. In the original Chekhov story, fifteen years of time are condensed into five short paragraphs. Film's ability to condense time stems from the medium itself. A motion picture consists of many hundreds of bits of celluloid linked together. Separating each shot from the subsequent shot is some form of cinematic transition. There are three basic kinds of transitions. Most fundamental is the cut. One picture ends; another image replaces it. As a director cuts from shot to shot, he leaves out details that would be time consuming. Whatever occurred in time between the two shots has been eliminated. Because there are hundreds of cuts, a considerable period of time can be condensed into the actual film running time.

A second kind of cinematic transition is the fade-out and fade-in. An image goes dark on the screen; then, the screen lights up with another image. Psychologically, a fade-out serves a purpose similar to the use of a curtain in a play, or the end of a chapter in a novel. It communicates to the audience the end of a sequence or scene; it also

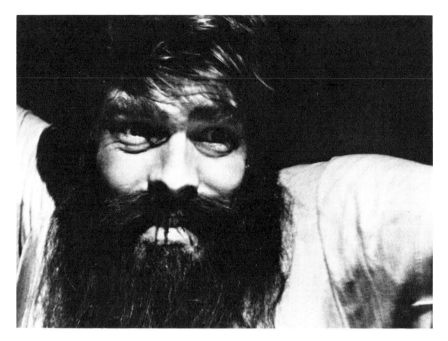

The Bet (1967) Each stage of hairlessness or hairiness signifies important psychological changes in the character. The external man reflects the interior man. *Still shots reproduced courtesy of Pyramid Films.*

implies the passage of time. However, it is not as distracting as the lowering and raising of a curtain and therefore can be used more frequently without obviously interrupting the flow of the action. In today's motion pictures, the fade-out technique is much less frequent than in older movies. Today's more sophisticated audiences can cope with the more abrupt cut.

The third transitional device is the dissolve. In this case, one image on screen gets lighter until it disappears. Simultaneously, another image comes on screen. For a short time, both images co-exist on the screen. Several time-oriented reasons may dictate the director's dcision to use a dissolve. First, the co-existence of two shots suggests a relationship between them. Thus, the technique could translate into "meanwhile" or "at the same time." A dissolve also can link the present with the past. A character in a film sees something happen; simultaneously, he recalls a parallel, related, or contrasting event of the past. On screen, the view of the current event fades while the past event slowly becomes a clear image, the image of a time gone past. While there are additional variations among the transitional devices of the filmmaker, these are the essential ones. Cuts are more contemporary than fades, which represent a style more popular in earlier movies.

Film and fiction can also expand time. Probably the best-known example of this among short stories and short films is *An Occurrence at Owl Creek Bridge* in which a brief instant between the initiation of Peyton Farquhar's execution and the moment of his death is expanded to many pages in the story and many minutes of reel time in the film.

If the filmmaker wishes, cinematic time can be expanded beyond real time for psychological purposes. Thus, instead of a shot of the murderer slipping a noose over the victim and tightening it with the victim collapsing several seconds later, the director could show the murderer slip the noose over the victim, then cut to a cat scampering away, then cut to a shot of the clock, cut again to a shot of the victim's brother drinking at some distant bar, cut back to the cat, and finally show the collapse of the victim. The real time needed for the act of murder would be expanded to a longer period of film time.

For the filmmaker, then, the manipulation of time is a significant part of his craft. He necessarily concerns himself with a motion picture's rhythm. In turn, rhythm of a film helps express its meaning. For example, in *The Loneliness of the Long Distance Runner*, the director uses a series of abrupt cuts to separate his shots. Psychologically, his decision is wise because the jolting rhythm of the film is appropriate to its theme. In contrast, *To Catch a Mockingbird* uses many slow fades and dissolves, thereby capturing the pace of events occurring in a sleepy

Southern community. In *The Bet,* with its emphasis on the psychological trauma of self-isolation, the rapidly alternating shots and abrupt cuts, particularly during early sequences of the film, increase the pressure and tension; the spectator is drawn into the film and experiences the emotional upheaval of the protagonist.

THE UPTURNED FACE

Stephen Crane

When Stephen Crane wrote "The Upturned Face," he knew he was dying of tuberculosis. Like his earlier novel, The Red Badge of Courage *(1895), the story probes the emotions of men under fire with pitiless accuracy. Crane described himself as a writer concerned with "realism." For him, this meant capturing the paradox of man, the contrasting pulls of ideals and realities.*

The ten-minute film adaptation by Edward Folger retains most of the dialogue of Crane's story. The film was released in 1973.

In addition to a shot analysis of Folger's movie, the book provides an unproduced screenplay by Jim Stinson. Written in 1973, the screenplay was rejected because Folger's film had only recently been released. The produced and unproduced films have enough significant differences to warrant comparative evaluations as screen adaptations of the Crane short story.

What will we do now?" said the adjutant, troubled and excited. "Bury him," said Timothy Lean.

The two officers looked down close to their toes where lay the body of their comrade. The face was chalk-blue; gleaming eyes stared at the sky. Over the two upright figures was a windy sound of bullets, and on the top of the hill Lean's prostrate company of Spitzbergen infantry was firing measured volleys.

Don't you think it would be better—" began the adjutant. "We might leave him until to-morrow."

"No," said Lean. "I can't hold that post an hour longer. I've got to fall back, and we've got to bury old Bill."

"Of course," said the adjutant, at once. "Your men got entrenching tools?"

Lean shouted back to his little line, and two men came slowly, one with a pick, one with a shovel. They stared in the direction of the Rostina sharpshooters. Bullets cracked near their ears. "Dig here," said Lean gruffly. The men, thus caused to lower their glances to the turf, became hurried and frightened, merely because they could not look to see whence the bullets came. The dull beat of the pick striking the earth sounded amid the swift snap of close bullets. Presently the other private began to shovel.

"I suppose," said the adjutant, slowly, "we'd better search his clothes for—things."

Lean nodded. Together in curious abstraction they looked at the body. Then Lean stirred his shoulders suddenly, arousing himself.

"Yes," he said, "we'd better see what he's got." He dropped to his knees, and his hands approached the body of the dead officer. But his hands wavered over the buttons of the tunic. The first button was brick-red with drying blood, and he did not seem to dare touch it.

"Go on," said the adjutant, hoarsely.

Lean stretched his wooden hand, and his fingers fumbled the bloodstained buttons. At last he rose with ghastly face. He had gathered a watch, a whistle, a pipe, a tobacco-pouch, a handkerchief, a little case of cards and papers. He looked at the adjutant. There was a silence. The adjutant was feeling that he had been a coward to make Lean do all the grisly business.

"Well," said Lean, "that's all, I think. You have his sword and revolver?"

"Yes," said the adjutant, his face working, and then he burst out in a sudden strange fury at the two privates. "Why don't you hurry up with that grave? What are you doing, anyhow? Hurry, do you hear? I never saw such stupid—"

Even as he cried out in his passion the two men were laboring for their lives. Ever overhead the bullets were spitting.

The grave was finished. It was not a masterpiece—a poor little shallow thing. Lean and the adjutant again looked at each other in a curious silent communication.

Suddenly the adjutant croaked out a weird laugh. It was a terrible laugh, which had its origin in that part of the mind which is first moved by the singing of the nerves. "Well," he said humorously to Lean, "I suppose we had best tumble him in."

"Yes," said Lean. The two privates stood waiting, bent over their implements. "I suppose," said Lean, "it would be better if we laid him in ourselves."

"Yes," said the adjutant. Then, apparently remembering that he had made Lean search the body, he stooped with great fortitude and took hold of the dead officer's clothing. Lean joined him. Both were particular that their fingers should not feel the corpse. They tugged away; the corpse lifted, heaved, toppled, flopped into the grave, and the two officers, straightening, looked again at each other—they were always looking at each other. They sighed with relief.

The adjutant said, "I suppose we should—we should say something. Do you know the service, Tim?"

"They don't read the service until the grave is filled in," said Lean, pressing his lips to an academic expression.

"Don't they?" said the adjutant, shocked that he had made the mistake. "Oh well," he cried, suddenly, "let us—let us say something —while he can hear us."

"All right," said Lean. "Do you know the service?"

"I can't remember a line of it," said the adjutant.

Lean was extremely dubious. "I can repeat two lines, but—"

"Well, do it," said the adjutant. "Go as far as you can. That's better than nothing. And the beasts have got our range exactly."

Lean looked at his two men. "Attention," he barked. The privates came to attention with a click, looking much aggrieved. The adjutant lowered his helmet to his knee. Lean, bareheaded, stood over the grave. The Rostina sharpshooters fired briskly.

"O Father, our friend has sunk in the deep waters of death, but his spirit has leaped toward Thee as the bubble arises from the lips of the drowning. Perceive, we beseech, O Father, the little flying bubble, and—"

Lean, although husky and ashamed, had suffered no hesitation up to this point, but he stopped with a hopeless feeling and looked at the corpse.

The adjutant moved uneasily. "And from Thy superb heights—" he began, and then he too came to an end.

"And from Thy superb heights," said Lean.

The adjutant suddenly remembered a phrase in the back of the Spitzbergen burial service, and he exploited it with the triumphant manner of a man who has recalled everything, and can go on.

"Oh God, have mercy—"

"Oh God, have mercy—" said Lean.

"Mercy," repeated the adjutant, in quick failure.

"Mercy," said Lean. And then he was moved by some violence of feeling, for he turned upon his two men and tigerishly said, "Throw the dirt in."

The fire of the Rostina sharpshooters was accurate and continuous.

One of the aggrieved privates came forward with his shovel. He, lifted his first shovel-load of earth, and for a moment of inexplicable hesitation it was held poised above this corpse, which from its chalk-blue face looked keenly out from the grave. Then the soldier emptied his shovel on—on the feet.

Timothy Lean felt as if tons had been swiftly lifted from off his forehead. He had felt that perhaps the private might empty the shovel on—on the face. It had been emptied on the feet. There was a great point gained there—ha, ha!—the first shovelful had been emptied on the feet. How satisfactory!

The adjutant began to babble. "Well, of course—a man we've messed with all these years—impossible—you can't, you know, leave your intimate friends rotting on the field. Go on, for God's sake, and shovel, you."

The man with the shovel suddenly ducked, grabbed his left arm with his right hand, and looked at his officer for orders. Lean picked the shovel from the ground. "Go to the rear," he said to the wounded man. He also addressed the other private. "You get under cover, too; I'll finish this business."

The wounded man scrambled hard still for the top of the ridge without devoting any glances to the direction from whence the bullets came, and the other man followed at an equal pace; but he was different, in that he looked back anxiously three times.

This is merely the way—often—of the hit and unhit.

Timothy Lean filled the shovel, hesitated, and then, in a movement which was like a gesture of abhorrence, he flung the dirt into the grave, and as it landed it made a sound—plop. Lean suddenly stopped and mopped his brow—a tired laborer.

"Perhaps we have been wrong," said the adjutant. (His glance wavered stupidly.) "It might have been better if we hadn't buried him just at this time. Of course, if we advance to-morrow the body would have been—".

"Damn you," said Lean, "shut your mouth." He was not the senior officer.

He again filled the shovel and flung the earth. Always the earth made that sound—plop. For a space Lean worked frantically, like a man digging himself out of danger.

Soon there was nothing to be seen but the chalk-blue face. Lean filled the shovel. "Good God," he cried to the adjutant. "Why didn't you turn him somehow when you put him in? This—" Then Lean began to stutter.

The adjutant understood. He was pale to the lips. "Go on, man," he cried, beseechingly, almost in a shout.

Lean swung back the shovel. It went forward in a pendulum curve. When the earth landed it made a sound—plop.

shot analysis
THE UPTURNED FACE

1. Pyramid Films on black.

2. Black. THE UPTURNED FACE.

FADE OUT:

3. CLOSE-UP: A man's hands opening a paper cylinder. He removes a pill from the cylinder and lifts it out of the frame.

CUT TO:

4. CLOSE-UP: The man, a soldier, sits against a tree. Another man flashes past. The man drinks from a canteen.

CUT TO:

5. MEDIUM SHOT: Two soldiers. The man with the canteen seated at left; the other (the adjutant) standing at right. He wears a sword. The adjutant speaks

ADJ.

Come on!

The adjutant exits behind trees in upper center of frame. The seated man spits out a mouthful of water and closes his canteen. He rises, grabbing his hat and rifle, and trots after the adjutant, meanwhile putting on his hat. He exits from frame. Hold on green Southern landscape.

CUT TO:

6. LONG SHOT: Pan fast right through trees. A man running. He runs toward camera into a close-up. He is the man with the canteen. A shot sounds; the man falls out of frame. Hold on trees in background. The adjutant's voice, off-screen, calls out.

ADJ.

Bill!

CUT TO:

7. LONG SHOT: Green background. The adjutant, running left, slows down and comes into a two-shot with the fallen body. He pauses and

looks down at the body; another officer, Lean, runs into frame from down left.

CUT TO:

8. CLOSE-UP: Two-shot. The adjutant and Lean looking down. Lean looks at the adjutant and back down. The adjutant removes his hat, wipes his face, and looks at Lean.

ADJ.

What do we do now?

Lean looks up, then down,

LEAN

Bury him.

ADJ.

Here? Now? I mean, couldn't we—

LEAN

Can't drag him back through the marsh.

ADJ.

Maybe if we come back tomorrow—

Lean pauses, shakes his head.

ADJ.

Your men got any trenching tools?

CUT TO:

9. LONG SHOT: Three men with their backs to the camera firing.

CUT TO:

10. CLOSE-UP: Lean, looking away from camera, calls two names. He turns to look at the body.

CUT TO:

11. LONG SHOT: Foliage. A man crosses right; another follows.

CUT TO:

12. TWO-SHOT: Lean and adjutant. Another man runs into frame. Sound of firing.

CUT TO:

13. Lean points.

LEAN
You men dig here.

CUT TO:

14. MEDIUM SHOT: Adjutant looks right. Two men cross in background. Sound of digging.

ADJ.
I suppose we ought to check his belongings.

CUT TO:

15. MEDIUM SHOT: Lean looks down left, nods, and bends to body.

CUT TO:

16. CLOSE-UP: Adjutant watching.

CUT TO:

17. CLOSE-UP: Lean's hands opening bloody pocket with a bullet hole in it. They remove a container of pills. Painstakingly, the hands close the pocket.

CUT TO:

18. CLOSE-UP: Adjutant watching.

CUT TO:

19. CLOSE-UP: Lean's bloodied hands close pocket and check another pocket. They remove a lady's photo.

CUT TO:

20. CLOSE-UP: Lean looking pained.

CUT TO:

21. CLOSE-UP: Photo of lady. Sounds of digging over.

CUT TO:

22. CLOSE-UP: Lean looking pained. He looks up.

LEAN
. . . guess that's it.

CUT TO:

23. MEDIUM SHOT: Adjutant, looking down, walks away. A shot rings out. A man crosses frame. There is a troop in the distance, firing. Voices over. An ax falls in the foreground.

CUT TO:

24. MEDIUM SHOT: A man with a gun runs right. He wears a farmer's straw hat.

CUT TO:

25. LONG SHOT: A field. A shot fired by a distant figure.

CUT TO:

26. MEDIUM SHOT: Farmer, on one knee, returns fire.

CUT TO:

27. LONG SHOT: Field. A small figure runs left.

CUT TO:

28. MEDIUM SHOT: Adjutant, back to camera. Firing over. He turns toward camera.

ADJ.
Hurry up with that grave!

CUT TO:

29. LONG SHOT: Field. Two men crossing toward camera. Firing over.

MAN
Now.

CUT TO:

30. LONG SHOT: Two men firing left.

CUT TO:

31. LONG SHOT: Brushy area. Two men fire back. One rises, cocks gun, fires.

CUT TO:

32. MEDIUM SHOT: Man, back to camera, crouching, moves away from camera.

CUT TO:

33. THREE-SHOT: Center man, finished with his digging, pants as he wipes his face with his left sleeve. He switches the shovel handle to his left hand and leans on it. He turns to the adjutant who crosses right to the body.

ADJ.

Put him in.

The adjutant bends down and takes the body by the cartridge belt. Another man enters frame. They drag the body toward the grave. Clanking sounds over. At the end of the shot, the dead man's face is in foreground of screen.

CUT TO:

34. MEDIUM SHOT: Two soldiers watching. One looks pained, the other disinterested.

CUT TO:

35. MEDIUM SHOT: Adjutant walks into frame.

ADJ.

We better say something: Do you know the regimental service?

LEAN

They don't say the service until the grave is filled.

ADJ.

Well, we better say something. While he can hear us.

LEAN

All right. Do you know the service?

ADJ.

No.

CUT TO:

36. MEDIUM SHOT: Two privates.

CUT TO:

37. MEDIUM SHOT: Adjutant and Lean.

LEAN

I can remember two lines.

ADJ.

Well, do it. It's better than nothing.

LEAN

All right.

CUT TO:

38. FOUR-SHOT.

                         LEAN

'Ten hut!

The men come to attention.

                         LEAN

Dear Father, our friend has sunk in the deep waters of death, but his spirit has leaped toward you like a bubble rising from the lips of the drowning. Receive, we beseech Thee, O Father, the little floating bubble, and—(a pause)

                         ADJ.

and from Thy superb heights—

                         LEAN

and from Thy superb heights—

A long pause. A white butterfly flutters from right to center and disappears in the background.

                         ADJ.

The Lord have mercy.

                         LEAN

The Lord have mercy.

                         ADJ.

. . . mercy—

CUT TO:

39. CLOSE-UP: Lean looks around, confused. He steps back; his face contorts.

                         LEAN

Throw the dirt in.

He puts on his hat.

CUT TO:

40. MEDIUM SHOT: Hands lifting shovels to fill grave.

CUT TO:

41. MEDIUM SHOT: Body. Dirt falls on it.

CUT TO:

42. MEDIUM SHOT: Lean. A shot rings out. Lean ducks.

CUT TO:

43. CLOSE-UP: Soldier. He grabs his bicep. Blood runs through his hand. (The soldier who was disinterested—see shot 34). He nearly collapses.

CUT TO:

44. MEDIUM SHOT: Lean. He straightens up.

LEAN

Get out of here, get out of here.

He takes off his hat, ducks, and crosses right.

LEAN

You can get your rifle and get out there. I'll finish this.

CUT TO:

45. MEDIUM SHOT: Private grabs hat, runs right, then left.

CUT TO:

46. MEDIUM SHOT: Lean. Shoveling rapidly.

CUT TO:

47. LONG SHOT: Private running.

ADJ. (voice-over)

I told you we shouldn't have buried him . . .

CUT TO:

48. CLOSE-UP: Adjutant.

ADJ.

. . . today. (He stutters) T, T, Tomorrow, tomorrow, there's going to be an advance and we could take care of it then—

CUT TO:

49. CLOSE-UP: Lean. He rises.

LEAN

Damn you, shut your mouth!

CUT TO:

50. CLOSE-UP: Adjutant. He turns, looks right.

CUT TO:

51. LONG SHOT: An armed man crosses right, running.

CUT TO:

52. MEDIUM SHOT: Lean. Looking down, he pauses in shoveling.

LEAN

Good God. (He looks up) Why didn't we turn him some way when we put him in?

CUT TO:

53. CLOSE-UP: Adjutant.

CUT TO:

54. CLOSE-UP: Corpse's face, eyes open.

CUT TO:

55. CLOSE-UP: Adjutant.

CUT TO:

56. CLOSE-UP: Lady's photo.

CUT TO:

57. CLOSE-UP: Adjutant.

CUT TO:

58. MEDIUM SHOT: Lean. He looks down at body.

CUT TO:

59. CLOSE-UP: Upturned face. Shovel comes into frame and dirt is shovelled onto face, covering it. Focus on dirt.

FADE OUT:

60. Black. Directed by EDWARD FOLGER.

CUT TO:

61. Screenplay by EDWARD FOLGER.

CUT TO:

62. Based on a story by STEPHEN CRANE

CUT TO:

63.–66. Credits.

screenplay

THE UPTURNED FACE

Jim Stinson

FADE IN:

1. VERY WIDE SHOT, WALKING: A peaceful, rural scene very early on a glorious Spring morning. A fence-bordered dirt road divides rolling farm meadows dotted with small copses 'of trees. The sun, just risen, is driving off the last dew sparkles and fingers of mist. A breeze rustles translucent leaves. Birds sing and chatter loudly; occasional barks and a distant cock-crow suggest a farmyard not far away.
We are striding briskly across a field, parallel to the road. Heavy foot-falls confirm that this is a point-of-view shot. A rough, energetic voice is humming the barracks tune "Beer, Beer, Beer."
The camera swings right, then left, surveying the scene, then returns to the line of travel.

>   BILL (Voice-Over)
>   (grumbling absent-mindedly)
>   . . . always get the bum details . . .

The shot continues, accompanied by the bird calls and Bill's own sounds, unnaturally clear and distinct.

>   BILL (Voice-Over)
>   (in the middle of his song)
>   . . . hm hm hm hm so queer,
>   In the Quar - ter - mas - ter's . . .

1a. CAMERA HALTS, centering a copse of trees about one hundred yards away.

>   BILL (Voice-Over)
>   (inspecting the copse)
>   Hmmm.

1b. WALKING RESUMES as he dismisses the copse of trees from his mind.

BILL (Voice-Over)
(finishing the verse)
. . . Corps!
(muttering)
Well, they gotta be *some*place.
(singing again)
My eyes - are dim,
I can - not see—ee-ee,

1c. CAMERA HALTS, centering another stand of trees on the far side of the road. The singing breaks off again, leaving the natural sounds loud on the track. Hold a moment, then

1d. WALKING RESUMES.

BILL (Voice-Over)
(singing)
There are - no - flies - on - meeeee!

2. JUMP CUT TO CLOSE ON TREES: a muzzle flash and smoke puff; sharp gunshot report.

3. WALKING SHOT: A sickening thud and the camera is knocked violently to a sitting position.

BILL (Voice-Over)
(breath only)
Uhhhh!!

The camera tilts very slowly forward to frame booted feet and khaki legs stretched out. The left leg pulls back out of the shot as Bill gets it under him and attempts to rise. He gets part-way up, then totters. A Lee-Enfield type rifle drops into the shot, onto the foot. A trickle of bright blood splashes the boot briefly, then stops. The birds resume their cheerful gabble.

Very slowly, the camera tilts upward, continuing steadily past horizontal and into the air. It jars slightly and stops, framing empty blue sky.

4. CLOSE-UP: A feisty blue jay scolds his way along a branch.
SUPERIMPOSE FIRST MAIN TITLE

5. CLOSE-UP: An energetic ground squirrel searches, gobbles, chews.
SUPERIMPOSE SECOND MAIN TITLE

6. CLOSE-UP: Translucent tree leaves sparkle in the sunshine. SUPERIMPOSE LAST MAIN TITLE

FADE TO BLACK. The sounds of nature continue a moment, unnaturally clear in the blackness. Then we hear

ADJUTANT
(still over black screen)

What'll we do now?

DIRECT CUT TO:

7. CLOSE-UP, HIGH ANGLE: Bill's blunt, seamed, dead face; a trickle of dried blood out of one corner of the mouth, through the dirty beard. Calm empty eyes staring sightlessly.

7a. ZOOM OUT, revealing the chunky head and shoulders of a grizzled veteran in his early fifties: longish hair, once blond; untidy olive uniform of officer rank. The widening shot shows the body lying on its back, feet nearest camera. Lean and the adjutant stand at the feet, backs to camera, framing the corpse. Bird and insect sounds continue. The hot light suggests mid-afternoon.

8. MEDIUM SHOT: Lean, a tall, rangy man of forty with a thatch of hair and beard. He replies as if giving the obvious answer to a self-evident question:

LEAN

Bury him.

9. MEDIUM SHOT: The adjutant is a slight man in his thirties, with an aggressive moustache that fails to toughen his soft face. His uniform is tidier than Lean's, and his sword indicates that he is the ranking officer. He is dismayed by the answer.

10. FULL SHOT, HIGH ANGLE: A gunshot, ricochet, splintering wood and a light branch falls across the body.

11. TWO-SHOT: The adjutant hits the dirt, leaving Lean in frame. Lean appears not to have noticed. He turns to look at the source of the firing, and we see the distant copse of trees.

LEAN

Sharpshooters. Out of range.

He turns back and looks down at the body.

LEAN

Almost.

He looks at the adjutant.

12. FULL SHOT: The adjutant is embarrassed at being caught lying down while Lean remains standing. Looking for an excuse, he spots the branch lying across the dead man's face. Angrily, he pulls it off.

13. CLOSE-UP: The impassive face is revealed again as the leaves wipe across it. The distant gunshots continue irregularly.

14. MEDIUM SHOT: Lean looks up from the body, toward the low hill opposite the distant copse of trees. The crest of the hill is obscured by trees and brush.

LEAN
(conversationally)

What do you say, boys?

As if in answer, the crest of the hill erupts in a disciplined volley of gunshots. An orderly rank of six or eight smoke puffs drifts away from the hill.

ADJUTANT (Voice-Over)
(hesitant)

Wouldn't it be better . . .

16. FULL SHOT: The adjutant is kneeling behind the body, holding the severed branch in front of him as if trying, unconsciously, to hide behind it.

ADJUTANT

We could leave him . . .

(qualifying)

. . . until tomorrow . . ?

17. MEDIUM SHOT (as in 15.): Lean is still looking toward the sharp-shooters.

LEAN

I can't hold that hill any longer. We're going to fall back.

He turns to look at the adjutant.

LEAN
(stating the obvious)

And we've got to bury old Bill.

18. STILL INSERT: Bill, seated on a log between Lean and the adjutant, ladling food from a pot in foreground, onto their tin plates. The adjutant

looks dubiously at his plate; Lean is making a face; Bill is laughing at them.

19. CLOSE-UP: The adjutant, afraid of appearing cowardly or callous, pulls himself together.

ADJUTANT
(forcefully)

Of course.

He registers on the tree branch, discards it, and, trying to conceal his fear, stands erect like Lean. (WIDEN as he rises.)

ADJUTANT
(being matter-of-fact)

Your men have tools?

20. TWO-SHOT: The adjutant is walking around the body to join Lean when, without warning, Lean shouts up the hill:

LEAN
(calling)

Cory!!

Appalled, the adjutant whips around to look at Lean, ducking as he does so. Two or three rounds racket through the branches above. Lean is totally oblivious to them.

LEAN
(continuing)

Send a burial detail!

21. MEDIUM SHOT: The adjutant straightens up, looking at Lean to see if his reaction has been noticed.

22. LONG SHOT: Two men emerge from the cover atop the hill and scuttle down the exposed meadow.

22a. ZOOM IN to frame them in full shot as a hail of fire comes from the sharpshooters. Bullets whistle over. One man falls, tumbles, regains his feet. Both men stop their crouching and zig-zagging; they pound toward the camera flat-out, terrified.

22b. ZOOM OUT to hold them in full shot as they rush up to the two officers and . . .

23. TWO-SHOT, LOW ANGLE: sink to the ground. We are looking across the corpse as the enlisted men, both nondescript privates in their

'teens, see the body. They freeze in momentary shock, then look at each other, at the officers—look anywhere but at the body.

24. MEDIUM SHOT: The adjutant straightens himself into a more military bearing, not quite sure of what to say to the privates.

LEAN (Voice-Over)

Dig here.

25. FULL SHOT: Lean is standing in a slightly more protected spot, about ten feet away.

26. TWO-SHOT: Dubiously, the privates look to the adjutant.

27. CLOSE-UP: Keeping a stern countenance, he looks away.

28. CLOSE-UP: Lean suddenly loses patience.

LEAN
(barking)

Dig!

29. FULL SHOT: Reluctantly, the privates rise and, still avoiding looking at the corpse, move to the spot indicated. Lean rejoins the adjutant.

30. TWO-SHOT: Lean and the adjutant look down at the body.

31. FULL SHOT: Smoke puffs drift out of the distant trees as the invisible sharpshooters maintain a brisk, irregular fire.

32. FULL SHOT: Lean's company, also invisible in the hilltop scrub, return measured volleys.

33. TWO-SHOT: The adjutant steals a glance at Lean, then tries to imitate his matter-of-fact attitude.

ADJUTANT
I guess we better search his clothes, for—things.

He looks at the body again.

34. STILL INSERT: Lean, the adjutant, and Bill are flaked out on the ground. Bill is swigging whiskey out of a bottle. The adjutant is reaching for the bottle, as if to save some. Lean watches, grinning.

35. MEDIUM SHOT: The corpse stares patiently upward. Beside its head, the adjutant's booted feet shift uneasily. The muffled, methodical *thunks* and *chunks* of digging can be heard.

36. TWO-SHOT: Lean emerges from his abstracted state, sighing.

LEAN

Yes, we better.

The adjutant looks at him anxiously, then shows relief as Lean moves toward the body.

37. LOW ANGLE: across the head and chest of the body as Lean drops, kneeling into medium shot. He lifts his hands toward the blood-stained tunic, then hesitates.

38. STILL INSERT: The three men playing poker on the ground. The adjutant watches in amusement as Lean rakes in a pot. Bill registers cheerful disgust at his cards.

39. LOW ANGLE MEDIUM SHOT: Suddenly, Lean's emotionless façade is cracked. He looks up at the adjutant, off-screen, then at the body. He lifts his hands toward the blood-stained tunic, then hesitates.

40. STILL INSERT: Bill waist-deep in a stream, scrubbing himself exuberantly with yellow soap and a rag.

41. CLOSE-UP: Lean is reluctant to touch the blood. He glances at the adjutant, then forces himself to make the effort. His arms move forward.

41a. TILT DOWN to frame his hands approaching the dead fist, loosening its grip on the tunic, fumbling the bloody buttons.

41b. TILT UP to frame Lean's face again. Now he is struggling to keep his composure. He concentrates grimly, blanking his mind to all but the mechanical task of searching the body.
A close ricochet makes him wince, but he keeps working.

ADJUTANT (Voice-Over)
(shouting, during the above)

Dig, you stupid . . . ! !

42. TIGHT CLOSE-UP: a pathetic pile of trivia gathers as Lean tosses items on the ground: a turnip watch with blood on it, a pipe and tobacco pouch, a pair of gold spectacles, a small, battered case of cards and letters, a dirty bandanna. We hear hasty footsteps and . . .

42a. ZOOM OUT to include the adjutant as he kneels by the pile and scoops the possessions into the bandanna. Rising, he looks at Lean,

43. MEDIUM SHOT: who proffers the dead man's belt, holster, and revolver.

44. FULL SHOT: The adjutant takes the belt and pistol; Lean rises.

They stare at each other. It is late afternoon now. A lull in the firing allows insect noises to be heard.

45. FULL SHOT: The privates watch, crouching in the completed grave.

46. MEDIUM-CLOSE SHOT: The dead face stares. A fly walks across the forehead.

47. CLOSE-UP: The adjutant croaks out a weird laugh. He is suppressing hysteria. He looks at Lean.

ADJUTANT

Guess we better . . . tumble him in.

48. STILL INSERT: A medium shot of Bill embracing a woman. Her back is to the camera; she has long, lustrous hair and wears a simple dress. Bill is giving her a bear-hug and buss on the ear. The effect is more cheerful than romantic.

49. CLOSE-UP: Lean nods, looking at the adjutant, then turns to the privates,

50. MEDIUM TWO-SHOT: . . . who obviously want no part of it.

51. CLOSE-UP: Lean looks reluctantly at the adjutant.

LEAN

Better if we laid him in ourselves.

52. STILL INSERT: A medium shot of Bill mending a sock with needle and thread.

53. CLOSE-UP: The adjutant hates to touch the body but pulls himself together.

53a. ZOOM TO FULL SHOT: He sets down the belongings and, forcing himself to be brisk, bends to take hold of the body. Lean moves to the corpse's head.

54. MEDIUM CLOSE-UP: Lean pulls the body's arms up over its head, then

55. TIGHT CLOSE-UP: grabs its hands. His hands jerk away from the dead flesh, fumble, and gain a purchase on the tunic sleeves. He lifts.

56. FULL SHOT: The adjutant has grabbed the dead feet. He heaves upward.

57. MEDIUM SHOT: Lean heaves too.

58. FULL SHOT: A boot comes off in the adjutant's hand. The feet flop to the ground,

59. FULL SHOT: and Lean is left holding up the arms of the now sitting corpse. Lean's face is ghastly.

60. CLOSE-UP: The adjutant is horror-stricken. He glances at Lean, then holds out the boot, as if to have Lean do something with it.

Three or four bullets racket through the branches overhead, sending down leaves and twigs.

60a. SNAP-ZOOM OUT as the adjutant, cursing inaudibly, drops the boot, grabs the feet again, and the two officers wrestle the body toward the grave. The privates scramble out of the grave.

61. FULL SHOT: The officers approach the grave in foreground, and heave the body toward it.

62. CLOSE-UP: The head bangs on the ground.

63. CLOSE-UP: A limp arm cartwheels through the frame.

64. CLOSE-UP: A tangle of legs slides down into the grave.

65. CLOSE-UP: The head scrapes down the side of the grave, flips over, and ends up staring at camera. Rivulets of loose dirt run down behind it, into its hair.

66. FULL SHOT: Lean scrambles around, pulling the arms down and straightening the legs.

67. MEDIUM SHOT: The adjutant has picked up the belongings again. He hands the boot to Lean, as if to have him replace it; but Lean takes the boot without noticing it. They look at each other, then down at the grave.

68. LOW ANGLE FULL SHOT: The body is decently arranged, except that the grave is so shallow that the toes are almost at ground level, the bootless, dirty-stockinged foot prominent near camera. The face stares straight up.

69. MEDIUM TWO-SHOT: The two officers are contemplating the body.

70. STILL INSERT: The three officers sitting together. Bill, center, is reading aloud from a letter, spindly glasses perched on his blunt nose.

71. MEDIUM TWO-SHOT: The two officers, as before. The adjutant looks at Lean.

ADJUTANT

I guess we should . . . say something.

Lean stares down at the corpse, unheeding.

72. STILL INSERT: Chin elevated, Bill is pulling a coarse comb through his beard. His rather dandyish pose is contradicted by his usual scruffy appearance.

73. CLOSE-UP: The adjutant looks again at Lean.

ADJUTANT

Do you know the service?

74. CLOSE-UP: Lean. He sighs.

LEAN

(as if patiently explaining the obvious)
They don't read the service till the grave is filled in.

75. CLOSE-UP: The adjutant reacts apologetically.

ADJUTANT

Don't they?

The adjutant looks down at the corpse, then back at Lean.

ADJUTANT

Well, but . . .

76. CLOSE-UP: The dead face stares upward.

ADJUTANT (Voice-Over)
(suddenly bursting out)
Well lets say *some*thing—while he can still hear us.

77. CLOSE TWO-SHOT, as before. Lean ponders this suggestion very seriously. Individual gunshots and answering volleys continue, distantly.

LEAN

All right. You know the service?

ADJUTANT

Not a line.

LEAN

(very dubious)
I know . . . two lines, maybe . . .

The bullets are suddenly closer again. The adjutant reacts.

ADJUTANT
(urgently)

Well *do* it!

Lean looks at him, and the adjutant is embarrassed by his outburst.
Lean nods agreement, then speaks over his shoulder to the two privates:

LEAN

Tennn-*hut!*

78. CLOSE TWO-SHOT: The two privates are incredulous: they look
toward the sharpshooters, then at each other. Clearly, the officers are
crazy.

79. CLOSE-UP: Lean glares at them.

LEAN
(barking)

Ten-*HUT!!*

80. CLOSE TWO-SHOT: Showing their feelings plainly, the privates
come reluctantly to a sort of attention . . .

80a. ZOOM OUT TO LONG SHOT: . . . still in the protection of a tree.
The grave lies across the foreground, with the two officers behind it,
facing camera. The privates are visible between the two officers, in the
background. The adjutant awkwardly clutches the bandanna and the
belt, holster, and pistol. Lean absent-mindedly dangles the boot. It is
now very late in the day: The light is amber and the men throw long,
dark shadows. Night sounds are just becoming audible.

LEAN
(mechanically)

O Father, our friend has sunk in the deep waters of death,
but his spirit has leaped toward thee . . .

81. CLOSE-UP: The adjutant is mouthing the words in unison, silently.

LEAN (Voice-Over)

. . . as the bubble arises from the lips of the drowning. Uh . . .
perceive, we beseech Thee, O Father, the little flying bubble,
and . . .

82. CLOSE-UP: Lean is beginning to lose control. He breaks off and,
looking at the corpse, tries to pull himself together.

83. CLOSE-UP: The dead face stares indifferently.

84. CLOSE-UP: The adjutant looks at Lean, then helps out:

ADJUTANT
(prompting)
. . . and from Thy superb heights . . .

85. CLOSE TWO-SHOT: Lean is grateful for the start:

LEAN
. . . and from Thy superb heights . . .

Bogging down again, he looks helplessly at the adjutant. The adjutant suddenly recalls another phrase.

ADJUTANT
(hastily)

O, God have mercy . . .

LEAN

O, God, have mercy . . .

ADJUTANT
(struggling)

. . . mercy . . .

86. CLOSE-UP: Lean gives up the attempt.

LEAN
(saying goodbye)

Mercy.

The sound of a volley from the hilltop seems like a salute.

87. CLOSE TWO-SHOT: Lean stands a moment, fighting for control. He looks at the adjutant, who is fighting to appear impassive, then wheels toward the privates.

LEAN

Throw the dirt in!

88. FULL SHOT: One of the privates scrambles over to the side of the grave, near the feet of the body. He picks up a spadeful of earth, prepares to toss it, then stops suddenly, shovel arrested at the end of its backswing.

89. MEDIUM SHOT: The private looks from the body to the officers.

90. CLOSE TWO-SHOT: They look from the corpse to the private,

91. CLOSE-UP: (Point of view): then trace the trajectory of the dirt from the shovel to the dead face.

92. FULL SHOT: The private twists his body and deposits the soil on the corpse's feet.

93. CLOSE-UP: The dirt cascades over the bootless sock.

94. CLOSE TWO-SHOT: The officers expel held breath. The adjutant actually smiles. Lean is obviously relieved.

95. FULL SHOT: The private has shifted his stance so that he can fill the grave from the feet up. He works desperately, stealing glances toward the sharpshooters.

96. MEDIUM SHOT: Several times, the full shovel passes over the upturned face to deposit its load out of frame. Each load lands with a loud *plop!*

ADJUTANT (Voice-Over)

Well . . . of course . . . when you've been together all this time . . . I mean, a friend like Bill . . . well, you can't just leave him . . . to rot, I mean.

97. TIGHT CLOSE-UP: A hand disappears under a spadeful of dirt: *plop!*

ADJUTANT (Voice-Over)

It's impossible, you know . . . just like that, without . . .

Lean is wincing visibly at each plop.

ADJUTANT (Voice-Over)
(babbling)

Some things you just have to . . . they have to be done. I . . .
(breaking)

Oh, for God's sake *shovel!*

98. MEDIUM SHOT: The dirt advances up the grave.

99. MEDIUM SHOT: The private lifts another shovelful. A shot; he jerks backwards.

100. CLOSE-UP: The shovel clatters into the grave, its handle falling across the corpse.

101. MEDIUM SHOT: The private grabs his arm. Both his hand and arm are bloody.

102. FULL SHOT: Lean scrambles to the grave and removes the shovel. Then he turns to the private.

LEAN

Bad?

103. CLOSE-UP: The private shakes his head, as much in shock as in denial. This sudden, close look reveals him as a distinct person.—no longer an anonymous enlisted man.

104. CLOSE-UP: Lean is brusque:

LEAN

Go to the rear.
                    (indicating the other private)
You too.

105. LONG SHOT: The two privates make their way back up the meadow toward the knoll.

105a. ZOOM TO FULL SHOT: The wounded private charges straight up the hill, as if to out-run any sniper bullets. His companion weaves his way up in a crouching run, glancing fearfully toward the sharp-shooters' trees. The sound and smoke of a volley as the company covers their retreat.

106. MEDIUM TWO-SHOT: Lean sighs and absent-mindedly hands the boot to the adjutant, who adds it to the other possessions clutched awkwardly in his arms.

107. CLOSE-UP: Lean sets his jaw,

107a. ZOOM TO FULL SHOT: and bends to scoop a spadeful of earth. Grimly, he resumes filling the grave.

108. MEDIUM SHOT: The adjutant stares dully across his armload of belongings.

ADJUTANT

Maybe we're wrong. (PLOP!) Maybe it'd be better (PLOP!)
if we didn't bury him . . . (PLOP!)

109. MEDIUM SHOT: The earth rises to the dead man's chest.

ADJUTANT (Voice-Over)

. . . just this time. (PLOP!) Course, if we move up tomorrow, (PLOP!)

110. FULL SHOT: Lean shovels methodically.

ADJUTANT (Voice-Over)

. . . the body'll be . . .

LEAN

(not pausing or looking at him)

Damn you, shut your mouth! (PLOP!)

111. CLOSE-UP: The dead face stares at us, then a load of earth falls into frame, covering the body to the chin. We hear the scrape of another load being filled, but no dirt appears.

112. LOW ANGLE CLOSE-UP: Lean looks down at the face.

LEAN

Good God! Why didn't you turn him over?

113. STILL INSERT: A close-up of Bill laughing uproariously as something.

114. CLOSE-UP: The stricken adjutant says nothing. He stares at the face.

115. FULL SHOT: Lean swings the shovel back, pauses,

116. CLOSE-UP: looks at the face.

117. CLOSE-UP: The face looks back.

118. CLOSE-UP: The adjutant breaks out of his stupor.

ADJUTANT

(shouting)

Go *on*, man!

119. CLOSE-UP: Lean stares down.

120. CLOSE-UP: The face stares up.

121. FULL SHOT: Lean forces himself to continue.

122. CLOSE-UP: The shovel blade swings back, hesitates, swings forward. The dirt arcs outward and

123. TIGHT CLOSE-UP: lands (PLOP!!) on the face, filling the open eyes . . .

124. TIGHT CLOSE-UP: . . . running into the nose and mouth . . .

125. TIGHT CLOSE-UP: . . . hiding all but some scraggly beard and a piece of ear.

FADE TO BLACK. Night sounds continue prominently on the sound track.

FADE IN CREDITS, OVER STILL INSERTS:

126. STILL INSERT: Bill serving the meal.

127. STILL INSERT: Bill swigging the whiskey.

128. STILL INSERT: Bill playing cards.

129. STILL INSERT: Bill embracing a girl.

130. STILL INSERT: Bill washing in a stream.

131. STILL INSERT: Bill mending his sock.

132. STILL INSERT: Bill reading a letter.

133. STILL INSERT: Bill combing his beard.

134. STILL INSERT: Bill laughing.

Sounds of frogs and night insects fade out as we
FADE TO BLACK.

THE UPTURNED FACE
QUESTIONS

1. In the short story, Stephen Crane does not explicitly describe the setting against which the action takes place. Filmmakers must necessarily include settings in which the action unfolds. Describe the setting employed in the film and assess its utility for the filmmaker's purposes. Is the film's setting appropriate to the themes and tone of the short story?

2. How does the story's opening dialogue foreshadow the characterization of the two officers? Is Crane's characterization maintained in the film? Has the filmmaker made any significant changes in dialogue?

3. In the film adaptation, the director alters the contents of Bill's pockets. How do you explain his modifications?

4. In the short story, Stephen Crane makes several references to the two officers "looking at each other." What significance do you assign to these references? In your judgment, has the filmmaker focused on these lines in preparing his adaptation?

5. Assess the different treatments of the two privates in the story and film versions of *The Upturned Face*.

6. How does the line, "This is merely the way—often—of the hit and unhit" affect point of view in the story? To what extent has the filmmaker made use of the line?

7. In the Stinson screenplay of *The Upturned Face*, what is the function of the still inserts (shots #18, 34, 38, etc.)?

8. Examine the following still inserts in the context of the juxtaposed shots: shot 40, shot 52, shot 115. What pattern does the screenwriter seem to be establishing?

9. In both film and story, Lean says, "Damn you. Shut your mouth." What significance do you find in this scene? Be specific.

THE UPTURNED FACE
SUGGESTIONS FOR PAPERS

1. Contrast the beginning of the Stephen Crane short story with the opening shots of the film adaptation. How do you account for the differences?

2. Analyze the language of the regimental service in the short story and film.

3. Describe the major differences between Folger's film and the screenplay by Stinson. Which do you find more effective cinematically? Explain your critical judgment.

4. Describe your reactions to the characterizations of Lean and the adjutant in the film version of *The Upturned Face*. How do you account for your specific responses?

5. Read Stephen Crane's short story, "The Open Boat." If you intended to write a screen adaptation, what would you anticipate as your major cinematic problems? Use specific story details to clarify your position.

DR. HEIDEGGER'S EXPERIMENT

Nathaniel Hawthorne

This early nineteenth-century story has elements of a popular modern genre, science fiction, with its "mad" scientist and Fountain of Youth elixir. Like most of Hawthorne's fiction, however, it is essentially moralistic in tone and ambiguous in style. More questions are raised than answered. Written in 1837, and adapted in 1969, it seems to be highly relevant to a contemporary audience.

Like other films in the "Short Story Showcase," Dr. Heidegger's Experiment was adapted, produced, and directed by Larry Yust. Clifton Fadiman collaborated in the production.

The screenplay which follows the story permits readers to assess the creative process of transforming this story to a film.

That very singular man, old Dr. Heidegger, once invited four venerable friends to meet him in his study.. There were three white-bearded gentlemen, Mr. Medbourne, Colonel Killigrew, and Mr. Gascoigne, and a withered gentlewoman, whose name was the Widow Wycherly. They were all melancholy old creatures, who had been unfortunate in life, and whose greatest misfortune it was that they were not long ago in their graves. Mr. Medbourne, in the vigor of his age, had been a prosperous merchant, but had lost his all by a frantic speculation, and was now little better than a mendicant. Colonel Killigrew had wasted his best years, and his health and substance, in the pursuit of sinful pleasures, which had given birth to a brood of pains, such as the gout, and divers other torments of soul and body. Mr. Gascoigne was a ruined politician, a man of evil fame, or at least had been so till time had buried him from the knowledge of the present generation, and made him obscure instead of infamous. As for the Widow Wycherly, tradition tells us that she was a great beauty in her day; but, for a long while past, she had lived in deep seclusion, on account of certain scandalous stories which had prejudiced the gentry of the town against her. It is a circumstance worth mentioning that each of these three old gentlemen, Mr. Medbourne, Colonel Killigrew, and Mr. Gascoigne, were early lovers of the Widow Wycherly, and had once been on the point of cutting each other's throats for her sake. And, before proceeding further, I will merely hint that Dr. Heidegger and all his four guests were sometimes thought to be a little beside themselves —as is not unfrequently the case with old people, when worried either by present troubles or woeful recollections.

"My dear old friends," said Dr. Heidegger, motioning them to be seated, "I am desirous of your assistance in one of those little experiments with which I amuse myself here in my study."

If all stories were true, Dr. Heidegger's study must have been a very curious place. It was a dim, old-fashioned chamber, festooned with cobwebs, and besprinkled with antique dust. Around the walls stood several oaken bookcases, the lower shelves of which were filled with rows of gigantic folios and black-letter quartos, and the upper with little parchment-covered duodecimos. Over the central bookcase was a bronze bust of Hippocrates, with which according to some authorities, Dr. Heidegger was accustomed to hold consultations in all difficult cases of his practice. In the obscurest corner of the room stood a tall and narrow oaken closet, with its door ajar, within which doubtfully appeared a skeleton. Between two of the bookcases hung a looking glass, presenting its high and dusty plate within a tarnished gilt frame. Among many wonderful stories related of this mirror, it was fabled that the spirits of all the doctor's deceased patients dwelt within its verge, and would stare him in the face whenever he looked thitherward. The opposite side of the chamber was ornamented with the full-length portrait of a young lady, arrayed in the faded magnificence of silk, satin, and brocade, and with a visage as faded as her dress. Above half a century ago, Dr. Heidegger had been on the point of marriage with this young lady; but, being affected with some slight disorder, she had swallowed one of her lover's prescriptions, and died on the bridal evening. The greatest curiosity of the study remains to be mentioned; it was a ponderous folio volume, bound in black leather, with massive silver clasps. There were no letters on the back, and nobody could tell the title of the book. But it was well known to be a book of magic; and once, when a chambermaid had lifted it, merely to brush away the dust, the skeleton had rattled in its closet, the picture of the young lady had stepped one foot upon the floor, and several ghastly faces had peeped forth from the mirror, while the brazen head of Hippocrates frowned, and said, "Forbear!"

Such was Dr. Heidegger's study. On the summer afternoon of our tale a small round table, as black as ebony, stood in the center of the room, sustaining a cut-glass vase of beautiful form and elaborate workmanship. The sunshine came through the window between the heavy festoons of two faded damask curtains, and fell directly across this vase; so that a mild splendor was reflected from it on the ashen visages of the five old people who sat around. Four champagne glasses were also on the table.

"My dear old friends," repeated Dr. Heidegger, "may I reckon on your aid in performing an exceedingly curious experiment?"

Now Dr. Heidegger was a very strange old gentleman, whose eccentricity had become the nucleus for a thousand fantastic stories. Some of these fables, to my shame be it spoken, might possibly be traced back to my own veracious self; and if any passages of the present tale should startle the reader's faith, I must be content to bear the stigma of a fiction monger.

When the doctor's four guests heard him talk of his proposed experiment, they anticipated nothing more wonderful than the murder of a mouse in an air pump, or the examination of a cobweb by the microscope, or some similar nonsense, with which he was constantly in the habit of pestering his intimates. But without waiting for a reply, Dr. Heidegger hobbled across the chamber, and returned with the same ponderous folio, bound in black leather, which common report affirmed to be a book of magic. Undoing the silver clasps, he opened the volume, and took from among its black-letter pages a rose, or what was once a rose, though now the green leaves and crimson petals had assumed one brownish hue, and the ancient flower seemed ready to crumble to dust in the doctor's hands.

"This rose," said Dr. Heidegger, with a sigh, "this same withered and crumbling flower, blossomed five and fifty years ago. It was given me by Sylvia Ward, whose portrait hangs yonder; and I meant to wear it in my bosom at our wedding. Five and fifty years it has been treasured between the leaves of this old volume. Now, would you deem it possible that this rose of half a century could ever bloom again?"

"Nonsense!" said the Widow Wycherly, with a peevish toss of her head. "You might as well ask whether an old woman's wrinkled face could ever bloom again."

"See!" answered Dr. Heidegger.

He uncovered the vase, and threw the faded rose into the water which it contained. At first, it lay lightly on the surface of the fluid, appearing to imbibe none of its moisture. Soon, however, a singular change began to be visible. The crushed and dried petals stirred, and assumed a deepening tinge of crimson, as if the flower were reviving from a deathlike slumber; the slender stalk and twigs of foliage became green; and there was the rose of half a century, looking as fresh as when Sylvia Ward had first given it to her lover. It was scarcely full blown; for some of its delicate red leaves curled modestly around its moist bosom, within which two or three dewdrops were sparkling.

"That is certainly a very pretty deception," said the doctor's friends: carelessly, however, for they had witnessed greater miracles at a conjurer's show. "Pray, how was it effected?"

"Did you ever hear of the Fountain of Youth," asked Dr. Heidegger, "which Ponce de León, the Spanish adventurer, went in search of two or three centuries ago?"

"But did Ponce de León ever find it?" said the Widow Wycherly.

"No," answered Dr. Heidegger, "for he never sought it in the right place. The famous Fountain of Youth, if I am rightly informed, is situated in the southern part of the Floridian peninsula, not far from Lake Macaco. Its source is overshadowed by several gigantic magnolias, which, though numberless centuries old, have been kept as fresh as violets by the virtues of this wonderful water. An acquaintance of mine, knowing my curiosity in such matters, has sent me what you see in the vase."

"Ahem!" said Colonel Killigraw, who believed not a word of the doctor's story. "And what may be the effect of this fluid on the human frame?"

"You shall judge for yourself, my dear colonel," replied Dr. Heidegger, "and all of you, my respected friends, are welcome to so much of this admirable fluid as may restore to you the bloom of youth. For my own part, having had much trouble in growing old, I am in no hurry to grow young again. With your permission, therefore, I will merely watch the progress of the experiment."

While he spoke, Dr. Heidegger had been filling the four champagne glasses with the water of the Fountain of Youth. It was apparently impregnated with an effervescent gas, for little bubbles were continually ascending from the depths of the glasses, and bursting in silvery spray at the surface. As the liquor diffused a pleasant perfume, the old people doubted not that it possessed cordial and comfortable properties; and though utter sceptics as to its rejuvenescent power, they were inclined to swallow it at once. But Dr. Heidegger besought them to stay a moment.

"Before you drink, my respectable old friends," said he, "it would be well that, with the experience of a lifetime to direct you, you should draw up a few general rules for your guidance, in passing a second time through the perils of youth. Think what a sin and shame it would be, if, with your peculiar advantages, you should not become patterns of virtue and wisdom to all the young people of the age!"

The doctor's four venerable friends made him no answer, except by a feeble and tremulous laugh; so very ridiculous was the idea that, knowing how closely repentance treads behind the steps of error, they should ever go astray again.

"Drink, then," said the doctor, bowing. "I rejoice that I have so well selected the subjects of my experiment."

With palsied hands, they raised the glasses to their lips. The liquor, if it really possessed such virtues as Dr. Heidegger imputed to it, could not have been bestowed on four human beings who needed it more woefully. They looked as if they had never known what youth or pleasure was, but had been the offspring of Nature's dotage, and always the gray, decrepit, sapless, miserable creatures, who now sat stooping round the doctor's table, without life enough in their souls or bodies to be animated even by the prospect of growing young again. They drank off the water, and replaced their glasses on the table.

Assuredly there was an almost immediate improvement in the aspect of the party, not unlike what might have been produced by a glass of generous wine, together with a sudden glow of cheerful sunshine brightening over all their visages at once. There was a healthful suffusion on their cheeks, instead of the ashen hue that had made them look so corpse-like. They gazed at one another, and fancied that some magic power had really begun to smooth away the deep and sad inscriptions which Father Time had been so long engraving on their brows. The Widow adjusted her cap, for she felt almost like a woman again.

"Give us more of this wondrous water!" cried they, eagerly. "We are younger—but we are still too old! Quick—give us more!"

"Patience, patience!" quoth Dr. Heidegger, who sat watching the experiment with philosophic coolness. "You have been a long time growing old. Surely, you might be content to grow young in half an hour! But the water is at your service."

Again he filled their glasses with the liquor of youth, enough of which still remained in the vase to turn half the old people in the city to the age of their own grandchildren. While the bubbles were yet sparkling on the brim, the doctor's four guests snatched their glasses from the table, and swallowed the contents at a single gulp. Was it delusion? Even while the draught was passing down their throats, it seemed to have wrought a change in their whole systems. Their eyes grew clear and bright; a dark shade deepened among their silvery locks; they sat around the table, three gentlemen of middle age, and a woman, hardly beyond her buxom prime.

"My dear widow, you are charming!" cried Colonel Killigrew, whose eyes had been fixed upon her face, while the shadows of age were flitting from it like darkness from the crimson daybreak.

The fair widow knew, of old, that Colonel Killigrew's compliments were not always measured by sober truth; so she started up and ran to the mirror, still dreading that the ugly visage of an old woman would meet her gaze. Meanwhile, the three gentlemen behaved in such a manner as proved that the water of the Fountain of Youth possssed some intoxicating qualities; unless, indeed, their exhilaration of spirits was merely a lightsome dizziness caused by the sudden removal of the weight of years. Mr. Gascoigne's mind seemed to run on political topics, but whether relating to the past, present, or future, could not easily be determined, since the same ideas and phrases have been in vogue these fifty years. Now he rattled forth full-throated sentences about patriotism, national glory, and people's right; now he muttered some perilous stuff or other, in a sly and doubtful whisper, so cautiously that even his own conscience could scarcely catch the secret; and now, again, he spoke in measured accents, and a deeply deferential tone, as if a royal ear were listening to his well-turned periods. Colonel Killigrew all this time had been trolling forth a jolly bottle song, and ringing his glass in symphony with the chorus, while his eyes wandered toward the buxom figure of the Widow Wycherly. On the other side of the table, Mr. Medbourne was involved in a calculation of dollars and cents, with which was strangely intermingled a project for supplying the East Indies with ice, by harnessing a team of whales to the polar icebergs.

As for the Widow Wycherly, she stood before the mirror curtsying and simpering to her own image, and greeting it as the friend whom she loved better than all the world beside. She thrust her face close to the glass, to see whether some long-remembered wrinkle or crow's foot had indeed vanished. She examined whether the snow had so entirely melted from her hair that the venerable cap could be safely thrown aside. At last, turning briskly away, she came with a sort of dancing step to the table.

"My dear old doctor," cried she, "pray favor me with another glass!"

"Certainly, my dear madam, certainly!" replied the complaisant doctor. "See! I have already filled the glasses."

There, in fact, stood the four glasses, brimful of this wonderful water, the delicate spray of which, as it effervesced from the surface, resembled the tremulous glitter of diamonds. It was now so nearly sunset that the chamber had grown duskier than ever; but a mild and moonlike splendor gleamed from within the vase, and rested alike on the four guests and on the doctor's venerable figure. He sat in a high-backed, elaborately carved, oaken armchair, with a gray dignity of aspect that might have well befitted that very Father Time, whose power had never been disputed, save by this fortunate company. Even while quaffing the third draught of the Fountain of Youth, they were almost awed by the expression of his mysterious visage.

But, the next moment, the exhilarating gush of young life shot through their veins. They were now in the happy prime of youth. Age, with its miserable train of cares and sorrows and diseases, was remembered only as the trouble of a dream, from which they had joyously awoke. The fresh gloss of the soul, so early lost, and without which the world's successive scenes had been but a gallery of faded pictures, again threw its enchantment over all their prospects. They felt like new-created beings in a new-created universe.

"We are young! We are young!" they cried exultingly.

Youth, like the extremity of age, had effaced the strongly marked characteristics of middle life, and mutually assimilated them all. They were a group of merry youngsters, almost maddened with the exuberant frolicsomeness of their years. The most singular effect of their gaiety was an impulse to mock the infirmity and decrepitude of which they had so lately been the victims. They laughed loudly at their old-fashioned attire, the wide-skirted coats and flapped waistcoats of the young men, and the ancient cap and gown of the blooming girl. One limped across the floor like a gouty grandfather; one set a pair of spectacles astride of his nose, and pretended to pore over the black-letter pages of the book of magic; a third seated himself in an armchair, and strove to imitate the venerable dignity of Dr. Heidegger. Then all shouted mirthfully, and leaped about the room. The Widow Wycherly—if so fresh a damsel could be called a widow—tripped up to the doctor's chair, with a mischievous merriment in her rosy face.

"Doctor, you dear old soul," cried she, "get up and dance with me!" And then the four young people laughed louder than ever, to think what a queer figure the poor old doctor would cut.

"Pray excuse me," answered the doctor quietly. "I am old and rheumatic, and my dancing days were over long ago. But either of these gay young gentlemen will be glad of so pretty a partner."

"Dance with me, Clara!" cried Colonel Killigrew.

"No, no, I will be her partner!" shouted Mr. Gascoigne.

"She promised me her hand fifty years ago!" exclaimed Mr. Medbourne.

They all gathered round her. One caught both her hands in his passionate grasp—another threw his arm about her waist—the third buried his hands among the glossy curls that clustered beneath the widow's cap. Blushing, panting, struggling, chiding, laughing, her warm breath fanning each of their faces by turns, she strove to disengage herself, yet still remained in their triple embrace. Never was there a livelier picture of youthful rivalship, with bewitching beauty for the prize. Yet, by a strange deception, owing to the duskiness of the chamber and the antique dresses which they still wore, the tall mirror is said to have reflected the figures of the three old, gray, withered grandsires, ridiculously contending for the skinny ugliness of a shriveled grandam.

But they were young; their burning passions proved them so. Inflamed to madness by the coquetry of the girl-widow, who neither granted nor quite withheld her favors, the three rivals began to interchange threatening glances. Still keeping hold of the fair prize, they grappled fiercely at one another's throats. As they struggled to and fro, the table was overturned, and the vase dashed into a thousand fragments. The precious Water of Youth flowed in a bright stream across the floor, moistening the wings of a butterfly, which, grown old in the decline of summer, had alighted there to die. The insect fluttered lightly through the chamber, and settled on the snowy head of Dr. Heidegger.

"Come, come, gentlemen! Come, Madame Wycherly," exclaimed the doctor, "I really must protest against this riot."

They stood still and shivered, for it seemed as if gray Time were calling them back from their sunny youth, far down into the chill and darksome vale of years. They looked at old Dr. Heidegger, who sat in his carved armchair, holding the rose of half a century, which he had rescued from among the fragments of the shattered vase. At the motion of his hand, the four rioters resumed their seats, the more readily, because their violent exertions had wearied them, youthful though they were.

"My poor Sylvia's rose!" ejaculated Dr. Heidegger, holding it in the light of the sunset clouds. "It appears to be fading again."

And so it was. Even while the party were looking at it, the flower continued to shrivel up, till it became as dry and fragile as when the doctor had first thrown it into the vase. He shook off the few drops of moisture which clung to its petals.

"I love it as well thus as in its dewy freshness," observed he, pressing the withered rose to his withered lips. While he spoke, the butterfly fluttered down from the doctor's snowy head, and fell upon the floor.

His guests shivered again. A strange chillness, whether of the body or spirit they could not tell, was creeping gradually over them all. They gazed at one another, and fancied that each fleeting moment snatched away a charm, and left a deepening furrow where none had been before. Was it an illusion? Had the changes of a lifetime been crowded into so brief a space, and were they now four aged people, sitting with their old friend, Dr. Heidegger?

"Are we grown old again, so soon?" cried they, dolefully.

In truth they had. The Water of Youth possessed merely a virtue more transient than that of wine. The delirium which it created had effervesced away. Yes! They were old again. With a shuddering impulse, that showed her a woman still, the widow clasped her skinny hands before her face, and wished that the coffin lid were over it, since it could be no longer beautiful.

"Yes, friends, ye are old again," said Dr. Heidegger, "and lo! the Water of Youth is all lavished on the ground. Well—I bemoan it not; for if the fountain gushed at my very doorstep, I would not stoop to bathe my lips in it—no, though its delirium were for years instead of moments. Such is the lesson ye have taught me!"

But the doctor's four friends had taught no such lesson to themselves. They resolved forthwith to make a pilgrimage to Florida, and quaff at morning, noon, and night, from the Fountain of Youth.

screenplay

DR. HEIDEGGER'S EXPERIMENT

Larry Yust

FADE TITLES.

1. The CAMERA comes to rest on a CLOSE-UP of Dr. Heidegger, silhouetted against the light of the window. He is a very old man and his face is quiet and watchful, with deep, searching eyes. He speaks directly to the CAMERA.

DR. HEIDEGGER

My dear old friends—I would like your assistance in one of those little experiments with which I amuse myself here in my study.

CUT TO:

2. Dr. Heidegger's POINT OF VIEW: His four guests are as old as he. Widow Wycherly, Colonel Killigrew, Mr. Medbourne and Mr. Gas-

coigne look, in fact, as if they had never known what youth or pleasure was, but have always been the gray, decrepit, sapless, miserable creatures we see before us. Slowly, the open door behind the four guests closes.

CUT TO:

3. SIDE ANGLE WIDE SHOT: Dr. Heidegger hobbles forward to assist the Widow Wycherly to a chair.

CUT TO:

4. SLOW MOTION, FOLLOWING CLOSE-UP as Dr. Heidegger assists the Widow Wycherly to one of the chairs grouped around the black table.

DR. HEIDEGGER
Please be seated, Madame Wycherly.

CUT TO:

5. SLOW MOTION CLOSE-UP as Mr. Medbourne moves haltingly toward the camera. Dr. Heidegger steps into frame and guides Mr. Medbourne to another of the chairs.

DR. HEIDEGGER
Mr. Medbourne.

PAN DOWN to end on a CLOSE-UP of Mr. Medbourne's ancient face.

CUT TO:

6. SLOW MOTION FOLLOWING CLOSE-UP as Dr. Heidegger approaches Mr. Gascoigne and shows him to another of the chairs placed about the black table.

DR. HEIDEGGER
I hope you will be comfortable there, Mr. Gascoigne.

CUT TO:

7. SLOW MOTION: Colonel Killigrew moves slowly toward the camera. In the background, a grinning skull's face peers out from its cabinet. As the camera moves with Colonel Killigrew, Dr. Heidegger steps into frame.

DR. HEIDEGGER
My dear Colonel Killigrew. You are looking well.

PULL BACK to a WIDE SHOT: Dr. Heidegger sits down in the high-backed chair across the table from the three old men and the old woman. The doctor observes his guests for several moments.

DR. HEIDEGGER

My dear old friends, may I depend upon your aid in performing an exceedingly curious experiment?

Several moments pass. Dr. Heidegger gets up and we go in to a close shot of his guests. The mild light diffused by a vase plays on the ashen faces of the four old people.

GO IN FAST to the glass vase. Through it, we see a distorted image of Dr. Heidegger as he lifts a big folio volume from its stand in front of the window.

CUT TO:

8. TRUCK with DR. HEIDEGGER as he hobbles back to the table, carrying the book. Continue trucking back to include his four guests. Dr. Heidegger resumes his seat and places the book across his bony knees.

DISSOLVE TO:

9. SLOW MOTION; EXTREME CLOSE-UP of Dr. Heidegger's hands as he opens one of the silver clasps that fasten the book.

DISSOLVE TO:

10. SLOW MOTION: Dr. Heidegger unfastens the second silver clasp. PAN LEFT to see book open.

DISSOLVE TO:

11. SLOW MOTION: Dr. Heidegger turns a page that reveals a pressed, dried rose. GO IN to flower.

CUT TO:

12. FULL FRAME CLOSE-UP of Dr. Heidegger gazing down at the flower.

CUT TO:

13. FOLLOWING CLOSE-UP of Dr. Heidegger's long-fingered, time-withered hand as he reaches for the faded rose and lifts it gently from the book. The ancient flower seems ready to crumble to dust between the doctor's fingers. He lifts the rose to his face, gazes at it for a moment, then raises his eyes to his guests. PULL BACK slowly, as he speaks, to reveal the portrait hanging on the wall behind him.

DR. HEIDEGGER

This rose–this same withered and crumbling flower—blossomed five and fifty years ago. It was given me by Sylvia Ward, whose portrait hangs there—I meant to wear it in my bosom at our wedding.

DISSOLVE TO:

14. CLOSE-UP of the paint-faded face of Sylvia Ward.

DR. HEIDEGGER (Voice-Over)

But my beautiful young Sylvia grew ill.

PAN from the portrait to a WIDE SHOT of the table and the five OLD PEOPLE sitting around it.

DR. HEIDEGGER

It was not a serious disorder. I prepared a prescription for her. She swallowed it—and died on our bridal evening.

CUT TO:

15. EXTREME CLOSE-UP. The eyes of Dr. Heidegger. Slowly PULL BACK to reveal his face, the withered rose, and the portrait behind him.

DR. HEIDEGGER

For five and fifty years, the rose she gave me has been treasured between the leaves of this old volume. Now—would you believe it possible that this rose of half a century could ever bloom again?

CUT TO:

16. CLOSE-UP of the Widow Wycherly.

WIDOW WYCHERLY

Nonsense! You might as well ask whether an old woman's withered face could ever bloom again.

CUT TO:

17. EXTREME CLOSE-UP of Dr. Heidegger's thin, bloodless lips.

DR. HEIDEGGER

See!

CUT TO:

18. The effervescent water in the glass vase glows with the light of the

afternoon sun. Dr. Heidegger hunches forward and carefully lowers the faded rose to the surface of the water. Gently he lets the flower float free. Slowly TRUCK around the vase until Dr. Heidegger's guests are seen in the background. All four of them are watching the floating, withered flower.

CUT TO:

19. TIME LAPSE PHOTOGRAPHY: EXTREME CLOSE-UP of the faded rose. After several moments, the crushed and dried petals begin to stir. Slowly they assume a deepening tinge of crimson, the stalk and twigs of foliage become green and, finally, we see before us the rose of half a century looking as fresh as when it was first picked.

CUT TO:

20. The restored crimson rose is big in the foreground. In the background we see the four guests. They are impressed, but only as by a clever trick.

MR. MEDBOURNE

That's a very pretty trick. Tell us—how is it done?

PAN and TILT to a CLOSE-UP of Dr. Heidegger.

DR. HEIDEGGER

Did you never hear of the Fountain of Youth—which the Spanish adventurer Ponce de León went in search of two or three centuries ago?

CUT TO:

21. CLOSE-UP of the Widow Wycherly.

WIDOW WYCHERLY

But did Ponce de León ever find it?

CUT TO:

22. CLOSE-UP of Dr. Heidegger.

DR. HEIDEGGER

No—for he never searched in the right place.

PAN away from Dr. Heidegger, past the restored rose and in CLOSE-UP across the faces of the four guests. They listen listlessly and skeptically.

DR. HEIDEGGER

The famous Fountain of Youth–if I am rightly informed— is located in the southern part of the Floridian peninsula— not far from Lake Macaco. Its source is hidden by several gigantic magnolias, which—though numberless centuries old —have been kept as fresh as violets by the virtues of this wonderful water. An acquaintance of mine—knowing my curiosity in such matters—has sent me what you see in the vase.

Colonel Killigrew clears his throat.

COLONEL KILLIGREW

And what may be the effect of this fluid on the human body?

As the PAN stops, the reflection of Dr. Heidegger's face is revealed in the tall mirror above Colonel Killigrew's shoulder.

DR. HEIDEGGER

You shall judge for yourself, my dear Colonel.

CUT TO:

23. EXTREME WIDE SHOT: The soft light diffused by the vase picks out from the surrounding darkness the dry whiteness of five faded faces.

DR. HEIDEGGER

And all of you—my respected friends–are welcome to as much of this admirable fluid as may restore to you the bloom of youth.

COLONEL KILLIGREW

And for you, my dear Dr. Heidegger?

Slowly GO IN toward Dr. Heidegger.

DR. HEIDEGGER

For my own part, having had so much trouble in growing old, I am in no hurry to grow young again. With your permission, therefore, I will merely watch the progress of the experiment.

The doctor closes the book.

DISSOLVE TO:

24. SLOW MOTION, FOLLOWING CLOSE-UP: Dr. Heidegger lifts the vase and fills one of the champagne glasses.

DISSOLVE TO:

25. SLOW MOTION: Dr. Heidegger's eyes watching, as he pours.

DISSOLVE TO:

26. SLOW MOTION, EXTREME CLOSE-UP of one of the champagne glasses. As it is filled with the water, we see little bubbles ascending from the depths of the glass and bursting in silvery spray above.

DISSOLVE TO:

27. SLOW MOTION: SHOOT DOWN along the faces of the four old guests, watching.

DISSOLVE TO:

28. SLOW MOTION: SHOOT STRAIGHT DOWN on a champagne glass as it is filled with the sparkling liquid.

DISSOLVE TO:

29. CLOSE-UP of the one remaining empty champagne glass. Through it, we can see the face of Colonel Killigrew watching. Dr. Heidegger fills the glass with the sparkling liquid.

COLONEL KILLIGREW

Well—it appears, at least, to be of good vintage. No doubt I've taken worse in my time.

Colonel Killigrew reaches for the glass.

CUT TO:

30. FULL FACE CLOSE-UP of Dr. Heidegger.

DR. HEIDEGGER

Wait a moment.

CUT TO:

31. WIDE SHOT of the five old people. Dr. Heidegger sits down.

DR. HEIDEGGER

Before you drink—my respectable old friends—would it not be well, that, with the experience of a lifetime to direct you, you should draw up a few general rules for your guidance, in passing a second time through the perils of youth?

Dr. Heidegger draws no reaction from his guests.

CUT TO:

32. SIDE ANGLE CLOSE-UP of DR. HEIDEGGER. He observes his guests and then continues.

DR. HEIDEGGER

Think what a sin and shame it would be, if with the particular advantages of your knowledge of life . . .

PAN to see the four guests.

DR. HEIDEGGER

. . . you should not, in second youth, become patterns of virtue and wisdom to all the young people of the age.

There is a listless silence of several moments before Widow Wycherly ventures to answer the doctor.

WIDOW WYCHERLY

Do you suggest that our lives have not been patterns of virtue and wisdom, my dear doctor?

CUT TO:

33. FULL FACE CLOSE-UP of DR. HEIDEGGER.

DR. HEIDEGGER

Come now, my dear old friends. Colonel Killigrew . . .

CUT TO:

34. EXTREME CLOSE-UP of COLONEL KILLIGREW, FRAMING inside his face. The CAMERA moves about, relentlessly exploring faults and weaknesses.

DR. HEIDEGGER (Voice-Over)

. . . had ever a young man a more promising future than yours? Family, wealth, a handsome face and a figure. Was it virtuous or wise in you to trample upon the advantages with which you were endowed, your fortune and your health squandered in the pursuit of sinful pleasures?

CUT TO:

35. CLOSE-UP of Dr. Heidegger. With surprising quickness, he turns to face Mr. Gascoigne.

DR. HEIDEGGER

And you . . .

CUT TO:

36. Mr. Gascoigne's wavering eye fills the FRAME. Slowly PULL BACK to reveal the weaknesses of his withered face.

DR. HEIDEGGER (Voice-Over)

. . . my respectable old friend. Were you not an honored leader of the people, a man chosen to positions of power and trust? Was it virtuous–or wise—in you to betray that trust in exchange for small quantities of money?

CUT TO:

37. The faces of Dr. Heidegger and Mr. Medbourne are SUPERIM-POSED so that one face seems to take form out of the other.

DR. HEIDEGGER

And my dear Medbourne—who would have believed forty years ago that all your shops and warehouses would be lost in one foolish speculation, and you left to live as best you could by cultivating the kindnesses of strangers.

CUT TO:

38. WIDE SHOT of the five old people.

DR. HEIDEGGER

And all three of you gentlemen—were you not once at the point of cutting each other's throats for the beauty of Madame Wycherly? And my dear widow, why have scandalous stories . . .

CUT TO:

39. SIDE ANGLE CLOSE-UP of the Widow Wycherly. The profiles of the three other guests can be seen dimly in the background.

DR. HEIDEGGER (Voice-Over)

. . . been told of you that so turn society against you that you have had to live these many years in such deep seclusion?

There is a silence of several moments before the Widow Wycherly speaks.

WIDOW WYCHERLY

If we have made mistakes, have we not learned from them? Do you imagine that we would ever repeat our errors?

CUT TO:

40. CLOSE-UP of Dr. Heidegger. He studies his guests in silence. He smiles.

CUT TO:

41. The four venerable guests. They join in a feeble and nervous laugh under Dr. Heidegger's gaze.

CUT TO:

42. Dr. Heidegger rises from his chair and bows. LOW ANGLE.

DR. HEIDEGGER
Drink then. I rejoice that I have so well selected the subjects of my experiment.

DISSOLVE TO:

43. SLOW MOTION: Four palsied hands reach for the four filled champagne glasses. FOLLOW in CLOSE-UP to see the glasses lifted to colorless lips.

DISSOLVE TO:

44. SLOW MOTION, EXTREME CLOSE-UP: Colonel Killigrew drinks.

DISSOLVE TO:

45. SLOW MOTION, EXTREME CLOSE-UP: Mr. Medbourne drinks.

DISSOLVE TO:

46. SLOW MOTION, EXTREME CLOSE-UP: The Widow Wycherly drinks.

DISSOLVE TO:

47. SLOW MOTION, EXTREME CLOSE-UP: Mr. Gascoigne drinks.

DISSOLVE TO:

48. SLOW MOTION: The glasses are placed, empty, back on the table.

CUT TO:

49. WIDE SHOT of the doctor and his four guests. The figures of the guests seem to be straighter than they were. A healthful color has replaced the ashen hue that had made them look so corpselike. Surreptitiously at first, they glance at one another, not daring to believe that a change really has taken place.

CUT TO:

50. CLOSE-UP of Mr. Medbourne. He turns to glance at his neighbor. Medbourne's eyes are brighter than they were, and his color is much improved. He holds himself straighter than he did, and his movements are more steady and controlled.

CUT TO:

51. CLOSE-UP of the Widow Wycherly. She is aware of Medbourne's glance and adjusts her cap, feeling almost like a woman again.
Her color also has improved. There is a sparkle in eyes that were dead before, and some of the deep lines which marked her face seem to have softened. She turns to glance toward Mr. Gascoigne.

CUT TO:

52. CLOSE-UP of Mr. Gascoigne. He also appears less old. A faint smile comes to his lips as he glances at the Widow Wycherly and sees the change that has taken place in her.

CUT TO:

53. CLOSE-UP of Colonel Killigrew. He, too, is younger. He turns toward his companions and gazes at them openly, and is amazed at what he sees. He turns quickly to Dr. Heidegger. ZOOM BACK FAST to a WIDE SHOT of Dr. Heidegger and his four guests.

COLONEL KILLIGREW

Give me more of this wonderful water. We are younger—
but we are still too old. Quick—give me more.

CUT TO:

54. EXTREME CLOSE-UP of Mr. Gascoigne.

MR. GASCOIGNE

Yes, give me more.

55. EXTREME CLOSE-UP of Mr. Medbourne.

MR. MEDBOURNE

More, please.

CUT TO:

56. EXTREME CLOSE-UP of the Widow Wycherly.

WIDOW WYCHERLY

Quickly, more.

CUT TO:

57. CLOSE-UP of Dr. Heidegger.

DR. HEIDEGGER

Patience. Patience.

CUT TO:

58. WIDE SHOT of the doctor and his four guests.

DR. HEIDEGGER

You have been a long time growing old. Surely you might be content to grow young in half an hour. But the water is at your service.

With the slowness of age, Dr. Heidegger reaches forward, lifts the vase and begins to fill the champagne glasses once more. His guests watch with a new eagerness.

CUT TO:

59. EXTREME CLOSE-UP of the crimson rose floating on the surface of the sparkling water.

PULL BACK to see Dr. Heidegger hunching forward, filling the champagne glasses. Occasionally, he glances up at his guests. INTERCUT several SIX FRAME CLOSE-UPS of his guests, watching eagerly. When Dr. Heidegger has filled the glasses, four hands reach forward to snatch them OUT OF FRAME.

CUT TO:

60. SLOW MOTION: The four guests drink. Dimly, in the background, we can see Dr. Heidegger's reflection in the tall mirror, watching.

DISSOLVE TO:

61. SLOW MOTION, EXTREME CLOSE-UP of Mr. Gascoigne, full face. He drinks.

SLOW DISSOLVE TO:

62. SLOW MOTION, EXTREME CLOSE-UP of Mr. Gascoigne, side angle. He finishes his drink and lowers the glass from his lips. His eyes have grown clear and bright, the white hair on his head and chin has darkened. His face is now that of a man in the prime of middle age.

CUT TO:

63. SLOW MOTION, EXTREME CLOSE-UP of the head of Mr. Medbourne. He is still old. He drinks.

SLOW DISSOLVE TO:

64. SLOW MOTION: Head of Mr. Medbourne. He finishes his drink, and now he is a man of middle-age.

DISSOLVE TO:

65. SLOW MOTION, FULL FRAME SIDE ANGLE CLOSE-UP of Colonel Killigrew. He is old. He drinks.

SLOW DISSOLVE TO:

66. SLOW MOTION: The same FRAME as the previous scene. The Colonel finishes his drink and turns to look past the CAMERA. He is a middle-aged man with dissipated good looks.

DISSOLVE TO:

67. SLOW MOTION, SIDE ANGLE CLOSE-UP of the Widow Wycherly. She is old. She drinks.

SLOW DISSOLVE TO:

68. SLOW MOTION, FULL FRAME CLOSE-UP of the Widow Wycherly. She finishes her drink. She is a middle-aged woman, hardly beyond her buxom prime.

CUT TO:

69. CLOSE-UP of Colonel Killigrew. He stares at the widow and smiles approvingly.

COLONEL KILLIGREW
My dear widow, you are charming.

70. CLOSE-UP of the Widow Wycherly. She turns to stare at Colonel Killigrew. She lifts an exploring hand to her face, not daring to believe what he says. Suddenly, she rises from her chair and rushes over toward the tall mirror, still dreading that the ugly face of an old woman will meet her gaze. TRUCK FAST to keep up with her.

CUT TO:

71. The Widow Wycherly's reflection in the mirror as she runs up to it. She stops close to the glass and examines her figure and face.

WIDOW WYCHERLY
Am I really pretty? Can it be that I am beautiful again?

PAN from the reflection to Widow Wycherly herself as she examines and admires her image. In the background, COLONEL KILLIGREW, watching her, breaks into song.

COLONEL KILLIGREW

When the landlord's daughter she came in,
And we kissed those rosy cheeks again,
We all sat down and then we'd sing,

CUT TO:

72. CLOSE-UP of Colonel Killigrew. He rings his glass in time with the chorus. LOW ANGLE.

COLONEL KILLIGREW

(Bang, bang, bang)
When Jones' ale was new, my boys,
When Jones' ale was new.

CUT TO:

73. EXTREME COSE-UP: A quill pen scratching out a calculation in dollars and cents.

MR. MEDBOURNE (Voice-Over)

The money is to be had for the taking. The initial investment is nothing when balanced against the potential profits to be made.

PULL BACK and TILT UP to an EXTREME CLOSE-UP of Medbourne. He quits scratching figures and speaks earnestly to an unseen associate.

MR. MEDBOURNE

Think of it. Ice, mountains of ice, floating in the Northern oceans. Ours for the taking. A sturdy ship (I know just the master in New Bedford)—or whales!

MR. MEDBOURNE

Yes! Teams of whales–to tow the ice to the Southern latitudes—to the East Indies—to be sold the sweltering natives at the highest prices possible!

MR. GASCOIGNE (Voice-Over)

This great republic . . . representative government . . . the people's wishes . . .

CUT TO:

74. A CLOSE-UP of Gascoigne from a LOW ANGLE. He continues rattling off full-throated phrases which seem literally to inflate his body, until he is obliged to rise to his feet, addressing the multitudes.

MR. GASCOIGNE

. . . justice and equality . . . blessings of liberty . . . wisdom of our forefathers . . . will of the people . . . inalienable rights . . .

SUPERIMPOSE:

75. Dr. Heidegger has pulled his armchair back from the table, and sits, isolated from the rest, observing the workings of his experiment with the gray dignity of Father Time himself. Dr. Heidegger's image will be held over the scenes which follow, and we will slowly MOVE IN toward his face.

CUT TO:

76. The Widow Wycherly stands before the mirror, curtsying and simpering to her own image, greeting it as the friend she loves best in all the world.

CUT TO:

77. CLOSE-UP of Gascoigne. His eyes shift nervously. The light of the lowering afternoon sun grows orange. Gascoigne mutters in a sly and doubtful whisper to an unseen co-conspirator.

MR. GASCOIGNE

I don't know if that could be arranged or not. You surely understand that there are risks.

Gascoigne glances nervously at Colonel Killigrew who continues his song.

MR. GASCOIGNE

If any hint of it should be made public, the most serious consequences would result. Also—there are highly placed people whose friendship we should have to win over. What you ask is very difficult, you must understand that—but perhaps it could be arranged—if your interest in the matter is sufficiently great—to provide—the necessary incentives . . .

CUT TO:

78. CLOSE-UP of Medbourne. He speaks directly to the CAMERA.

MR. MEDBOURNE

Those without vision laugh at every great scheme, when it is first proposed. Do you imagine I could have reached my present position in life without vision?

PAN FAST to a CLOSE-UP of Colonel Killigrew.

COLONEL KILLIGREW

When Jones' ale was new.

CUT TO:

79. HIGH ANGLE: Gascoigne approaches the CAMERA, and speaks to it in measured accents and in a deeply deferential tone.

MR. GASCOIGNE

Thank you, Senator. I am forever grateful to you for your assistance in this matter. And you may rest assured that I would never have approached you with an additional burden —I know what a great weight of duties you have—had I not known that you would be moved by your great patriotism to look . . .

CUT TO:

80. The Widow Wycherly thrusts her face close to the glass.

WIDOW WYCHERLY

Is there a shadow left there?

MR. GASCOIGNE (Voice-Over)

. . . favorably on any project that promised so great a benefit for the people of this great republic . . .

WIDOW WYCHERLY

No. Gone. All gone.

The widow smiles in relief. The CAMERA has MOVED IN so close to the SUPERIMPOSED image of Dr. Heidegger that we are now inside one of his eyes. Slowly the image FADES away. The Widow Wycherly glances at her hair and examines it underneath her cap.

WIDOW WYCHERLY

And my hair—has the color come back completely? Is it really true that I can throw this hateful cap away?

She turns briskly from the mirror. TRUCK with her as she moves with a dancing step up to the place where Dr. Heidegger sits.

WIDOW WYCHERLY

My dear old doctor—give me another glass—please.

CUT TO:

81. CLOSE-UP of Dr. Heidegger. He studies the Widow Wycherly for a moment before answering.

DR. HEIDEGGER

Certainly, my dear madame, certainly.

ZOOM IN FAST to a CLOSE-UP of the doctor's lips.

DR. HEIDEGGER

See!

CUT TO:

82. CLOSE-UP of the four champagne glasses filled to the brim with the effervescent water. The doctor's image is seen through each of the glasses.

DR. HEIDEGGER

I have already filled the glasses.

CUT TO:

83. Widow Wycherly as she looks down at the filled glasses. Gascoigne, Medbourne and Colonel Killigrew approach the table where the glasses wait. It is now nearly sunset, and the study has grown darker than ever. But a mild and moonlight splendor gleams from within the vase and rests on the four guests and on the doctor's venerable figure. The four guests look up at him in wondering awe.

CUT TO:

84. CLOSE-UP of Dr. Heidegger. Mildly, he returns the stares of his guests.

DR. HEIDEGGER

Drink!

CUT TO:

85. EXTREME WIDE SHOT: The guests reach for their glasses and drink. They lower their glasses from their lips and look at one another. Colonel Killigrew cries out with a young man's voice.

COLONEL KILLIGREW

We are young! We *are* young!

CUT TO:

86. A CLOSE SHOT of the four guests. They are young, the oldest still in his early twenties. The Widow Wycherly breaks from the group, races to the mirror and looks.

WIDOW WYCHERLY

I am beautiful!

She spins from the mirror, turning to face her friends, folding her arms to her breasts in a tight, girlish embrace that enfolds all the world.

WIDOW WYCHERLY

How beautiful everything is!

CUT TO:

87. Medbourne hurries forward into an EXTREME CLOSE-UP.

MR. MEDBOURNE

I can do anything in the world! Look!

CUT TO:

88. SLOW MOTION: Medbourne leaps up into the air, as high as he can go, and floats gently back down to earth.

CUT TO:

89. FAST FOLLOWING CLOSE-UP of Gascoigne.

MR. GASCOIGNE

See how strong I am!

CUT TO:

90. SLOW MOTION: Gascoigne reaches for a table and lifts it by one leg until he holds it even with his shoulders at arm's length.

CUT TO:

91. FAST FOLLOWING CLOSE-UP of Killigrew as he strides forward to join the Widow Wycherly. He touches the shoulder of her ancient dress, grinning. He turns to the others with mocking, laughing eyes. The Widow Wycherly steps forward into a CLOSE-UP and the CAM-

ERA swings around to see her light-heartedly examining the clothes of an old man which Killigrew wears.
She hurries forward to join the others, examining them and laughing as she goes. The CAMERA TRUCKS with her.

CUT TO:

92. EXTREME CLOSE-UP of the young Widow Wycherly. She laughs with girlish delight.

CUT TO:

93. CLOSE-UP of Gascoigne.

CUT TO:

94. TRUCK back with Gascoigne as he limps painfully forward, mocking the gouty gait of a grandfather.

CUT TO:

95. Medbourne affects the mannerism and voice of an old man as he stoops over Dr. Heidegger's ponderous book.

CUT TO:

96. Killigrew has sat in an armchair, and is skillfully mocking the venerable dignity of Dr. Heidegger. We can see the doctor, in an identical pose, reflected in the tall mirror to one side of the frame. Killigrew imitates the doctor's voice.

CUT TO:

97. CLOSE-UP of the Widow Wycherly. She laughs delightedly, then turns at the sound of music.

CUT TO:

98. Medbourne dances forward, playing a gay waltz on Dr. Heidegger's dust-covered violin.

CUT TO:

99. TRUCK to keep the Widow Wycherly in full face as she pivots lightly in time to the music. She sees the quiet, watchful figure of Dr. Heidegger and dances over to him with mischievous merriment in her rosy face.

WIDOW WYCHERLY

Doctor, you dear old soul, get up and dance with me!

CUT TO:

100. CLOSE-UP of Dr. Heidegger. He studies the laughing young people quietly before he answers.

DR. HEIDEGGER

Pray excuse me. I am old and rheumatic. My dancing days were over long ago. But either of these handsome young gentlemen would be glad of so pretty a partner.

CUT TO:

101. TRUCK BACK to keep Killigrew in CLOSE-UP as he steps forward into a tight TWO-SHOT with the girl.

COLONEL KILLIGREW

Dance with me, Clara.

CUT TO:

102. TRUCKING CLOSE-UP of Gascoigne as he steps forward.

MR. GASCOIGNE

No, no! I'll be her partner.

CUT TO:

103. Medbourne stops playing. FOLLOW him in tight CLOSE-UP as he hurries forward.

MR. MEDBOURNE

She promised to marry me—fifty years ago!

CUT TO:

104. EXTREME CLOSE-UP of the Widow Wycherly's beautiful face.

WIDOW WYCHERLY

Fifty years ago!

She laughs and spins coquettishly away from the three young men.

CUT TO:

105. FOLLOWING CLOSE-UP of Medbourne as he hurries to catch up with her.

MR. MEDBOURNE

Clara, your laughter is like music.

WIDOW WYCHERLY

Is it, Mr. Medbourne?

She smiles at him, and then with a gesture as sensuous as if she were stripping herself naked, she tears the old woman's cap from her head, and her brilliant red hair cascades down about her shoulders.

CUT TO:

106. FOLLOWING CLOSE-UP of Gascoigne as he hurries close to the flame-haired beauty.

MR. GASCOIGNE

Your hair is like fire.

WIDOW WYCHERLY

Mr. Gascoigne.

Smiling, she slips away from him.

CUT TO:

107. FOLLOWING CLOSE-UP of Killigrew as he hurries up to the Widow Wycherly.

COLONEL KILLIGREW

You are beautiful, Clara.

She turns to him, smiling.

WIDOW WYCHERLY

Who can believe what you say to a young girl, Mr. Killigrew?

She twists away from him, laughing.

COLONEL KILLIGREW

You know it's the truth. You are beautiful.

Turning again into CLOSE-UP, the girl's magnificent smile flashes through FRAME.

CUT TO:

108. FULL SHOT: The three young men are gathered around the girl. One catches her hands. Another throws his arm about her waist. The third buries his hand in the richness of her flaming hair. Blushing, panting, struggling, chiding, laughing, her warm breath fanning each of their faces by turns, she strives to disengage herself, yet still remains in their triple embrace. PAN to the tall mirror. The image we see

Dr Heidegger's Experiment (1969) In the tall mirror, we see reflected three withered grandfathers contending for the skinny ugliness of a shriveled grandmother. Contrasting images of youth and age co-exist within the frame, thereby capturing Hawthorne's tone of ambiguity *Still shot reproduced courtesy of Encyclopaedia Britannica Educational Corporation.*

reflected there is that of the figures of three old, gray, withered grandfathers, ridiculously contending for the skinny ugliness of a shriveled
grandmother.

CUT TO:

109. In this and the following scenes, the four young people continue
to move together led by the beautiful widow who, coquettishly, neither
grants nor quite withholds her favors from the young men. CLOSE-UP
of Killigrew.

COLONEL KILLIGREW

Come with me.

The group moves so that we follow the girl in CLOSE-UP.

WIDOW WYCHERLY

Oh, that would be lovely, but these other young gentlemen
are so demanding of my time.

CUT TO:

110. FOLLOWING CLOSE-UP of Gascoigne. The other faces move in
and out of FRAME, punctuated by the swirling red of the beautiful
girl's hair.

MR. GASCOIGNE

My lovely Clara, you are my life. Only when you appear
does the sun rise for me. When you leave me, the dark of
night falls over my spirit.

CUT TO:

111. FOLLOWING EXTREME CLOSE-UP of the Widow Wycherly.

WIDOW WYCHERLY

A speech for me, too, Mr. Gascoigne? How charming you are.

MR. GASCOIGNE

I mean what I say.

CUT TO:

112. FOLLOWING CLOSE-UP of Medbourne.

MR. MEDBOURNE

I shall be rich, Clara. I shall be able to give you everything
your beauty deserves. You must be mine. I will buy you . . .

The Widow Wycherly steps forward into CLOSE-UP, turning to face the three young men. The CAMERA TRUCKS to keep her in profile.

WIDOW WYCHERLY

But how can I choose one of you, when you are all so charming, and so handsome, and so young?

She smiles beautifully.

CUT TO:

113. FOLLOWING CLOSE-UP of Killigrew, as he hurries forward to the girl, and catches her hard by the arm.

COLONEL KILLIGREW

What he promises in the future, I can give you now. Come with me. We're well suited to each other.

CUT TO:

114. Medbourne angrily steps forward into CLOSE-UP.

MR. MEDBOURNE

No, no. She promised to marry me fifty years ago!

CUT TO:

115. CLOSE-UP of Gascoigne. He speaks angrily to Medbourne.

MR. GASCOIGNE

We're speaking of today!

He turns to the girl.

MR. GASCOIGNE

I will be famous, honored. You will share my successes. All the world will admire you.

CUT TO:

116. EXTREME CLOSE-UP of Killigrew.

COLONEL KILLIGREW

More promises for tomorrow. What I offer you is mine today!

CUT TO:

117. EXTREME WIDE SHOT: In the foreground, his back toward us, Dr. Heidegger is silhouetted against the fading light of the dying sun.

Quietly, he watches the figures of the young girl and the three young men.

MR. MEDBOURNE

Yes, inherited wealth and position. Not a day's work have you done for it!

COLONEL KILLIGREW

Mine just the same. Clara?

MR. GASCOIGNE

Don't listen to him. I need you. A man in my position must have a wife.

MR. MEDBOURNE

You see? For him you're only a convenience by which he hopes to advance his ridiculous strivings for public notice.

MR. GASCOIGNE

Ridiculous strivings! You pompous shopkeeper!

COLONEL KILLEGREW

Both of you are ridiculous. Clara, come with me.

CUT TO:

118. EXTREME CLOSE-UP of the Widow Wycherly. She turns her brilliant smile toward Killigrew.

CUT TO:

119. EXTREME WIDE SHOT as before.

MR. GASCOIGNE

I love you.

CUT TO:

120. EXTREME CLOSE-UP of the Widow Wycherly. She smiles at Gascoigne.

CUT TO:

121. EXTREME WIDE SHOT.

MR. MEDBOURNE

Take your hands off her!

MR. GASCOIGNE

Don't touch me!

COLONEL KILLIGREW

Both of you, let her alone!

MR. MEDBOURNE

You stay out of this!

Medbourne shoves Killigrew.

CUT TO:

122. EXTREME CLOSE-UP of Killigrew.

COLONEL KILLIGREW

I will not have that!

He slaps Medbourne.

CUT TO:

123. EXTREME CLOSE-UP of the beautiful girl. She screams in a mixture of fear and delight.

CUT TO:

124. SLOW MOTION: A MONTAGE of several shots. The three young men fight with each other over the girl.

CUT TO:

125. SLOW MOTION: The Widow Wycherly turns among the struggling men. She is frightened, but pleasurably excited.

CUT TO:

126. SLOW MOTION, LOW ANGLE: The delicate black table in the foreground. Beyond it, the young men struggle. The battle surges toward us and the table is overturned. The glass vase, full of the wonderful water, falls slowly.

CUT TO:

127. SLOW MOTION, SIDE ANGLE CLOSE-UP: The vase toppling forward off the tilting table.

CUT TO:

128. SLOW MOTION: The men look down at the table.

CUT TO:

129. SLOW MOTION, STRAIGHT DOWN CLOSE-UP: The vase strikes the floor and smashes. The water spreads, carrying the crimson rose with it.

CUT TO:

130. HIGH ANGLE: The three young men and the young woman stare down at the destroyed vase and the wasted water. Dr. Heidegger can be seen watching his guests from the background.

CUT TO:

131. WIDE SHOT: Dr. Heidegger observes the suddenly quiet young people for several moments before speaking.

DR. HEIDEGGER

Come, come, gentlemen. Come, Madame Wycherly. I really must protest against this sort of thing.

The room is almost in darkness. Only a shaft of weak red light from sunset clouds passes the window and streaks across the fallen table.

CUT TO:

132. CLOSE SHOT of the four young people. They stand in the shadow and the Widow Wycherly shudders with a sudden chill.

CUT TO:

133. CLOSE-UP of Dr. Heidegger.

DR. HEIDEGGER

Sit down.

Dr. Heidegger rises and hobbles past the young people who are seating themselves in shadowed chairs, to the place where the fallen rose has come to rest. With difficulty, the doctor stoops down and picks it up. He holds the flower in the dim red light of sunset. GO IN to a TIGHT CLOSE-UP of the doctor and the rose. The rose has lost its freshness.

DR. HEIDEGGER

My poor Sylvia's rose. It appears to be fading again.

Dr. Heidegger returns slowly to his chair. We PAN with him until the CAMERA comes to a CLOSE FRAME of his four guests. They sit in deep shadow, but after a moment, we can see that they are once again middle-aged.

CUT TO:

134. Dr. Heidegger sits in his chair, and holds the faded rose up to his face.

DR. HEIDEGGER

I love it as well thus as in its dewy freshness.

Dr. Heidegger presses the rose to his withered lips. GO IN to an EX-TREME CLOSE-UP. The rose is faded again as it was when we first saw it.

CUT TO:

135. The four guests in shadow. The Widow Wycherly shivers again. She turns to look at Colonel Killigrew.

DISSOLVE TO:

136. CLOSE-UP of Colonel Killigrew. He is an old man again. He turns slowly toward the Widow Wycherly.

DISSOLVE TO:

137. The Widow Wycherly. She is old again.
The faces of the other old people can be seen in dim silhouette beyond her. She looks up at Dr. Heidegger.

WIDOW WYCHERLY

Are we grown old again, so soon?

With a shuddering impulse, she clasps her fleshless hands over her face to hide its ugliness.

CUT TO:

138. WIDE SHOT: The five aged people sitting in the shadows around the fallen table.

DR. HEIDEGGER

Yes, friends, you are old again. And look, the water of youth is all wasted on the ground.

He points, and they slowly, painfully, turn to look.

CUT TO:

139. CLOSE-UP of Dr. Heidegger, the faded rose in his hands, the dim portrait behind him. LOW ANGLE.

DR. HEIDEGGER

Well, I do not regret it. For if the fountain gushed at my very doorstep, I would not stoop to bathe my lips in it—no, though its delirium lasted for years instead of moments.

CUT TO:

140. EXTREME LOW ANGLE WIDE SHOT: The smashed vase in the foreground. The last of the water is gone.

The Widow Wycherly bends painfully to look. Mr. Medbourne, Mr. Gascoigne and Colonel Killigrew stand behind her, also looking down at the shattered vase. Dr. Heidegger watches them all from his chair in the shadowed background.

WIDOW WYCHERLY

He's right. It's gone. All gone.

Mr. Medbourne turns to Colonel Killigrew.

MR. MEDBOURNE

You spilled it.

Colonel Killigrew does not respond. The Widow Wycherly turns to him.

WIDOW WYCHERLY

You must get me more.

Once again, Colonel Killigrew fails to respond. After several moments, Mr. Gascoigne speaks in a voice that is slow and barely audible.

MR. GASCOIGNE

Yes, we must have more. We must go to Florida and find this fountain and stay close by so that we may drink the water continually.

MR. MEDBOURNE

Yes, we must go.

COLONEL KILLIGREW

Yes.

WIDOW WYCHERLY

Quickly.

The four old people stand quietly, staring down with dim eyes at that which is lost.

SLOW DISSOLVE TO:

141. It is night. Dr. Heidegger sits watching his guests, the faded rose held in his withered hands.

DR. HEIDEGGER'S EXPERIMENT
QUESTIONS

1. In the opening shot of the film, Dr. Heidegger seems to be addressing us, the audience. Moments later, it becomes apparent that he is actually addressing Colonel Killigrew, Mr. Medbourne, Madame Wycherly, and Mr. Gascoigne. How does the opening shot fit into one of the central themes of both film and story?

2. Much of the expository background preceding the experiment appears on the opening page of the short story. Describe and evaluate the filmmaker's use of this exposition in his adaptation.

3. What is the significance of Sylvia Ward in the story and film?

4. In the short story, the head of Hippocrates was reported to have frowned and said, "Forbear!" What significance do you assign to this detail? What does the filmmaker do with this detail? Why?

5. Hawthorne describes Dr. Heidegger as a "strange old gentleman" who is eccentric. How does this description affect the tone of the short story? Does the filmmaker create a similar tone? Explain.

6. Hawthorne describes Dr. Heidegger as being "in the habit of pestering his intimates." What are the connotations of "pestering"? How do you account for Hawthorne's language?

7. In the closing three paragraphs, Hawthorne uses the word "delirium" twice. What differences do you find in the two uses of the word? Which of the two "deliriums" did the filmmaker utilize? How do you explain it?

8. The short story closes in highly didactic style. Is the film equally didactic? Support your judgment with relevant film details.

9. Compare and contrast the rhythm of film and story.

DR. HEIDEGGER'S EXPERIMENT
SUGGESTIONS FOR PAPERS

1. Compare and contrast the ways in which Hawthorne uses description to create mood and Yust uses images to create mood.

2. In the short story Hawthorne writes, ". . . the tall mirror is said to have reflected the figures of three old, gray, withered grand-sires, ridiculously contending for the skinny ugliness of a shriveled grandam." What other examples of ambiguity does Hawthorne use? What cinematic techniques does Yust use to convey Hawthorne's ambiguities? How successful are they? Explain.

3. In the short story, the newly-rejuvenated Medbourne, Gascoigne, Killigrew, and Wycherly "mock the infirmity and decrepitude of which they had so lately been the victims." What is the function of this scene in the short story? The scene does not occur in the film. Assess its deletion in the context of the film's final form.

4. Compare and contrast the attitudes of Nathaniel Hawthorne and Larry Yust toward the characterization of Dr. Heidegger.

5. In Hawthorne's story, the water from the Fountain of Youth seems to be exhilirating in its effects. Mr. Gascoigne's mind runs on "political topics," while Colonel Killigrew trolls a "jolly bottle song." Widow Wycherly stands before a mirror "curtsying and simpering" while Mr. Medbourne calculates a "polar" project. In Yust's film, two of his sequences cover the same materials. Assess the tone of story and film as each deals with this segment of the narrative.

THE BET

Anton Chekhov

(translated from the Russian by M. S. Kidd.)

Anton Chekhov is regarded today as one of the world's greatest short story writers. He wrote "The Bet" in 1888. This very brief short story spans a period of fifteen years.

Released in 1967, Ron Waller's film uses the credit "inspired by" instead of the more conventional credit, "adapted from." While borrowing a basic plot idea from Chekhov, Waller's film departs radically in style, tone, and philosophy from its literary predecessor.

While the movie depicts an isolation extended over a five year period, it runs for only 24 minutes. Following the short story is a film continuity.

It was a dark autumn night. The old banker paced from corner to corner of his study and recalled how, fifteen years ago in the fall, he held a soirée. That evening, there had been many clever people and interesting discussions. Among other things, they touched on capital punishment. The guests, among whom there were several scholars and journalists, disapproved of the death penalty. They considered that method of punishment outmoded, unsuited to a Christian government, and immoral. In the opinion of several of them, capital punishment should in all cases be replaced by life imprisonment.

"I don't agree with you," said the banker-host. I have suffered neither the death penalty nor life imprisonment, but if one is to judge *a priori*, then in my opinion, capital punishment is a more moral and humane choice. It kills you at once, but life imprisonment does it slowly. Which executioner is the more humane, one who kills you in a few minutes, or the one who draws out your life for many years?"

"They are each equally immoral," observed one of the guests, "because each has the same goal—the deprivation of life. A government is not God. It does not have the right to take away that which it cannot replace if it wishes."

There was a lawyer among the guests, a young man of twenty-five. When they asked his opinion, he replied, "The death penalty and life imprisonment are equally immoral, but if you press me to choose between the death penalty and life imprisonment, then I should, of course, choose the second. To be alive, in whatever manner, is better than nothing."

This produced an animated discussion. The banker, who was then younger and more highly strung, was suddenly beside himself. Turning to the young lawyer, he struck the table with his fist and cried, "It's not so! I will bet two million rubles that you couldn't stay shut away for even five years."

"If you are serious," replied the lawyer, "then I will bet that I can remain not five, but fifteen years."

"Fifteen? Done!" exclaimed the banker. "Gentlemen, I'll wager two million rubles."

"Agreed! You bet millions, and I, my freedom," said the lawyer.

And that queer senseless bet was on. The spoilt and callow banker, who at that time didn't even count his millions, was delighted with the bet. During supper, he made fun of the lawyer and said, "Be reasonable, young man, while it's not too late. For myself, two million is a trifle, but you risk losing three or four of the best years of your life. I say three or four, because you won't last longer. Don't forget, unhappy soul, that voluntary incarceration is by far more burdensome than if it were compulsory. The thought that at any minute, you have the right to regain your freedom can poison your whole existence in confinement. I feel sorry for you."

The banker, now pacing from side to side, recalled all this and asked himself, "What was the point of the bet? Who benefits from it, the lawyer losing fifteen years of his life, or I, throwing away two million? Was it to show people that the death sentence is better or worse than life imprisonment? Absolutely not. Stuff and nonsense! For me, it was the whim of a well-fed man, and for the lawyer, it was pure greed."

Then he thought of what had happened after the evening described. It was decided that the lawyer would serve out his imprisonment under strict supervision in one of the cottages in the banker's garden. They agreed that for the duration of fifteen years, he would be deprived of the right to cross the threshold of the cottage, see human beings, hear a human voice, or receive letters and newspapers. He was allowed to have a musical instrument, read books, write letters, drink wine and smoke tobacco. According to the conditions, he was not allowed to communicate with the outside world other than silently, through a little window built expressly for the purpose. All that he needed, books, paper, wine, and so on, he could receive in any amount he pleased, as agreed, but only through the window. The agreement enumerated all conditions and details, which stipulated a confinement absolutely solitary, and obliged the lawyer to endure exactly fifteen years, from twelve o'clock, November 14, 1870, to twelve o'clock, November 14, 1885. The least attempt on the part of the lawyer to infringe on the conditions, even two minutes from the end of the term, would release the banker from his obligation to pay two million rubles.

In the first year, the lawyer, as far as they could judge from his short notes, suffered greatly from solitude and boredom. Day and night, the sounds of a piano were heard constantly from his cottage. He refrained from wine and tobacco. "Wine," he wrote, "arouses longings, and longings are the first enemy of the prisoner; and besides, there is nothing more boring than to drink good wine and not see anyone." And tobacco spoiled the air of his room. During that first year, they sent the lawyer books mainly of a light character: novels with complicated love intrigues, crime stories, fantasies, and the like.

In the second year, there was no music from the cottage, and in his notes, the lawyer demanded only classics. In the fifth year, music was heard again, and the prisoner asked for wine. Those who observed him through the little window said that all that year, he only ate, drank, and lay on the bed, often yawned and talked irritably to himself. He read no books. Sometimes at night, he would sit down to write, scribble for a long time, and towards morning, would rip all he had written into shreds. At times, they heard him weep.

In the second half of the sixth year, the prisoner assiduously began the study of languages, philosophy and history. He embarked so avidly on these studies that the banker scarcely had time to order the books for him. In the following four years, almost six hundred volumes were ordered at his request. In that period of enthusiasm, the banker received from his prisoner the following note: "My dear jailor! I am writing you these lines in six languages. Show them to scholars. They will be able to read them. If they find not one mistake, then I beg you, order a gun fired in the garden. That shot will tell me that my efforts have not been for nothing. Geniuses of all ages and countries have spoken in divers tongues, but there burns in all of them the same flame. Oh, if only you knew what unearthly happiness fills my soul that I can understand them!" The wishes of the prisoner were fulfilled; the banker ordered a gun fired twice in the garden.

Thereupon, after the tenth year, the lawyer sat in his chair and read only one book, the Gospel. It seemed strange to the banker that a man who in four years had conquered six hundred abstruse tomes, should expend almost a year on the reading of one easily understood and not very thick book. To replace the Gospel came history, religion, and theology.

In the last two years of confinement, the prisoner read an extraordinary amount, without discrimination. Now he studied natural science, now he demanded Byron or Shakespeare. There were notes from him requesting chemistry, medical treatises, novels, and all kinds of philosophical or theological tracts at the same time. His reading was as though he swam among the wreckage of a ship at sea, and desirous of saving his life, eagerly snatched at first one piece of debris, then another.

II

The old banker recalled all this and thought, "At twelve o'clock tomorrow, he will gain his freedom, and I must pay him two million rubles, as we agreed. If I pay him, then everything is finished. I am absolutely ruined."

Fifteen years ago, he had not counted his millions, but now he was afraid to ask himself which he had more of—money or debts. Gambling on the stock market, risky speculations, and a recklessness which even in old age he could not renounce had led little by little to the decline of his business; and the intrepid, self-sufficient rich man was reduced to a mediocre banker, trembling at each rise and fall of the market.

"That damnable bet!" muttered the old man, slapping his head in despair. "Why didn't he die? He is but forty years old. He'll have my last kopeck, marry, enjoy life, play the market, while I like a beggar, will look on enviously and every day will hear the same words from him: "I am indebted to you for my life's happiness. Allow me to help you." No—that's too much. My only salvation from bankruptcy and disgrace is that man's death."

Three o'clock struck. The banker listened intently. Everyone in the house was asleep and the only sound to be heard was the chilly rustle of the trees through the window. Trying to make no sound, he took from his strongbox the key to the door which had not been opened for fifteen years, put on his coat, and left the house.

The garden was dark and cold. It was raining. A damp thin wind rushed howling throughout the garden and gave the trees no rest. The banker strained his eyes, but could see neither the ground, the white statues, the cottage, nor the trees. Going toward the place where the cottage stood, he twice hailed the watchman. There was no answer. Evidently the watchman was sheltering from the weather and now slept somewhere in the kitchen or in the orangerie.

"If I have the courage to do what I intend," thought the old man, "suspicion will fall on the watchman first."

He groped for the step and doorway in the darkness, and went into the entrance hall of the cottage, where he made his fumbling way to a small passage and struck a match. There was not a soul there. In a corner, a cast-iron stove was visible, and a bedstead of some sort, without covers. Seals were affixed to the door leading to the prisoner's room.

When the match went out, the old man, trembling with nervousness, peered through the little window.

A candle gleamed dimly in the prisoner's room. He himself was seated at the table. Only his back, the hair on his head, and his hand were visible. Open books lay on the table, on two armchairs, and on the carpet near the table.

Five minutes passed and the prisoner did not once stir. Fifteen years of imprisonment had taught him to sit motionless. The banker tapped his fingers on the window, but the prisoner made no move in answer. Then the banker gingerly tore the seals from the door and put the key in the keyhole. The rusty lock grated and the door creaked. The banker expected a cry of astonishment and immediate footsteps, but three minutes passed and it was as quiet as before beyond the doorway. He decided to enter the room.

The man sitting motionless on the chair was not like normal folk. He was a skeleton covered with skin, with long feminine curls and a shaggy beard. The color of his face was yellow, with a sallow hue, his cheeks were sunken, his back was long and thin, and the hand with which he held his hairy head was so drawn and thin that it was terrible to look upon. There were already silver threads in his hair, and gazing at his aging emaciated face, no one would believe that this was a man of only forty years. He was asleep . . . on the table near his bowed head lay a sheet of paper on which something was written in a cramped hand.

"Poor soul!" thought the banker. "He is asleep and assuredly sees millions in his dreams. I have only to take this half-dead man, throw him on the bed and gently smother him with a pillow. The most conscientious expert will find no sign of a violent death. First, however, I had better read over what he has written."

The banker took the page from the table and read the following: "Tomorrow at twelve o'clock noon, I shall receive my freedom and the right of intercourse with people. But before I leave this room and see the sun, I consider it necessary to tell you several things. With the clearest conscience and before God who sees me, I declare to you that

I despise freedom, life, health, and all things which in your books are accounted the blessings of the world.

"For fifteen years, I have carefully studied life on this earth. True, I did not see the earth or people, but through your books, I drank full-bodied wines, sang songs, hunted deer and the savage wild boar through the woods, loved women . . . Exquisite beauties, ephemeral as clouds, created by the brilliance of your inspired poets, came to me at night and whispered marvelous tales which rose to my head like wine. In your books, I scaled the summits of Elbrus and Mont Blanc and saw from there how the sun rose in the morning and in the evening flooded the heavens, ocean, and mountain heights with crimson gold; there I saw above me the sundered clouds, the flashing lightning; I saw green forests, fields, rivers, lakes, cities; heard the song of the Sirens and the shepherd's pipe, felt the wings of splendid demons flying to me to talk of God. In your books, I threw myself down bottomless abysses, performed wonders, destroyed and sacked cities, propounded new religions, conquered whole kingdoms. . . .

"Your books gave me wisdom. All that which human thought has tirelessly created throughout the ages is contained in my mind in one small lump. I know that I have more wisdom than all of you.

"And I despise your books, despise wisdom and all the happiness of the world! All is nothing, perishable, illusory, deceptive as a mirage. Though you be proud, wise and beautiful, death will shake you from the face of the earth even as the mice scrabbling in their burrows; but your posterity, your history, the immortality of your geniuses will freeze or flame together with the earthly sphere.

"You have gone mad, and do not walk in those paths. You accept lies as truth and ugliness as beauty. If, for some reason, apple and orange trees suddenly brought forth frogs and lizards instead of fruit, or roses began to stink like a sweating horse, you would be amazed, even as I marvel at you, who have bartered heaven for earth. I do not wish to understand you.

"In order to make my contempt for the way you live quite plain, I decline the two million rubles of which I once dreamed as of Paradise, and which I now despise. To deprive myself to the right to them, I shall leave here five hours before the appointed time and by so doing, shall violate the agreement . . ."

Upon reading this, the banker laid the paper on the table, kissed the head of this strange man, and weeping, left the cottage. Never at any other time, even after dangerous losses on the stock market had he felt so much contempt for himself as now. Returned home, he lay on his bed; but for a long time, emotion and tears gave him no rest.

The morning of the next day, white-faced watchmen came running up to inform him that they had seen someone like the man who had been living in the cottage climb through the window into the garden, slip to the gate and then steal away. The banker immediately set off with the servants and verified the flight of his prisoner. To prevent unnecessary rumors, he took the note of renunciation from the table, and upon returning to his room, locked it in his strongbox.

film continuity

THE BET

1. Fade in: Black. A door opens from left to right and reveals two shadowy figures, Ron and Mike. They pause in the doorway, hesitant.

RON: What's the piano for? I haven't touched one since I was a kid.

MIKE: Yes, I know. The books you asked for are on the shelf. You recall what we discussed about the telephone? It's a direct line to the office switchboard.

RON: Yeah, I know. Everything looks fine.

MIKE: Ron—

RON: Mike! Don't start again. We've been all through . . .

MIKE: Call it off.

RON: No!

MIKE: You're a fool.

Ron smiles. Mike looks at him for a moment; then he exits. The door closes to black.

2. Fade in: Beyond Ron's shadow, there is a calendar on the wall. Over a year has been marked off. Ron's shadow remains visible in right foreground. He is smoking a cigar. He takes a drink, moves left, and marks off part of March of the second year. He recalls an earlier conversation.

VOICE-OVERS

MIKE: Hmm. Don't you ever feel like just being alone instead of all these other people down here?

RON: Well, I don't know. At different times.

MIKE: Like when?

RON: Like this morning; I think I was alone for (pause) an hour.

MIKE: Why, when you were bathing?

Ron has moved to the cupboard; he takes another drink.

RON: Still, I was alone.

He opens the lazy susan and takes out a bag.

RON: No, I'm talking about being alone. You're alone where you just kind of do things that you want to do to improve yourself.

Ron takes a fifth of whisky and a bottle of wine out of the paper bag. He works at opening the bottle of wine.

MIKE: You're the last one in the world that should talk about being alone.

RON: Why, how do you figure that?

MIKE: You've got broads around you all the time.

RON: (laughs) Oh that.

MIKE: I've never seen you come down here yet that you didn't have a broad with you, or one coming.

RON: Yeah, well, I wonder where she is.

Ron crosses to a rumpled bed carrying a bottle and a bag. The table in front of the bed contains glasses, whisky, beer, and a coffee cup. The bed has only a sheet and pillow.

RON: —and I maintain that if a person is allowed to be alone by himself without any interruptions or any social pressures, not having to worry about food or clothing or anything like that, he would manage to make himself a better human being.

Ron sits. He takes a pizza from a bag, puts out his cigar, and begins opening the wine bottle with a corkscrew.

MIKE: It's a very beautiful theory, Walden and Thoreau and being off in Brook Pond, but—

RON: The length of time (pause) oh, I think a man, if he is really going to do anything with his mind would have to be alone at least five years. That's a lot of time.

MIKE: Five years? You realize what you're saying? It's like saying you're going to put yourself in jail for five years.

RON: No—

MIKE: Worse than jail, you're cutting yourself off from all human contact.

Ron tries a different corkscrew to get the wine cork out of the bottle.

MIKE: Well, so—that clears—

RON: No, no, no! I mean to be alone and allowed to study and learn.

Ron is getting increasingly frantic trying to open the bottle.

MIKE: Oh, that sounds great. It sounds great.

RON: Anyway, I still maintain and insist that it would work.

Ron tries a knife and then his finger and still can't budge the cork.

MIKE: I don't think it would work. In fact, I'll tell you what I'll do. I want to bet you something.

Ron tries his little finger.

RON: How's that?

Ron succeeds in pushing the cork into the bottle.

MIKE: A little wager, and you can break it any time you want. No problem. I've got a shack on some property I own, really isolated, out in the country.

RON: Well?

Ron fills his glass from the bottle.

MIKE: Now, what we'll do is we'll board up all the windows; there's to be no outside communication, food will be brought to you, but you won't see who brings it. Sort of a lazy susan thing, from one side, and you can leave a note for supplies, what you want. Everything will be supplied, but, as soon as you open that door or if you lift the telephone and break the seal on it—

Ron continues to drink. He sets the glass down revealing the calendar as before.

RON: What telephone?

Ron sits on the bed. The room is terribly cluttered and untidy.

MIKE: I'm going to have a telephone installed with a seal. As soon as you break that seal and make a telephone call on the outside, you lose.

Ron reclines on the bed.

MIKE: How's that.

RON: What's the stake? (He munches on the pizza.)

MIKE: Oh, let's make it interesting. Fifty thousand?

RON: For five years? Not enough.

MIKE: No, that's right, too. What about this boat? Think it's worth it?

RON: Sure it's worth it. You know it's worth it. I know what this boat's worth. (He sits up and pours another drink.)

MIKE: Well, all right.

RON: I've always kind of liked this boat, too, as a matter of fact. And you never use the damn thing. You don't even take it out and play with it.

MIKE: I'll put it in writing, have it notarized, the whole thing. You still want to go through with it?

RON: You're gonna bet me this boat, against five years of my life—

MIKE: In complete isolation. No letters, no communication whatsoever, no radio. You can have anything else you ask for.

Ron turns out the bedside lamp and lies down. He covers himself with the single sheet and wads his pillow under his head.

RON: Hmm. You, my dear sir, have a bet.

MIKE: Think it over, my friend, think it over.

3. Diffused shot of ashtray. Camera moves back to reveal the ashtray filled with butts and paper. Liquor bottles jam the table. Ron, vaguely visible, thrashes about on the bed in the background. He rises, hairy, bearded, disheveled, and seizes a bottle. He pours a drink, feverishly. He shakes, pants, and continues drinking. He crosses over to a clock that says 12:08. The dim sound of a tone begins; it increases in intensity as he fumbles for a cigarette.

PHONE OPERATOR'S VOICE: The time is 12:08, exactly.

Ron crosses over to the calendar and marks off March of the third year. He circles about the room drinking, pouring more. His physical condition has deteriorated. He searches for a cigarette; they are all gone. He finds another pack and rips it open. He sees a clock. The tone sound ceases.

VOICE: The time is 12:08, exactly. (Tone resumes).

He picks up the clock and shakes it vehemently.

VOICE: The time is twelve, eight, twelve, eight, twelve, eight—

He sits down heavily and tries to take the clock apart.

VOICE: (faster) Twelve, eight, twelve, eight (tone)—thirty-two—

He shakes the clock close to his ear.

VOICE: exactly (tone continues). The time is one, two, (tone)—

Ron takes another drink.

VOICE: three, four, five, six, seven-thirty—

Ron looks about desperately for another bottle with liquor in it.

VOICE: exactly (tone, still louder).

He races to the lazy susan hitting his head on the overhead lamp. He says "Damn!" The lamp oscillates; he removes a bag. It contains a loaf of bread. He flings it away. The tone continues bleeping with increasing rapidity and loudness. Ron groans; he staggers past the bookcase. He smashes bottles and heaves books from the shelves. He grabs the phone, nearly lifts the receiver, fights his inclination, and moans. The swinging light alternately lights and darkens the room. The insistent tone persists—louder and louder.

A series of fast cuts: Ron falls on the bed; he pours another drink; he drinks, convulsively; he cries; he screams; then, he hurls his glass; he throws the clock. He rises from the bed. Crying, he walks barefoot over the broken glass on the floor. He rips the calendar off the wall and tears it apart. His bloody feet stomp over the glass-littered floor. He curls up on the bed in a fetal position sobbing convulsively. While the camera focuses on his heaving body and bloody feet, the screen continues to reflect the flashing light.

4. Fade in: black. Ron's sobbing over. A dead branch. The camera pans over many bottles of liquor. A yacht (color). The camera backs away to reveal a "toy" boat in a tiny sea set in a desert locale.

VOICE: (distorted) Five years. I bet my yacht—you go mad—get, get, get, bet, bet, bet, (maniacal laughter over).

A barren landscape (color). Camera pans right while a yellow filter moves across the screen left. The creaking sound of a rocking chair over. The camera zooms in to a red glow, an isolated rocking chair rocking—a woman's face—his mother. She smiles. Dissolve to a smiling girl who puts her thumb in her mouth, sucks it, slowly withdraws her thumb, and smiles, sensually. From above, the camera sees the girl; she seems to be lying on her back, laughing. The camera zooms in on her open mouth; she screams. In a medium shot Ron sits up from his lying position. He screams. Black out.

5. Fade in. Diffused shot of a filigreed candelabra (part of a lamp). Ron's laughter over. The camera pans along well-ordered bookcases, around the room, now neat, and across the carefully made bed to the empty table. Ron, well-dressed, hair combed, beard and moustache trimmed, is reading a book and laughing. Piano and metronome sound over.

Ron playing the piano, with some hesitation. Camera moves back, across the books. Sound-over of piano playing becoming more assured. Pan to Ron on the floor doing pushups.

RON: 31, 32, 33, 34, 35, 36—

Camera pans around room. Music accompanies exercises; camera reveals bed where Ron is doing situps.

RON: (voice-over) 37, 38, 39—

RON: (counting pushups) 40, 41, 42, 43, 44, 45, 46, 47, 48, 49, 50. (counting of situps, in bed) 45 (pause), 46 (pause), 47—48—49—50.

Music stops. Ron sits up after last situp.

RON: Whew! (He laughs, self-satisfied.)

6. Ron in a dressing gown, eating a salad, and reading a book on hypnosis.

RON: (reads) Time distortion is one of the most interesting and clinically valuable phenomena of hypnosis. It can be induced readily through post-hypnotic suggestions. Ten minutes of clock time can be condensed in one minute of subjective or experimental time. Hmm.

He rises, whistles, and dances into the bathroom. Sound of running water. Diffused shot (screen has blue tint). Music up. Clean ashtray with a pipe in it. Ron, back to camera, is at the piano, writing music. He rises, lights his pipe. He opens the lazy susan and takes out a stock of books. He puts them on the table. He selects one book and settles back on his bed to read. Back to scene.

RON: (reads) In time distortion, the subject must concentrate on a phenomenon that is devoid of relation to time. This sublimation will therefore allow condensation or expansion of events without references to chronological conditioning. Close your eyes. Your eyes are getting very heavy and you're going to relax. Relax completely all over and you're concentrating, concentrating on a very vivid color. You can see a color—

Close-up of Ron's closed eyes. A blue spot begins on his right eye and becomes bigger, filling more screen space.

RON: a color that's becoming brighter and brighter and larger and larger. A color that is going to engulf you—

VOICE-OVER: In your mind's eye you will see a color; you can live and breathe inside this color (shot of clock); concentrate on color. Time means nothing to you at all. Just concentrate on the color blue, indigo blue. Time will no longer be—

RON: In auto-hypnosis—

VOICE: with you. You will not be able to even think about time. You will not know what time is anymore. You're so very very relaxed and the blue is so rich.

RON: Concentrate on color, on beautiful, blue, rich color.

VOICE: Concentrate. Relax. (Long thin crystals of blue). Relax (Piano over).

Flash cuts of Ron and piano. Raindrops on a bush. Pine needles with lights filtering through. Music gets richer. Ron's face, clean shaven. Piano keys. Piano hammers moving on strings (they turn blue).

Ron's face, concentrating.

Pencil tip moving on paper.

7. Ron is playing a piano concerto. Ron at table writing in foreign language.

RON: During the time that I've been in this room, I have learned Italian, French, Greek, and words of various other languages. (Foreign words under).

Loud, abrupt telephone ringing. Camera zooms to phone; close-up of Ron's eyes; close-up of phone ringing with a normal sound. Ron, calmer, more collected, answers the phone.

RON: Go to Hell! I'll call you back later.

Ron hangs up the phone and begins writing.

Close-ups: hands writing, yacht, Ron's face, girl's face in black and white, papers placed in an "out" file above which is an Oscar Wilde quotation, as follows, "When the gods wish to punish us, they answer our prayers."

8. Ron sits and thinks. He turns out the desk light and walks to the other side of the room. Shots of him remembering his earlier experiences. This is a black montage; the screen is primarily black with bits of light flashing the following images: Ron with a short beard eating; Ron with a shaggy beard at table with liquor bottles; Ron at table with a long but trimmed beard reading and then exercising. Ron turns out a second lamp and walks to the piano. He plays a few bars and turns out the last light. Screen goes black; sounds of Ron walking across the room, quick cuts of the phone.

RON: (on the telephone) I'm ready.

RON: What time?

RON: Huh! (Laughs) Dawn! (Phone down).

Door creaks open. Mike peers in and waits as we hear Ron approaching. Ron and Mike look at each other in silhouette; Mike tips his head back in a moment of apprehension. Ron smiles; Mike smiles. Mike steps back to allow Ron to pass. In a long shot from outside the house, Ron begins to emerge, hands over his eyes. He blinks and slowly moves his fingers from his face. He smiles as he sees an idyllic sunrise. Music up. Freeze; credits over.

THE BET
QUESTIONS

1. In Chekhov's short story, the lawyer rejects those material values that originally prompted him to make the bet. He also rejects non-material values that are widely accepted. Compare the lawyer's and Ron's values.

2. Did you find the changes in the lawyer and/or Ron from beginning to end psychologically sound? Defend any positions you take.

3. In his credits, Ron Waller elected to describe his film as "inspired by" a Chekhov story rather than the more conventional credit, "adapted from." Would you agree with Waller's choice of verb? Explain.

4. Because a film engages the senses of sight and sound together, it can depict past and present simultaneously. How does the film-maker link past and present in this film?

5. Compare Chekhov's use of the banker with the filmmaker's use of Mike as antagonists to those undertaking the bet.

6. To what extent does physical appearance indicate the state of a man's interior life in the short story and film?

7. The end of the film is ambiguous; the end of the short story is didactic. Which ending seemed to you more effective? Why?

8. Analyze the role of music in the short story and film.

9. Assess the closing line of the short story and the closing shot of the film.

10. In his story, Chekhov covers a fifteen-year period in five short paragraphs. In the film, Waller encompasses five years in twenty-four minutes of film. How effective is each in using his medium to convey the passing of time?

THE BET
SUGGESTIONS FOR PAPERS

1. The passing of time is depicted both visually and aurally in Waller's film. Describe the many ways in which he accomplishes this.

2. Both Chekhov and Waller use a flashback technique for expository purposes. Compare their methods and effectiveness.

3. In Chekhov's short story, the lawyer's final written statement asserts, "Your books gave me wisdom." In your judgment, how wise is the lawyer? Does the filmmaker's protagonist, Ron, become wiser as a result of his incarceration? Support your judgments.

4. Describe Waller's use of color in *The Bet*. What inferences can you draw from your description?

5. Describe, in detail, your own reactions to Ron's experiences during his first two-and-a-half years in confinement. Use specific cinematic examples to explain your personal responses.

6. Describe, in detail, the role of food and drink in the film. What inferences do you draw from your observations?

chapter 3

Point of View
and Tone
in Film and Fiction

A short story writer determines his point of view very deliberately. Conventionally, he has two basic options. He may elect to use a third-person voice or a first-person voice. Within these options, further sub-divisions exist. If he chooses a third-person omniscient voice, the story narrator can describe what each character does, feels, and thinks. If the author prefers, the speaker can emphasize the actions and thoughts of a central character while limiting himself merely to a description of other characters' actions. Some writers, like Hemingway, for example, often use a detached third-person voice that describes events while minimizing or eliminating any descriptions of the feelings or thoughts of the characters; thus, the events and characters stand objectively on their words and deeds.

In contrast to the third-person voice, a writer may choose to have one of the characters in his story serve as the narrator. Again, there are subdivisions. The first-person narrator may be a central character in the action, as in Herman Melville's story, "Bartleby." On the other hand, the author might use a first-person narrator who is on the fringes of the story, or even one who remains outside the plot but describes events. Examples would be Washington Irving's story, "The Legend of Sleepy Hollow," or Edgar Allan Poe's story, "The Masque of the Red Death."

What considerations dictate a writer's choice of point of view?

What advantages or disadvantages inhere in each alternative? The omniscient voice has the definite advantage of allowing the reader maximum information. The narrator of the story can enter the minds and report the feelings of every character. The omniscient voice tends to be detached and more distant from the events than a first-person narrator who is close to events he himself observes. The first-person narrator is necessarily limited to the experiences of the narrator himself; he can only report what he knows first hand. Because the first-person narrator is so close to the action, it is very easy for a reader to identify with such a character. In turn, this increases the reader's involvement in the events of the narrative. The first-person point of view also lends itself to irony. As the speaker describes events and draws conclusions, the reader learns about the events but may come to conclusions entirely different from those of the narrator. A reader weighs the words of a first-person narrator by assessing his character and his interpretations of the events he reports.

Some writers have meshed first- and third-person points of view in a story, but this is relatively rare. Once a writer determines a point of view, he usually maintains a consistent pattern. On this point, cinematic practice differs sharply from literary practice.

Filmmakers, by the very nature of their medium, make use of two points of view. The basic camera shot is objective. The cameraman photographs what he sees before him. Motion pictures, since their inception, have benefited from seeming to mirror reality. It has been said that the camera doesn't lie. Moreover, the inability of the camera to reject some physical surfaces while photographing other surfaces strengthens the idea of a film's reality. The viewer expects objectivity. This explains why filmmakers go to such elaborate pains to make even their science fiction films credible. (In fact, the camera can be used manipulatively, and the fact that films seem objective makes such manipulation all the more effective.)

In contrast to an objective or omniscient point of view, the film director also uses subjective shots. This represents, as the name indicates, a perception as seen through the eyes of a character in the movie. A common, almost stereotyped, subjective shot might begin with the unfocused ceiling and lights seen by a hospital patient as he comes to after an operation; slowly, the room comes back into focus. Not all subjective shots, however, are out of focus. A standard subjective shot occurs when the prior shot shows a character looking at something outside the frame. The subsequent shot reveals what he sees—as he sees it. In any film adapted from fiction, you can expect to see many objective and subjective shots. Rarely does a filmmaker, except a documentarist, fail to blend both kinds of shots in his film. Subjective shots may range from realistic perceptions to distorted images. They tell us what the character sees and allows us to see through his eyes.

Another common shot in the filmmaker's lexicon is the reaction shot, one of the techniques of the cinematic medium for which fiction does not have an exact equivalent. For example, in Saki's short story, "The Open Window," Vera tells Framton Nuttel an outrageous tale. The writer cannot simultaneously relate Vera's words and Nuttel's reaction to those words. One necessarily precedes the other. In the film adaptation, directed by Richard Patterson, Vera speaks her words off-screen; simultaneously, on-screen, we observe Framton's response to those words. As an audience, we have no difficulty in accepting Vera's off-screen voice. From the film's context, we extrapolate her presence.

The contrast between sound and image can also be used for ironic effect. For example, in *The Lady or the Tiger,* an off-screen narrator describes the king: ". . . whenever there was a little hitch, he was blander and more genial still, for nothing pleased him so much as to make the crooked straight and to crush down uneven places." On screen, we observe rioting and images of police bludgeoning protestors.

Both reaction shots and ironic screen images are objective. The bludgeoning in *The Lady or the Tiger* represents reality, a reality we accept because we see what is occurring. In film, seeing is not only believing; seeing also means suspending disbelief.

Film, Fiction, and Tone

A different aspect of point of view is the attitude a writer or filmmaker takes toward his subject. The tone a writer chooses influences a reader's reaction. If, for example, he describes a character as a "little" man, he may mean literally 5' 2" in height, but the connotation of "little" extends beyond physical description to characterization. If the word "short" is substituted for "little," the negative connotation is reduced. Even word order affects tone. Describe a child as "cute but fat" and the cuteness becomes secondary. Alter the description to "fat but cute" and the fatness is forgiven.

In describing the "tone and style" of fiction, the present author has observed:

> . . . Two writers with a common slate of characters and a given plot would create different stories, out of their distinctive tech-

niques, their unique visions. One writer chooses narrative. He concentrates on detailed background—the exposition—and the flow of events. Another prefers dialogue; he places his characters in stress situations, producing dramatic conflicts. One writer tells all; another implies. One colors the setting; another neglects it. Even sentence structure separates writers along a broad spectrum of choices. Hemingway uses taut sentences stripped of modifiers. Faulkner's involuted sentences reflect the complexity of his characters.

Tone tells of feelings conjured up by language choices. One writer seeks subtle nuances; he adds metaphor for quiet contrasts. Another evokes experience by allusion, or by the more direct use of expressed comparison through similes. Writers choose stances by their choices of language. One detaches himself from the action; he expects the reader to draw inferences from the events. Another engages the reader through direct address. Language rhythms may vary significantly. One writer uses formal sentences; another exploits realistic, colloquial speech patterns. One chooses visual images; another leans heavily upon sound. The range of choices is very great.[1]

Filmmakers also set a tone with a variety of cinematic techniques. One director uses close-ups to create intimate effects; another prefers to use primarily long shots. One uses extended takes; another cuts frequently. For example, although both *The Open Window* and *The Legend of Sleepy Hollow* are satirical in tone, each film establishes that tone in a different way. The director of *The Open Window*, Richard Patterson, uses many shots that remain on screen for some seconds while Sam Weiss, director of *The Legend of Sleepy Hollow*, uses shorter shots. As a result, the pace of *The Open Window* is slower than that of *The Legend of Sleepy Hollow*.

Filmmakers make considerable use of cinematic manipulation. Some of their methods have become stereotyped. The clean-cut Western hero contrasts all too obviously with his scruffy opponent. Angles of shooting and lighting techniques also affect the tone of a scene. Shooting up at a character makes him look powerful, even menacing. At the beginning of David Lean's *Great Expectations*, a sequence takes place from young Pip's point of view. When he encounters the convict, Magwitch, we are terrified as we too seem to be whirled about. Different directors elect to use different proportions of objective and subjective point-of-view shots.

[1]Fred H. Marcus, *Perception and Pleasure* (Lexington, Mass.: D. C. Heath, 1967), p. 94.

An Occurrence at Owl Creek Bridge (1962) "Angles of shooting . . . can color a scene, too. Shooting up at a character makes him more powerful; it can also add menace." *Still shot reproduced courtesy of Contemporary/ McGraw-Hill Films.*

Backlighting an actress' face produces a flattering halo which gives her an angelic look. Underlighting, on the other hand, creates an ominous appearance. Thus, a filmmaker's apparent objectivity can mask cinematic slanting. One telling illustration occurs in *Pygmalion*, a film adapted from the play by George Bernard Shaw. Early in the picture, Professor Higgins announces, "I shall make a duchess of this draggle-tailed guttersnipe." The cameraman shoots him from the point of view of Eliza's cowering position; he seems to tower over her. Later, when he says, "If you're naughty and idle you will sleep in the back kitchen among the black beetles," he stands on the stairs, again dominating the girl. The filmmaker brings this technique to a climax when Higgins says, "If you refuse this offer, you will be a most ungrateful and wicked girl." The words are accompanied by his walking between her and the camera so that she is completely obliterated from view.

Film's apparent objectivity makes it a strong medium for reporting the exterior world. As a medium, movies handle sociological themes very effectively. Because psychological studies emphasize interior worlds, films have greater difficulty in showing such states. As Michael Roemer points out in "The Surfaces of Reality," film can occasionally give us sensitive insights beyond the limits of words. He cites an example from *Marty*. In an encounter between a lonely man and girl, she says, "I'm twenty-nine years old. How old are you?" He answers, "Thirty-six." Roemer notes:

> On the stage or the printed page these lines would fall ludicrously flat. But on the screen . . . they instantly convey—as they would in life itself—a complex web of feeling: the girl's fear that she might be too old for the man, her need to come right to the point, her relief when he turns out to be older, and finally a mutual delight that their relationship has crossed its first hurdle.[2]

One final question merits attention. When a critic assesses a motion picture adapted from a fictional source, what assumptions can he make? First, a negative injunction. Statements like, "The movie was better," or, "The book was better," assume a non-existent parallelism between the two media. Just as it would be foolish to say that Auden's poem, "Musée des Beaux Arts," is better—or worse—than his source, Breughel's painting, *Landscape with the Fall of Icarus*, or that the Romeo and Juliet ballet is better—or worse—than Shakespeare's play or Zeffirelli's film adaptation, so it would be meaningless to say that Edgar Allan Poe's short story is superior—or inferior—to the prize-winning animated film, *The Masque of the Red Death*. What minimal similarities might a critic legitimately expect when a filmmaker adapts a short story? In *Reflections on the Screen*, George W. Linden puts it precisely.

> . . . a director can change the plot of a novel, he can eliminate certain characters and scenes, and he can include scenes not included in the novel without violating it. But he cannot seriously violate the theme of the novel, and the one thing he must be able to translate into his new medium is its tone. If the tone of a work is lost, the work is lost; but the tone of a novel must be rendered in an aural-visual patterning instead of by the use of descriptive dialogue or other narrative device.[3]

Linden's perceptive prescription suggests a valuable critical stance for assessing films adapted from fiction. In *The Legend of Sleepy Hollow*, the filmmaker deletes most of the allusions to American history

---

[2]Michael Roemer, "The Surfaces of Reality," in *Film and Literature*, p. 42.
[3]Linden, *Reflections on the Screen*, p. 49.

found in the story. He drops minor characters such as Katrina's parents and Hans Van Ripper. He also deletes any reference to the story's postscript and alters many other details. For example, the note inviting Ichabod to a party at the Van Tassels is delivered by a child instead of a Negro. When Ichabod receives the note, he dashes from his schoolhouse immediately rather than dismissing his students an hour early. In his haste, he doesn't dismiss them at all. Early in the film, a pie sequence not present in the story is added. One reference by Irving is embellished. The author alludes to Ichabod's visits to the homes of students whose mothers were "noted for the comforts of the cupboard"; the filmmaker actually *shows* us Ichabod demolishing a vast quantity of food at breakneck speed while a puffing and panting overweight mother watches in amazement.

Do these changes—deletion, invention, alteration—modify the tone of the story? Not at all. Irving's fundamental tone is one of gentle mockery, of urbane, tongue-in-cheek satire. He describes Ichabod as "esteemed by the women as a man of great erudition for he had read several books quite through." These are the same country wives "who are the best judges of these matters, [and] maintain to this day that Ichabod was spirited away by supernatural means."

The film's preoccupation with food is derived from Irving's food metaphors. Ichabod is described as looking like "the genius of famine descending upon the earth, or some scarecrow eloped from a cornfield." Katrina Van Tassel is described as "a blooming lass of fresh eighteen; plump as a partridge; ripe and melting and rosy cheeked as one of her father's peaches . . . ." Ichabod has "the dilating powers of an anaconda." Irving uses food imagery when he discusses Ichabod's superstitious credulity: "His appetite for the marvelous, and his powers of digesting it, were equally extraordinary. . . . No tale was too gross or monstrous for his capacious swallow."

One final example of how the film captures the flavor of the story merits attention. Ichabod is described as assisting the farmers in the "lighter labors of their farms; helped to make hay; mended the fences; took the horses to water; drove the cows from pasture; and cut wood for the winter fire." Obviously, the phrase "lighter labors" is used ironically. Irving's humor is verbal, but the filmmaker needs, as Linden notes, "aural-visual" patterns. One film example suffices. In the scene following his huge meal, Ichabod helps with the clean-up chores. The voice-over states, ". . . knowing that his rustic patrons were apt to consider schoolmasters as mere drones, he would render himself useful and agreeable." What do we see on screen? Ichabod washes dishes, rocks the baby's cradle, sings, dries dishes, and stacks them—all at once. As the voice-over hits the word "useful," we see a dish smashing to the floor. At this moment, word and image produce an ironic contrast, and the aural-visual pattern succeeds in duplicating Washington Irving's humorous tone.

In contrast to *The Legend of Sleepy Hollow* is *The Bet*, a short film based on a short story by Anton Chekhov. In *The Bet*, Ron Waller changes the plot of the story substantially. The film is set in America of the 1960's instead of Russia in the years 1870–1885. Chekhov's unnamed banker and lawyer are replaced by Mike and Ron respectively. The fifteen years of isolation willingly undertaken by Chekhov's lawyer are reduced to five years in the film version. But the plot changes are far less significant than the thematic and tonal changes. Chekhov's lawyer takes the bet for only one reason: unmitigated greed. In contrast, Ron's motives are dual. While he seizes on the opportunity to win a boat worth appreciably more than $50,000, his primary motive is idealistic. He says, "I maintain that if a person is allowed to be alone by himself without any interruptions or any social pressures, not having to worry about food or clothing or anything like that, he would manage to make himself a better human being." Ironically, as Ron recalls saying this, he is putting down a cigar, taking a pizza out of a sack, and opening a bottle of cheap wine with a corkscrew. The ending of the film is very different from that of the Chekhov story. Chekhov's lawyer demonstrates his contempt not only for money but for life itself on the last day of his confinement. But Waller's protagonist survives the five-year ordeal. Indeed, he thrives on his isolation after a few terribly destructive years. At the film's end, he has demonstrated the legitimacy of his earlier prediction. He has become "a better human being." When he emerges into a beautiful glowing dawn, it contrasts with the dark, cold, rain, and wind of the early morning hours of the lawyer's last day.

The change in tone from story to film also merits attention. Chekhov's chief character is really the banker. Except for what the lawyer reveals in his long letter of renunciation, we know relatively little about him. We do know, however, a great deal about the banker. We know his character, his values, his fears, his thought processes. Chekhov's story deals with social and philosophical ideas. The film, in contrast, virtually ignores Mike except for his expository function. Centering on Ron as he attempts to cope with his isolation and the passing of time, the movie emphasizes his physical and psychological changes. The terrible trauma of the first two years is pictured in detail; the vivid particulars draw the audience into sympathy with the nearly demented and suffering protagonist. Given these substantive changes, it is neither

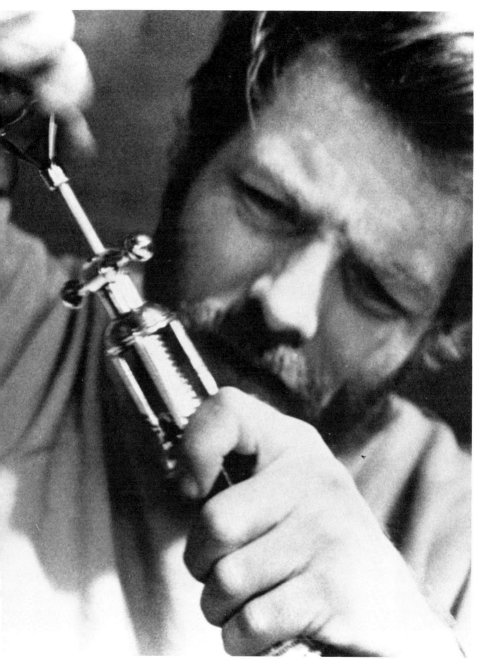

The Bet (1967) As Ron talks about making himself "a better human being," the visuals ironically picture him opening a bottle of cheap wine with a cork-screw. Film encourages directors to achieve irony by juxtaposing contrasting verbal and visual elements. *Still shot reproduced courtesy of Pyramid Films.*

surprising nor inappropriate for the filmmaker to use the phrase "inspired by" in crediting Chekhov rather than the more conventional phrase, "adapted from." By Linden's definition, Waller's film cannot be considered a film adaptation at all.

All of the films represented by stories in this book, except *The Bet*, are closely related to their progenitors. Some are almost literal in their fidelity to the originals while others modify or alter plots considerably. As you read the stories, assess the related film materials, and see the movies, you need to go beyond a recognition of plot differences to the more crucial questions of point of view, theme, and tone. This critical process calls for close study of the stories' literary techniques complemented by a careful scrutiny of the films' cinematic patterns.

THE LADY OR THE TIGER

Frank Stockton

Born in 1834, Frank Stockton initially wrote humorous and fanciful stories before turning to fairy tales for children. In 1882, he wrote his most famous story, "The Lady or the Tiger," which appeared in The New Century. *The open-ended story drew a torrent of response, mostly from readers who demanded an answer to the story's unanswered question.*

In 1969, Larry Yust adapted and directed a highly contemporary film for Encyclopaedia Britannica's "Short Story Showcase." The film combines modern cinematic techniques and documentary footage with a voice-over narration of Frank Stockton's story. The fidelity of the film to the story and its visual imaginativeness earned it several film festival awards.

In the very olden time, there lived a semibarbaric king, who was a man of exuberant fancy and of an authority so irresistible that, at his will, he turned his varied fancies into facts. He was greatly given to self-communing, and when he and himself agreed upon anything, the thing was done. When everything moved smoothly, his nature was bland and genial; but whenever there was a little hitch, he was blander and more genial still, for nothing pleased him so much as to make the crooked straight, and crush down uneven places.

Among his borrowed notions was that of the public arena, in which, by exhibitions of manly and beastly valor, the minds of his subjects were refined and cultured.

But even here the exuberant and barbaric fancy asserted itself. This vast amphitheater, with its encircling galleries, its mysterious vault, and its unseen passages, was an agent of poetic justice, in which crime was punished, or virtue rewarded, by the decrees of an impartial and incorruptible chance.

When a subject was accused of a crime of sufficient importance to interest the king, public notice was given that on an appointed day the fate of the accused person would be decided in the king's arena.

When all the people had assembled in the galleries, and the king, surrounded by his court, sat high up on his throne of royal state on one side of the arena, he gave a signal, a door beneath him opened, and the accused subject stepped out into the amphitheater. Directly opposite him, on the other side of the enclosed space, were two doors, exactly alike and side by side. It was the duty and the privilege of the person on trial to walk directly to these doors and open one of them. He could open either door he pleased. He was subject to no guidance or influence but that of the aforementioned impartial and incorruptible chance. If he opened the one, there came out of it a hungry tiger, the fiercest and most cruel that could be procured, which immediately sprang upon him and tore him to pieces as a punishment for his guilt. The moment that the case of the criminal was thus decided, doleful iron bells were clanged, great wails went up from the hired mourners posted on the outer rim of the arena, and the vast audience, with bowed heads and downcast hearts, wended slowly their homeward way, mourning greatly that one so young and fair, or so old and respected, should have merited so dire a fate.

But if the accused person opened the other door, there came forth from it a lady, the most suitable to his years and station that His Majesty could select among his fair subjects; and to this lady he was immediately married, as a reward of his innocence. It mattered not that he might already possess a wife and family, or that his affections might be engaged upon an object of his own selection. The king allowed no such arrangements to interfere with his great scheme of punishment and reward. The exercises, as in the other instance, took place imme-diately, and in the arena. Another door opened beneath the king, and a priest, followed by a band of choristers, and dancing maidens blowing joyous airs on golden horns, advanced to where the pair stood side by side, and the wedding was promptly and cheerily solemnized. Then the gay brass bells rang forth their merry peals, and the people shouted glad hurrahs, and the innocent man, preceded by children strewing flowers on his path, led his bride to his home.

This was the king's semibarbaric method of administering justice. Its perfect fairness is obvious. The criminal could not know out of which door would come the lady. He opened either he pleased, without having the slightest idea whether, in the next instant, he was to be devoured or married. On some occasions the tiger came out of one door, and on some, out of the other. The decisions were not only fair —they were positively decisive. The accused person was instantly pun-ished if he found himself guilty, and if innocent, he was rewarded on the spot, whether he liked it or not. There was no escape from the judgments of the king's arena.

The institution was a very popular one. When the people gathered together on one of the great trial days, they never knew whether they were to witness a bloody slaughter or a hilarious wedding. This element of uncertainty lent an interest to the occasion which it could not otherwise have attained. Thus the masses were entertained and pleased, and the thinking part of the community could bring no charge of unfairness against this plan; for did not the accused person have the whole matter in his own hands?

This semibarbaric king had a daughter as blooming as his most rosy fancies, and with a soul as fervent and imperious as his own. As is usual in such cases, she was the apple of his eye, and was loved by him above all humanity. Among his courtiers was a young man of that fineness of blood and lowness of station common to the heroes of romance who love royal maidens. This royal maiden was well satisfied with her lover, for he was handsome and brave to a degree unsurpassed in all this kingdom, and she loved him with an ardor that had enough of barbarism in it to make it exceedingly warm and strong. This love affair moved on happily for many months, until, one day, the king happened to discover its existence. He did not hesitate nor waver in regard to his duty. The youth was immediately cast into prison, and a day was appointed for his trial in the king's arena. This, of course, was an especially important occasion, and His Majesty, as well as all the people, was greatly interested in the workings and development of this trial. Never before had such a case occurred—never before had a subject dared to love the daughter of a king. In afteryears such things became commonplace enough, but then they were, in no slight degree, novel and startling.

The tiger cages of the kingdom were searched for the most savage and relentless beasts, from which the fiercest monster might be selected for the arena, and the ranks of maiden youth and beauty throughout the land were carefully surveyed by competent judges, in order that the young man might have a fitting bride in case fate did not determine for him a different destiny. Of course, everybody knew that the deed with which the accused was charged had been done. He had loved the princess, and neither he, she, nor anyone else thought of denying the fact. But the king would not think of allowing any fact of this kind to interfere with the workings of the court of judgment, in which he took such great delight and satisfaction. No matter how the affair turned out, the youth would be disposed of, and the king would take pleasure in watching the course of events which would determine whether or not the young man had done wrong in allowing himself to love the princess.

The appointed day arrived. From far and near the people gathered and thronged the great galleries of the arena, while crowds, unable to gain admittance, massed themselves against its outside walls. The king and his court were in their places, opposite the twin doors—those fateful portals, so terrible in their similarity!

All was ready. The signal was given. A door beneath the royal party opened, and the lover of the princess walked into the arena. Tall, beautiful, fair, his appearance was greeted with a low hum of admiration and anxiety. Half the audience had not known so grand a youth had lived among them. No wonder the princess loved him! What a terrible thing for him to be there!

As the youth advanced into the arena, he turned, as the custom was, to bow to the king. But he did not think at all of that royal personage; his eyes were fixed upon the princess, who sat to the right of her father. Had it not been for the barbarism in her nature, it is probable that lady would not have been there. But her intense and fervid soul would not allow her to be absent on an occasion in which she was so terribly interested. From the moment that the decree had gone forth that her lover should decide his fate in the king's arena, she had thought of nothing, night or day, but this great event and the various subjects connected with it. Possessed of more power, influence, and force of character than anyone who had ever before been interested in such a case, she had done what no other person had done—she had possessed herself of the secret of the doors. She knew in which of the two rooms behind those doors stood the cage of the tiger, with its open front, and in which waited the lady. Through these thick doors, heavily curtained with skins on the inside, it was impossible that any noise or suggestion should come from within to the person who should approach to raise the latch of one of them. But gold, and the power of a woman's will, had brought the secret to the princess.

Not only did she know in which room stood the lady, ready to emerge, all blushing and radiant, should her door be opened, but she knew who the lady was. It was one of the fairest and loveliest of the damsels of the court who had been selected as the reward of the accused youth, should he be proved innocent of the crime of aspiring to one so far above him; and the princess hated her. Often had she seen, or imagined that she had seen, this fair creature throwing glances of admiration upon the person of her lover, and sometimes she thought these glances were perceived and even returned. Now and then she had seen them talking together. It was but for a moment or two, but much can be said in a brief space. It may have been on most unimportant topics, but how could she know that? The girl was lovely, but she had dared to raise her eyes to the loved one of the princess, and, with all the intensity of the savage blood transmitted to her through long lines of wholly barbaric ancestors, she hated the woman who blushed and trembled behind that silent door.

When her lover turned and looked at her, and his eye met hers as she sat there paler and whiter than anyone in the vast ocean of anxious faces about her, he saw, by that power of quick perception which is given to those whose souls are one, that she knew behind which door crouched the tiger, and behind which stood the lady. He had expected her to know it. He understood her nature, and his soul was assured that she would never rest until she had made plain to herself this thing, hidden to all other lookers-on, even to the king. The only hope for the youth in which there was any element of certainty was based upon the success of the princess in discovering this mystery, and the moment he looked upon her, he saw she had succeeded.

Then it was that his quick and anxious glance asked the question, "Which?" It was as plain to her as if he shouted it from where he stood. There was not an instant to be lost. The question was asked in a flash; it must be answered in another.

Her right arm lay on the cushioned parapet before her. She raised her hand, and made a slight, quick movement toward the right. No one but her lover saw her. Every eye but his was fixed on the man in the arena.

He turned, and with a firm and rapid step he walked across the empty space. Every heart stopped beating, every breath was held, every eye was fixed immovably upon that man. Without the slightest hesitation, he went to the door on the right and opened it.

Now, the point of the story is this: Did the tiger come out of that door, or did the lady?

The more we reflect upon this question, the harder it is to answer. It involves a study of the human heart which leads us through roundabout pathways of passion, out of which it is difficult to find our way. Think of it, fair reader, not as if the decision of the question depended upon yourself, but upon that hot-blooded, semibarbaric princess, her soul at a white heat beneath the combined fires of despair and jealousy. She had lost him, but who should have him?

How often, in her waking hours and in her dreams, had she started in wild horror and covered her face with her hands as she thought of her lover opening the door on the other side of which waited the cruel fangs of the tiger!

But how much oftener had she seen him at the other door! How in her grievous reveries had she gnashed her teeth and torn her hair when she saw his start of rapturous delight as he opened the door of the lady! How her soul had burned in agony when she had seen him rush to meet that woman, with her flushing cheek and sparkling eye of triumph; when she had seen him lead her forth, his whole frame kindled with the joy of recovered life; when she had heard the glad shouts from the multitude, and the wild ringing of the happy bells; when she had seen the priest, with his joyous followers, advance to the couple, and make them man and wife before her very eyes; and when she had seen them walk away together upon their path of flowers, followed by the tremendous shouts of the hilarious multitude, in which her one despairing shriek was lost and drowned!

Would it not be better for him to die at once, and go to wait for her in the blessed regions of semibarbaric futurity?

And yet, that awful tiger, those shrieks, that blood!

Her decision had been indicated in an instant, but it had been made after days and nights of anguished deliberation. She had known she would be asked, she had decided what she would answer, and without the slightest hesitation, she had moved her hand to the right.

The question of her decision is one not to be lightly considered, and it is not for me to presume to set up myself as the one person able to answer it. So I leave it with all of you: Which came out of the opened door—the lady or the tiger?

film continuity

THE LADY OR THE TIGER

1. Sequence: dry lake; limousine and six motorcycles; close-up of king; cheering crowds; close-up of king.

NARRATOR

In the very olden time, there lived a semibarbaric king whose ideas, though somewhat polished and sharpened by the progressiveness of distant neighbors, were still large, florid, and untrammeled, as became the half of him which was barbaric. When every member of his domestic and political systems moved smoothly in its appointed course, his nature was bland and genial.

2. Sequence: rioting mobs; close-up of king; war scene, bombs exploding; cemetery.

But whenever there was a little hitch, he was blander and more genial still, for nothing pleased him so much as to make the crooked straight and to crush down uneven places.

3. Sequence: arena; parking lot; people entering arena; audience; close-ups of individuals in arena; floor of arena with two doors.

Among the borrowed notions by which the king's barbarism had become diluted was that of the public arena, in which the minds of his subjects were refined and cultured. This vast amphitheater was an agent of poetic justice, in which crime was punished or virtue rewarded by the decrees of an impartial and incorruptible chance.

4. Sequence: patrol wagon rushing to arena; prisoner being led by guard into arena; sign, "The People vs Harold Simpson"; audience; king and court seated above people; doorkeeper talking into radio.

When a subject was accused of a crime of sufficient importance to interest the king, public notice was given that on an appointed day the fate of the accused person would be decided in the king's arena. When all the people had assembled in the galleries, and the king, surrounded by his court, sat high up on his throne of royal state, he gave a signal . . .

DOORKEEPER

Now.

5. Sequence: prisoner in arena; spotlights; prisoner bowing to king; king nodding.

NARRATOR

. . . and the accused subject stepped out into the amphitheater.

6. Sequence: prisoner looking at the two doors; close-ups of audience; prisoner going to right door, stopping; close-up of king; close-ups of audience; prisoner going to left door; tiger jumping out; close-ups of audience.

Directly opposite the accused, on the other side of the enclosed space, were two doors. It was the duty and privilege of the person on trial to walk directly to these doors and open one of them. He could open either door he pleased. He was subject to no guidance or influence but that of the aforementioned impartial and incorruptible chance.

7. Sequence: close-up of king; close-ups of audience; bell tolling; audience leaving arena; montage of funeral processions.

If the accused opened the one door, there came out of it a hungry tiger, the fiercest and most cruel that could be procured, which immediately tore him to pieces as a punishment for his guilt. The moment that the case of the criminal was thus decided, doleful bells were clanged, great wails went up from hired mourners, and the vast audience, with downcast hearts, wended slowly their homeward way, mourning greatly that one so young and fair, or so old and respected, should have merited so dire a fate.

8. Sequence: reverse film action, bringing audience back into arena; prisoner opening right door; lady stepping out; close-up of prisoner; king applauding; audience applauding; prisoner and lady being married, kissing.

But if the accused person opened the other door, there came forth from it a lady, the most suitable to his years and station that his majesty could select from among his fair subjects: and to this lady the accused was immediately married, as a reward of his innocence. The exercises, as in the other instance, took place immediately.

9. Sequence: organist playing; montage of wedding shots; bells ringing; close-up of king; prisoner and lady; doorkeeper throwing meat to tiger; workman removing sign.

This was the king's semibarbaric method of administering justice. Its perfect fairness is obvious. On some occasions the tiger came out of one door, and on some out of the other. The criminal could open either door he pleased. The whole matter was in his own hands.

10. Sequence: cars leaving arena; king and princess riding in limousine; close-up of chauffeur, limousine.

Thus the masses were entertained and pleased, and the thinking part of the community could bring no charge of unfairness against the king's justice. This semibarbaric king had a daughter as blooming as his most florid fancies. Among the king's court was a young man of that fineness of blood and lowness of station common to the conventional heroes of romance who love royal maidens.

11. Sequence: princess and her lover on merry-go-round, running along beach, kissing, driving in limousine; king in helicopter watching; princess's lover being taken out of patrol wagon and to cell.

This royal maiden was well satisfied with her lover, for he was handsome and brave to a degree unsurpassed in all the kingdom; and she loved him with an ardor that had enough of barbarism in it to make it exceedingly warm and strong. This love affair moved on happily for many months, until one day the king happened to discover its existence. He did not hesitate nor waver in regard to his duty. The youth was immediately cast into prison, and a day was appointed for his trial in the king's arena.

12. Sequence: montage of tiger shots; montage of beauty pageants; close-ups of people talking.

The tiger cages of the kingdom were searched for the most savage and relentless beasts, from which the fiercest monster might be selected. And the ranks of maiden youth and beauty throughout the land were carefully surveyed by competent judges, in order that the young man might have a fitting bride in case fate did not determine for him a different destiny. Of course, everybody knew that the deed with which the accused was charged had been done. He had loved the princess, and neither he, she, nor anyone else thought of denying it.

13. Sequence: king getting out of car, walking through park with guards, catching ball, giving it back to little girl.

But the king would not think of allowing any fact of this kind to interfere with the working of the tribunal. No matter how the affair turned out, the king would take an aesthetic pleasure in watching the course of events which would determine whether or not the young man had done wrong in allowing himself to love the princess.

LITTLE GIRL

Thank you.

14. Sequence: spotlights on arena; cars jamming parking lot; filled stands; king surrounded by court; floor of arena; two doors; crowd; close-up of king nodding; doorkeeper talking; princess's lover stepping into arena.

NARRATOR

The appointed day arrived. From far and near the people gathered, and thronged the great galleries of the arena. The king and his court were in their places, opposite the twin doors—those fateful portals, so terrible in their similarity. All was ready. The signal was given.

DOORKEEPER

Now.

NARRATOR

Half the audience had not known that so grand a youth had lived among them. No wonder the princess loved him! What a terrible thing for him to be there!

15. *Sequence: arena floor; close-ups of audience; princess's lover bowing to king; close-up of princess's lover; negative images (close-up of princess driving car, going to arena, talking with doorkeeper).*

Following custom, the youth bowed to the king. But he was not thinking at all of that royal personage. From the moment that the decree had gone forth that her lover should decide his fate in the king's arena, the princess had thought of nothing but this great event and the various subjects connected with it. Possessed of more power, influence, and force of character than anyone who had ever before been interested in such a case, she had done what no other person had done— she had possessed herself of the secret of the doors.

16. *Sequence: negative images (close-up of princess; close-up of doorkeeper; princess putting her hand on his arm, handing him money; figures of princess and doorkeeper); close-up of princess; floor of arena; close-up of princess.*

Gold, and the power of a woman's will, had brought the secret to the princess. She knew in which of the two rooms that lay behind the doors stood the open cage of the tiger and in which waited the lady. And not only did she know that, but she also knew who the lady was.

17. *Sequence: negative images (close-up of lady; close-up of princess; lady looking at princess's lover, who returns the look).*

It was one of the fairest and loveliest maidens of the court who had been selected as the reward of the accused youth,

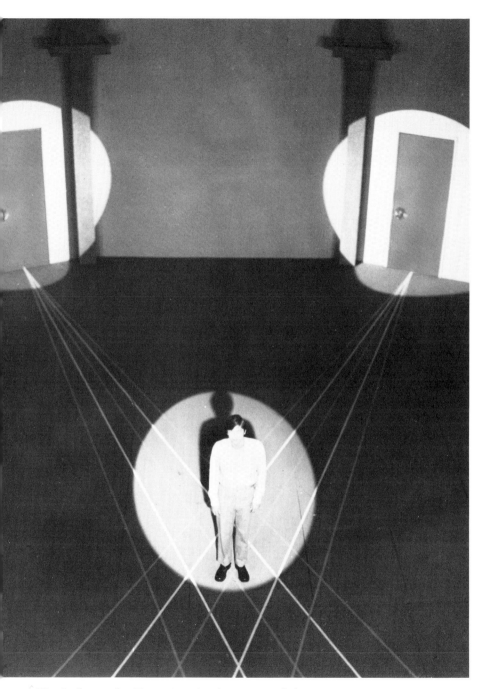

The Lady or the Tiger (1969) The open-ended story continues to intrigue readers/viewers. *Still shot reproduced courtesy of Encyclopaedia Britannica Educational Corporation.*

should he be proved innocent of the crime of aspiring to one so far above him; and the princess hated her. Often had she seen this fair creature throwing glances of admiration upon the person of her lover, and sometimes she thought those glances were perceived.

18. Sequence: negative images (princess golfing; princess's lover and lady talking; close-ups of princess, lady, princess's lover); close-up of princess.

Now and then she had seen them talking together; it was but for a moment or two, but much can be said in a brief space. The girl had dared to raise her eyes to the loved one of the princess; and with all the intensity of her savage blood, the princess hated the woman who waited behind that silent door.

19. Sequence: princess's lover in front of two doors; negative images (princess sitting up in bed; princess's lover opening door, smiling at lady; lady smiling; crowds; close-up of princess; crowd; clergyman performing marriage ceremony; princess's lover and lady kissing).

How often she had started in wild horror as she thought of her lover opening the door behind which waited the cruel fangs of the tiger! But how much oftener she had seen him at the other door!

20. Sequence: negative images (close-ups of princess, tiger); alternate close-ups of princess and her lover.

And yet—that awful tiger, those shrieks, that blood! When the accused looked at the princess and his eyes met hers, he saw, by that quick power of perception which is given to those whose souls are one, that she knew behind which door crouched the tiger and behind which stood the lady. He had expected her to know it.

21. Sequence: princess's lover; princess and court; princess raising her right hand and signaling; princess's lover walking to door at right and starting to open it.

PRINCESS'S LOVER (*thinking*)

Which one?

NARRATOR

Now, the point of the story is this: Did the tiger come out of that door, or did the lady?

THE LADY OR THE TIGER
QUESTIONS

1. In the opening shots of the film, the audience views the king and his motorcycle escort in the middle of a vast desert. What purpose does this setting serve? What inferences can be drawn from the motorcycle escort? Are any of these inferences applicable to the short story? Explain.

2. What functions are served by the newsreel shots in the film? Are these functions also operative in the story?

3. The visual violence on screen runs a gamut of types as well as a range of geographical places. What inferences flow from the filmmaker's technique?

4. In the short story, the princess's lover is described as having that ". . . fineness of blood and lowness of station common to conventional heroes." How would you describe the tone of the storyteller here? To what extent is this tone reflected in the film?

5. What is the purpose of the film scene in which the king bends down on one knee to return a ball to a little girl?

6. Under usual circumstances—not in the case of the princess's lover —how fair and impartial is the king's "justice"? Compare the attitudes of writer and filmmaker toward the king's justice.

7. Many viewers would recognize the Los Angeles Forum as the film's arena. How appropriate is such a choice—the Forum is best known for competitive athletic events—for the arena?

8. The filmmaker uses many negative images in the screen version of *The Lady or the Tiger*. Why? Assess their effectiveness in the context of the film's themes and tone.

9. What verbal irony do you find in the short story? What verbal to visual (contrasts) irony do you find in the film? What verbal irony—if any—do you find in the film? On the basis of your responses, what inferences might you draw?

THE LADY OR THE TIGER
SUGGESTIONS FOR PAPERS

1. Evaluate the director's decision to use a voice-over (off-screen) narrator in the film. Support your opinions with appropriate details from the story and film.

2. Compare and contrast the film and story endings. Both writer and director attempt to balance the princess's motives so delicately that there is an equally good argument for selecting the tiger as the lady. Do both succeed in maintaining an untilted equilibrium? Support your judgments with concrete details from the film and story.

3. How did you react to the cinematic special effects of *The Lady or the Tiger*? How do you account for your responses?

4. The short story takes place in "olden times." The film director places his picture in a contemporary setting. To what extent do you find his change of setting consistent with the tone of the story? Justify your judgments.

5. Compare and contrast the rhythm of film and story.

THE OPEN WINDOW
Saki

In many of his stories, Saki combines a hint of the supernatural with a witty and satirical view of British respectability. He characterizes children as inventive, imaginative, and unceasingly hostile to adults, especially adults who are pompous or priggish. "The Open Window" combines the best features of Saki's whimsy and social criticism.

Richard Patterson, who was at the American Film Institute when he directed a twelve-minute adaptation of the story, wrote several screenplays en route to the actual shooting of the film. His creative thought processes are revealed in the progressive changes from his initial conception to the film itself.

The Open Window was produced in 1972 and won a Cine Golden Eagle. Viewers will find that its use of music and slow motion merit critical attention. The film was selected for presentation at the Edinburgh Film Festival and received a Gold Medal Special Jury Award at the Atlanta International Film Festival.

"My aunt will be down presently, Mr. Nuttel," said a very self-possessed young lady of fifteen; "in the meantime you must try and put up with me."

Framton Nuttel endeavored to say the correct something which should duly flatter the niece of the moment without unduly discounting the aunt that was to come. Privately he doubted more than ever whether these formal visits on a succession of total strangers would do much towards helping the nerve cure which he was supposed to be undergoing.

"I know how it will be," his sister had said when he was preparing to migrate to this rural retreat; "you will bury yourself down there and not speak to a living soul, and your nerves will be worse than ever from moping. I shall just give you letters of introduction to all the people I know there. Some of them, as far as I can remember, were quite nice."

Framton wondered whether Mrs. Sappleton, the lady to whom he was presenting one of the letters of introduction, came into the nice division.

"Do you know many of the people round here?" asked the niece, when she judged that they had had sufficient silent communion.

"Hardly a soul," said Framton. "My sister was staying here, at the rectory, you know, some four years ago, and she gave me letters of introduction to some of the people here."

He made the last statement in a tone of distinct regret.

"Then you know practically nothing about my aunt?" pursued the self-possessed young lady.

"Only her name and address," admitted the caller. He was wondering whether Mrs. Sappleton was in the married or widowed state. An undefinable something about the room seemed to suggest masculine habitation.

"Her great tragedy happened just three years ago," said the child; "that would be since your sister's time."

"Her tragedy?" asked Framton; somehow in this restful country spot tragedies seemed out of place.

"You may wonder why we keep that window wide open on an October afternoon," said the niece, indicating a large French window that opened on to a lawn.

"It is quite warm for the time of the year," said Framton, "but has that window got anything to do with the tragedy?"

"Out through that window, three years ago to a day, her husband and her two young brothers went off for their day's shooting. They never came back. In crossing the moor to their favorite snipe-shooting ground they were all three engulfed in a treacherous piece of bog. It had been that dreadful wet summer, you know, and places that were safe in other years gave way suddenly without warning. Their bodies were never recovered. That was the dreadful part of it." Here the child's voice lost its self-possessed note and became falteringly human. "Poor aunt always thinks that they will come back some day, they and the little brown spaniel that was lost with them, and walk in at that window just as they used to do. That is why the window is kept open every evening till it is quite dusk. Poor dear aunt, she has often told me how they went out, her husband with his white waterproof coat over his arm, and Ronnie, her youngest brother, singing, 'Bertie, why do you bound?' as he always did to tease her, because she said it got on her nerves. Do you know, sometimes on still, quiet evenings like this, I almost get a creepy feeling that they will all walk in through that window—"

She broke off with a little shudder. It was a relief to Framton when the aunt bustled into the room with a whirl of apologies for being late in making her appearance.

"I hope Vera has been amusing you?" she said.

"She has been very interesting," said Framton.

"I hope you don't mind the open window," said Mrs. Sappleton briskly; "my husband and brothers will be home directly from shooting, and they always come in this way. They've been out for snipe in the marshes today, so they'll make a fine mess over my poor carpets. So like you menfolk, isn't it?"

She rattled on cheerfully about the shooting and the scarcity of birds, and the prospects for duck in the winter. To Framton it was all purely horrible. He made a desperate but only partially successful effort to turn the talk on to a less ghastly topic; he was conscious that his hostess was giving him only a fragment of her attention, and her eyes were constantly straying past him to the open window and the lawn beyond. It was certainly an unfortunate coincidence that he should have paid his visit on this tragic anniversary.

"The doctors agree in ordering me complete rest, an absence of mental excitement, and avoidance of anything in the nature of violent physical exercise," announced Framton, who labored under the tolerably wide-spread delusion that total strangers and chance acquaintances are hungry for the least detail of one's ailments and infirmities, their cause and cure. "On the matter of diet they are not so much in agreement," he continued.

"No?" said Mrs. Sappleton, in a voice which only replaced a yawn at the last moment. Then she suddenly brightened into alert attention —but not to what Framton was saying.

"Here they are at last!" she cried. "Just in time for tea, and don't they look as if they were muddy up to the eyes!"

Framton shivered slightly and turned towards the niece with a look intended to convey sympathetic comprehension. The child was staring out through the open window with dazed horror in her eyes. In a chill shock of nameless fear Framton swung round in his seat and looked in the same direction.

In the deepening twilight three figures were walking across the lawn towards the window; they all carried guns under their arms, and one of them was additionally burdened with a white coat hung over his shoulders. A tired brown spaniel kept close at their heels. Noiselessly they neared the house, and then a hoarse young voice chanted out of the dusk: "I said, Bertie, why do you bound?"

Framton grabbed wildly at his stick and hat; the hall-door, the gravel-drive, and the front gate were dimly noted stages in his headlong retreat. A cyclist coming along the road had to run into the hedge to avoid imminent collision.

"Here we are, my dear," said the bearer of the white mackintosh, coming in through the window; "fairly muddy, but most of it's dry. Who was that who bolted out as we came up?"

'A most extraordinary man, a Mr. Nuttel," said Mrs. Sappleton; "could only talk about his illnesses, and dashed off without a word of goodby or apology when you arrived. One would think he had seen a ghost."

"I expect it was the spaniel," said the niece calmly; "he told me he had a horror of dogs. He was once hunted into a cemetery somewhere on the banks of the Ganges by a pack of pariah dogs, and had to spend the night in a newly dug grave with the creatures snarling and grinning and foaming just above him. Enough to make anyone lose their nerve."

Romance at short notice was her specialty.

screenplay

THE OPEN WINDOW

Richard Patterson

1. EXTERIOR, COUNTRYSIDE; LATE NINETEENTH-CENTURY ENGLAND.

The late afternoon autumn light fights a losing battle with the gathering mists as Framton Nuttel makes his way across the English countryside to the Sappleton estate.

Framton pauses when he rounds the corner to behold the Sappleton country house. There is something distinctly uninviting about its facade and the woods bordering the house. Framton, at best an indecisive individual, and now recovering from a severe nervous breakdown, contemplates the house with genuine misgivings, then turns resolutely to retrace his steps. As soon as he starts, he is swamped by second thoughts and self-reproach. Once again he strikes out towards the house, collecting himself as he walks.

TITLE: THE OPEN WINDOW

2. EXTERIOR, SAPPLETON COUNTRY HOUSE.

Framton refortifies himself before knocking on the door and almost forgets to take out a letter in his coat pocket.

A maid answers the door and ushers Framton into a large gloomy hallway where scattered remnants of daylight are dying for lack of human support.

3. INTERIOR, HALLWAY.

Framton is nervous and unsure of himself even with the maid.

FRAMTON

Framton Nuttel to see Mrs. Sappleton

He gives her the letter.

FRAMTON

My sister . . . sends her regards and suggested I call.

There is something disturbing and even sinister about the maid's quiet propriety as she leads Framton through another equally gloomy hallway to the sitting room.

4. INTERIOR, SITTING ROOM.

The sitting room is a large, comfortably furnished room with French windows out onto the lawn and garden. One of the windows is open, and the edge of the forest can be seen through the mist beyond the lawn. At one end of the room is what appears to be a man's desk, and there is something about the slightly dishevelled furniture which suggests the presence of a man in the household.

Framton sits down wrapping his coat around himself more snugly to protect himself from the draft coming through the open window. Gradually he begins to relax as he surveys the room indulging his proclivity for observing human society rather than participating in it. He becomes so absorbed in his inspection of the room that he is quite startled by the entrance of a 15 year old girl.

VERA

My aunt will be down presently, Mr. Nuttel. In the meantime you must try and put up with me.

Vera seems precociously self-possessed, and this combines with Framton's natural awkwardness to shatter whatever peace of mind he had gathered while alone in the room.

FRAMTON

Yes, well, I'm sure it will be a pleasure.

They sit in silence until Vera finally comes to his rescue.

VERA

Do you know many of the people round here?

FRAMTON

Hardly a soul. My sister was staying here, at the rectory, you know, some four years ago, and she gave me letters of introduction to some of the people here.

There is a tone of distinct regret in his last statement.

VERA

Then you know practically nothing about my aunt?

FRAMTON

Only her name and address.

VERA

Her great tragedy happened just three years ago. That would be since your sister's time.

Framton's misgivings about his visit are doubled.

FRAMTON

Her tragedy?

VERA

You may wonder why we keep that window wide open on an October afternoon.

FRAMTON

It is quite warm for the time of year, but has that window got anything to do with the tragedy?

Vera rises and starts to walk towards the open window searching for the right words with which to relate a delicate matter.

VERA

Out through that window, three years ago to a day, her husband and two young brothers went off for their day's shooting. They never came back.

Framton is moved but he wishes he had not let himself in for this.

VERA

In crossing the moor to their favorite snipe-shooting ground they were all three engulfed in a treacherous piece of bog. It had been that dreadful wet summer, you know, and places that were safe in other years gave way suddenly without warning. Their bodies were never recovered. That was the dreadful part of it.

Her voice loses its self-possession and becomes falteringly human as she returns to her seat.

VERA

Poor aunt always thinks that they will come back some day, they and the little brown spaniel that was lost with them, and walk in at that window just as they used to do. That is why the window is kept open every evening till it is quite dusk. Poor dear aunt, she has often told me how they went out, her husband with his white waterproof coat over his arm, and Ronnie, her youngest brother, singing, "Bertie, why do you bound?" as he always did to tease her, because she said it got on her nerves.

Framton has quite forgotten his nervousness in his commiseration with the child. As she sits, she looks into his eyes with a look that pierces to the bottom of his soul.

VERA

Do you know, sometimes on still, quiet evenings like this, I almost get a creepy feeling that they will all walk in through that window . . .

Her voice breaks off in a shudder and Framton is once again thrown into a state of utter turmoil. He glances at the open window and starts to rise, searching for an excuse to leave.

MRS. SAPPLETON

I'm sorry to have kept you waiting. It was most ungracious of me.

Mrs. Sappleton bustles into the room, catching Framton completely off guard.

MRS. SAPPLETON

I hope Vera has been amusing you?

FRAMTON

She has been very interesting.

Framton watches Mrs. Sappleton a little apprehensively as she straightens a few things up in the room before sitting down.

MRS. SAPPLETON

I hope you don't mind the open window. My husband and brothers will be home directly from shooting and they always come in this way. They've been out for snipe in the marshes today, so they'll make a fine mess over my poor carpets. So like you men-folk, isn't it.

Framton does not have the presence of mind to reply with anything more than an inarticulate grunt. Mrs. Sappleton continues to rattle on cheerfully.

MRS. SAPPLETON

I don't know why they insist on wallowing around in the marshes when everyone knows there are no snipe to be had this fall. I suppose that only increases the excitement of the hunt.

FRAMTON

I'm not a hunter myself.

MRS. SAPPLETON

I'm told, though, that there should be an abundance of duck this winter.

Framton is desperately trying to change the topic of conversation.

FRAMTON

I'm here for my health, actually . . . had a rather bad case of nerves.

Mrs. Sappleton has ceased talking, but she is giving Framton only a fragment of her attention. As he talks, her eyes are constantly straying past him to the open window and the lawn beyond.

FRAMTON

The doctors agree in ordering me complete rest, an absence of mental excitement, and avoidance of anything in the nature of violent physical exercise.

Framton sincerely believes it will be possible to interest Mrs. Sappleton in his plight and thereby distract her from her preoccupation with the window behind him.

FRAMTON

On the matter of diet they are not so much in agreement.

Mrs. Sappleton is unable to completely suppress a yawn.

MRS. SAPPLETON

No?

Suddenly her face brightens into alert attention.

MRS. SAPPLETON

Here they are at last! Just in time for tea, and don't they look as if they were muddy up to the eyes!

Framton shivers slightly and turns toward Vera with a look intended to convey sympathetic comprehension.

Vera is staring out through the open window with dazed horror in her eyes. In a chill shock of nameless fear Framton swings around in his seat and looks in the same direction.

In the deepening twilight three figures are walking across the lawn towards the window. They all carry guns under their arms, and one of them has a white coat hung over his shoulders. A tired brown spaniel keeps close at their heels. Noiselessly they near the house, and then a hoarse young voice chants out of the dusk.

RONNIE
(Singing)

I said, Bertie, why do you bound?

Framton grabs wildly at his stick and hat.

5. EXTERIOR, SAPPLETON COUNTRY HOUSE.

In no time Framton is out the hall door, down the gravel drive and through the front gate. A cyclist coming along the road runs into the hedge to avoid imminent collision.

6. INTERIOR, SITTING ROOM.

The bearer of the white mackintosh comes in through the window.

MR. SAPPLETON

Here we are, my dear, fairly muddy, but most of it's dry. Who was that who bolted out as we came up?

MRS. SAPPLETON
A most extraordinary man, a Mr. Nuttel. Could only talk about his illnesses and dashed off without a word of good-bye or apology when you arrived. One would think he had seen a ghost.

VERA
I expect it was the spaniel. He told me he had a horror of dogs. He was once hunted into a cemetery somewhere on the banks of the Ganges by a pack of pariah dogs, and had to spend the night in a newly dug grave with the creatures snarling and grinning and foaming just above him. Enough to make anyone lose their nerve.

Her expression reflects an unusual degree of understanding for someone her age.

revised screenplay

THE OPEN WINDOW

Richard Patterson

FADE IN

1. EXTERIOR, CLOSE-UP: Front Door Knocker.

SUPERIMPOSE TITLE: THE OPEN WINDOW.

FADE OUT TITLE. Framton's hand reaches up to knock on the door, hesi-tates, and then grabs the knocker resolutely and knocks three times.

2. EXTERIOR, MEDIUM SHOT: Framton at the front door (from behind Framton). He steps back after knocking. He straightens his coat, adjusts his hat, and tries to loosen his collar as he waits for someone to answer the door. No one answers. He decides to go and turns with a look of relief on his face. The door opens catching him off guard. He turns to see the open door but sees no one inside. He enters cautiously.

3. INTERIOR, ENTRANCE HALL; LONG SHOT: Framton and the maid. Framton steps inside, and the door closes behind him. He turns to discover the maid. He smiles weakly at her for a moment and then retrieves his presence of mind. The maid begins to glare at him contemptuously as he introduces himself and fishes a letter out of his coat pocket.

FRAMTON

I'm Framton Nuttel. I'm staying at the inn, and my sister gave me this letter of introduction to Mrs. Sappleton.

The maid waits for him to give her the letter. Framton continues to explain himself. When he finally places the letter in the maid's hand, she starts to walk off without waiting for him to finish.

FRAMTON

My doctor insisted I take a rest in the country and my sister . . .

Framton does not understand where the maid is going. She opens the door to the sitting room and then steps back. Framton finally realizes he is supposed to enter the room.

4. INTERIOR, SITTING ROOM DOOR; MEDIUM SHOT: Framton and the maid. Framton gathers up his courage as he enters the room, expecting to see Mrs. Sappleton. The maid glares at him from behind with snobbish amazement. He is surprised by what he sees.

5. INTERIOR, SITTING ROOM; LONG SHOT: Framton at the far end of the empty room. The door closes behind him.

6. INTERIOR, SITTING ROOM; MEDIUM SHOT: Framton reacts to the door shutting behind him. He then turns and the CAMERA DOLLIES BACK as he ventures into the room. He tries to decide where he should stand in the room or whether he should sit down. Eventually he sits in a chair by the fireplace with his back to the door to the hall. The chair is lower than he expects it to be. He collects himself again and glances around the room as he waits. The CAMERA DOLLIES into a CLOSE-UP of Framton. He hears a door close somewhere in the house and the sound of footsteps approaching the room. He gets up.

6A. INTERIOR, SITTING ROOM; INSERT PAN OF ROOM: Framton's point of view.

7. INTERIOR, SITTING ROOM; FULL FRONTAL SHOT: Framton rises to greet the person coming to the room. The footsteps go past the door and into the back part of the house. He decides not to sit back down in the same chair and looks around for a moment before sitting in a chair facing the door to the hall. As he sits the CAMERA DOLLIES into a CLOSE-UP of Framton with the open window in the background behind him. Framton notices a draft on the back of his neck, wraps his coat tighter around him as he glances at the window, and finally decides to get up and close the window. He peers out the window and debates whether he should close it a little. Just as his hand is about to touch the window he is startled by Vera's voice.

VERA (Voice-Over)

My aunt will be down presently, Mr. Nuttel.

8. INTERIOR, SITTING ROOM; FULL FRONTAL SHOT: Vera is standing just inside the door to the hall.

VERA

In the meantime you must try and put up with me.

9. MEDIUM SHOT: Framton.

FRAMTON

Yes, well I'm sure it will be a pleasure.

The CAMERA PANS as he walks back towards his chair revealing Vera as she sits in the chair facing his. He sits down and there is a long silence before Vera speaks. As she speaks the CAMERA DOLLIES very slowly towards her and Framton's back.

VERA

Do you know many of the people round here?

FRAMTON

Hardly a soul. My sister was staying here, at the rectory, you know, some four years ago, and she gave me letters of introduction to some of the people here.

VERA

Then you know practically nothing about my aunt?

FRAMTON

Only her name and address.

VERA

Her great tragedy happened just three years ago. That would be since your sister's time.

9A. The CAMERA PANS AND DOLLIES to a CLOSE-UP of Framton with the window in the background.

FRAMTON

Her tragedy?

VERA (Voice-Over)

You may wonder why we keep that window wide open on an October afternoon.

FRAMTON

It is quite warm for the time of year, but has that window got anything to do with the tragedy?

10. MEDIUM SHOT: Vera. DOLLY BACK as she rises and walks towards the camera (past Framton and towards the window). DOLLY BACK and PAN to reveal the window as she approaches it.

VERA

Out through that window, three years ago to a day, her husband and brother went off for their day's shooting. They never came back.

11. MEDIUM SHOT: Framton.

VERA (Voice-Over)

In crossing the moor to their favorite snipe shooting ground they were both engulfed in a treacherous piece of bog.

12. MEDIUM SHOT: Vera looking back at Framton.

VERA

It had been that dreadful wet summer, you know, and places that were safe in other years gave way suddenly without warning. Their bodies were never recovered. That was the dreadful part of it.

Her voice loses its self-possession and becomes falteringly human.

VERA

Poor aunt thinks they will come back home some day . . .

13. CLOSE-UP: Framton.

VERA (Voice-Over)

. . . they and the little brown spaniel that was lost with them, and walk in at that window just as they used to do.

14. MEDIUM SHOT: Vera.

VERA

That is why the window is kept open every evening till it is quite dusk.

She begins to walk back towards Framton and as she moves out of the frame the CAMERA DOLLIES toward the open window.

VERA

Poor dear aunt, she has often told me how they went out, her husband with his white waterproof coat over his arm and Ronnie, her brother, singing, "Bertie, why do you bound?" as he always did to tease her, because she said it got on her nerves.

15. CLOSE-UP: Framton gazing out the window and then looking at Vera.

16. CLOSE-UP: Vera looking straight into Framton's eyes.

VERA

Do you know, sometimes on still, quiet evenings like this, I almost get a creepy feeling that they will all walk in through that window . . .

17. CLOSE-UP: Framton reacting to Vera. He reaches for his hat and cane and starts to rise. He is thrown off balance by Mrs. Sappleton's entrance.

18. MEDIUM SHOT: Mrs. Sappleton. CAMERA DOLLIES BACK as she enters the room.

MRS. SAPPLETON

I'm so sorry to have kept you waiting. It was most ungracious of me.

She moves around the room straightening things up and gesturing for Framton to sit down. Framton watches her apprehensively from the background.

MRS. SAPPLETON

I hope Vera has been amusing you?

FRAMTON.

She has been very interesting.

CAMERA PANS with MRS. SAPPLETON so that Framton is no longer in the frame.

MRS. SAPPLETON

I hope you don't mind the open window. My husband and brother will be home directly from shooting, and they always come in this way.

19. CLOSE-UP: Framton reacting to Mrs. Sappleton and looking to Vera.

20. CLOSE-UP: Vera.

21. MEDIUM SHOT: Framton with Mrs. Sappleton in the background.

MRS. SAPPLETON

They've been out for snipe in the marshes today, so they'll make a fine mess over my poor carpets. So like you men-folk, isn't it?

Mrs. Sappleton exits frame and the CAMERA DOLLIES in to CLOSE-UP of Framton trying to say something and then looking at Vera.

MRS. SAPPLETON (Voice-Over)

I don't know why they insist on wallowing around in the marshes when everyone knows there are no snipe to be had this fall.

22. CLOSE-UP: Vera lowering her eyes.

MRS. SAPPLETON (Voice-Over)

But I suppose that only increases the excitement of it all.

23. CLOSE-UP: Framton trying to get Mrs. Sappleton to sit down.

FRAMTON

I'm not a sportsman myself.

The CAMERA DOLLIES BACK and PANS to include Mrs. Sappleton in the frame as she walks towards the chair facing Framton.

MRS. SAPPLETON

I'm told though that there should be an abundance of duck this winter.

FRAMTON
I'm here for my health actually . . . had a rather bad case
of nerves.

Mrs. Sappleton sits and the CAMERA DOLLIES into a MEDIUM
SHOT of her. She is looking out the window.

FRAMTON (Voice-Over)
The doctors agree in ordering me complete rest, an absence
of mental excitement, and avoidance of anything in the
nature of violent physical exercise.

24. CLOSE-UP: Framton.

FRAMTON
On the matter of diet they are not so much in agreement.

25. CLOSE-UP: Mrs. Sappleton suppressing a yawn.

MRS. SAPPLETON
No?

Suddenly her face brightens into alert attention as she looks toward
the window.

MRS. SAPPLETON
Here they are at last!

26. CLOSE-UP: Framton shivering and then looking to Vera. PAN
and ZOOM to a CLOSE-UP of VERA staring out through the open
window with dazed horror in her eyes.

27. CLOSE-UP: Framton turning to look towards the window. PAN
to window and ZOOM to a LONG SHOT of Mr. Sappleton and
Ronnie walking towards the house. They are carrying guns under
their arms and Mr. Sappleton has a white coat hung over his shoulders.
A tired brown spaniel keeps close at their heels. Noiselessly, they
near the house, and then a hoarse young voice chants out of the dusk.

RONNIE (SINGING)
I said, Bertie, why do you bound?

28. MEDIUM SHOT: Framton grabbing wildly at his hat and cane.
CAMERA DOLLIES BACK as he gets up to run out of the room
(SLOW MOTION?)

29. HALLWAY; MEDIUM SHOT: Framton running out of the living
room towards the front door. The CAMERA DOLLIES BACK to a

LONG SHOT of FRAMTON as he approaches the door and the maid comes around the corner carrying the tea. (SLOW MOTION?)

30. EXTERIOR, FRONT DOOR; MEDIUM SHOT: Framton as he bursts out of the door. He exits frame slamming the door behind him (SLOW MOTION?)

31. INTERIOR, SITTING ROOM; MEDIUM SHOT: Mr. Sappleton and Ronnie entering the room via the French window. CAMERA DOLLIES BACK and PANS to reveal Mrs. Sappleton and the maid.

MR. SAPPLETON
Here we are, my dear, fairly muddy, but most of it's dry. Who was that who bolted out as we came up?

MRS. SAPPLETON
A most extraordinary man, a Mr. Nuttel. Could only talk about his illness and dashed off without a word of good-bye or apology when you arrived. One would think he had seen a ghost.

VERA (Voice-Over)
I expect it was the spaniel . . .

PAN and DOLLY into a CLOSE-UP of Vera.

VERA
He told me he had a horror of dogs. He was once hunted into a cemetery somewhere on the banks of the Ganges by a pack of pariah dogs, and had to spend the night in a newly dug grave with the creatures snarling and grinning and foaming just above him. Enough to make anyone lose their nerve.

FREEZE FRAME ON CLOSE-UP of Vera and ROLL UP CREDITS.

THE OPEN WINDOW
QUESTIONS

1. Saki's short story begins with Vera speaking to Framton Nuttel about the imminent appearance of her aunt while Patterson's film begins with Framton Nuttel standing outside the front door of the house. Do you think the invention of three sequences (Framton at the door, Framton and the maid in the hallway, and Framton alone in the sitting room prior to Vera's entrance) helps the film?

Explain. Do you find these sequences consistent with the tone of Saki's story? Explain.

2. Unlike the writer, a filmmaker can make use of slow motion or freeze a single image. Both techniques are used in the film, *The Open Window*. What functions do they serve in the film? Are they consistent with the tone and themes of the short story?

3. If you look at two of the characters' names, you discover that the first syllables give you "Nut" and "Sap." Do these seem to be appropriate as colloquial characterizations of Framton Nuttel and Mrs. Sappleton? Explain. In which medium, short story or film, were you more aware of the name symbolism? Why?

4. Saki's last line in the story reads, "Romance at short notice was her specialty." Explain the function of this line in the story. Do you think its non-appearance in the film makes any difference? Explain.

5. In the film, when the front door swings inward without apparent human assistance, we may momentarily share Framton Nuttel's uncertainty. However, an objective camera shot from inside the house reveals the maid who opened the door. Patterson uses the technique of hinting at the supernatural and then using objective reality to deflate the mysterious. In what other sequence is a similar technique employed?

6. The film has an interesting recurrent pattern. Each time Framton Nuttel is about to take a decisive action, something intervenes to stop him, reducing him to his typical indecisive state. The swinging open of the front door prevents him from walking away from the house; just as he is about to close the open window, Vera's unexpected voice interrupts him; similarly, when Vera finishes the story about her aunt, the sudden appearance of Mrs. Sappleton reverses his inclination to leave. To what extent does this cinematic pattern conform to the plot and/or tone of Saki's story?

7. Compare and contrast the conversation between Framton Nuttel and Mrs. Sappleton in the short story and film. Assess the quality of their conversation.

8. In the film, we see Framton Nuttel "bolt" from the room in slow motion. Then, Mrs. Sappleton's husband and brother stride into the room. The three adults form a group, with Vera positioned

outside of the group. How is the placement of the characters relevant to the way the filmmaker concludes his film? To what extent has the filmmaker invented his visuals for this scene? To what extent has he benefited from clues in Saki's story?

THE OPEN WINDOW
SUGGESTIONS FOR PAPERS

1. In a wry observation, the French with, La Rochefoucauld, once observed, "We all of us have an infinite capacity with which to withstand the suffering of others." To what extent do the story and film versions of *The Open Window* demonstrate the accuracy of his tongue-in-cheek observation? What specific story and film details support your conclusions?

2. Compare and contrast the attitudes of Saki and Richard Patterson toward Vera.

3. The director of *The Open Window*, Richard Patterson, wrote several screenplays prior to shooting his film. Comparing the first screenplay to the actual film, which changes seem most substantive? Support your judgments with relevant particulars from story, screenplay, and film.

4. Write a paper describing your initial reactions to the "ghostly" elements in *The Open Window*. How do you account for your responses?

5. Select another short story by Saki and prepare a screen adaptation of it. Be prepared to justify your adaptation.

chapter 4

The Art of Animation

Four short films, all adapted from fictional sources, testify to the artistic diversity of animation as a specialized film medium. In 1953, William Hurtz directed *The Unicorn in the Garden*, a seven-minute adaptation of James Thurber's modern fable. The film's drawings parallel Thurber's visual style. The tone of the film captures the humorist's attitude toward the battle of the sexes. Superficially, the film resembles the conventional cartoon short subject. However, its subtleties of color and imagery carry it well beyond convention to a very high level of verbal and pictorial sophistication. For example, the small, henpecked husband appears in sunshine or bright light throughout the picture; his shrewish wife is always seen in shade or shadows. Thus, the tone of Thurber's story is skillfully expressed in cinematic images. The filmmaker's personification of Dr. I. Ego enhanced Thurber's skeptical view of psychoanalysis, implied but not developed in the fable.

Contrasting sharply with Thurber's colorful and witty tale is the strange story about a man who lost his nose. Alexandre Alexeieff adapted Gogol's short story, "The Nose," in 1963. The tone of the film was haunting and strangely surrealistic, far removed from the familiar images of cartoon humor. Alexeieff's unorthodox style, pinboard animation, consisted of many hundreds of pins on a board arranged so that shadows cast by lighting them from the side produced black, white, and grey images resembling a steel engraving or lithograph. This austere technique seemed particularly appropriate for the grotesque subject matter.

In 1970, animators of the Zagreb studios in Yugoslavia created *The Masque of the Red Death,* an adaptation of the short story by Edgar Allan Poe. This brilliantly conceived film captured the sombre and macabre mood of its literary progenitor. Using oil paintings rather than line drawings, the film's powerful images recreated Poe's world of pestilence and devastation; the plague sweeps inexorably across the countryside despite man's efforts to stop it. The film's sound effects produce the same eerie and chilling impact as Poe's sound imagery. While the original story stressed the efforts of aristocrats to escape the devastation of the Red Death, the film expanded on Poe's initial paragraph to reveal the omnipresence of death among farmers, craftsmen, and monks. Not even religious self-flagellants could keep the Red Death at bay. Inside the castle inhabited by the Duke and his entourage, the Red Death is personified as an attractive masked woman. This cinematic modification reinforces Poe's hints that the gaiety of the nobility is irresponsible and immoral in the face of pestilence beyond the castle walls.

In 1972, Stephen Bosustow co-produced an animated version of Washington Irving's story, "The Legend of Sleepy Hollow," written in 1819. Unlike *The Masque of the Red Death,* which uses only music and sound effects, or *The Unicorn in the Garden* which uses dialogue, *The Legend of Sleepy Hollow* has a voice-over narration, which parallels the tongue-in-cheek style of the story. While the modern cartoon adaptation reflects the rapid rhythms of contemporary culture, it nevertheless maintains the major themes and mood of the early nineteenth-century story. Genial satire and urbane sophistication dominate the pages of Washington Irving's sketch; similarly, the filmmakers poke fun at Ichabod Crane's superstitions, vanity, and self-serving shrewdness.

In what ways do animated films differ from live-action motion pictures? In his historically-oriented book, Stephenson defines animation. He writes, ". . . an animated film is one that is created frame-by-frame."[1] What does this observation mean? Film's normal projection rate is 24 frames per second. Therefore, one minute of film requires 24x60 (seconds) or 1,440 separate frames. Theoretically, a ten-minute animated film would contain 14,400 separate drawings. Each drawing

[1]Ralph Stephenson, *The Animated Film* (New York: A. S. Barnes, 1973), p. 15.

would be slightly different in order to produce the illusion of motion as the images were projected on a screen.

In actual practice, animators have reduced their work load through several developments, particularly cell animation. The animator begins with several layers of celluloid; on one sheet he paints or draws scenic backgrounds. On another sheet, he draws an arm or leg of a character. Each piece of celluloid can be moved to a slightly different position as needed while other layers remain the same. Thus, it is not necessary to re-draw all of each separate picture to be photographed. Even with labor-saving techniques, however, it is obvious that animation is a time-consuming method of filmmaking; it also demands meticulous planning. Nothing accidentally happens into any frame.

Live-action film evolved from photography, but animation owes its beginnings to the graphic arts. The animator tends to keep his works less complex than those of a painter. Because his drawings "move," he has one immediate advantage over even a rich and complex painting. Each drawing is seen in the context of the others, and a rich content stems from the moving images. For example, in *The Masque of the Red Death*, a procession of monks raise aloft a huge white cross in a vain supplication that the spread of the pestilence be halted. The subsequent shot shows the church cemetery filled with small white crosses over graves, mute but potent evidence of the failure of religion to ward off, even momentarily, the onslaught of the Red Death. In *The Legend of Sleepy Hollow*, Ichabod Crane looks over Katrina's father's rich farm when he comes to court her. Each animal he sees—a duck, a pig, a turkey—he imagines served up on a steaming platter. This juxtaposition of images gives viewers a picture of the "real" world conjoined to Ichabod's fantasy world.

Obviously, the seemingly "real" world of animated drawings is not literally real. However, the viewer easily sheds his disbelief. A live-action film gives a very strong impression that it is depicting real events, and, to some extent, this effect is present in animated films as well. An audience has no difficulty in accepting and enjoying the animals with human qualities which so frequently appear in cartoons. In reading Thurber's fable, "The Unicorn in the Garden," a skeptic may well accept its symbolic meanings but reject any literal belief in the existence of the unicorn itself. Like the wife of the fable, he is likely to retort, "The unicorn is a mythical beast." In the animated film, however, we actually "see" the unicorn. We also see the husband's reaction to it and we watch him touch his finger to its golden horn. Not least important, we see the trail left by the unicorn after it has gone. All of these visual details testify to the reality of its existence.

The Masque of the Red Death (1970) Film art benefits from an adroit juxta-position of images. These shots reveal the "failure of religion to ward off, even momentarily, the onslaught of the Red Death." *Still shots reproduced courtesy of Contemporary/McGraw-Hill Films.*

Indeed, its reality allows us to align ourselves more readily with the husband of the fable.

Because animation is simultaneously "not real," we accept deviations from actuality that would be challenged in a live-action film. For example, when the wife of *The Unicorn in the Garden* tiptoes across a room in a parody of a ballerina's dance, we do not challenge her ability to move in such a spritely fashion. In *The Legend of Sleepy Hollow*, Ichabod's St. Vitus-like dancing generates more amusement than skepticism because of the extravagance of his movements. When Ichabod finishes consuming a multi-course meal at his student's home, he tilts back comfortably from the table and we see his slightly distended belly reflecting his gastronomical prowess. The animator does not need to justify his exaggeration. The medium condones such imagery.

In order that his animated film benefit from the conventions available to live-action photography, the animator draws in cuts and dissolves as necessary. Much as a live-action director selects bits of celluloid to be spliced together, so the animation director shoots individual frames which he organizes into sequential patterns. For a live-action film, shooting a scene with one character or a host of characters is equally feasible. For the animator, however, adding more characters means adding more drawings; a crowd scene makes greater demands of time and effort than a simpler scene. This fact of animated life tends to push toward simplification of line and the elimination of any unnecessary footage.

Color film usually adds realism to live-action photography. The animation director also controls color to set a tone. In *The Legend of Sleepy Hollow*, the red interior of Ichabod's schoolhouse suggests the traditional little red schoolhouse; the red, blood-shot eyes of Brom Bones reflect his anger with Ichabod. In one dramatic scene, the camera focuses on the severed head carried by the apparition on horseback. After a furious chase, the ghostly figure rises in its stirrups to heave its "head" at Ichabod and send him sprawling. The camera then pans over to the battered orange and black pumpkin. The next shot cuts to the wedding of Brom Bones and Katrina Van Tassel; this is a long shot dominated by an orange and black gazebo. Color thus links the two scenes and serves as the major transitional device. In *The Unicorn in the Garden*, the film opens with a blue bird flying upside-down and backwards. Later in the picture, Dr. I. Ego describes the tied-up wife as "crazy as a jaybird." Suddenly, the erratic flight of the blue bird makes sense. Similarly, color plays a significant role in *The Masque of the Red Death*. Squawking ravens appear early in the picture, and

The Legend of Sleepy Hollow (1972) "The animator does not need to justify his exaggeration. The medium condones such imagery." The viewer willingly suspends his disbelief. *Still shot reproduced courtesy of Stephen Bosustow Productions and Pyramid Films.*

their inky blackness foreshadows death. Each time a death occurs, the film's eerie sound effects are accompanied by flashes of red across the screen. Thus, red and black serve as harbingers of pestilence throughout the film. The tolling of a bell and the swinging of a bronze-colored pendulum augment the other symbols of death.

One final observation about animation merits attention. While the stage performer is limited to real space and real time, and the live-action performer is limited to real space and real time within a shot, the animator has greater flexibility. Since he draws and photographs each individual frame, he can manipulate the speed of movement as he chooses. Normally, animated action moves at a rapid pace. In *The Unicorn in the Garden*, the husband sees the unicorn and races up the stairs at appreciably greater than normal speed to announce the phenomenon to his wife. After she jeers at him, he plods down those same stairs. The speed of action is controlled entirely by the animator. In *The Legend of Sleepy Hollow*, Ichabod devours a meal so rapidly he seems to sprout extra arms to shovel in the food more expeditiously. Indeed, animation encourages an audience's suspension of disbelief.

At the Van Tassel party, Ichabod's jaws seem to become unhinged in order to accommodate the great quantity of food he devours and this is appropriate to Irving's description of him as having the dilating powers of an anaconda.

Like the live-action filmmaker, the adapter who uses animation can be held accountable for the major themes and tone of his work and the extent to which it reflects the original fictional source. Also like the live-action filmmaker, he depends on visuals and the organization of images in imaginative patterns. Both Washington Irving and Edgar Allan Poe were masters of literary style, each with clearly identifiable language patterns. In his adaptation of *The Masque of the Red Death*, the filmmaker chose to do without words entirely. In *The Legend of Sleepy Hollow*, the filmmaker reduced a very long short story to a relatively short film. While some use was made of Irving's language, visual imagery played a major role in capturing Irving's themes and tone.

A final word on the steps used to create an animated film may be helpful. After finding a subject or story, the producer will commission a writer to prepare a brief treatment. This is a short verbal description of what the film will contain (see treatments, p. 306 to 310 and p. 310 to 316). The next step is the preparation of a storyboard (see p. 317 to 358). Then come the actual drawings, the addition of color, the conjoining of words to actions, the addition of music and sound effects, and the final editing. The process is complex and carefully controlled. The final product, when it is as well-done as *The Unicorn in the Garden*, or *The Legend of Sleepy Hollow*, is a work of cinematic art meriting the same kind of critical attention as an equally sustained live-action film.

THE LEGEND OF SLEEPY HOLLOW
Washington Irving

In 1819–20, Washington Irving published a collection of sketches and stories under the title of The Sketch Book of Geoffrey Crayon. Included in the book were two of the earliest American short stories, "The Legend of Sleepy Hollow" and "Rip Van Winkle." An American romantic, Irving was the first New World writer to achieve significant literary stature abroad.

In 1972, Stephen Bosustow Productions, a three-time Academy Award winner for animation, collaborated with Pyramid Films to produce a new version of this much-anthologized story. The film has received a series of international film festival awards and much critical acclaim.

It took over a year to produce the thirteen-minute film. Two initial treatments were rejected. Then, following the development of a high-quality treatment and a stimulating storyboard, an editorial-cinematic team began work on the film. The writer-adapter, two co-producers, a literary supervisor, and a director-animator co-operated to create the final film.

FOUND AMONG THE PAPERS OF THE LATE
DIEDRICH KNICKERBOCKER

A pleasing land of drowsy head it was,
 Of dreams that wave before the half-shut eye;
And of gay castles in the clouds that pass,
 For ever flushing round a summer sky.

CASTLE OF INDOLENCE

In the bosom of one of those spacious coves which indent the eastern shore of the Hudson, at that broad expansion of the river denominated by the ancient Dutch navigators the Tappan Zee, and where they always prudently shortened sail, and implored the protection of St. Nicholas when they crossed, there lies a small market-town or rural port, which by some is called Greensburgh, but which is more generally and properly known by the name of Tarry Town. This name was given, we are told, in former days, by the good housewives of the adjacent country, from the inveterate propensity of their husbands to linger about the village tavern on market days. Be that as it may,

I do not vouch for the fact, but merely advert to it, for the sake of being precise and authentic. Not far from this village, perhaps about two miles, there is a little valley, or rather lap of land, among high hills, which is one of the quietest places in the whole world. A small brook glides through it, with just murmur enough to lull one to repose; and the occasional whistle of a quail, or tapping of a woodpecker, is almost the only sound that ever breaks in upon the uniform tranquillity.

I recollect that, when a stripling, my first exploit in squirrel-shooting was in a grove of tall walnut-trees that shades one side of the valley. I had wandered into it at noon time, when all nature is peculiarly quiet, and was startled by the roar of my own gun, as it broke the Sabbath stillness around, and was prolonged and reverberated by the angry echoes. If ever I should wish for a retreat, whither I might steal from the world and its distractions, and dream quietly away the remnant of a troubled life, I know of none more promising than this little valley.

From the listless repose of the place, and the peculiar character of its inhabitants, who are descendants from the original Dutch settlers, this sequestered glen has long been known by the name of SLEEPY HOLLOW, and its rustic lads are called the Sleepy Hollow Boys throughout all the neighboring country. A drowsy, dreamy influence seems to hang over the land, and to pervade the very atmosphere. Some say that the place was bewitched by a high German doctor, during the early days of the settlement; others, that an old Indian chief, the prophet or wizard of his tribe, held his powwows there before the country was discovered by Master Hendrick Hudson. Certain it is, the place still continues under the sway of some witching power, that holds a spell over the minds of the good people, causing them to walk in a continual reverie. They are given to all kinds of marvellous beliefs; are subject to trances and visions; and frequently see strange sights, and hear music and voices in the air. The whole neighborhood abounds with local tales, haunted spots, and twilight superstitions; stars shoot and meteors glare oftener across the valley than in any other part of the country, and the nightmare, with her whole nine fold, seems to make it the favorite scene of her gambols.

The dominant spirit, however, that haunts this enchanted region, and seems to be commander-in-chief of all the powers of the air, is the apparition of a figure on horseback without a head. It is said by some to be the ghost of a Hessian trooper, whose head had been carried away by a cannon-ball, in some nameless battle during the Revolutionary War; and who is ever and anon seen by the country folk, hurrying along in the gloom of night, as if on the wings of the

The Legend of Sleepy Hollow (1972) "The whole neighborhood abounds with local tales, haunted spots, and twilight superstitions. . . ." The animator's super-imposed images allow the viewer to "see into" the mental processes of the characters. *Still shot reproduced courtesy of Stephen Bosustow Productions and Pyramid Films.*

wind. His haunts are not confined to the valley, but extend at times to the adjacent roads, and especially to the vicinity of a church at no great distance. Indeed, certain of the most authentic historians of those parts, who have been careful in collecting and collating the floating facts concerning this spectre, allege that the body of the trooper, having been buried in the church-yard, the ghost rides forth to the scene of battle in nightly quest of his head; and that the rushing speed with which he sometimes passes along the Hollow, like a midnight blast, is owing to his being belated, and in a hurry to get back to the church-yard before daybreak.

   Such is the general purport of this legendary superstition, which has furnished materials for many a wild story in that region of shadows; and the spectre is known, at all the country firesides, by the name of the Headless Horseman of Sleepy Hollow.

It is remarkable that the visionary propensity I have mentioned is not confined to the native inhabitants of the valley, but is unconsciously imbibed by everyone who resides there for a time. However wide awake they may have been before they entered that sleepy region, they are sure, in a little time, to inhale the witching influence of the air, and begin to grow imaginative—to dream dreams, and see apparitions.

I mention this peaceful spot with all possible laud; for it is in such little retired Dutch valleys, found here and there embosomed in the great State of New York, that population, manners, and customs remain fixed; while the great torrent of migration and improvement, which is making such incessant changes in other parts of this restless country, sweeps by them unobserved. They are like those little nooks of still water which border a rapid stream; where we may see the straw and bubble riding quietly at anchor, or slowly revolving in their mimic harbor, undisturbed by the rush of the passing current. Though many years have elapsed since I trod the drowsy shades of Sleepy Hollow, yet I question whether I should not still find the same trees and the same families vegetating in its sheltered bosom.

In this by-place of nature, there abode, in a remote period of American history, that is to say, some thirty years since, a worthy wight of the name of Ichabod Crane; who sojourned, or, as he expressed it, "tarried," in Sleepy Hollow, for the purpose of instructing the children of the vicinity. He was a native of Connecticut; a State which supplies the Union with pioneers for the mind as well as for the forest, and sends forth yearly its legions of frontier woodsmen and country schoolmasters. The cognomen of Crane was not inapplicable to his person. He was tall, but exceedingly lank, with narrow shoulders, long arms and legs, hands that dangled a mile out of his sleeves, feet that might have served for shovels, and his whole frame most loosely hung together. His head was small, and flat at top, with huge ears, large green glassy eyes, and a long snipe nose, so that it looked like a weather-cock, perched upon his spindle neck, to tell which way the wind blew. To see him striding along the profile of a hill on a windy day, with his clothes bagging and fluttering about him, one might have mistaken him for the genius of famine descending upon the earth, or some scarecrow eloped from a cornfield.

His school-house was a low building of one large room, rudely constructed of logs; the windows partly glazed, and partly patched with leaves of old copy-books. It was most ingeniously secured at vacant hours, by a withe twisted in the handle of the door, and stakes set against the window shutters; so that, though a thief might get in with perfect ease, he would find some embarrassment in getting out; an idea most probably borrowed by the architect, Yost Van Houten, from the mystery of an eel-pot. The school-house stood in a rather lonely but pleasant situation, just at the foot of a woody hill, with a brook running close by, and a formidable birch tree growing at one end of it. From hence the low murmur of his pupils' voices, conning over their lessons, might be heard in a drowsy summer's day, like the hum of a bee-hive; interrupted now and then by the authoritative voice of the master, in the tone of menace or command; or, peradventure, by the appalling sound of the birch, as he urged some tardy loiterer along the flowery path of knowledge. Truth to say, he was a conscientious man, and ever bore in mind the golden maxim, "Spare the rod and spoil the child."—Ichabod Crane's scholars certainly were not spoiled.

I would not have it imagined, however, that he was one of those cruel potentates of the school, who joy in the smart of their subjects; on the contrary, he administered justice with discrimination rather than severity; taking the burthen off the backs of the weak, and laying it on those of the strong. Your mere puny stripling, that winced at the least flourish of the rod, was passed by with indulgence; but the claims of justice were satisfied by inflicting a double portion on some little, tough, wrong-headed, broad-skirted Dutch urchin, who sulked and swelled and grew dogged and sullen beneath the birch. All this he called "doing his duty by their parents"; and he never inflicted a chastisement without following it by the assurance, so consolatory to the smarting urchin, that "he would remember it, and thank him for it the longest day he had to live."

When school hours were over, he was even the companion and playmate of the larger boys; and on holiday afternoons would convoy some of the smaller ones home, who happened to have pretty sisters, or good housewives for mothers, noted for the comforts of the cupboard. Indeed it behooved him to keep on good terms with his pupils. The revenue arising from his school was small, and would have been scarcely sufficient to furnish him with daily bread, for he was a huge feeder, and though lank, had the dilating powers of an anaconda; but to help out his maintenance, he was, according to country custom in those parts, boarded and lodged at the houses of the farmers, whose children he instructed. With these he lived successively a week at a time; thus going the rounds of the neighborhood, with all his worldly effects tied up in a cotton handkerchief.

That all this might not be too onerous on the purses of his rustic patrons, who are apt to consider the costs of schooling a grievous burden, and schoolmasters as mere drones, he had various ways of rendering himself both useful and agreeable. He assisted the farmers occasionally in the lighter labors of their farms; helped to make hay; mended the fences; took the horses to water; drove the cows from pasture; and cut wood for the winter fire. He laid aside, too, all the dominant dignity and absolute sway with which he lorded it in his little empire, the school, and became wonderfully gentle and ingratiating. He found favor in the eyes of the mothers, by petting the children, particularly the youngest; and like the lion bold, which whilom so magnanimously the lamb did hold, he would sit with a child on one knee, and rock a cradle with his foot for whole hours together.

In addition to his other vocations, he was the singing-master of the neighborhood, and picked up many bright shillings by instructing the young folks in psalmody. It was a matter of no little vanity to him, on Sundays, to take his station in front of the church gallery, with a band of chosen singers; where, in his own mind, he completely carried away the palm from the parson. Certain it is, his voice resounded far above all the rest of the congregation; and there are peculiar quavers still to be heard in that church, and which may even be heard half a mile off, quite to the opposite side of the mill-pond, on a still Sunday morning, which are said to be legitimately descended from the nose of Ichabod Crane. Thus, by divers little makeshifts in that ingenious way which is commonly denominated "by hook and by crook," the worthy pedagogue got on tolerably enough, and was thought, by all who understood nothing of the labor of headwork, to have a wonderfully easy life of it.

The schoolmaster is generally a man of some importance in the female circle of a rural neighborhood; being considered a kind of idle gentlemanlike personage, of vastly superior taste and accomplishments to the rough country swains, and, indeed, inferior in learning only to the parson. His appearance, therefore, is apt to occasion some little stir at the tea-table of a farmhouse, and the addition of a supernumerary dish of cakes or sweetmeats, or, peradventure, the parade of a silver tea-pot. Our man of letters, therefore, was peculiarly happy in the smiles of all the country damsels. How he would figure among them in the church-yard, between services on Sundays! gathering grapes for them from the wild vines that overrun the surrounding trees; reciting for their amusement all the epitaphs on the tombstones; or sauntering, with a whole bevy of them, along the banks of the adjacent mill-pond; while the more bashful country bumpkins hung sheepishly back, envying his superior elegance and address.

From his half itinerant life, also, he was a kind of travelling gazette, carrying the whole budget of local gossip from house to house;

so that his appearance was always greeted with satisfaction. He was, moreover, esteemed by the women as a man of great erudition, for he had read several books quite through, and was a perfect master of Cotton Mather's history of New-England Witchcraft, in which, by the way, he most firmly and potently believed.

He was, in fact, an odd mixture of small shrewdness and simple credulity. His appetite for the marvellous, and his powers of digesting it, were equally extraordinary; and both had been increased by his residence in this spellbound region. No tale was too gross or monstrous for his capacious swallow. It was often his delight, after his school was dismissed in the afternoon, to stretch himself on the rich bed of clover, bordering the little brook that whimpered by his school-house, and there con over old Mather's direful tales, until the gathering dusk of the evening made the printed page a mere mist before his eyes. Then, as he wended his way, by swamp and stream and awful wood-land, to the farmhouse where he happened to be quartered, every sound of nature, at that witching hour, fluttered his excited imagination: the moan of the whip-poor-will from the hill-side; the boding cry of the tree-toad, that harbinger of storm; the dreary hooting of the screech-owl, or the sudden rustling in the thicket of birds frightened from their root. The fire-flies, too, which sparkled most vividly in the darkest places, now and then startled him, as one of uncommon brightness would stream across his path; and if, by chance, a huge blockhead of a beetle came winging his blundering flight against him, the poor varlet was ready to give up the ghost, with the idea that he was struck with a witch's token. His only resource on such occasions, either to drown thought, or drive away evil spirits, was to sing psalm tunes;—and the good people of Sleepy Hollow, as they sat by their doors of an evening, were often filled with awe, at hearing his nasal melody, "in linked sweetness long drawn out," floating from the distant hill, or along the dusky road.

Another of his sources of fearful pleasure was to pass long winter evenings with the old Dutch wives, as they sat spinning by the fire, with a row of apples roasting and spluttering along the hearth, and listen to their marvellous tales of ghosts and goblins, and haunted fields, and haunted brooks, and haunted bridges, and haunted houses, and particularly of the headless horseman, or galloping Hessian of the Hollow, as they sometimes called him. He would delight them equally by his anecdotes of witchcraft, and of the direful omens and portentous sights and sounds in the air, which prevailed in the earlier times of Connecticut; and would frighten them woefully with specula-tions upon comets and shooting stars; and with the alarming fact that the world did absolutely turn round, and that they were half the time topsy-turvy!

But if there was a pleasure in all this, while snugly cuddling in the chimney corner of a chamber that was all of a ruddy glow from the crackling wood fire, and where, of course, no spectre dared to show his face, it was dearly purchased by the terrors of his subsequent walk homewards. What fearful shapes and shadows beset his path amidst the dim and ghastly glare of a snowy night!—With what wistful look did he eye every trembling ray of light streaming across the waste fields from some distant window—How often was he appalled by some shrub covered with snow, which, like a sheeted spectre, beset his very path!—How often did he shrink with curdling awe at the sound of his own steps on the frosty crust beneath his feet; and dread to look over his shoulder, lest he should behold some uncouth being tramping close behind him!—and how often was he thrown into complete dismay by some rushing blast, howling among the trees, in the idea that it was the Galloping Hessian on one of his nightly scourings!

All these, however, were mere terrors of the night, phantoms of the mind that walk in darkness; and though he had seen many spectres in his time, and been more than once beset by Satan in divers shapes, in his lonely perambulations, yet daylight put an end to all these evils; and he would have passed a pleasant life of it, in despite of the devil and all his works, if his path had not been crossed by a being that causes more perplexity to mortal man than ghosts, goblins, and the whole race of witches put together, and that was—a woman.

Among the musical disciples who assembled, one evening in each week, to receive his instructions in psalmody, was Katrina Van Tassel, the daughter and only child of a substantial Dutch farmer. She was a blooming lass of fresh eighteen; plump as a partridge; ripe and melting and rosy cheeked as one of her father's peaches, and universally famed, not merely for her beauty, but her vast expectations. She was withal a little of a coquette, as might be perceived even in her dress, which was a mixture of ancient and modern fashions, as most suited to set off her charms. She wore the ornaments of pure yellow gold, which her great-great-grandmother had brought over from Saardam; the tempting stomacher of the olden time; and withal a provokingly short petticoat, to display the prettiest foot and ankle in the country round.

Ichabod Crane had a soft and foolish heart towards the sex; and it is not to be wondered at, that so tempting a morsel soon found favor in his eyes; more especially after he had visited her in her paternal mansion. Old Baltus Van Tassel was a perfect picture of a thriving, contented, liberal-hearted farmer. He seldom, it is true, sent either his eyes or his thoughts beyond the boundaries of his own farm; but within those every thing was snug, happy, and well-conditioned. He was satisfied with his wealth, but not proud of it; and piqued himself upon the hearty abundance, rather than the style in which he lived. His stronghold was situated on the banks of the Hudson, in one of those green, sheltered, fertile nooks, in which the Dutch farmers are so fond of nestling. A great elm-tree spread its broad branches over it; at the foot of which bubbled up a spring of the softest and sweetest water, in a little well, formed of a barrel; and then stole sparkling away through the grass, to a neighboring brook, that bubbled along among alders and dwarf willows. Hard by the farmhouse was a vast barn, that might have served for a church; every window and crevice of which seemed bursting forth with the treasures of the farm; the flail was busily resounding within it from morning to night; swallows and martins skimmed twittering about the eaves; and rows of pigeons, some with one eye turned up, as if watching the weather, some with their heads under their wings, or buried in their bosoms, and others swelling, and cooing, and bowing about their dames, were enjoying the sunshine on the roof. Sleek unwieldy porkers were grunting in the repose and abundance of their pens; whence sallied forth, now and then, troops of sucking pigs, as if to snuff the air. A stately squadron of snowy geese were riding in an adjoining pond, convoying whole fleets of ducks; regiments of turkeys were gobbling through the farm-yard, and guinea fowls fretting about it, like ill-tempered housewives, with their peevish, discontented cry. Before the barn door strutted the gallant cock, that pattern of a husband, a warrior, and a fine gentleman, clapping his burnished wings, and crowing in the pride and gladness of his heart—sometimes tearing up the earth with his feet, and then generously calling his ever-hungry family of wives and children to enjoy the rich morsel which he had discovered.

The pedagogue's mouth watered, as he looked upon this sump-tuous promise of luxurious winter fare. In his devouring mind's eye, he pictured to himself every roasting-pig running about with a pudding in his belly, and an apple in his mouth; the pigeons were snugly put to bed in a comfortable pie, and tucked in with a coverlet of crust; the geese were swimming in their own gravy; and the ducks pairing cosily in dishes, like snug married couples, with a decent competency of onion sauce. In the porkers he saw carved out the future sleek side of bacon, and juicy relishing ham; not a turkey but he beheld daintily trussed up, with its gizzard under its wing, and, peradventure, a necklace of savory sausages; and even bright chanticleer himself lay sprawling on his back, in a side-dish, with uplifted claws, as if craving that quarter which his chivalrous spirit disdained to ask while living.

As the enraptured Ichabod fancied all this and as he rolled his great green eyes over the fat meadow-lands, the rich fields of wheat, of rye, of buckwheat, and Indian corn, and the orchards burthened with ruddy fruit, which surrounded the warm tenement of Van Tassel, his heart yearned after the damsel who was to inherit these domains, and his imagination expanded with the idea, how they might be readily turned into cash, and the money invested in immense tracts of wild land, and shingle palaces in the wilderness. Nay, his busy fancy already realized his hopes, and presented to him the blooming Katrina, with a whole family of children, mounted on the top of a wagon loaded with household trumpery, with pots and kettles dangling beneath; and he beheld himself bestriding a pacing mare, with a colt at her heels, setting out for Kentucky, Tennessee, or the Lord knows where.

When he entered the house the conquest of his heart was complete. It was one of those spacious farmhouses, with high-ridged, but low-sloping roofs, built in the style handed down from the first Dutch settlers; the low projecting eaves forming a piazza along the front, capable of being closed up in bad weather. Under this were hung flails, harness, various utensils of husbandry, and nets for fishing in the neighboring river. Benches were built along the sides for summer use; and a great spinning-wheel at one end, and a churn at the other, showed the various uses to which this important porch might be devoted. From this piazza the wondering Ichabod entered the hall, which formed the centre of the mansion and the place of usual residence. Here, rows of resplendent pewter, ranged on a long dresser, dazzled his eyes. In one corner stood a huge bag of wool ready to be spun; in another a quantity of linsey-woolsy just from the loom; ears of Indian corn, and strings of dried apples and peaches, hung in gay festoons along the walls, mingled with the gaud of red peppers; and a door left ajar gave him a peep into the best parlor, where the claw-footed chairs and dark mahogany tables shone like mirrors; and irons, with their accompanying shovel and tongs, glistened from their covert of asparagus tops; mock-oranges and conch-shells decorated the mantelpiece; strings of various colored birds' eggs were suspended above it: a great ostrich egg was hung from the centre of the room, and a corner cupboard, knowingly left open, displayed immense treasures of old silver and well-mended china.

From the moment Ichabod laid his eyes upon these regions of delight, the peace of his mind was at an end, and his only study was how to gain the affections of the peerless daughter of Van Tassel. In this enterprise, however, he had more real difficulties than generally fell to the lot of a knight-errant of yore, who seldom had any thing but giants, enchanters, fiery dragons, and such like easily-conquered adversaries, to contend with; and had to make his way merely through gates of iron and brass, and walls of adamant, to the castle keep, where the lady of his heart was confined; all which he achieved as easily as a man would carve his way to the centre of a Christmas pie; and then the lady gave him her hand as a matter of course. Ichabod, on the contrary, had to win his way to the heart of a country coquette, beset with a labyrinth of whims and caprices, which were forever presenting new difficulties and impediments; and he had to encounter a host of fearful adversaries of real flesh and blood, the numerous rustic admirers, who beset every portal to her heart; keeping a watchful and angry eye upon each other, but ready to fly out in the common cause against any new competitor.

Among these the most formidable was a burly, roaring, roystering blade, of the name of Abraham, or, according to the Dutch abbreviation, Brom Van Brunt, the hero of the country round, which rang with his feats of strength and hardihood. He was broad-shouldered and double-jointed, with short curly black hair, and a bluff, but not unpleasant countenance, having a mingled air of fun and arrogance. From his Herculean frame and great powers of limb, he had received the nickname of BROM BONES, by which he was universally known. He was famed for great knowledge and skill in horsemanship, being as dexterous on horseback as a Tartar. He was foremost at all races and cock-fights; and, with the ascendency which bodily strength acquires in rustic life, was the umpire in all disputes, setting his hat on one side, and giving his decisions with an air and tone admitting of no gainsay or appeal. He was always ready for either a fight or a frolic; but had more mischief than ill-will in his composition; and, with all his overbearing roughness, there was a strong dash of waggish good humor at bottom. He had three or four boon companions, who regarded him as their model, and at the head of whom he scoured the country, attending every scene of feud or merriment for miles round. In cold weather he was distinguished by a fur cap, surmounted with a flaunting fox's tail; and when the folks at a country gathering descried this well-known crest at a distance, whisking about among a squad of hard riders, they always stood by for a squall. Sometimes his crew would be heard dashing along past the farmhouses at midnight, with whoop and halloo, like a troop of Don Cossacks; and the old dames, startled out of their sleep, would listen for a moment till the hurry-scurry had clattered by, and then exclaim, "Ay, there goes Brom Bones and his gang!" The neighbors looked upon him with a mixture of awe, admiration, and good-will; and when any madcap prank, or rustic brawl, occurred in the vicinity, always shook their heads, and warranted Brom Bones was at the bottom of it.

This rantipole hero had for some time singled out the blooming Katrina for the object of his uncouth gallantries, and though his amorous toyings were something like the gentle caresses and endearments of a bear, yet it was whispered that she did not altogether discourage his hopes. Certain it is, his advances were signals for rival candidates to retire, who felt no inclination to cross a lion in his amours; insomuch, that when his horse was seen tied to Van Tassel's paling, on a Sunday night, a sure sign that his master was courting, or, as it is termed, "sparking," within, all other suitors passed by in despair, and carried the war into other quarters.

Such was the formidable rival with whom Ichabod Crane had to contend, and, considering all things, a stouter man than he would have shrunk from the competition, and a wiser man would have despaired. He had, however, a happy mixture of pliability and perseverance in his nature; he was in form and spirit like a supplejack—yielding, but tough; though he bent, he never broke; and though he bowed beneath the slightest pressure, yet, the moment it was away—jerk! he was erect, and carried his head as high as ever.

To have taken the field openly against his rival would have been madness; for he was not a man to be thwarted in his amours, any more than that stormy lover, Achilles. Ichabod, therefore, made his advances in a quiet and gently-insinuating manner. Under cover of his character of singing-master, he made frequent visits at the farmhouse; not that he had anything to apprehend from the meddlesome interference of parents, which is so often a stumbling-block in the path of lovers. Balt Van Tassel was an easy indulgent soul; he loved his daughter better even than his pipe, and, like a reasonable man and an excellent father, let her have her way in everything. His notable little wife, too, had enough to do to attend to her housekeeping and manage her poultry; for, as she sagely observed, ducks and geese are foolish things, and must be looked after, but girls can take care of themselves. Thus while the busy dame bustled about the house, or plied her spinning-wheel at one end of the piazza, honest Balt would sit smoking his evening pipe at the other, watching the achievements of a little wooden warrior, who, armed with a sword in each hand, was most valiantly fighting the wind on the pinnacle of the barn. In the meantime, Ichabod would carry on his suit with the daughter by the side of the spring under the great elm, or sauntering along in the twilight, that hour so favorable to the lover's eloquence.

I profess not to know how women's hearts are wooed and won. To me they have always been matters of riddle and admiration. Some seem to have but one vulnerable point, or door of access; while others have a thousand avenues, and may be captured in a thousand different ways. It is a great triumph of skill to gain the former, but a still greater proof of generalship to maintain possession of the latter, for the man must battle for his fortress at every door and window. He who wins a thousand common hearts is therefore entitled to some renown; but he who keeps undisputed sway over the heart of a coquette, is indeed a hero. Certain it is, this was not the case with the redoubtable Brom Bones; and from the moment Ichabod Crane made his advances, the interests of the former evidently declined; his horse was no longer seen tied at the palings on Sunday nights, and a deadly feud gradually arose between him and the preceptor of Sleepy Hollow.

Brom, who had a degree of rough chivalry in his nature, would fain have carried matters to open warfare, and have settled their pretensions to the lady, according to the mode of those most concise and simple reasoners, the knights-errant of yore—by single combat; but Ichabod was too conscious of the superior might of his adversary to enter the lists against him: he had overheard a boast of Bones, that he would "double the schoolmaster up, and lay him on a shelf of his own school-house"; and he was too wary to give him an opportunity. There was something extremely provoking in this obstinately pacific system; it left Brom no alternative but to draw upon the funds of rustic waggery in his disposition, and to play off boorish practical jokes upon his rival. Ichabod became the object of whimsical persecution to Bones, and his gang of rough riders. They harried his hitherto peaceful domains; smoked out his singing school, by stopping up the chimney; broke into the school-house at night, in spite of its formidable fastenings of withe and window stakes, and turned every thing topsy-turvy: so that the poor schoolmaster began to think all the witches in the country held their meetings there. But what was still more annoying, Brom took all opportunities of turning him into ridicule in presence of his mistress, and had a scoundrel dog whom he taught to whine in the most ludicrous manner, and introduced as a rival of Ichabod's to instruct her in psalmody.

In this way matters went on for some time, without producing any material effect on the relative situation of the contending powers. On a fine autumnal afternoon, Ichabod, in pensive mood, sat enthroned on a lofty stool whence he usually watched all the concerns of his little literary realm. In his hand he swayed a ferule, that sceptre of despotic power; the birch of justice reposed on three nails, behind the throne, a constant terror to evildoers; while on the desk before him might be seen sundry contraband articles and prohibited weapons, detected upon the persons of idle urchins; such as half-munched apples, popguns, whirligigs, fly-cages, and whole legions of rampant little paper game-cocks. Apparently there had been some appalling act of justice recently inflicted, for his scholars were all busily intent upon their books, or slyly whispering behind them with one eye kept upon the master; and a kind of buzzing stillness reigned throughout the school-room. It was suddenly interrupted by the appearance of a Negro, in tow-cloth jacket and trousers, a round-crowned fragment of a hat, like the cap of Mercury, and mounted on the back of a ragged, wild, half-broken colt, which he managed with a rope by way of halter. He came clattering up to the school door with an invitation to Ichabod to attend a merry-making or "quilting frolic," to be held that evening at Mynheer Van Tassel's; and having delivered his message with that air of importance, and effort at fine language, which a Negro is apt to display on petty embassies of the kind, he dashed over the brook, and was seen scampering away up the hollow, full of the importance and hurry of his mission.

All was now bustle and hubbub in the late quiet school-room. The scholars were hurried through their lessons, without stopping at trifles; those who were nimble skipped over half with impunity, and those who were tardy had a smart application now and then in the rear, to quicken their speed, or help them over a tall word. Books were flung aside without being put away on the shelves, inkstands were overturned, benches thrown down, and the whole school was turned loose an hour before the usual time; bursting forth like a legion of young imps, yelping and racketing about the green, in joy at their early emancipation.

The gallant Ichabod now spent at least an extra half hour at his toilet, brushing and furbishing up his best, and indeed only suit of rusty black, and arranging his locks by a bit of broken looking-glass, that hung up in the school-house. That he might make his appearance before his mistress in the true style of a cavalier, he borrowed a horse from the farmer with whom he was domiciliated, a choleric old Dutchman, of the name of Hans Van Ripper, and, thus gallantly mounted, issued forth, like a knight-errant in quest of adventures. But it is meet I should, in the true spirit of romantic story, give some account of the looks and equipments of my hero and his steed. The animal he bestrode was a broken-down plough-horse, that had outlived almost everything but his viciousness. He was gaunt and shagged, with a ewe neck and a head like a hammer; his rusty mane and tail were tangled and knotted with burrs; one eye had lost its pupil, and was glaring and spectral; but the other had the gleam of a genuine devil in it. Still he must have had fire and mettle in his day, if we may judge from the name he bore of Gunpowder. He had, in fact, been a favorite steed of his master's, the choleric Van Ripper, who was a furious rider, and had infused, very probably, some of his own spirit into the animal; for, old and broken-down as he looked, there was more of the lurking devil in him than in any young filly in the country.

Ichabod was a suitable figure for such a steed. He rode with short stirrups, which brought his knees nearly up to the pommel of the saddle; his sharp elbows stuck out like grasshoppers'; he carried his whip perpendicularly in his hand, like a sceptre, and, as his horse jogged on, the motion of his arms was not unlike the flapping of a pair of wings. A small wool hat rested on the top of his nose, for so his scanty strip of forehead might be called; and the skirts of his black coat fluttered out almost to the horse's tail. Such was the appearance of Ichabod and his steed, as they shambled out of the gate of Hans Van Ripper, and it was altogether such an apparition as is seldom to be met with in broad daylight.

It was, as I have said, a fine autumnal day, the sky was clear and serene, and nature wore that rich and golden livery which we always associate with the idea of abundance. The forests had put on their sober brown and yellow, while some trees of the tenderer kind had been nipped by the frosts into brilliant dyes of orange, purple, and scarlet. Streaming files of wild ducks began to make their appearance high in the air; the bark of the squirrel might be heard from the groves of beech and hickory nuts, and the pensive whistle of the quail at intervals from the neighboring stubble-field.

The small birds were taking their farewell banquets. In the fulness of their revelry, they fluttered, chirping and frolicking, from bush to bush, and tree to tree, capricious from the very profusion and variety around them. There was the honest cock-robin, the favorite game of stripling sportsmen, with its loud querulous note; and the twittering blackbirds flying in sable clouds; and the golden-winged woodpecker, with his crimson crest, his broad black gorget, and splendid plumage; and the cedar bird, with its red-tipt wings and yellow tipt tail, and its little montero cap of feathers; and the blue jay, that noisy coxcomb, in his gay light-blue coat and white under-clothes; screaming and chattering, nodding and bobbing and bowing, and pretending to be on good terms with every songster of the grove.

As Ichabod jogged slowly on his way, his eye, ever open to every symptom of culinary abundance, ranged with delight over the treasures of jolly autumn. On all sides he beheld vast stores of apples; some hanging in oppressive opulence on the trees; some gathered into baskets and barrels for the market; others heaped up in rich piles for the cider-press. Farther on he beheld great fields of Indian corn, with its golden ears peeping from their leafy coverts, and holding out the promise of cakes and hasty pudding; and the yellow pumpkins lying beneath them, turning up their fair round bellies to the sun, and giving ample prospects of the most luxurious of pies; and anon he passed the fragrant buckwheat fields, breathing the odor of the bee-hive, and as he beheld them, soft anticipation stole over his mind of dainty slapjacks, well buttered, and garnished with honey or treacle, by the delicate little dimpled hand of Katrina Van Tassel.

Thus feeding his mind with many sweet thoughts and "sugar suppositions," he journeyed along the sides of a range of hills which look out upon some of the goodliest scenes of the mighty Hudson. The sun gradually wheeled his broad disk down into the west. The wide bosom of the Tappan Zee lay motionless and glassy, excepting that here and there a gentle undulation waved and prolonged the blue shadow of the distant mountain. A few amber clouds floated in the sky, without a breath of air to move them. The horizon was of a fine golden tint, changing gradually into a pure apple green, and from that into the deep blue of the mid-heaven. A slanting ray lingered on the woody crests of the precipices that overhung some parts of the river, giving greater depth to the dark-gray and purple of their rocky sides. A sloop was loitering in the distance, dropping slowly down with the tide, her sail hanging uselessly against the mast; and as the reflection of the sky gleamed along the still water, it seemed as if the vessel was suspended in the air.

It was toward evening that Ichabod arrived at the castle of the Heer Van Tassel, which he found thronged with the pride and flower of the adjacent country. Old farmers, a spare leathern-faced race, in homespun coats and breeches, blue stockings, huge shoes, and magnificent pewter buckles. Their brisk withered little dames, in close crimped caps, long-waisted short-gowns, homespun petticoats, with scissors and pincushions, and gay calico pockets hanging on the outside. Buxom lasses, almost as antiquated as their mothers, excepting where a straw hat, a fine ribbon or perhaps a white frock, gave symptoms of city innovation. The sons, in short square-skirted coats with rows of stupendous brass buttons, and their hair generally queued in the fashion of the times, especially if they could procure an eel-skin for the purpose, it being esteemed, throughout the country, as a potent nourisher and strengthener of the hair.

Brom Bones, however, was the hero of the scene, having come to the gathering on his favorite steed Daredevil, a creature, like himself, full of mettle and mischief, and which no one but himself could manage. He was, in fact, noted for preferring vicious animals, given to all kinds of tricks, which kept the rider in constant risk of his neck, for he held a tractable well-broken horse as unworthy of a lad of spirit.

Fain would I pause to dwell upon the world of charms that burst upon the enraptured gaze of my hero, as he entered the state parlor of Van Tassel's mansion. Not those of the bevy of buxom lasses, with their luxurious display of red and white: but the ample charms of a genuine Dutch country tea-table, in the sumptuous time of autumn. Such heaped-up platters of cakes of various and almost indescribable kinds, known only to experienced Dutch housewives! There was the doughty doughnut, the tenderer oly koek, and the crisp and crumbling cruller; sweet cakes and short cakes, ginger cakes and honey cakes, and the whole family of cakes. And then there were apple pies and peach pies and pumpkin pies; besides slices of ham and smoked beef; and moreover delectable dishes of preserved plums, and peaches, and pears, and quinces; not to mention broiled shad and roasted chickens; together with bowls of milk and cream, all mingled higgledy-piggledy, pretty much as I have enumerated them, with the motherly tea-pot sending up its clouds of vapor from the midst—Heaven bless the mark! I want breath and time to discuss this banquet as it deserves, and am too eager to get on with my story. Happily, Ichabod Crane was not in so great a hurry as his historian, but did ample justice to every dainty.

He was a kind and thankful creature, whose heart dilated in proportion as his skin was filled with good cheer, and whose spirits rose with eating as some men's do with drink. He could not help, too, rolling his large eyes round him as he ate, and chuckling with the possibility that he might one day be lord of all this scene of almost unimaginable luxury and splendor. Then, he thought, how soon he'd turn his back upon the old school-house; snap his fingers in the face of Hans Van Ripper, and every other niggardly patron, and kick any itinerant pedagogue out of doors that should dare to call him comrade!

Old Baltus Van Tassel moved about among his guests with a face dilated with content and good humor, round and jolly as the harvest moon. His hospitable attentions were brief, but expressive, being confined to a shake of the hand, a slap on the shoulder, a loud laugh, and a pressing invitation to "fall to, and help themselves."

And now the sound of the music from the common room or hall, summoned to the dance. The musician was an old grayheaded Negro, who had been the itinerant orchestra of the neighborhood for more than half a century. His instrument was as old and battered as himself. The greater part of the time he scraped on two or three strings, accompanying every movement of the bow with a motion of the head; bowing almost to the ground, and stamping with his foot whenever a fresh couple were to start.

Ichabod prided himself upon his dancing as much as upon his vocal powers. Not a limb, not a fibre about him was idle; and to have seen his loosely hung frame in full motion, and clattering about the room, you would have thought Saint Vitus himself, that blessed patron of the dance, was figuring before you in person. He was the admiration of all the Negroes; who having gathered, of all ages and sizes, from the farm and the neighborhood, stood forming a pyramid of shining black faces at every door and window, gazing with delight at the scene, rolling their white eye-balls, and showing grinning rows of ivory from ear to ear. How could the flogger of urchins be otherwise than animated and joyous? the lady of his heart was his partner in the dance; and smiling graciously in reply to all his amorous oglings; while Brom Bones, sorely smitten with love and jealousy, sat brooding by himself in one corner.

When the dance was at an end, Ichabod was attracted to a knot of the sager folks, who, with old Van Tassel, sat smoking at one end of the piazza, gossiping over former times, and drawing out long stories about the war.

This neighborhood, at the time of which I am speaking, was one of those highly-favored places which abound with chronicle and great men. The British and American line had run near it during the war; it had, therefore, been the scene of marauding, and infested with refugees, cow-boys, and all kinds of border chivalry. Just sufficient time had elapsed to enable each story-teller to dress up his tale with a little becoming fiction, and, in the indistinctness of his recollection, to make himself the hero of every exploit.

There was the story of Doffue Martling, a large blue-bearded Dutchman, who had nearly taken a British frigate with an old iron nine-pounder from a mud breastwork, only that his gun burst at the sixth discharge. And there was an old gentleman who shall be nameless, being too rich a mynheer to be lightly mentioned, who, in the battle of White Plains, being an excellent master of defence, parried a musket ball with a small sword, insomuch that he absolutely felt it whiz round the blade, and glance off at the hilt: in proof of which, he was ready at any time to show the sword, with the hilt a little bent. There were several more that had been equally great in the field, not one of whom but was persuaded that he had a considerable hand in bringing the war to a happy termination.

But all these were nothing to the tales of ghosts and apparitions that succeeded. The neighborhood is rich in legendary treasures of the kind. Local tales and superstitions thrive best in these sheltered long-settled retreats; but are trampled under foot by the shifting throng that forms the population of most of our country places. Besides, there is no encouragement for ghosts in most of our villages, for they have scarcely had time to finish their first nap, and turn themselves in their graves, before their surviving friends have travelled away from the neighborhood; so that when they turn out at night to walk their rounds, they have no acquaintance left to call upon. This is perhaps the reason why we so seldom hear of ghosts except in our long-established Dutch communities.

The immediate cause, however, of the prevalence of supernatural stories in these parts, was doubtless owing to the vicinity of Sleepy Hollow. There was a contagion in the very air that blew from that haunted region; it breathed forth an atmosphere of dreams and fancies infecting all the land. Several of the Sleepy Hollow people were present at Van Tassel's, and, as usual, were doling out their wild and wonderful legends. Many dismal tales were told about funeral trains, and mourning cries and wailings heard and seen about the great tree where the unfortunate Major André was taken, and which stood in the neighborhood. Some mention was made also of the woman in white, that haunted the dark glen at Raven Rock, and was often heard to shriek · on winter nights before a storm, having perished there in the snow. The chief part of the stories, however, turned upon the favorite spectre of Sleepy Hollow, the headless horseman, who had been heard several times of late, patrolling the country; and, it was said, tethered his horse nightly among the graves in the church-yard.

The sequestered situation of this church seems always to have made it a favorite haunt of troubled spirits. It stands on a knoll, surrounded by locust-trees and lofty elms, from among which its decent, whitewashed walls shine modestly forth, like Christian purity beaming through the shades of retirement. A gentle slope descends from it to a silver sheet of water, bordered by high trees, between which, peeps may be caught at the blue hills of the Hudson. To look upon its grass-grown yard, where the sunbeams seem to sleep so quietly, one would think that there at least the dead might rest in peace. On one side of the church extends a wide woody dell, along which raves a large brook among broken rocks and trunks of fallen trees. Over a deep black part of the stream, not far from the church, was formerly thrown a wooden bridge; the road that led to it, and the bridge itself, were thickly shaded by overhanging trees, which cast a gloom about it, even in the daytime; but occasioned a fearful darkness at night. This was one of the favorite haunts of the headless horseman; and the place where he was most frequently encountered. The tale was told of old Brouwer, a most heretical disbeliever in ghosts, how he met the horseman returning from his foray into Sleepy Hollow, and was obliged to get up behind him; how they galloped over bush and brake, over hill and swamp, until they reached the bridge; when the horseman suddenly turned into a skeleton, threw old Brouwer into the brook, and sprang away over the tree-tops with a clap of thunder.

This story was immediately matched by a thrice marvellous adventure of Brom Bones, who made light of the galloping Hessian as an arrant jockey. He affirmed that, on returning one night from the neighboring village of Sing Sing, he had been overtaken by this midnight trooper; that he had offered to race with him for a bowl of punch, and should have won it too, for Daredevil beat the goblin horse all hollow, but, just as they came to the church bridge, the Hessian bolted, and vanished in a flash of fire.

All these tales, told in that drowsy undertone with which men talk in the dark, the countenances of the listeners only now and then receiving a casual gleam from the glare of a pipe, sank deep in the mind of Ichabod. He repaid them in kind with large extracts from his invaluable author, Cotton Mather, and added many marvellous events that had taken place in his native State of Connecticut, and fearful sights which he had seen in his nightly walks about Sleepy Hollow.

The revel now gradually broke up. The old farmers gathered together their families in their wagons, and were heard for some time rattling along the hollow roads, and over the distant hills. Some of the damsels mounted on pillions behind their favorite swains, and their light-hearted laughter, mingling with the clatter of hoofs, echoed along the silent woodlands, sounding fainter and fainter until they gradually died away—and the late scene of noise and frolic was all silent and deserted. Ichabod only lingered behind, according to the custom of country lovers, to have a tête-à-tête with the heiress; fully convinced that he was now on the high road to success. What passed at this interview I will not pretend to say, for in fact I do not know. Something, however, I fear me, must have gone wrong, for he certainly sallied forth, after no very great interval, with an air quite desolate and chop-fallen.—Oh these women! these women! Could that girl have been playing off any of her coquettish tricks?—Was her encouragement of the poor pedagogue all a mere sham to secure her conquest of his rival?—Heaven only knows, not I!—Let it suffice to say, Ichabod stole forth with the air of one who had been sacking a hen-roost, rather than a fair lady's heart. Without looking to the right or left to notice the scene of rural wealth, on which he had so often gloated, he went straight to the stable, and with several hearty cuffs and kicks, roused his steed most uncourteously from the comfortable quarters in which he was soundly sleeping, dreaming of mountains of corn and oats, and whole valleys of timothy and clover.

It was the very witching time of night that Ichabod, heavy-hearted and crest-fallen, pursued his travel homewards, along the sides of the lofty hills which rise above Tarry Town, and which he had traversed so cheerily in the afternoon. The hour was as dismal as himself. Far below him, the Tappan Zee spread its dusky and indistinct waste of waters, with here and there the tall mast of a sloop, riding quietly at anchor under the land. In the dead hush of midnight, he could even hear the barking of the watch dog from the opposite shore of the Hudson; but it was so vague and faint as only to give an idea of his distance from this faithful companion of man. Now and then, too, the long-drawn crowing of a cock, accidentally awakened, would sound far, far off, from some farmhouse away among the hills—but it was like a dreaming sound in his ear. No signs of life occurred near him, but occasionally the melancholy chirp of a cricket, or perhaps the guttural twang of a bull-frog, from a neighboring marsh, as if sleeping uncomfortably, and turning suddenly in his bed.

All the stories of ghosts and goblins that he had heard in the afternoon, now came crowding upon his recollections. The night grew darker and darker; the stars seemed to sink deeper in the sky, and driving clouds occasionally hid them from his sight. He had never felt so lonely and dismal. He was, moreover, approaching the very place where many of the scenes of the ghost stories had been laid. In the centre of the road stood an enormous tulip-tree, which towered like a giant above all the other trees of the neighborhood, and formed a kind of landmark. Its limbs were gnarled, and fantastic, large enough to form trunks for ordinary trees, twisting down almost to the earth, and rising again into the air. It was connected with the tragical story of the unfortunate André, who had been taken prisoner hard by; and was universally known by the name of Major André's tree. The common people regarded it with a mixture of respect and superstition, partly out of sympathy for the fate of its ill-starred namesake, and partly from the tales of strange sights and doleful lamentations told concerning it.

As Ichabod approached this fearful tree, he began to whistle; he thought his whistle was answered—it was but a blast sweeping sharply through the dry branches. As he approached a little nearer, he thought he saw something in white, hanging in the midst of the tree—he paused and ceased whistling; but on looking more narrowly, perceived that it was a place where the tree had been scathed by lightning, and the white wood laid bare. Suddenly he heard a groan—his teeth chattered and his knees smote against the saddle: it was but the rubbing of one huge bough upon another, as they were swayed about by the breeze. He passed the tree in safety, but new perils lay before him.

About two hundred yards from the tree a small brook crossed the road, and ran into a marshy and thickly-wooded glen, known by the name of Wiley's swamp. A few rough logs, laid side by side, served for a bridge over this stream. On that side of the road where the brook entered the wood, a group of oaks and chestnuts, matted thick with wild grapevines, threw a cavernous gloom over it. To pass this bridge was the severest trial. It was at this identical spot that the unfortunate André was captured, and under the covert of those chestnuts and vines were the sturdy yeomen concealed who surprised him. This has ever since been considered a haunted stream, and fearful are the feelings of the schoolboy who has to pass it alone after dark.

As he approached the stream, his heart began to thump; he summoned up, however, all his resolution, gave his horse half a score of kicks in the ribs, and attempted to dash briskly across the bridge; but instead of starting forward, the perverse old animal made a lateral movement, and ran broadside against the fence. Ichabod, whose fears increased with the delay, jerked the reins on the other side, and kicked lustily with the contrary foot: it was all in vain; his steed started, it is true, but it was only to plunge to the opposite side of the road into a thicket of brambles and alder bushes. The schoolmaster now bestowed both whip and heel upon the starveling ribs of old Gunpowder, who dashed forward, snuffling and snorting, but came to a stand just by the bridge, with a suddenness that had nearly sent his rider sprawling over his head. Just at this moment a plashy tramp by the side of the bridge caught the sensitive ear of Ichabod. In the dark shadow of the grove, on the margin of the brook, he beheld something huge, mis-shapen, black and towering. It stirred not, but seemed gathered up in the gloom, like some gigantic monster ready to spring upon the traveller.

The hair of the affrighted pedagogue rose upon his head with terror. What was to be done? To turn and fly was now too late; and besides, what chance was there of escaping ghost or goblin, if such it was, which could ride upon the wings of the wind? Summoning up, therefore, a show of courage, he demanded in stammering accents— "Who are you?" He received no reply. He repeated his demand in a still more agitated voice. Still there was no answer. Once more he cudgelled the sides of the inflexible Gunpowder, and, shutting his eyes, broke forth with involuntary fervor into a psalm tune. Just then the shadowy object of alarm put itself in motion, and, with a scramble and a bound, stood at once in the middle of the road. Though the night was dark and dismal, yet the form of the unknown might now in some degree be ascertained. He appeared to be a horseman of large dimensions, and mounted on a black horse of powerful frame. He made no offer of molestation or sociability, but kept aloof on one side of the road, jogging along on the blind side of old Gunpowder, who had now got over his fright and waywardness.

Ichabod, who had no relish for this strange midnight companion, and bethought himself of the adventure of Brom Bones with the Galloping Hessian, now quickened his steed, in hopes of leaving him behind. The stranger, however, quickened his horse to an equal pace. Ichabod pulled up, and fell into a walk, thinking to lag behind—the other did the same. His heart began to sink within him; he endeavored to resume his psalm tune, but his parched tongue clove to the roof of his mouth, and he could not utter a stave. There was something in the moody and dogged silence of this pertinacious companion, that was mysterious and appalling. It was soon fearfully accounted for. On mounting a rising ground, which brought the figure of his fellow-traveller in relief against the sky, gigantic in height, and muffled in a cloak, Ichabod was horror-struck, on perceiving that he was headless!— but his horror was still more increased, on observing that the head, which should have rested on his shoulders, was carried before him on the pommel of the saddle: his terror rose to desperation; he rained a shower of kicks and blows upon Gunpowder, hoping, by a sudden movement, to give his companion the slip—but the spectre started full jump with him. Away then they dashed, through thick and thin; stones flying, and sparks flashing at every bound. Ichabod's flimsy garments fluttered in the air, as he stretched his long lank body away over his horse's head, in the eagerness of his flight.

They had now reached the road which turns off to Sleepy Hollow; but Gunpowder, who seemed possessed with a demon, instead of keeping up it, made an opposite turn, and plunged headlong down hill to the left. This road leads through a sandy hollow, shaded by trees for about a quarter of a mile, where it crosses the bridge famous in goblin story, and just beyond swells the green knoll on which stands the whitewashed church.

As yet the panic of the steed had given his unskilful rider an apparent advantage in the chase; but just as he had got half way through the hollow, the girths of the saddle gave way, and he felt it slipping from under him. He seized it by the pommel, and endeavored to hold it firm, but in vain; and had just time to save himself by clasping old Gunpowder round the neck, when the saddle fell to the earth, and he heard it trampled under foot by his pursuer. For a moment the terror of Hans Van Ripper's wrath passed across his mind—for it was his Sunday saddle; but this was no time for petty fears; the goblin was hard on his haunches; and (unskilful rider that he was!) he had much ado to maintain his seat; sometimes slipping on one side, sometimes on another, and sometimes jolted on the high ridge of his horse s backbone, with a violence that he verily feared would cleave him asunder.

An opening in the trees now cheered him with the hopes that the church bridge was at hand. The wavering reflection of a silver star in the bosom of the brook told him that he was not mistaken. He saw the walls of the church dimly glaring under the trees beyond. He recollected the place where Brom Bones' ghostly competitor had disappeared. "If I can reach that bridge," thought Ichabod, "I am safe." Just then he heard the black steed panting and blowing close behind him; he even fancied that he felt his hot breath. Another convulsive kick in the ribs, and old Gunpowder sprang upon the bridge; he thundered over the resounding planks; he gained the opposite side; and now Ichabod cast a look behind to see if his pursuer should vanish, according to rule, in a flash of fire and brimstone. Just then he saw the goblin rising in his stirrups, and in the very act of hurling his head at him. Ichabod endeavored to dodge the horrible missile, but too late. It encountered his cranium with a tremendous crash—he was tumbled headlong into the dust, and Gunpowder, the black steed, and the goblin rider, passed by like a whirlwind.

The next morning the old horse was found without his saddle, and with the bridle under his feet, soberly cropping the grass at his master's gate. Ichabod did not make his appearance at breakfast— dinner-hour came, but no Ichabod. The boys assembled at the school-house, and strolled idly about the banks of the brook; but no school-master. Hans Van Ripper now began to feel some uneasiness about the fate of poor Ichabod, and his saddle. An inquiry was set on foot, and after diligent investigation they came upon his traces. In one part of the road leading to the church was found the saddle trampled in the dirt; the tracks of horses' hoofs deeply dented in the road, and evidently at furious speed, were traced to the bridge, beyond which, on the bank of a broad part of the brook, where the water ran deep and black, was found the hat of the unfortunate Ichabod, and close beside it a shattered pumpkin.

The brook was searched, but the body of the schoolmaster was not to be discovered. Hans Van Ripper, as executor of his estate, examined the bundle which contained all his worldly effects. They consisted of two shirts and a half; two stocks for the neck; a pair or two of worsted stockings; an old pair of corduroy small-clothes; a rusty razor; a book of psalm tunes, full of dogs' ears; and a broken pitchpipe. As to the books and furniture of the school-house, they belonged to the community, excepting Cotton Mather's *History of Witchcraft*, a *New England Almanac*, and a book of dreams and fortune-telling; in which last was a sheet of foolscap much scribbled and blotted in several fruitless attempts to make a copy of verses in honor of the heiress of Van Tassel. These magic books and the poetic scrawl were forthwith consigned to the flames by Hans Van Ripper; who from that time forward determined to send his children no more to school; observing, that he never knew any good come of this same reading and writing. Whatever money the schoolmaster possessed, and he had received his quarter's pay but a day or two before, he must have had about his person at the time of his disappearance.

The mysterious event caused much speculation at the church on the following Sunday. Knots of gazers and gossips were collected in the churchyard, at the bridge, and at the spot where the hat and pumpkin had been found. The stories of Brouwer, of Bones, and a whole budget of others, were called to mind; and when they had diligently considered them all, and compared them with the symptoms of the present case, they shook their heads, and came to the conclusion that Ichabod had been carried off by the galloping Hessian. As he was a bachelor, and in nobody's debt, nobody troubled his head any more about him. The school was removed to a different quarter of the hollow, and another pedagogue reigned in his stead.

It is true, an old farmer, who had been down to New York on a visit several years after, and from whom this account of the ghostly adventure was received, brought home the intelligence that Ichabod Crane was still alive; that he had left the neighborhood, partly through fear of the goblin and Hans Van Ripper, and partly in mortification at having been suddenly dismissed by the heiress; that he had changed his quarters to a distant part of the country; had kept school and studied law at the same time, had been admitted to the bar, turned politician, electioneered, written for the newspapers, and finally had been made a justice of the Ten Pound Court. Brom Bones too, who, shortly after his rival's disappearance, conducted the blooming Katrina in triumph to the altar, was observed to look exceedingly knowing whenever the story of Ichabod was related, and always burst into a hearty laugh at the mention of the pumpkin; which led some to suspect that he knew more about the matter than he chose to tell.

The old country wives, however, who are the best judges of these matters, maintain to this day that Ichabod was spirited away by supernatural means; and it is a favorite story often told about the neighborhood round the winter evening fire. The bridge became more than ever an object of superstitious awe, and that may be the reason why the road has been altered of late years, so as to approach the church by the border of the millpond. The school-house being deserted, soon fell to decay, and was reported to be haunted by the ghost of the unfortunate pedagogue; and the plough boy, loitering homeward of a still summer evening, has often fancied his voice at a distance, chanting a melancholy psalm tune among the tranquil solitudes of Sleepy Hollow.

POSTSCRIPT, FOUND IN THE HANDWRITING

OF MR. KNICKERBOCKER

The preceding Tale is given, almost in the precise words in which I heard it related at a Corporation meeting of the ancient city of Man-hattoes, at which were present many of its sagest and most illustrious burghers. The narrator was a pleasant, shabby, gentlemanly old fellow, in pepper-and-salt clothes, with a sadly humorous face; and one whom I strongly suspected of being poor,—he made such efforts to be enter-taining. When his story was concluded, there was much laughter and approbation, particularly from two or three deputy aldermen, who had been asleep the greater part of the time. There was, however, one tall, dry-looking old gentleman, with beetling eyebrows, who maintained a grave and rather severe face throughout: now and then folding his arms, inclining his head, and looking down upon the floor, as if turning a doubt over in his mind. He was one of your wary men, who never laugh, but upon good grounds—when they have reason and the law on their side. When the mirth of the rest of the company had subsided, and silence was restored, he leaned one arm on the elbow of his chair, and sticking the other akimbo, demanded, with a slight, but exceedingly sage motion of the head, and contraction of the brow, what was the moral of the story, and what it went to prove?

The story-teller, who was just putting a glass of wine to his lips, as a refreshment after his toils, paused for a moment, looked at his inquirer with an air of infinite deference, and lowering the glass slowly to the table, observed, that the story was intended most logically to prove:—

"That there is no situation in life but has its advantages and pleasures—provided we will but take a joke as we find it:

"That, therefore, he that runs races with goblin troopers is likely
to have rough riding of it.

"Ergo, for a country schoolmaster to be refused the hand of a
Dutch heiress, is a certain step to high preferment, in the state."

The cautious old gentleman knit his brows tenfold closer after this
explanation, being sorely puzzled by the ratiocination of the syllogism;
while, methought, the one in pepper-and-salt eyed him with something
of a triumphant leer. At length he observed, that all this was very well,
but he thought the story a little on the extravagant—there were one or
two points on which he had his doubts.

"Faith, sir," replied the story-teller, "as to that matter, I don't believe one-half of it myself."

treatment

THE LEGEND OF SLEEPY HOLLOW

June 13, 1971

METHOD: Irving's words will be used for the narration of all descriptive passages, e.g., Ichabod's appearance, the characteristics of Sleepy
Hollow. For the sake of condensation, short bridge statements necessary
to describe the action and forward the plot will be written by the present
author.

In order to provide a tie-in with Irving's postscript, the film will
begin in a tavern, with the narrator telling the story to his listeners.
Some simplification of Irving's postscript comment will also be rendered.
Irving's nonsense syllogism is a put-down to the overly analytical
listener. It is fairly clearly a statement to the effect that, though persons
like Ichabod may be overly imaginative, it's not good to be too literal
and fact-oriented either. The film will express the same idea—but using
a less ambiguous means than the syllogism and the attendant conversation. Synch sound will be used in the tavern among the storyteller and
his listeners; voice-over narration for the body of the story.

Irving didn't seem to be pointing out any particular moral, and the film won't either. Perhaps the most original aspects of the tale are that its main characters, Ichabod and Brom Bones, are given both negative and positive qualities, and that the causes of events are shown to be multiple, complex and therefore undramatically out-of-focus, e.g., Ichabod leaves the Hollow not only because he was frightened by the Headless Horseman, but also partly because the lovely Katherine has spurned his love. In this Irving anticipates the later realist and psychological writers.

THE STORY

1. IN THE TAVERN: Open on a close-up of a pumpkin as a hand comes in with knife to cut a face in it. Pop on and off credits during this time. Camera zooms out to reveal cutter as the story teller. Tavern owner grouchily berates him for ruining a good pumpkin that's needed for pie. "The face will keep away ghosts," responds the story teller. "I don't believe in ghosts," says the owner. "Oh, but belief in ghosts is very important." "Bah! Superstition!" "Oh?" says the story teller, "Well I know a ghost story that might change your mind." Dissolve to Sleepy Hollow and the story.

2. SLEEPY HOLLOW AND ENVIRONS: Here we let Irving take over with his descriptions of the Hollow, the Dutch farmers, the history of the place, etc. Lots of lovely landscape and Brueghel-like peasants leading the lusty, simple life. The camera now moves over some of the gloomier corners of the Hollow and past nervous groups of old ladies, as the narrator describes the superstitions and ghost legends so prevalent in the valley. Then the camera picks up a small school house and zooms in on it.

3. DESCRIPTION OF ICHABOD CRANE: In the school house we see Ichabod teaching. The kids are mischievous, and Ichabod punishes them with a few raps and slashes of his birch stick. At the same time some simple reading or arithmetic lesson goes on in a random, comical fashion. Again the narrator quotes Irving, to the effect that Ichabod is, though stern, no sadist and flogs only the older boys hard. Ichabod dismisses the students for the day. They all rush out joyously, followed by Ichabod himself. We now dissolve to Ichabod at the home of the farmer he's boarding with and watch how he makes himself useful by doing chores, taking care of the baby, etc. At the same time, Irving tells us about the material situation of a rural teacher in those days, that he had to stay in the good graces of the people boarding and paying him, that he was constantly moving from one farm to the next, and so forth.

  We dissolve to Ichabod in other situations as Irving tells of his work as a singing teacher, his warm reception among the womenfolk as the reigning local intellectual, and, most important, of the long nights of ghost story-telling he and the women thrill to. Here the scene gets spooky and lots of surrealistic ghosts dissolve into and over the story-tellers. End on close-up of Ichabod's face looking nervous. Match dissolve to next.

4. DESCRIPTION OF KATHERINE VAN TASSEL: Closeup of Ichabod's face looking happy, this time as the narrator tells us that he has more pleasant activities as well, namely, the courting of the lovely Kathy. Zoom out to reveal Ichabod talking to Kathy. Now hold on her as Irving describes her. Meanwhile, the father and mother are briefly introduced, and then the two walk outdoors. Ichabod's face really lights up when he beholds the prosperous farm and reflects that this will all be his if he wins Kathy's hand. Various scenes of bulging corn cribs, ripe fields, and fat animals as this is being narrated. At the end of this sequence, the camera picks up a fierce black bull and zooms into a close-up of his tossing head. Match dissolve to next.

5. DESCRIPTION OF BROM BONES: Match dissolve from bull to head of Brom Bones. Zoom out to reveal him drinking with his buddies and then wrestling two of them at a time. Lots of background noise and shouting as the narrator tells of the redoubtable Brom. The scene ends with all of them jumping on their horses and riding off to some mischief. Along the way the point is made that Brom also wants Kathy, that he knows Ichabod is his rival, and that what he would like to do to that rival is tie him into a ball and roll him out of town.

6. BROM'S HARASSMENT OF ICHABOD: "Now Ichabod knew Brom was out to get him, but knowing the futility of pitting his strength against the mighty Brom Bones, he did his best to avoid him," says the narrator. But though Brom doesn't challenge Ichabod outright, he plays all kinds of rough tricks on him. As Ichabod enters his school one morning, a pail of water falls on his head from over the door. He steps on a loosened board and it flies up and hits him in the head. The stove coughs smoke because of its stuffed chimney, etc. As this is going on, we cut to shots of Brom and his crew peeking through the window and sniggering. Dissolve to next.

7. ICHABOD DRESSES UP FOR THE BIG PARTY AT THE VAN TASSEL'S: As we watch Ichabod's ludicrous efforts to dress himself up to look handsome—dust billows from his Sunday coat, his shirt is too short, his hair keeps sticking up, etc.—the narrator tells us that this is the big day for Ichabod; it is the perfect opportunity to ask for Kathy's

hand. Cut to fantasy of Ichabod waltzing with her; he looks as handsome as he *wishes* he looked. Then cut back to him riding an old swayback, borrowed horse to party. Just then Brom Bones gallops by on his magnificent black horse shouting insults at Ichabod. Big cloud of dust envelops him; use this as the transition to next scene.

8. PARTY AT THE VAN TASSEL'S: Much gaiety, dancing, fiddle music in the background. We see Ichabod dancing, awkwardly, but confidently, neverthless. Cut to table laden with food, everybody eating. Old Van Tassel talks to Brom Bones who is without his gang and on his good behavior.

Dissolve to same scene later. The dancing and eating has tired people, and they've settled down to less strenuous activities. Some men play cards, some drink, some sleep. In one corner a group of elderly ladies exchange ghost stories. Ichabod is with them. The story being told as we look in is that of the Headless Hessian or Headless Horseman who is supposed to have lost his head to a cannonball during the Revolutionary War and who is supposed to ride through the Hollow on certain nights carrying his head under his arm. Close-up of Ichabod hearing and getting very frightened. Cut then to Brom Bones observing that Ichabod is frightened. Narrator then provides a verbal bridge to the next scene with the simple statement that finally it becomes quite late and everybody goes home except Ichabod who stays to talk to Kathy. Dissolve to next.

9. ICHABOD RIDES HOME: From the depressed look on Ichabod's face it's obvious that the interview went badly. Here the narrator quotes a nice bit by Irving on the fickleness of women. Meanwhile, Ichabod's appearance slowly becomes less sad and more fearful: he's entering the haunted regions of Sleepy Hollow. Various scary things happen: an owl opens his eyes and hoots, a fox yaps, branches reach out like claws and tear at Ichabod's clothes, etc.

Then a black shape materializes out of the darkness. For a while it follows Ichabod in silence. Then he sees it's a horseman—and a horseman apparently carrying his head under his arm! He tries to flee, but the headless horseman keeps right behind him. The chase is hot and exciting. Finally the horseman throws the thing under his arm and hits Ichabod in the head with it. At the last second we see it's a pumpkin. When it hits Ichabod in the head, he screams and the pumpkin breaks into many orange shards which completely fill up the frame. Cut abruptly from this to the next.

10. BROM BONES MARRIES KATHERINE: As the two walk down the aisle and are wed, the narrator says that Ichabod hasn't been seen

since the night of the party, that there is speculation that the Headless
Horseman got him, and that Brom Bones seems to know something
about the affair but won't talk. The narrator then describes the life
ahead of Brom and Kathy, and the scene ends with Brom giving his new
bride a robust kiss. Dissolve to next.

11.   BACK IN THE TAVERN: We're back to synch sound, and the
storyteller is taking a drink to wet his throat. The innkeeper asks him,
"So was it Brom who threw the pumpkin at him or was it really a
ghost?" "Brom, of course." "Well, then that was no ghost story after all,
and you said you were going to prove to me that ghosts were real." "No,
I didn't. I said ghosts are real to people who think they're real. If Ichabod
hadn't believed in ghosts he wouldn't have let himself be frightened into
running away from Sleepy Hollow." "That brings up another point:
whatever happened to him?" "Oh, he went to New York City, studied
law and became quite a successful judge. You might say, believing in
ghosts didn't do him so much harm after all." End on close-up of story
teller's slyly smiling face. Dissolve to logo or silhouette of Ichabod
fleeing on his horse.

treatment
THE LEGEND OF SLEEPY HOLLOW
Joseph C. Cavella

1.   We zoom in slowly with an aerial view of Sleepy Hollow. The narrator (reading from Irving) tells us it is sleepy and quiet, which we see.
      But it is also enchanted and spooky.
      Some say it is bewitched by a High German doctor. Others say it
was the favored spot of a magic Indian wizard.
      The good inhabitants are given to telling all kinds of supernatural
stories. They say they see strange sights, hear spooky music and voices
in the air.
      Visuals for the above narration may be sequences from later ghost
scenes, particularly those with the Headless Horseman. Perhaps scenes

showing his decapitation by a cannonball. Opticals may be added to create a mood of stormy terror.

It should scare the hell out of the audience.

Now that we have their attention, we can start our story.

2. The narrator introduces Ichabod Crane. We see him striding along in all his clodhopping glory. Tall, lanky, shovel feet, hung together like a skeleton, his clothes flapping in the wind, he looks like an escaped scarecrow!

His face is foolish, smug, vain, venal, and above all, comical. He is poor, poor, poor, and continuously, ravenously hungry.

3. We see him in his little schoolhouse at the head of his class and know he is a schoolteacher.

We see how he regards his little scholars by the embroidered sampler on the wall: "Spare the rod and spoil the child."

Crack! we see the rod whacking little hands, bottoms, backs, legs. Ichabod does his duty with enthusiasm!

He swats one particular little boy, but then remembers something. He checks his pockets and finds that, as usual, he's penniless. He screws his face into a grin and pats the head of the boy he recently injured.

4. Ichabod is walking home with the same little tyke. We can see he despises the tot, but he clumsily butters him up, which tells us Ichabod is unprincipled.

5. And this is why he played up to the little shaver. He's sitting at a broad country table shoveling food into his bottomless mouth.

The boy's mother, the best cook in the valley, is racing back and forth with plates, trying to stay ahead of his voracity.

In amazement, people line up to watch him. He eats his way right into the night.

When he's finished, he's not ungrateful. He does chores—and at the same time shows off his ambidexterity. He washes the dishes, rocks a cradle, amuses a toddler, sings and dances, all at the same time.

6. Later, in his room, he enjoys his favorite pastime, reading Cotton Mather's *History of New England Witchcraft*.

We see by his shaking hands that he believes every word of it.

He takes a kind of foolish pleasure in frightening himself.

7. He goes out of his way to get spooked. We see him on a winter night, sitting by the fire listening to an old Dutch wife tell tales of ghosts and goblins and haunted fields and houses, and especially, especially of the Galloping Hessian.

The Legend of Sleepy Hollow (1972) "While listening, all snug by the chimney, Ichabod is only mildly apprehensive." Ichabod almost seems to solicit the thrill of apprehension. His superstitious credulity leads to his being hoist by his own petard. *Still shot reproduced courtesy of Stephen Bosustow Productions and Pyramid Films.*

While listening, all snug by the chimney, Ichabod is only mildly apprehensive. But afterwards, on his way home, what fearful shapes and shadows beset his path amidst the dim and ghostly glare of the snowy night!

How wistfully he eyes the yellow light from a distant window.

He shrinks from the lonely sound of his own feet.

Every sound of nature at that witching hour makes his heart beat wildly.

The foreboding cry of a tree toad.

The dreary hooting of a screech owl.

The sudden rustle of birds frightened from a thicket.

A demonic-looking snow-covered shrub.

Terrified, he looks over his shoulder, expecting to see the Galloping Hessian close behind him!

But all is still and white . . . then, there is a sudden, screaming blast of wind and his hands fly to his throat.

8.   Later, on a fine summer day, Ichabod is giving singing lessons to the blooming Katrina Van Tassel at the sumptuous farmhouse of her wealthy Dutch father.

Ichabod loves to watch her tender face form sweet, round vowels.

But we can see she is a coquette and quite capable, on a whim, of breaking his foolish heart.

And who watches from outside the window?

He's broad-shouldered, with black, curly hair and a pleasant Dutch face. He's Brom Bones, who, until Ichabod's arrival, was the hero of the countryside and Katrina's betrothed.

And he's fuming with jealousy!

Brom knows he cannot regain Katrina's affections by physically assaulting an obviously weaker opponent, so he employs his natural inclination for fun and mischief.

He prods his talented dog to mimic Ichabod with a ludicrous howl.

Katrina is displeased, and sends Brom on his way. Brom leaves, but he is burning with the hot fires of jealousy and revenge.

Ichabod is smug and joyful. Katrina has brushed aside the main impediment to his pursuit of her affections.

9.   Passing through the Van Tassel property on his way home, Ichabod has visions of successfully courting the fair Katrina. He makes up his mind then and there to seek her hand in marriage—and soon!

His eye roams over the well-stocked Dutch farm.

He spies little porkers and immediately imagines each on a spit with an apple in its mouth.

Strutting turkeys are suddenly on plates swimming in gravy.

Ducks roasted to a succulent brown.

Hogs carved into bacon and juicy hams.

Hens daintily trussed up on serving dishes.

After relishing the livestock, Ichabod assesses the fat meadowlands.

Rich fields of wheat, rye, and Indian corn.

Orchards laden with ripe fruit.

How he sighs and yearns for the blooming Katrina Van Tassel— who is an only daughter and will inherit these domains!

10.   Some time later, Ichabod, sitting at the head of his class, is handed a note. It is an invitation from Katrina to attend a party at her father's mansion. He is all hustle and bustle.

Ichabod drives his scholars through their lessons.

The nimble students skip over their lessons. The tardy ones get their rears cracked!

Finally, Ichabod can wait no longer, and releases the class an hour early.

The children pour out of the schoolhouse screaming with joy.

11.   Ichabod gets himself ready for the party. He washes and brushes, scrapes and scours.

He imagines himself appearing before his mistress in the true style of a cavalier, and sees an admiring Van Tassel bestow upon him his total wealth.

He is certain that tonight he will win the heiress's hand.

Before a cracked piece of looking-glass, he arranges his scraggly hair into curled locks. Tonight's the night!

12.   Ichabod is gallantly mounted on his borrowed steed—a broken-down plow-horse, gaunt, scraggly, with a knotted mane, a head like a hammer, and one good eye in which lurks the devil.

Ichabod is a suitable rider for such a steed, for he lurches along with his long bony limbs folded up like a grasshopper's, his arms flapping like wings.

As he approaches the Van Tassel mansion, his eye cannot resist ranging over the culinary treasure of the farm.

Vast stores of apples. Great fields of corn. Plump yellow pumpkins.

He sees visions of Katrina's dimpled hand serving him buttered flapjacks dripping with honey.

He races toward his goal!

13.   Ichabod enters the mansion. He is immediately enraptured.

Not by the bevy of buxom lasses, but by the real Dutch food set out on stout tables.

Platters of boiled shad. Roasted chickens. Cakes. Doughnuts. Pies and preserves of every kind.

Ichabod grows faint from the aroma alone.

He starts at one end of the table and systematically works his way to the other end, doing justice to every dish.

He rolls his eyes and chuckles. Soon he will be lord of all this luxury and splendor.

14.   The music starts. Ichabod chooses for his partner the lady of his heart.

Katrina smiles graciously in reply to all his amorous oglings.

Ichabod grows ecstatic.

His dancing grows more splendiferous.

He prides himself on his dancing. When he's inspired, not a fiber in him is idle. To see his loosely hung frame in full motion, clattering about the room, is to see Saint Vitus himself before you!

He is the admiration of all present.

Except Brom Bones, who, smitten with love and jealousy, sits brooding in a corner.

15.   When the dance ends, the good Dutch country folks fall naturally to telling tales of ghosts and apparitions.

Ichabod's eyes grow wide as he absorbs every detail.

Soon the very air seems to speak of haunted regions and funeral trains and mourning cries and inhuman wailings and women in white shrieking in the dark glen at Raven Rock.

Ichabod trembles in every limb.

Then comes their favorite spectre—the Headless Horseman. It is clearly established that he has been heard recently in the churchyard among the graves.

Brom Bones, alert to Ichabod's total credulity, adds to the tales his own personal encounter with the ghost. He relates how just last night he raced the Horseman home. And just before he reached the church bridge, the spirit bolted and vanished in a flash of fire!

To Brom's satisfaction and delight, Ichabod is terror-stricken.

16.   The revel breaks up. Old farmers with their families are heard rattling off in their wagons toward home.

Ichabod lingers behind with the heiress, fully convinced that tonight she will accept him. But after a brief conversation, he turns, quite desolate and crestfallen, and leaves. Was her encouragement all a sham? Did she use him to make Brom Bones jealous?

17.   The heavy-hearted Ichabod goes to the stable and arouses his steed with several hardy cuffs and kicks.

18.   He is plodding toward home. It is the witching hour. The night is quiet except for a far-off cock crowing and the melancholy chirp of the crickets.

All the stories of ghosts and goblins come crowding into his brain.

The night grows darker and darker.

He approaches the very place where many of the ghosts were said to appear.

He begins to whistle.

He sees something white hanging in a tree.

Looking more carefully, he observes that it is a white place where the bark was stripped.

He hears a groan. It is two large branches rubbing together.

His teeth begin to chatter.

His heart begins to pound.

He gives his horse a kick in the sides.

The horse plunges from one side of the road to the other, then finally forward, then skids to a stop.

In the dark shadow of a grove of trees, Ichabod beholds a huge, misshapen mass. Black and towering.

His hair stands on end. What should he do?

He shuts his eyes tightly, he beats his horse, and involuntarily bursts forth into a fervent psalm-tune. The old horse lumbers forward.

Ichabod feels momentarily relieved, until he cautiously opens one eye and spies none other than the Headless Horseman trotting alongside!

He is terrified.

He quickens his pace. The Horseman does likewise. He slows to a walk. The apparition does the same.

He tries to sing, but his tongue is glued to the roof of his mouth.

He flails the horse into a sudden gallop.

This puts him momentarily out front, but it also slides the saddle loose. Ichabod clasps the charging animal around the neck and hangs on.

He looks over his shoulder and sees the goblin right behind him.

Then, looking ahead, he sees the church bridge, where Brom Bones said the headless phantom vanished in a flash of fire.

He looks back, expecting to see this very spectacle, but to his horror, he sees instead the horseman hurling his head at him. He tries to dodge, but the horrible missile clouts him in the back of the neck.

Ichabod is completely terrified. He loses his grip and tumbles off the horse and runs for his life.

The head rolls to a stop. We see it is actually a pumpkin!

19.   We see Katrina and Brom Bones at their wedding party.

The narrator tells us that since Ichabod's encounter with the headless horseman, he was never seen again in Sleepy Hollow. There is much speculation about what happened to him. The old Dutch wives say he was carried off by the Galloping Hessian. And what about the pumpkin found at the scene the next morning? Whenever it is mentioned, Brom Bones breaks into laughter—which leads some to believe he knows more about it than he will say.

1

2

In a remote period of American history, there was among the high hills, not far from Tarrytown, a

drowsy little Dutch settlement long known as Sleepy Hollow.

3

4

There are some who say that this enchanted region was bewitched. By a High German doctor.

Music

5

6

7

8

9

10
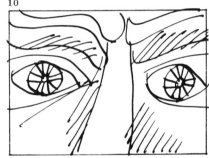

Others say that an Indian wizard held his pow-wows here.

11

12

Music

13

Certain it is that some power held a spell over the minds of the good people.

14

The whole neighborhood abounded with local tales of haunted spots and twilight superstitions and the

15

most fearsome spirit of all—the Headless Horseman.

16

Music

17

Now it happened that a very peculiar school teacher came to Sleepy Hollow. His name was Ichabod Crane.

18

And to see him striding along with his tattered clothes fluttering about him, one might have mistaken him for the spectre of Famine descending upon the earth.

19

20

Music

21

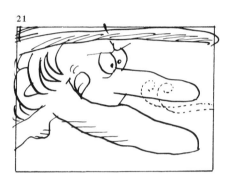

22

23

24

25

26

His schoolhouse, on a crisp winter day, buzzed with the low murmur of his

pupils' voices, interrupted now and then by the authoritative voice of the master, accompanied by the

27

28

crack of a birch stick. (wack)

(wack)

29

30

 (wack)

(wack)

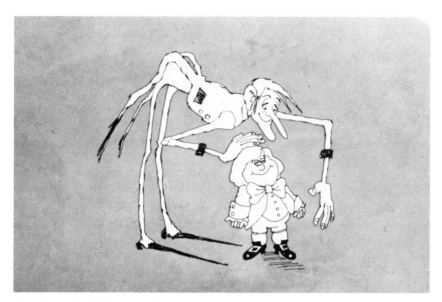

The Legend of Sleepy Hollow (1972) Utilizing the art of juxtaposition, the filmmaker sets up a contrast between the tattered skinny kids birched by Ichabod Crane and the chubby well-dressed student whose mother is "noted for the comforts of the cupboard." The juxtaposition also characterizes Ichabod as opportunistic. *Still shot reproduced courtesy of Stephen Bosustow Productions and Pyramid Films.*

31

(wack)

32

(wack)

33

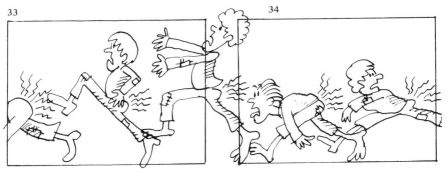

34

Ichabod's scholars were not spoiled.

And all of this he called "doing his duty."

35

36

He was not, as you may have imagined, one of those cruel potentates

37

38

of the school who joy in the smarting
of his subjects.

39

40

He administered justice with discrimination rather than severity.

41

42

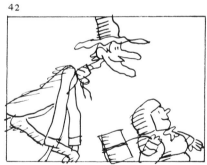

When school hours were over, he
would often walk a student home.

43

44

Especially the ones who had mothers who were noted

for the comforts of the cupboard.

45

46

(Music)

47

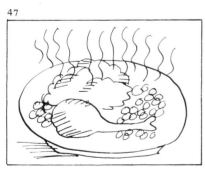

48

49

50

51

52

53

54

55

56

57

58

59
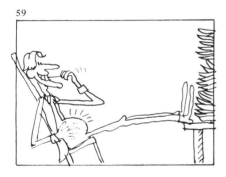

60

61

62
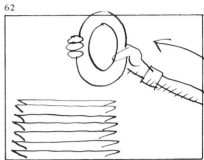

And knowing that his rustic patrons   masters as mere drones, he would
were apt to consider school-

63

render himself useful and agreeable.

64

65

(Then late at night,)   sitting by the fire, he listened to old
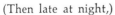

66

Dutch wives' tales of ghosts and

67

goblins

68

and haunted fields and

69

especially

70

the tale of the Headless

71

Horseman.

72

73

While listening, all snug by the chimney, Ichabod was only mildly apprehensive.

But afterwards, on his walk homeward, what fearful shapes and shadows beset his path.

74

Music

75

76

77

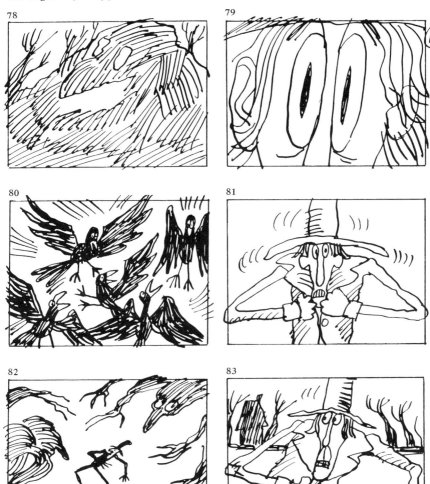

84

85

86

87
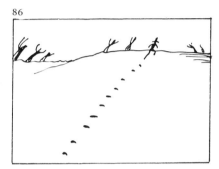

Music turns pastoral.

88

89

Among Ichabod's musical disciples was Katrina Van Tassel, the daughter and only heir of a substantial Dutch farmer.

On his way to her house, Ichabod rolled his great green eyes over her father's fat meadowlands.

90

91

92

93

94

95

How he sighed and yearned for the   who would inherit all these domains!
blooming Katrina Van Tassel

102

(Music)

103

(Ichabod singing)

104

(Katrina singing)

105

106

107

Ichabod's most formidable rival was Brom Bones, who until Ichabod's arrival was the hero of the countryside and Katrina's suitor.

108

109

110

111

Ichabod loved to watch her tender face form sweet round vowels.

Brom fumed with jealousy, but he knew he could not regain Katrina's affections by physically assaulting an obviously weaker opponent,

112

113

so he employed his natural inclination for fun and mischief.

(Ichabod singing)

114

(Dog howling)

115

(Howl)

116

Katrina sent Brom away.

117

Brom left, but he vowed revenge.

118

Ichabod rejoiced. Katrina had brushed aside the main impediment to his pursuit of her affections.

119

(Transition music)

120

121

Some time later,

122

123

Ichabod was handed a note.

124

125

An invitation to attend a party at the   (woosh)
Van Tassel mansion.

126

127

(Music)

128

129

130

131

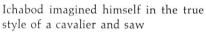

Ichabod imagined himself in the true style of a cavalier and saw an admiring Van Tassel bestowing upon him his total wealth.

132

133

(Music)

134

135

He was certain that tonight he would win the heiress's hand.

136

137

Ichabod, gallantly mounted on a borrowed steed, lurched along toward the Van Tassel estate.

It was toward evening

138

when Ichabod arrived.

139

When he entered, the conquest of his heart was complete.

140

A world of charms burst upon his enraptured gaze—not those of the bevy of buxom lasses, but the ample charms of a genuine Dutch country table.

141

142

Ichabod was a peculiar creature

143

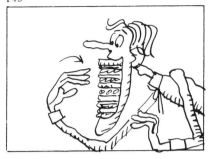

whose spirits rose with eating

144

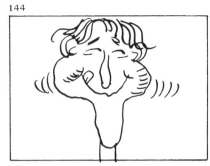

as some men's do with drink.

145

(Music)

146

147

Ichabod prided himself on his
dancing

148

as much as on his vocal powers.

149

150

Not a limb, not a fibre about him was idle. To see his loosely hung

151

frame in full motion, clattering

152

about the room, you would think

153

Saint Vitus himself was whirling

154

before you in person.

155

156

He was the admiration of all present

157

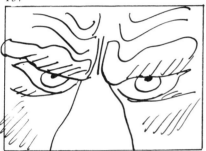

158

—except Brom Bones.   When the dance was at an end, Icha-
                                        bod was attracted to a group of

159

older folks who sat and doled out their wild and wonderful legends.

160

161

Many dismal tales were told about

funeral trains and mourning cries and wailings.

162

163

Some mention was made of the Woman in White who haunted the dark glen at Raven Rock. She

was often heard to shriek on winter nights before a storm.

164

165

Brom Bones, seeing Ichabod trembling in every limb, immediately added a tale of his own, an encounter with their favorite spectre

166

—the Headless Horseman of
Sleepy Hollow.

167

He affirmed that returning one

168

night from a neighboring village,

169

he had been overtaken by the
midnight trooper himself!

170
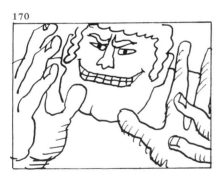

He raced him home,

171

and just as

172

they came to the church bridge, the Headless Horseman bolted and vanished

173

in a flash of fire.

174

To Brom's satisfaction and delight, Ichabod was terror-stricken!

175

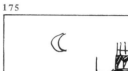

(Transition music—people saying goodbye)

176

Ichabod lingered behind, according to the custom of country lovers,

177

fully convinced that he had won her heart. What passed between them no one knows.

178

179

But something went wrong. Was her encouragement of the poor pedagogue all a

mere sham to secure her conquest of his rival?

180

181

Ichabod, heavy-hearted and crest-fallen, pursued his way homeward.

182

183

It was the witching hour.

All the stories of ghosts and goblins now came crowding upon his recollections.

184

185

The night grew darker and darker.

He had never felt so lonely and dismal.

186

187

He was, moreover, approaching the very place where many of the scenes of the ghost stories had been laid.

188

189

(Music)

190

191

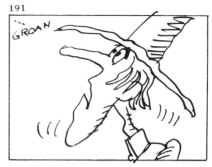

(Groan)

192

193

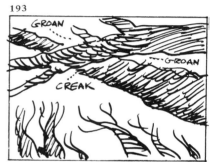

(Groan—Creak—Groan)   (Groan)

194

195

196

197

198

199

200

201

202

203

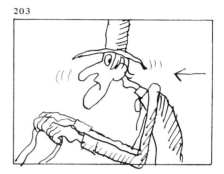

204

205

(Music cue)

206

AHEM ....

207

208

209

210

211

212

213

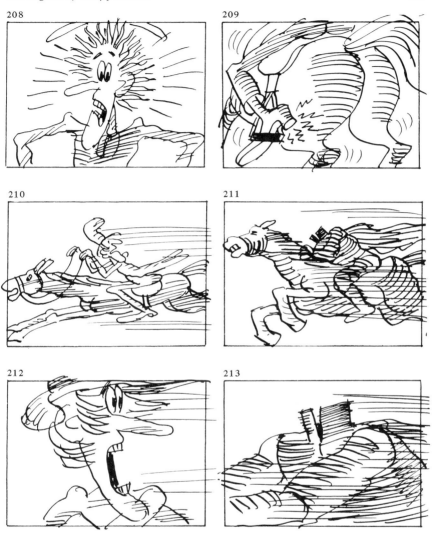

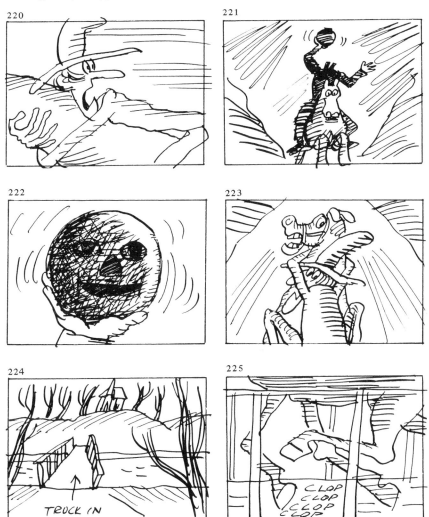

220

221

222

223

224

TRUCK IN

225

CLOP
CLOP
CLOP
CLOP

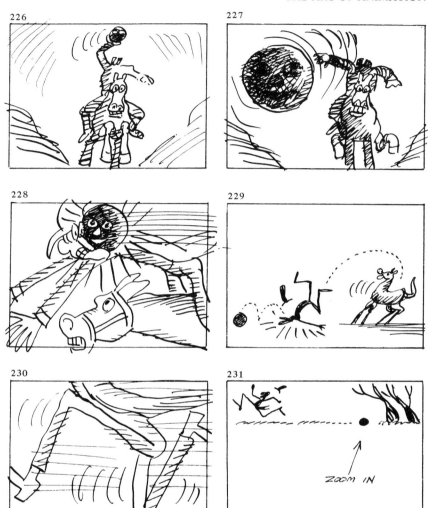

232

233

(Wedding music)

234

Ichabod was never again seen in that region.

235

The event caused much speculation.

236

Many stories were called to mind and diligently considered and compared.

237

But in the end, the old Dutch wives, who are the best judges in these matters, maintained that Ichabod was spirited away by the Headless Horseman.

238

239

| STORYBOARD/DIRECTION: SAM WEISS |
| FINISHED ART: BILL DAVIS |
| ANIMATION: VICENTE BASSOLS |

And to this day, it is a favorite story
often told about the neighborhood.

THE LEGEND OF SLEEPY HOLLOW
QUESTIONS

1. Washington Irving's short story appeared in 1819; the film adapta-
    tion was released in 1972. In what significant ways does each
    reflect its time period?

2. The filmmaker incorporated a pie sequence at the beginning of the
    movie. What major functions does this invented sequence have?

3. Assess the decision to use animation in the film adaptation of the
    story.

4. The film version of *The Legend of Sleepy Hollow* uses an off-
    screen narrator. How closely does the tone of his narration parallel
    the narration in Washington Irving's story?

5. How has the filmmaker handled those aspects of the Washington
    Irving story that could be described as male chauvinism and racial
    bigotry?

6. Are there elements in Washington Irving's portrayal of Ichabod
    Crane that anticipate Mark Twain's Connecticut Yankee, Herman
    Melville's Confidence Man, or the historic Daniel Boone? If so,
    have any of these elements been incorporated into the film version
    of *The Legend of Sleepy Hollow?*

7. To what extent do both the short story and the film intermingle
    humor and terror in their chase sequences?

8. Do the film and story use similar or different proportions of understatement and exaggeration for comic purposes?

9. What judgment did the filmmaker come to regarding the use of Washington Irving's postscript in his adaptation? Assess the merit of his judgment.

10. Compare the student Ichabod accompanies home to the ones he whacks in the film version. Contrast the filmmaker's treatment of this incident with Washington Irving's treatment. What inferences flow from each?

11. Irving describes Ichabod's listening to ghost stories at night as a source of "fearful pleasure." Given Ichabod's propensity, is there a kind of poetic justice in what happens to him? Does the filmmaker retain Washington Irving's point of view toward Ichabod's predilection for "fearful pleasure"?

THE LEGEND OF SLEEPY HOLLOW
SUGGESTIONS FOR PAPERS

1. Washington Irving describes Ichabod Crane as "an odd mixture of shrewdness and simple credulity." To what extent does the filmmaker illustrate Irving's characterization? Support your position with relevant particulars from the film.

2. Compare and contrast the use of food imagery in film and story.

3. Prior to seeing the screen adaptation, what were your expectations? In what ways did the actual film differ from your expectations?

4. Both Washington Irving and the filmmakers elected not to use any dialogue in the scene in which Katrina Van Tassel rejects Ichabod. Assume you are writing a scene for a stage production; re-create the scene using dialogue.

5. Read Washington Irving's short story, "Rip Van Winkle." What cinematic problems would this story present to a filmmaker? How would you cope with the difficulties?

film critique

THE LEGEND OF SLEEPY HOLLOW

Mahlon Woirhaye

Joseph Cavella, in his animated film version of "The Legend of Sleepy Hollow," boldly characterizes the bony schoolmaster and briefly runs through the plot of Washington Irving's leisurely tale, cleverly adapting the short story to the film medium with appropriate additions and deletions.

In the film, Ichabod Crane is the epitome of a gluttonous, vain, superstitious, bullying hypocrite. In the story, Crane (as in whooping) is caricatured as having "hands that dangled a mile out of his sleeves, feet that might have served for shovels, . . . and a long snipe nose that looked like a weathercock." No cartoonist is likely to go beyond Irving's hyperbolic description. The film's pipe-stem scarecrow with its elongated nose and chin recreates the spirit of Irving's characterization more faithfully than a living actor would ever be able to.

The unwary reader does not realize that gluttony is Ichabod's main characteristic until half way through the story. Irving spends some twenty lines describing Katrina Van Tassel, but devotes more than six times that space to her father's farm and livestock. Ichabod imagines the animals transformed into various sumptuous dishes. Many of Ichabod's characteristics are described in terms of food: "His appetite for the marvellous, and his powers of digesting it, were equally extraordinary. . . . No tale was too gross or monstrous for his capacious swallow." Katrina is "plump as a partridge: ripe and melting and rosy cheeked as one of her father's peaches." She was "so tempting a morsel." Ichabod is "feeding his mind with many sweet thoughts and 'sugar supposi-tions.'" In the film Ichabod's first action, which is the filmmaker's invention, is to follow his nose to a pie which is cooling on a window sill. Just as he reaches out, the pie is snatched away. This scene alerts us to his appetite and his hypocrisy, and is a foreshadowing of his ultimate failure as a suitor of Katrina. Three additional scenes hilariously portray Ichabod's incredible appetite and concern for food. (More time is spent emphasizing his gluttony than on all his other characteristics put together.) The film ignores the story's more subtle hints of gluttony, but does full justice to the story's major eating scenes.

We see evidence of Ichabod's vanity in the singing, bathing, and dancing scenes. Ichabod is a ludicrous figure in the singing and the dancing scenes to both the reader and the viewer. Actually hearing him sing a few notes and watching him dance is perhaps even funnier than reading that "his voice resounded far above the rest of the congregation; and there are peculiar quavers still to be heard in the church. . . ." The filmmaker invents a shot in which Ichabod intervenes to prevent Brom Bones from dancing with Katrina. In both media, however, the narrator says, "You would think Saint Vitus himself was whirling before you in person." In the bathing scene the film is clearly more comic than the story. Irving informs us in mock-heroic tone that, "The gallant Ichabod now spent an extra half hour at his toilet . . ." followed by four lines of particulars. The filmmaker invents a bath scene. A skinny man vaingloriously scrubbing himself in a laundry tub is a ridiculously funny figure indeed.

Both the film and the story make several references to the mysterious legends handed down by the folks of Sleepy Hollow and the superstitious nature of Ichabod Crane. The film uses surrealistic visual effects to create spooky scenes but, in keeping with the story, the narration hints that the viewer should take these with a pinch of salt. Both film and story emphasize the Headless Horseman legend. Seeing the nervous reaction of Ichabod to the fireside stories, and his fear when he encounters the Horseman, affected me more than reading about them. This was probably because the sudden appearance of scary images on the screen frightened me; then I could laugh a little at my fright, and a little more at Ichabod's frightened appearance.

In the early part of the story when I read that Ichabod did not spare the rod, I did not absolutely decide that he was a bully. In both versions the narrator says, "I would not have it imagined, however, that he was one of those cruel potentates of the school." In the story this line is playfully sarcastic. The film amuses us because during this comment, Ichabod is laying on the birch, and right afterwards spares the rod so that he can fill his stomach. The inconguity of what we see and hear is the filmmaker's approximation of the story's sarcasm. When our amusement ends, we clearly realize that Ichabod is an out and out villain on this score. It would be inappropriate to leave any doubts about this, because unless the viewer perceives that Ichabod is a bully, he will not be able to fully relish Brom Bones's treatment of Ichabod later in the film.

Three scenes in the film emphasize Ichabod's hypocrisy. In the pie scene, the schoolmaster who supposedly is a model of rectitude is revealed as a potential thief. In the bully scene, Ichabod's favoritism toward the plump boy is clearly unfair. Irving writes that Ichabod tells a "smarting urchin that he would remember it, and thank him for it the longest day he had to live," and the reader is amused at the half-truth of this remark. The final example of Ichabod's hypocrisy comes in the gluttony scene: we see that Ichabod is more impressed by the richness of the farm and the food potential of the livestock than he is by Katrina's beauty. We realize Katrina is only a means to the end of filling his stomach. The film narrator amuses us by intoning, "How he sighed and yearned for the blooming Katrina who would inherit all this domain." Irving's humor is compactly and not unsuitably captured in this scene.

There is a third-person narration in both the story and film. The filmmaker resisted any temptations he might have felt to let the characters speak. All we hear from Ichabod is a few notes of song. Had the characters begun speaking, the filmmaker would have put himself in the difficult position of inventing dialogue for the entire film, which would make the film more his story than Irving's, or he would have had to switch from dialogue to narration, which might have had a jarring effect on the viewer. Finally, he would have lost the irony which comes through when the narrator makes a comment about the "gallant" Ichabod while on screen we see him behaving in a gluttonous, vain, or bullying manner. The film, surprisingly enough, contains almost all of the plot elements and scenes which are portrayed in the twenty-six–page story.

My final comments concern the additions and deletions of foreshadowing elements, comic elements, and the postscript.

The pie scene, the scenes in which Ichabod hears of the Headless Horseman, and the suspended hearts scene all foreshadow future events. Only the Headless Horseman scenes appear in the story. I earlier expressed approval of the pie scene. I do not like the suspended hearts scene, however. It clearly indicates that Katrina loves only Brom. The story gives no such clear indication of her feelings; the reader, of course, forms an opinion on the matter. If the filmmaker felt it was necessary to make a statement about Katrina's feelings, he should have found a method that was more in keeping with the tone of the story.

The story contains one foreshadowing element that I especially enjoyed. As Ichabod is on his way to the party, he passes through fields where "small birds were taking their farewell banquets," and a patch containing almost human pumpkins that "turn their fair bellies to the sun." The story also tells of Brom Bones's horsemanship, his midnight rides, and his pranks. The film, rightly I believe, underplays these, revealing his prankishness in the scene with the howling hound.

The filmmaker added several comic incidents that I enjoyed. The rollicking old-time banjo music was perhaps suggested by Irving's description of the Negro fiddler at the party. Upon receiving the party invitation, Ichabod, in very fast action, leaves the school for his bath. In the story Ichabod dismisses school an hour early. The fast eating shots and the spider arm shots were also very amusing.

The film left out the postscript. This is appropriate inasmuch as readers may have some confusion about its meaning. Some readers suspect that the narrator is poking fun at a high personage at the table who started from a low background. It could be that this "tall" gentleman with "beetling-eyebrows" and elbows sticking "akimbo" was in his youth a schoolmaster.

THE MASQUE OF THE RED DEATH
Edgar Allan Poe

A major figure in the emergence of the early American short story, Poe frequently accentuated the bizarre and grotesque. "The Masque of the Red Death" first appeared in 1842 in Graham's Magazine.

Among contemporary animators, none has achieved the cinematic reputation for artistic and creative excellence earned by the filmmakers at the Zagreb school of animation in Yugoslavia. Their ten-minute film based on the Poe story has garnered awards at prestigious film festivals. It was produced in 1970.

Following the short story is a shot analysis of the film, a written detailed description of each individual shot in the motion picture. The purpose of a shot analysis is to re-create for the viewer the sequence of images he has previously seen. A shot analysis is not a substitute for the movie. It does, however, come as close as possible to reproducing in verbal terms the visual experience.

The "Red Death" had long devastated the country. No pestilence had ever been so fatal, or so hideous. Blood was its Avator and its seal—the redness and the horror of blood. There were sharp pains, and sudden dizziness, and then profuse bleeding at the pores, with dissolution. The scarlet stains upon the body and especially upon the face of the victim, were the pest ban which shut him out from the aid and from the sympathy of his fellowmen. And the whole seizure, progress and termination of the disease, were the incidents of half an hour.

But the Prince Prospero was happy and dauntless and sagacious. When his dominions were half depopulated, he summoned to his presence a thousand hale and lighthearted friends from among the knights and dames of his court, and with these retired to the deep seclusion of his castellated abbeys. This was an extensive and magnificent structure, the creation of the prince's own eccentric yet august taste. A strong and lofty wall girdled it in. This wall had gates of iron. The courtiers, having entered, brought furnaces and massy hammers and welded the bolts. They resolved to leave means neither of ingress or egress to the sudden impulses of despair or of frenzy from within. The abbey was amply provisioned. With such precautions the courtiers might bid defiance to contagion. The external world could take care of itself. In the meantime it was folly to grieve, or to think. The prince had provided all the appliances of pleasure. There were buffoons, there were improvisatori, there were ballet-dancers, there were musicians, there was Beauty, there was wine. All these and security were within. Without was the "Red Death."

It was toward the close of the fifth or sixth month of his seclusion, and while the pestilence raged most furiously abroad, that the Prince Prospero entertained his thousand friends at a masked ball of the most unusual magnificence.

It was a voluptuous scene, that masquerade. But first let me tell of the rooms in which it was held. There were seven—an imperial suite. In many palaces, however, such suites form a long and straight vista, while the folding doors slide back nearly to the walls on either hand, so that the view of the whole extent is scarcely impeded. Here the case was very different; as might have been expected from the duke's love of the *bizarre*. The apartments were so irregularly disposed that the vision embraced but little more than one at a time. There was a sharp turn at every twenty or thirty yards, and at each turn a novel effect. To the right and left, in the middle of each wall, a tall and narrow Gothic window looked out upon a closed corridor which pursued the windings of the suite. These windows were of stained glass whose color varied in accordance with the prevailing hue of the decorations of the chamber into which it opened. That at the eastern extremity was hung, for example, in blue—and vividly blue were its windows. The second chamber was purple in its ornaments and tapestries, and here the panes were purple. The third was green throughout, and so were the casements. The fourth was furnished and lighted with orange—the fifth with white— the sixth violet. The seventh apartment was closely shrouded in black velvet tapestries that hung all over the ceiling and down the walls, falling in heavy folds upon a carpet of the same material and hue. But in this chamber only, the color of the windows failed to correspond with the decorations. The panes here were scarlet—a deep blood color. Now in no one of the seven apartments was there any lamp or candelabrum, amid the profusion of golden ornaments that lay scattered to and fro or depended from the roof. There was no light of any kind emanating from lamp or candle within the suite of chambers. But in the corridors that followed the suite, there stood, opposite to each window, a heavy tripod, bearing a brazier of fire that projected its rays through the tinted glass and so glaringly illumined the room. And thus were produced a multitude of gaudy and fantastic appearances. But in the western or black chamber the effect of the firelight that streamed upon the dark hangings through the blood-tinted panes, was ghastly in the extreme, and produced so wild a look upon the countenances of those who entered, that there were few of the company bold enough to set foot within its precincts at all.

It was in this apartment, also, that there stood against the western wall, a gigantic clock of ebony. Its pendulum swung to and fro with a dull, heavy, monotonous clang; and when the minute-hand made the circuit of the face, and the hour was to be stricken, there came from the brazen lungs of the clock a sound which was clear and loud and deep and exceedingly musical, but of so peculiar a note and emphasis that, at each lapse of an hour, the musicians of the orchestra were constrained to pause, momentarily, in their performance, to hearken to the sound; and thus the waltzers perforce ceased their evolutions; and there was a brief disconcert of the whole gay company; and, while the chimes of the clock yet rang, it was observed that the giddiest grew pale, and the more aged and sedate passed their hands over their brows as if in confused revery or meditation. But when the echoes had fully ceased, a light laughter at once pervaded the assembly; the musicians looked at each other and smiled as if at their own nervousness and folly, and made whispering vows, each to the other, that the next chiming of the clock should produce in them no similar emotion; and then, after the lapse of sixty minutes (which embrace three thousand and six hundred seconds of the Time that flies), there came yet another chiming of the clock, and then were the same disconcert and tremulousness and meditation as before.

But, in spite of these things, it was a gay and magnificent revel. The tastes of the duke were peculiar. He had a fine eye for colors and effects. He disregarded the *decora* of mere fashion. His plans were bold and fiery, and his conceptions glowed with barbaric lustre. There are some who would have thought him mad. His followers felt that he was not. It was necessary to hear and see and touch him to be *sure* that he was not.

He had directed, in great part, the movable embellishments of the seven chambers, upon occasion of this great *fête;* and it was his own guiding taste which had given character to the masqueraders. Be sure they were grotesque. There were much glare and glitter and piquancy and phantasm—much of what has been since seen in "Hernani." There were arabesque figures with unsuited limbs and appointments. There were delirious fancies such as the madman fashions. There was much of the beautiful, much of the wanton, much of the *bizarre,* something of the terrible, and not a little of that which might have excited disgust. To and fro in the seven chambers there stalked, in fact, a multitude of dreams. And these—the dreams—writhed in and about, taking hue from the rooms, and causing the wild music of the orchestra to seem as the echo of their steps. And, anon, there strikes the ebony clock which stands in the hall of the velvet. And then, for a moment, all is still, and all is silent save the voice of the clock. The dreams are stiff-frozen as they stand. But the echoes of the chime die away—they have endured but an instant—and a light, half-subdued laughter floats after them as they depart. And now again the music swells, and the dreams live, and writhe to and fro more merrily than ever, taking hue from the many tinted windows through which stream the rays from the tripods. But to the chamber which lies most westwardly of the seven, there are now none of the maskers who venture, for the night is waning away; and there flows a ruddier light through the blood-colored panes; and the blackness of the sable drapery appalls; and to him whose foot falls upon the sable carpet, there comes from the near clock of ebony a muffled peal more solemnly emphatic than any which reaches *their* ears who indulge in the more remote gayeties of the other apartments.

But these other apartments were densely crowded, and in them beat feverishly the heart of life. And the revel went whirlingly on, until at length there commenced the sounding of midnight upon the clock. And then the music ceased, as I have told; and the evolutions of the waltzers were quieted; and there was an uneasy cessation of all things as before. But now there were twelve strokes to be sounded by the bell of the clock, and thus it happened, perhaps, that before the last echoes of the last chime had utterly sunk into silence, there were many individuals in the crowd who had found leisure to become aware of the presence of a masked figure which had arrested the attention of no single individual before. And the rumor of this new presence having spread itself whisperingly around, there arose at length from the whole company, a buzz, or murmur, expressive of disapprobation and surprise—then, finally, of terror, of horror, and of disgust.

In an assembly of phantasms such as I have painted, it may well be supposed that no ordinary appearance could have excited such sensation. In truth the masquerade license of the night was nearly unlimited; but the figure in question had out-Heroded Herod, and gone beyond the bounds of even the prince's indefinite decorum. There are chords in the hearts of the most reckless which cannot be touched without emotion. Even with the utterly lost, to whom life and death are equally jests, there are matters of which no jest can be made. The whole company, indeed, seemed now deeply to feel that in the costume and bearing of the stranger neither wit nor propriety existed. The figure was tall and gaunt, and shrouded from head to foot in the habiliments of the grave. The mask which concealed the visage was made so nearly to resemble the countenance of a stiffened corpse that the closest scrutiny must have had difficulty in detecting the cheat. And yet all this might have been endured, if not approved, by the mad revellers around. But the mummer had gone so far as to assume the type of the Red Death. His vesture was dabbled in *blood*—and his broad brow, with all the features of the face, was besprinkled with the scarlet horror.

When the eyes of Prince Prospero fell upon this spectral image (which with a slow and solemn movement, as if more fully to sustain its *rôle*, stalked to and fro among the waltzers) he was seen to be convulsed, in the first moment, with a strong shudder either of terror or distaste; but, in the next, his brow reddened with rage.

"Who dares?" he demanded hoarsely of the courtiers who stood near him—"who dares insult us with this blasphemous mockery? Seize him and unmask him—that we may know whom we have to hang at sunrise, from the battlements!"

It was in the eastern or blue chamber in which stood the Prince Prospero as he uttered these words. They rang throughout the seven rooms loudly and clearly—for the prince was a bold and robust man, and the music had become hushed at the waving of his hand.

It was in the blue room where stood the prince, with a group of pale courtiers by his side. At first, as he spoke, there was a slight rushing movement of this group in the direction of the intruder, who at the moment was also near at hand, and now, with deliberate and stately step, made closer approach to the speaker. But from a certain nameless awe with which the mad assumptions of the mummer had inspired the whole party, there were found none who put forth hand to seize him; so that, unimpeded, he passed within a yard of the prince's person; and, while the vast assembly, as if with one impulse, shrank from the centres of the room to the walls, he made his way uninterruptedly, but with the same solemn and measured step which had distinguished him from the first, through the blue chamber to the purple—through the purple to the green—through the green to the orange—through this again to the white—and even thence to the violet, ere a decided movement had been made to arrest him. It was then, however, that Prince Prospero, maddening with rage and the shame of his own momentary cowardice, rushed hurriedly through the six chambers, while none followed him on account of a deadly terror that had seized upon all. He bore aloft a drawn dagger, and had approached, in rapid impetuosity, to within three or four feet of the retreating figure, when the latter, having attained the extremity of the velvet apartment, turned suddenly and confronted his pursuer. There was a sharp cry—and the dagger dropped gleaming upon the sable carpet, upon which, instantly afterwards, fell prostrate in death the Prince Prospero. Then, summoning the wild courage of despair, a throng of the revellers at once threw themselves into the black apartment, and, seizing the mummer, whose tall figure stood erect and motionless within the shadow of the ebony clock, gasped in unutterable horror at finding the grave-cerements and corpse-like mask which they handled with so violent a rudeness, untenanted by any tangible form.

And now was acknowledged the presence of the Red Death. He had come like a thief in the night. And one by one dropped the revellers in the blood-bedewed halls of their revel, and died each in the despairing posture of his fall. And the life of the ebony clock went out with that of the last of the gay. And the flames of the tripods expired. And Darkness and Decay and the Red Death held illimitable dominion over all.

shot analysis
THE MASQUE OF THE RED DEATH

1. FADE IN: Titles on red background.

A
McGRAW-HILL
CONTEMPORARY
FILM

2. Music. A medieval instrumental type of music used at various times in the film. It includes violin, horn, and harpsichord.

Blue background.

Zagreb Film	Contemporary Films
Zagreb	McGraw-Hill
	New York

Production Supervision
Leo R. Dratfield

FADE OUT:

3.   FADE IN:

CLOSE-UP: A bronze pendulum occupies about one quarter of the frame. It swings from right to left and stops. It makes a gong-like sound similar to that of a large grandfather clock. The gong sound stops; we hear a swishing sound, as though someone switched a stick through the air twice.

CUT TO:

4.   The screen turns red to the accompaniment of a twanging sound over the sound of a high wind. The gong sound is muted in the background.

CUT TO:

5.   Titles. On red background, storm-sound under combined with the sound of a whip lash interposed at each title cut.
                maska crvene smrt:

CUT TO:

6.   Masque of the red death

CUT TO:

7.   le masque de la mort rouge

CUT TO:

8.   die maske des roten todes

CUT TO:

9.   Screen red. Wind sound. Screen becomes darker.

FADE TO:

10.   LONG SHOT: Still. A bluish grey screen. At the left is a horseman in a pale grey cowled monk's robe seated on a pale grey horse. The camera moves in slowly to a close-up of the rider's faceless head in cowl. Wind sound over.

CUT TO:

11.   LONG SHOT: A brownish-grey screen suggesting a plain or countryside. The rider, in lower left foreground, crosses to the right, diagonally lower, and exits frame. Wind sound with gong in background.

CUT TO:

12.   Dark brown countryside. Camera pans right. Crow appears in right corner foreground; another crow appears as squawks are heard.

PAN TO:

13. Crows in center of frame. They fly up, diagonally right, out of frame. Camera pans with them. Wind and flapping sounds. Screeching.

CUT TO:

14. Camera pans right across brown countryside.

CUT TO:

15. LONG SHOT: Three men with hoes are bent over in the center of screen. They wear blue and white against a bluish sky. They fill frame diagonally from lower left to upper right. For a moment, they do not move. Then, they hoe four strokes in unison.

CUT TO:

16. THREE-SHOT: The man at left looks up; then the other two look up together as swish/swish sounds are heard over.

CUT TO:

17. CLOSE-UP: One man's face centered in frame; he looks up awed and stricken, his face sepia. The sky is red. Wind sound over.

CUT TO:

18. CLOSE-UP: The man screams. He throws his hands up. Wind sound.

CUT TO:

19. CLOSE-UP: He covers his face with his hands. Wind sound.

CUT TO:

20. CLOSE-UP: Man's forearm and hand in center of frame on dark background. Wind sound.

CUT TO:

21. CLOSE-UP: Rippling wire sounds over. The arm sinks and the hand drops out of frame. The background dissolves to a brownish red, and then red. The camera pulls away to reveal . . .

CUT TO:

22. LONG SHOT: Three white corpses sprawled across the lower part of the frame, their hoes dropped at random around them. Black background. Erratic drumming and wind sounds.

CUT TO:

23. LONG SHOT: Brown countryside. Wind hiss and hushed gong sounds in distance. The pendulum appears superimposed over countryside in top half of frame. The pendulum swings; camera pans right across countryside with the swinging pendulum superimposed over.

CUT TO:

24. LONG SHOT: Two carpenters. They are planing and hammering a long wooden beam. Pendulum and wind sounds over. They look up and left.

CUT TO:

25. Frame turns red at upper left corner, the rest blue.

CUT TO:

26. Screen goes red. Wind sound.

CUT TO:

27. LONG SHOT: The carpenters looking up. A scream.

CUT TO:

28. Frame fades through shades of red to brown. Wind sound and muted scream over.

CUT TO:

29. LONG SHOT: The men lie dead, looking almost skeletal. A bell sounds. A shadow of the upper portion of the horseman enters frame from lower left and crosses right. Wind hissing sound. Sound of crows echo.

CUT TO:

30. LONG SHOT: Sepia screen. Bloated dead animal; outskirts of farm or town. Low wind sound over.

CUT TO:

31. LONG SHOT: Camera pans right across sepia countryside past ruins from which black smoke is rising. Sound of a strong wind building up.

PAN TO:

32. Smoke coming from a ruin; a crow in lower right corner of frame. Wind sound over.

CUT TO:

33. MEDIUM SHOT: Three crows in center of frame. Crows squawk. Pause. The crows fly up right abruptly and out of frame. Squawks merge into a dirge-like hymn.

CUT TO:

34. CLOSE-UP: A large white wooden cross diagonally across screen; its top is up left. Continuing gong sound and dirge-like chant.

CUT TO:

35. CLOSE-UP: The cross is carried out of frame. Sound of church bell.

CUT TO:

36. LONG SHOT: Three monks, the one at right in yellow bearing the cross, and two others in white moving right behind him. Sound becomes dirge-like hymn. Wind sound and bells tolling.

CUT TO:

37. LONG SHOT: Monks move right. More enter frame from left. It is a procession. Hymn and bell sounds.

CUT TO:

38. LONG SHOT: Procession of monks. Two in left foreground with hands upraised. Three monks pass behind, two in yellowish habits, one in reddish-brown. One monk in right background with hands raised heavenward. Hymn and bell sounds.

CUT TO:

39. LONG SHOT: Procession of monks crossing right in background. In center foreground, a shirtless hooded flagellant lashes himself with a whip. Sounds of whip, hymn, and bell.

CUT TO:

40. LONG SHOT: Procession, led by the bearer of the cross, mounts a hill. In the background, a white chapel stands on a smaller hill. Sounds of hymns and bells.

CUT TO:

41. CLOSE-UP: Chapel bell tower. Bell rings; its rope is pulled from below. Bell clangs rapidly over hymn.

PAN TO:

42. LONG SHOT: Camera pans down to reveal a cowled monk tugging at the rope. Clanging sounds of bell merge with hymn.

CUT TO:

43. LONG SHOT: Still. Black smoke is billowing from a fire in center. It seems to be moving closer, encompassing more and more of the screen. Monks still are left center; they lift the cross, as in supplication. The camera zooms in.

CUT TO:

44. CLOSE-UP: Cross. The screen goes red behind the white cross. Wild rushing sounds over.

CUT TO:

45. LONG SHOT: The monks below the huge cross look up in terror. Red background and wind sound.

CUT TO:

46. LONG SHOT: Chapel graveyard filled with small white crosses.

CUT TO:

47. CLOSE-UP: Bell tower. Fast pan down from tower and camera pulls back to reveal the horseman in foreground riding from center to right and out of frame. Gong sound like pendulum.

FADE OUT:

48. Black. Fade in on full front view of a pale castle with the drawbridge lowered. Crow sounds over. The camera closes in. The drawbridge closes with a clang. A reddish blotch appears. The camera moves in to a CLOSE-UP on the closed drawbridge.

DISSOLVE TO:

49. Reddish blotch is revealed to be a door. Camera zooms in on inner door in the castle. It clangs shut.

CUT TO:

50. CLOSE-UP: Another door clangs shut.

CUT TO:

51. CLOSE-UP: Another door slams shut.

CUT TO:

52. CLOSE-UP: Exterior castle window slammed shut. Sounds of slamming windows and doors. Music: harpsichord, then violins.

CUT TO:

53. CLOSE UP: Bronze chalice. A skeletal white hand with four opulent rings reaches out for it from left, clasps it, and lifts it out of frame. Music over.

CUT TO:

54. CLOSE-UP: Prospero. He holds the chalice as if for a toast. He drinks.

CUT TO:

55. MEDIUM SHOT: Prospero flanked by two bodies in blue.

CUT TO:

56. LONG SHOT: Color. Banquet room. Nobles seated at a long table in background; others on sides. A bearer brings in a tray to the duke from right.

CUT TO:

57. LONG SHOT: Focus left. People drinking.

CUT TO:

58. LONG SHOT: Focus right. People drinking.

CUT TO:

59. LONG SHOT: People toast each other.

CUT TO:

60. CLOSE-UP: Duke. Center. Drinking.

CUT TO:

61. CLOSE UP: Group of three looking right. Center man in red tapping forefinger and thumb together.

CUT TO:

62. CLOSE-UP: Right. Two men.

CUT TO:

63. CLOSE-UP: Center. A nobleman.

CUT TO:

64.   Same as 63, reverse angle.

CUT TO:

65.   CLOSE-UP: A couple facing left.

CUT TO:

66.   MEDIUM SHOT: Center. Two men face each other and drink.

CUT TO:

67.   MEDIUM SHOT: Center. A man lies drunk, his head across the table. A woman to his right raises her glass as if to toast him. She drinks. The man raises his head and reaches for his glass. He knocks it over and the wine spills in a large dark red stain that runs down the table-cloth right. Music stops as wine spills and stain spreads.

CUT TO:

68.   MEDIUM SHOT: Prospero. He claps his hands: once, twice. Sound of clapping over.

CUT TO:

69.   LONG SHOT: Banquet room. A bright red jester takes three leaps across the room from right to left, placing himself before the duke, his back to the camera. We hear the thumps his feet make on the floor. He does a flip and leaps onto the table, picks up a lute, flips back to the floor, bows to the duke, and begins to strum the instrument.

CUT TO:

70.   CLOSE-UP: Lute. Jester's hand completes strumming stroke.

CUT TO:

71.   MEDIUM SHOT: Jester plays lute and begins a ballad in French. Melody is dirge-like. Some cacophonous sounds are combined with it.

CUT TO:

72.   LONG SHOT: Banquet hall. Grey group. Camera moves in from lower left diagonally up to duke in background partly blocked by jester with his back to camera in foreground.

CUT TO:

73.   CLOSE-UP: Jester's face facing right and singing.

The Masque of the Red Death (1970) The jester's melody is dirgelike, fore-shadowing events to come. Thematically, death is no respecter of rank. *Still shot reproduced courtesy of Contemporary/McGraw-Hill Films.*

CUT TO:

74.   THREE-SHOT: Two women face left. A man turns his head as the jester reaches the sobbing part of his song.

CUT TO:

75.   MEDIUM SHOT: Jester, left, faces diagonally right as he sings. Wind sound.

CUT TO:

76.   LONG SHOT: Pan right to left across nobles (greyish) and MEDIUM SHOT of jester with back to camera. Wind sounds become louder, but music returns. The duke is barely visible over the jester. The jester sings, "Et quoi?"

CUT TO:

77.   LONG SHOT: Same scene. Jester's words are, "Et que vois tu la?" Pan right to left across nobles. Man on left raises his left hand toward his heart.

CUT TO:

78. CLOSE-UP: Jester's hand picking lute.

CUT TO:

79. MEDIUM SHOT: Jester sings, "Je vois des milles gens ensemble."

CUT TO:

80. LONG SHOT: Colorful group of nobles. Man and woman face away from camera. Woman moves her head in time with music. Man moves his head nodding to his partner. Third man moves his hand.

CUT TO:

81. CLOSE-UP: Jester singing.

CUT TO:

82. CLOSE-UP: Jester's hand as he plays lute.

CUT TO:

83. CLOSE-UP: Same as 81. Jester singing. Pan to nobles at table. Camera pulls back to LONG SHOT.

CUT TO:

84. LONG SHOT: Jester. In center, he bows, rises; his face seems to be a grinning skull. Gasps from his audience.

CUT TO:

85. LONG SHOT: Prospero at center table, shocked. Horrified grey nobles at his side.

CUT TO:

86. CLOSE-UP: Jester's hand holding skull mask before his face. He pulls the mask away and reveals his own face, grinning. Moments of silence.

CUT TO:

87. MEDIUM SHOT: The duke smiles and then claps twice. Laughter and applause over.

CUT TO:

88. LONG SHOT: Four grey musicians playing. Lilting, medieval music.

CUT TO:

89. MEDIUM SHOT: Prospero, standing. He holds a mask to his face. Gong sound.

CUT TO:

90. MEDIUM SHOT: Lady in blue lifts a mask to her face. Gong sound.

CUT TO:

91. MEDIUM SHOT: A man lifts mask also. Gong sound.

CUT TO:

92. LONG SHOT: A large hall. Pillar left. A procession of nobles in couples dance into frame from right to left. Music of dance dominant.

CUT TO:

93. MEDIUM SHOT: Dancers remove masks to the beat of the music and look forward. Swishing sound comes at the end of their movement.

CUT TO:

94. LONG SHOT: A lady, masked, moves from left to right and approaches the dancers. Swishing sounds continue.

CUT TO:

95. LONG SHOT: Dancers facing center in muted tones of red and brown. The masked lady passes in front of them moving toward right. She is dressed in grey-white.

CUT TO:

96. MEDIUM SHOT: Prospero. He sees the masked lady; he raises his hand to stop others who have approached from left side of frame toward masked lady. Then, he exits from frame after her. Music is atonal.

CUT TO:

97. LONG SHOT: Curtains swish. Masked lady is down right. The duke enters frame from between the curtains, far up center left. Sound of wire brushes across cymbals. Lilting music up; atonal music stops.

CUT TO:

98. CLOSE-UP: Masked woman raises her glass and drinks.

CUT TO:

99. CLOSE UP: Prospero, facing right, raises his glass and drinks.

CUT TO:

100. TWO-SHOT: They toast each other.

CUT TO:

101. CLOSE-UP: As the duke drinks, his glass covers his face.

CUT TO:

102. LONG SHOT: Castle hall. Pillars lower left and upper right. The masked woman moves behind the upper pillar. The duke pursues.

CUT TO:

103. MEDIUM SHOT: Castle hall in brown. Camera pulls back to LONG SHOT. The woman and duke walk with arms linked from left to right.

CUT TO:

104. MEDIUM SHOT: Prospero and masked woman look into each other's eyes. They cross right and stop. He kisses her hand. She exits frame right.

CUT TO:

105. LONG SHOT: Castle hall. The woman crosses right out of frame.

CUT TO:

106. A dark curtain. The duke parts the curtains.

CUT TO:

107. LONG SHOT: A dark room. The woman stands in the right corner. She lifts her arm.

CUT TO:

108. CLOSE-UP: Woman removes her mask and smiles.

CUT TO:

109. MEDIUM SHOT: The duke looks right. Then, he smiles.

CUT TO:

110. MEDIUM SHOT: The woman holds her arm outstretched. She drops her necklace; sound of the necklace as it hits the floor.

CUT TO:

111.   MEDIUM SHOT: Prospero's back. The curtains fall closed.

CUT TO:

112.   MEDIUM SHOT: The duke bends over, hands clasped.

CUT TO:

113.   MEDIUM SHOT: The woman's head disappears behind a door on the right. The door closes with a muted slam.

CUT TO:

114.   MEDIUM SHOT: The duke crosses the room to the right quickly and stealthily. He holds his hands expectantly before him.

CUT TO:

115.   LONG SHOT: The duke stands at a tiny door in the upper right corner of the frame. He knocks; there is no response. As he hunches his shoulders preparatory to breaking in, the music rises. He crashes in.

CUT TO:

116.   MEDIUM SHOT: Prospero looking right. His hands are clasped expectantly.

CUT TO:

117.   LONG SHOT: A bedroom. A curtained bed in upper right section of frame, an apparently nude woman reclining on it. The camera closes to a MEDIUM SHOT. The sound of curtains on rods is heard as the bed curtains fall closed.

CUT TO:

118.   CLOSE-UP: Bed from reverse angle. Pillow and part of the sheets. As the camera pulls away, the curtains at right part and reveal the duke. The camera zooms back; the bed is empty. To the left is the open side of the bed; to the right is a pillar. The woman disappears behind the pillar.

CUT TO:

119.   CLOSE-UP: Grey curtains part to reveal a pendulum on high. The music stops. As curtains part, there is a tolling sound like a church bell. The camera moves down to reveal the duke below holding the curtains open. The pendulum beat gets louder.

CUT TO:

120. LONG SHOT: A red tile floor. The camera moves up center frame to reveal a woman's feet and legs in the upper right hand corner; then, the whole woman. Music is up as a flute and guitar expand on the pendulum's beating sound. The sound intensity increases through the entire shot. The back of the duke's head appears and rises up in the center of the screen until his head fills the frame. The duke moves away from the camera to a MEDIUM SHOT. The woman's hands come over the duke's shoulders and they embrace. Then they sink down out of the frame. As they drop from sight, the swishing whip-like sound recurs. The black background flickers to red. There are discordant sounds that become a hissing. The woman rises into the center of a frame in a CLOSE-UP. She grins.

DISSOLVE TO:

121 CLOSE-UP. Her face becomes thin, dark, demonic.

DISSOLVE TO:

122. CLOSE-UP: Her face becomes a grinning skull.

CUT TO:

123. CLOSE-UP: The empty hood, the figure of death, faces left.

CUT TO:

124. MEDIUM SHOT: Prospero stares up, horrified. He screams and raises his hand defensively.

CUT TO:

125. LONG SHOT: Prospero. He backs up left. He pulls out a knife, begins to raise it, drops it, and collapses. Sound of knife clanking on tiles followed by wild rushing sounds.

CUT TO:

126. MEDIUM SHOT: Cowled faceless figure moves out of frame. Music including sound of pendulum beating.

CUT TO:

127. LONG SHOT: Prospero's skeletal body up center. The shadow of the hooded figure is lower left crossing from right to left. It exits frame. Pendulum beat increases. Focus on the duke's body and pan up.

CUT TO:

128. CLOSE UP: Pendulum. Still. Pendulum begins to swing with wider and wider sweeps; it maintains the beat.

CUT TO:

129. LONG SHOT: Exterior of castle in upper left background. The hooded horseman in lower center rides off right out of frame. Music ceases, pendulum beat continues.

FADE OUT TO:

130–135. Credits on black. Single musical tone.

FADE OUT

THE MASQUE OF THE RED DEATH
QUESTIONS

1. In the film version of *The Masque of the Red Death*, the story title appears in four languages. What inferences might flow from this procedure? Are there additional cinematic details that further support such inferences?

2. The opening shots of the film focus on objects, sounds, and colors. What symbolic significance do you find in these opening shots? To what extent do these objects, sounds, and colors play significant roles in the rest of the film?

3. In Edgar Allan Poe's short story, the opening paragraph alludes to the devastation of the countryside. By paragraph two, the emphasis has shifted to Prospero's "castellated abbey." Compare and contrast the filmmaker's portrayal of the effects of the Red Death. Is there any specific pattern in the visual portrayal of the onward march of death?

4. Identify the major symbols of death in story and film.

5. Poe's language establishes much of the tone of his story. In the first paragraph, he uses words like "devastated," and "pestilence." What problems in adaptation does this language pose?

6. In the short story, the final chamber with its blood-colored panes is described as the "western or black chamber." Why might Poe have described it in these terms? This is also the chamber in which Prospero dies. What elements from the story has the filmmaker

retained? What has he deleted or altered? What has he invented? In your judgment, how closely does the tone of the film parallel the tone of the story?

7. Three of Poe's patterns of imagery cluster around redness/blood, blackness/death and time. How are each of these patterns introduced into early sequences of the film? In the closing sequences of the film?

8. The bronze pendulum in the film is both a visual and aural symbol. Trace its role in the film.

9. The short story reveals Poe's interest in the "Gothic" tale. How "Gothic" is the film? Do any other periods (i.e. Renaissance) seem to play a role in the visuals or music of the film?

10. In the film adaptation, the duke has dissipated himself in the idle pleasures of wine, women, and song. How much support does Poe's story offer for this characterization? In addition to the sequences of the duke and the beautiful woman, what other visuals testify to his dissipation in the film?

THE MASQUE OF THE RED DEATH
SUGGESTIONS FOR PAPERS

1. Using a dictionary, find several meanings assigned to the word, "masque." Which of these meanings are relevant to the film? Which are relevant to the short story? Support your judgments with pertinent illustrations from film and story.

2. Assess the decision to use animation in this film adaptation of the Edgar Allan Poe story.

3. Compare and contrast the use of sound effects in the story and film.

4. To what extent was the substitution of the masked woman as a symbol of death consistent with the tone of the short story? Defend your view with appropriate details from the story and film.

5. What was your initial reaction to the red-clad jester in the film? Did your original response change? How do you account for your responses to the film's jester?

6. Select any Poe short story and prepare a treatment for a film adaptation. Be prepared to justify your cinematic approach.

film critique
THE MASQUE OF THE RED DEATH
Thomas Lew

Most successful adaptations of story into film result from the film-maker's skillful translation of ideas and descriptive material in the source story into appropriate visual analogues which retain the human meaning, tonal quality, and major themes of the story. The filmmaker's problem is how to convert ideas (verbal and often abstract) into sights and sounds (visual and concrete). The solution to this problem may take many forms.

In the film adaptation of Poe's "The Masque of the Red Death," the filmmaker resorts to major departures from the story narrative to recreate the mood and significant themes of the Poe work. There are, consequently, several excellent examples of visual invented sequences to facilitate the exposition and represent a number of abstract ideas.

The first, and most obvious, example of the filmmaker's success in visualizing descriptive material is seen in the opening sections of the film, a sort of prologue in which the viewer is shown the destructiveness and far-reaching devastation of the Red Death. The viewer sees the plague ravaging, in succession, three farmers, two carpenters, and finally a group of monks. Though there is no narration in the film, no dialogue (except for a short ballad sung in French later in the film), there is little doubt that it *is* a plague–a quick and lethal one—which destroys these people. The filmmaker reinforces this assumption in several ways. The countryside is portrayed in muted, ominous, and harsh browns. The victims scream quickly in terror and fall in ashen corpses. Black crows hover over the countryside. Dark smoke rises in the distance, a sure sign that the cremating of diseased bodies is in progress. Hymns are sung and a cross is erected as a church bell rings its foreboding death knell.

In the film, the Red Death is represented by a faceless, hooded horseman, an ominous presence whose appearance on screen (accom-panied by an all-pervasive red hue and haunting background sounds of swishing or thrashing) always foreshadows death.

In Poe's short story the Red Death and its effects on its victims are described in his first paragraph: "The 'Red Death' had long devastated the country. No pestilence had ever been so fatal, or so hideous," and so forth. The author's use of a general description here permits the filmmaker the freedom of his own invention. Still, the opening segments of the film are in keeping with the grotesque, macabre style of the story.

It is also interesting to note how well the three major patterns of imagery in the Poe story—redness/blood, blackness/darkness, and time are introduced and integrated in the film's opening segments. Red, signifying blood, terror, and the plague, appears and then dominates the screen as a prelude to all the death scenes. Black, traditionally a symbol of death and decay, is conspicuous in the crows and the burning columns of smoke. The concept of relentless and emotionless time, symbolic of the transitory aspect of life and the inevitability of death, is represented by the bronze pendulum and its broad, heavy sweeps. When the pendulum appears, it too announces death. In this way the film conveys the spirit of Poe's images, although it may not duplicate them exactly.

The vivid images in Poe's story are expressed through his diction and syntax. References to redness, blood, and the Red Death occur often in Poe's descriptions of the plague, decor, characters, etc.: "His vesture was dabbled in blood—and his broad brow . . . was besprinkled with the *scarlet* horror." Black is present in the furnishings of the seventh apartment, the color of the clock, the darkness of midnight, etc. And lastly, the passing of time (as symbolized by the ebony clock itself) actually exerts a visible influence on the revellers: "And then, for a moment, all is still, and all is silent save the voice of the clock." These three image patterns are merged in the tale's concluding paragraph, when the life of the clock goes out and darkness and the Red Death hold dominion over all.

The corresponding patterns of imagery developed in the film also merge during the Duke's death scene. The pendulum, red tiles, blackness, the sound of crows screeching, and the swishing sounds all combine to herald the Duke's death. The basic difference, of course, is that Poe's Prospero dies after stalking a ghoulish intruder, while the film's Duke succumbs after an amorous embrace with a beautiful woman.

Prospero's attempt to shut out the plague by withdrawing to the seclusion of one of his "castellated abbeys" is depicted cinematically by the closing of the castle drawbridge and the shutting and clanking of a series of doors within the castle. Thus we have an economic and effective rendition of Poe's wall with "gates of iron" whose bolts are welded by "furnaces and massy hammers."

With the securing of the castle, the story proper begins. The faceless horseman has laid waste the first two levels of medieval society: the peasantry and the clergy. The last level, the nobility, has taken elaborate precautions to wall out the Red Death. In this section of the film we see not only more elaboration by the filmmaker, but also significant departures from Poe's narrative.

First, the filmmaker has chosen to give less emphasis than Poe to spectacle and the highly exotic. The film does not depict the seven elegant suites of various colors, the braziers of fire, the thousand teeming revellers, and only some elements of "glare and glitter and piquancy and phantasm." This may have been done to cut production costs, but more likely to make the film more concentrated and centralized, allowing the character of the Duke to carry the central thematic thrust of the action.

The second major departure from the story, and by far the most interesting bit of invention, is the depiction of the spectre of Death (earlier presented as the faceless rider) as a beautiful, sensual woman who abruptly appears at the masque given by the Duke. As far as fidelity of film to story goes, this appears to be in direct contradiction to Poe's purposes. Death is beautiful and desired by the Duke (and indeed, by some of the nobles), not ominous and ugly and feared by all as in the short story: "The figure was tall and gaunt, and shrouded . . . in the habiliments of the grave. The mask . . . was made . . . to resemble the countenance of a stiffened corpse."

The change, however, seems justified. One of the central themes of both the story and film is the inescapability of death, and in the Duke's encounter with death there is a more specific application of this theme: death and time will surely ravage the wealthy and powerful along with the poor and pious, perhaps with a taunting and more insidious zeal, because the wealthy, like the Duke, have dissipated themselves in pursuit of drink, idle pleasures, and lust. There seems to be adequate support for this interpretation in the Poe story. Prospero is depicted as eccentric, selfish, a bit arrogant, rumored by many to be "mad." He has sought to avoid the misfortunes of life by isolating himself from the outside world, hoping to pass life pleasantly. In an indirect way, he creates the setting for his own doom by constructing the seven apartments to satisfy his macabre and bizarre fancies.

If anything, the film picks up this theme and develops it more thoroughly. The Duke and many of his guests are portrayed in different tones of grey, hinting not only at the moral dissolution of their characters, but also contributing to Poe's dream-like atmosphere of the bizarre. The Duke is first seen reaching with a grey, skeletal hand, ornamented with four opulent rings, toward a chalice filled with wine. The dissipation theme is here first indicated. The inference is further reinforced by attention to the large amount of drinking and overdrinking by his guests (another chalice is knocked over by an unsteady hand). Finally the masque begins. The guests go through their dance steps with ennui. Then the beautiful, masked woman appears, accompanied by the same foreboding music that preceded the other appearances of the Red Death.

The woman's entrance has been foreshadowed by the capers of a subsidiary character—a jester clothed in red. Poe writes: "There were buffoons, . . . there were musicians, there was Beauty, there was wine. . . . Without was the 'Red Death'." The filmmaker has expanded these bits of information imaginatively to sustain the strange and grotesque atmosphere that Poe has developed elsewhere in his story. The red jester who entertains, then momentarily startles his audience by donning a skull mask, is a nice bit of invention and foreshadowing. One can even assume that the jester is again actually Death himself in another of his many guises.

Because of the substitution of the woman for the gruesome masked figure, the chase or pursuit portion of the short story takes a different form in the film. In the story, the masked figure is pursued by Prospero through the seven suites. The figure's frightening appearance creates an immediate tension culminating in Prospero's death before the ebony clock. With the introduction of a lovely, voluptuous woman who is quickly desired by the Duke, the film sets in motion a series of wry ironies. A merry chase takes the two figures through a number of rooms, and a coy, sexual game of hide-and-seek is played between bed chambers and bed curtains. But the Duke is, in fact, pursuing his own doom. The woman's dropping of her pearl necklace not only serves as a prologue to her undressing, but also hints at her sinister intentions: the pearls, symbols of purity and beauty, are left behind in the chase.

The opening and closing of doors and curtains reinforces another pattern of images developed in the film, that of masking and unmasking, reality and illusion. The devastation of the Red Death outside is "masked" by the festive banquet within the castle. The lethal mission of the beautiful woman is concealed by her wanton beauty and Mona Lisa smile. The illusion the Duke entertains of shutting out the plague and the torments of the world is shattered by the reality of death which no mortal can escape.

Much of the mood and atmosphere of the Poe story is ably transferred to the film version by methods already mentioned. Moreover, the filmmaker has devised effective Renaissance style paintings. Some works of well-known Renaissance artists, among them Da Vinci and Titian are recognizable. The static life of a decadent nobility conveyed so well in the Poe story, is expressed in the film by imitating these painting styles and by portraying the Duke's castle in the massive and cavernous Gothic style. Muted browns and greys dominate many of the castle scenes, adding to the Gothic mood. Much of the gaiety of the guests is subdued; their laughter controlled. Background music, that of the lute, horn, and harpsichord, assists in fostering this somber, brooding atmosphere.

    To conclude, the film adaptation of "The Masque of the Red Death" has succeeded in creating a strong sense of mood and atmosphere accurately reflecting Poe's love of the Gothic and grotesque. In the narrative sense, however, the film is not an entirely faithful adaptation. It has eliminated Poe's spectacular element of the seven suites and substituted a beautiful woman for the ominous, masked figure of Death. But these departures from the story allow the film to express, in its own terms, the themes of human transiency and dissolution. Both film and story are splendid examples of the possibilities of each medium. Each work has its own interlocking and integrated themes and patterns of imagery, and each is able to exist independently of the other.

chapter 5
Short Stories
Adapted to Film

PICKETS
Robert W. Chambers

In 1895, Chambers published The Haunts of Man. *"Pickets," the second story in the collection, describes a brief truce during the Civil War, a truce involving two Union soldiers and a Confederate. In 1954, Denis and Terry Sanders, two UCLA students, adapted the Chambers story. They called their twenty-two minute black- and-white film* A Time Out of War. *The new title has an ironic connotation. The words "time out" are used in games and sports contests. The filmmakers are suggesting that war is an adult game, a stupid game in the context of the wonderfully human events that occur during the truce.*

In 1954, the picture won the Academy Award for best short live-action movie of the year. It also received the Silver Dolphin Award at the Venice International Film Festival and the British Film Academy Award. In Hollywood, the Screen Producers Guild selected A Time Out of War *as the best student film of the decade.*

391

"Hi, Yank!"

"Shut up!" replied Alden, wriggling to the edge of the rifle-pit. Connor also crawled a little higher and squinted through the chinks of the pine logs.

"Hey, Johnny," he called across the river, "are you that clay-eatin' Cracker with green lamps on your pilot?"

"Oh, Yank! Are yew the U. S. mewl with a C. S. A. brand on yewr head-stall?"

"Go to hell!" replied Connor sullenly.

A jeering laugh answered him from across the river.

"He had you there, Connor," observed Alden with faint interest.

Connor took off his blue cap and examined the bullet hole in the crown.

"C. S. A. brand on my head-stall, eh!" he repeated savagely, twirling the cap between his dirty fingers.

"You called him a clay-eating Cracker," observed Alden; "and you referred to his spectacles as green lanterns on his pilot."

"I'll show him whose head-stall is branded," muttered Connor, shoving his smoky rifle through the log crack.

Alden slid down to the bottom of the shallow pit and watched him apathetically.

The silence was intense; the muddy river, smooth as oil, swirled noiselessly between its fringe of sycamores; not a breath of air stirred the leaves around them. From the sun-baked bottom of the rifle-pit came the stale smell of charred logs and smoke-soaked clothing. There was a stench of sweat in the air and the heavy odour of balsam and pine seemed to intensify it. Alden gasped once or twice, threw open his jacket at the throat, and stuffed a filthy handkerchief into the crown of his cap, arranging the ends as a shelter for his neck.

Connor lay silent, his right eye fastened upon the rifle-sight, his dusty army shoes crossed behind him. One yellow sock had slipped down over the worn shoe heel and laid bare a dust-begrimed ankle.

In the heated stillness Alden heard the boring of weevils in the logs overhead. A tiny twig snapped somewhere in the forest; a fly buzzed about his knees. Suddenly Connor's rifle cracked; the echoes rattled and clattered away through the woods; a thin cloud of pungent vapour slowly drifted straight upward, shredding into filmy streamers among the tangled branches overhead.

"Get him?" asked Alden, after a silence.

"Nope," replied Connor. Then he addressed himself to his late target across the river:

"Hello, Johnny!"

"Hi, Yank!"

"How close?"

"Hey?"

"How close?"

"What, sonny?"

"My shot, you fool!"

"Why, sonny!" called back the Confederate in affected surprise, "was yew a shootin' at me?"

Bang! went Connor's rifle again. A derisive catcall answered him, and he turned furiously to Alden.

"Oh, let up," said the young fellow; "it's too hot for that."

Connor was speechless with rage, and he hastily jammed another cartridge into his long, hot rifle, while Alden roused himself, brushed away a persistent fly, and crept up to the edge of the pit again.

"Hello, Johnny!" he shouted.

"That you, sonny?" replied the Confederate.

"Yes. Say, Johnny, shall we call it square until four o'clock?"

"What time is it?" replied the cautious Confederate; "all our expensive gold watches is bein' repaired at Chickamauga."

At this taunt, Connor showed his teeth, but Alden laid one hand on his arm and sang out: "It's two o'clock, Richmond time; Sherman has just telegraphed us from your State-house."

"Wa-al, in that case this crool war is over," replied the Confederate sharpshooter; "we'll be easy on old Sherman."

"See here!" cried Alden; "is it a truce until four o'clock?"

"All right! Your word, Yank!"

"You have it!"

"Done!" said the Confederate, coolly rising to his feet and strolling down to the river bank, both hands in his pockets.

Alden and Connor crawled out of their ill-smelling dust wallow, leaving their rifles behind them.

"Whew! It's hot, Johnny," said Alden pleasantly. He pulled out a stained pipe, blew into the stem, polished the bowl with his sleeve, and sucked wistfully at the end. Then he went and sat down beside Connor who had improvised a fishing pole from his ramrod, a bit of string, and a rusty hook.

The Confederate rifleman also sat down on his side of the stream, puffing luxuriously on a fragrant corn-cob pipe.

Presently the Confederate soldier raised his head and looked across at Alden.

"What's yewr name, sonny?" he asked.

"Alden," replied the young fellow briefly.

"Mine's Craig," observed the Confederate; "what's yewr regiment?"

A Time Out of War (1954) The peaceful river serves as a divider. Even when the men learn to cooperate, the river ironically continues to separate them. Under normal circumstances, the river might be perceived as reflecting nature's calm placidity in contrast with man's violence. *Still shot reproduced courtesy of Pyramid Films.*

"Two hundred sixtieth New York; what's yours, Mr. Craig?"

"Ninety-third Maryland, *Mister* Alden."

"Quit that throwin' sticks in the water!" growled Connor; "how do you s'pose I'm goin' to catch anythin'?"

Alden tossed his stick back into the brush-heap and laughed.

"How's your tobacco, Craig?" he called out.

"Bully! How's yewr coffee 'n 'tack, Alden?"

"First-rate!" replied the youth.

After a silence he said: "Is it a go?"

"You bet," said Craig, fumbling in his pockets. He produced a heavy twist of Virginia tobacco, laid it on a log, hacked off about three inches with his sheath knife, and folded it up in a big green sycamore leaf. This again he rolled into a corn-husk, weighted with a pebble, then stepping back, he hurled it into the air, saying: "Deal squar, Yank!"

The tobacco fell at Alden's feet. He picked it up, measured it carefully with his clasp-knife, and called out: "Three and three-quarters, Craig. What do you want, hard-tack or coffee?"

" 'Tack," replied Craig; "don't stint!"

Alden laid out two biscuits. As he was about to hack a quarter from the third he happened to glance over the creek at his enemy. There was no mistaking the expression in his face. Starvation was stamped on every feature.

When Craig caught Alden's eye, he spat with elaborate care, whistled a bar of the "Bonny Blue Flag," and pretended to yawn.

Alden hesitated, glanced at Connor, then placed three whole biscuits in the corn husk, added a pinch of coffee, and tossed the parcel over to Craig.

That Craig longed to fling himself upon the food and devour it was plain to Alden, who was watching his face. But he didn't; he strolled leisurely down the bank, picked up the parcel, weighed it critically before opening it, and finally sat down to examine the contents. When he saw that the third cracker was whole, and that a pinch of coffee had been added, he paused in his examination and remained motionless on the bank, head bent. Presently he looked up and asked Alden if he had made a mistake. The young fellow shook his head and drew a long puff of smoke from his pipe, watching it curl out of his nose with interest.

"Then I'm obliged to yew, Alden," said Craig; " 'low, I'll eat a snack to see it ain't pizened."

He filled his lean jaws with the dry biscuit, then scooped up a tin-cup full of water from the muddy river and set the rest of the cracker to soak.

"Good?" queried Alden.

"Fair," drawled Craig, bolting an unchewed segment and choking a little. "How's the twist?"

"Fine," said Alden; "tastes like stable-sweepings."

They smiled at each other across the stream.

"Sa-a-y," drawled Craig with his mouth full, "when yew're out of twist, jest yew sing out, sonny."

"All right," replied Alden. He stretched back in the shadow of a sycamore and watched Craig with pleasant eyes.

Presently Connor had a bite and jerked his line into the air.

"Look yere," said Craig, "that ain't no way foh to ketch 'red-horse.' Yew want a ca'tridge on foh a sinker, sonny."

"What's that?" inquired Connor suspiciously.

"Put on a sinker."

"Go on, Connor," said Alden.

Connor saw him smoking and sniffed anxiously. Alden tossed him the twist, telling him to fill his pipe.

Presently Connor found a small pebble and improvised a sinker. He swung his line again into the muddy current with a mechanical sidelong glance to see what Craig was doing, and settled down again on his haunches, smoking and grunting.

"Enny news, Alden?" queried Craig after a silence.

"Nothing much—except that Richmond has fallen," grinned Alden.

"Quit foolin'," urged the Southerner; "ain't thar no news?"

"No. Some of our men down at Long Pond got sick eating catfish. They caught them in the pond. It appears you Johnnys used the pond as a cemetery, and our men got sick eating the fish."

"That so?" grinned Craig; "too bad. Lots of yewr men was in Long Pond, too, I reckon."

In the silence that followed, two rifle-shots sounded faint and dull from the distant forest.

" 'Nother great Union victory," drawled Craig. "Extry! extry! Richmond is took!"

Alden laughed and puffed at his pipe.

"We licked the boots off of the 30th Texas last Monday," he said.

"Sho!" exclaimed Craig. "What did you go a lickin' their boots for?—blackin'?"

"Oh, shut up!" said Connor from the bank, "I can't ketch no fish if you two fools don't quit jawin'."

The sun was dipping below the pine-clad ridge, flooding river and wood with a fierce radiance. The spruce needles glittered, edged with gold; every broad leaf wore a heart of gilded splendour, and the muddy waters of the river rolled onward like a flood of precious metal, heavy, burnished, noiseless.

From a balsam bough a thrush uttered three timid notes; a great gauzy-winged grasshopper drifted blindly into a clump of sun-scorched weeds, click! click! cr-r-r-r!

"Purty, ain't it," said Craig, looking at the thrush. Then he swallowed the last morsel of muddy hard-tack, wiped his beard on his cuff, hitched up his trousers, took off his green glasses, and rubbed his eyes.

"A he-cat-bird sings purtier though," he said with a yawn.

Alden drew out his watch, puffed once or twice, and stood up, stretching his arms in the air.

"It's four o'clock," he began, but was cut short by a shout from Connor.

"Gee-whiz!" he yelled, "what have I got on this here pole!"

The ramrod was bending, the line swaying heavily in the current.

"It's four o'clock, Connor," said Alden, keeping a wary eye on Craig.

"That's all right!" called Craig; "the time's extended till yewr friend lands that there fish!"

"Pulls like a porpoise," grunted Connor, "damn it! I bet it busts my ramrod!"

"Does it pull?" grinned Craig.

"Yes,—a dead weight!"

"Don't it jerk kinder this way an' that?" asked Craig, much interested.

"Naw," said Connor, "the bloody thing jest pulls steady."

"Then it ain't no 'red-horse,' it's a catfish!"

"Huh!" sneered Connor,—"don't I know a catfish? This ain't no catfish, lemme tell yer!"

"Then it's a log," laughed Alden.

"By gum! here it comes," panted Connor; "here, Alden, jest you ketch it with my knife,—hook the blade, blame ye!"

Alden cautiously descended the red bank of mud, holding on to roots and branches, and bent over the water. He hooked the big-bladed clasp knife like a scythe, set the spring, and leaned out over the water.

"Now!" muttered Connor.

An oily circle appeared upon the surface of the turbid water,— another and another. A few bubbles rose and floated upon the tide.

Then something black appeared just beneath the bubbles and Alden hooked it with his knife and dragged it shoreward.

It was the sleeve of a man's coat.

Connor dropped his ramrod and gaped at the thing: Alden would have loosed it, but the knifeblade was tangled in the sleeve.

He turned a sick face up to Connor.

"Pull it in," said the older man,—"here, give it to me, lad—"

When at last the silent visitor lay upon the bank, they saw it was the body of a Union cavalryman. Alden stared at the dead face, fascinated; Connor mechanically counted the yellow chevrons upon the blue sleeve, now soaked black. The muddy water ran over the baked soil, spreading out in dust-covered pools; the spurred boots trickled slime. After a while both men turned their heads and looked at Craig. The Southerner stood silent and grave, his battered cap in his hand. They eyed each other quietly for a moment, then, with a vague gesture, the Southerner walked back into his pit and presently reappeared, trailing his rifle.

Connor had already begun to dig with his bayonet, but he glanced up at the rifle in Craig's hands. Then he looked suspiciously into the eyes of the Southerner. Presently he bent his head again and continued digging.

It was sunset before he and Alden finished the shallow grave, Craig watching them in silence, his rifle between his knees. When they were ready they rolled the body into the hole and stood up.

Craig also rose, raising his rifle to a "present." He held it there while the two Union soldiers shovelled the earth into the grave. Alden went back and lifted the two rifles from the pit, handed Connor his, and waited.

"Ready!" growled Connor, "aim!"

Alden's rifle came to his shoulder. Craig also raised his rifle.

"Fire!"

Three times the three shots rang out in the wilderness, over the unknown grave. After a moment or two Alden nodded good night to Craig across the river and walked slowly toward his rifle-pit. Connor shambled after him. As he turned to lower himself into the pit he called across the river, "Good night, Craig!"

"Good night, Connor," said Craig.

AN OCCURRENCE AT OWL CREEK BRIDGE

Ambrose Bierce

"An Occurrence at Owl Creek Bridge" first appeared in a collection, Tales of Soldiers and Civilians, *published in 1891. Like many of Bierce's realistic and cynical stories, it deals with the Civil War in which he had fought.*

Robert Enrico, a French filmmaker, earned two of the most prestigious film festival awards with his adaptation. In 1962, the picture won the Grand Prize at the Cannes Film Festival. The following year, it received the Academy Award as the Best Live-Action Short Subject. Undoubtedly this film is the best known and most widely distributed of all 16 mm movies adapted from short fiction.

I

A man stood upon a railroad bridge in northern Alabama, looking down into the swift water twenty feet below. The man's hands were behind his back, the wrists bound with a cord. A rope closely encircled his neck. It was attached to a stout cross-timber above his head and the slack fell to the level of his knees. Some loose boards laid upon the sleepers supporting the metals of the railway supplied a footing for him and his executioners—two private soldiers of the Federal army, directed by a sergeant who in civil life may have been a deputy sheriff. At a short remove upon the same temporary platform was an officer in the uniform of his rank, armed. He was a captain. A sentinel at each end of the bridge stood with his rifle in the position known as "support," that is to say, vertical in front of the left shoulder, the hammer resting on the forearm thrown straight across the chest—a formal and unnatural position, enforcing an erect carriage of the body. It did not appear to be the duty of these two men to know what was occurring at the center of the bridge; they merely blockaded the two ends of the foot planking that traversed it.

Beyond one of the sentinels nobody was in sight; the railroad ran straight away into a forest for a hundred yards, then, curving, was lost to view. Doubtless there was an outpost farther along. The other bank of the stream was open ground—a gentle acclivity topped with a stockade of vertical tree trunks, loopholed for rifles, with a single embrasure through which protruded the muzzle of a brass cannon commanding the bridge. Midway of the slope between the bridge and fort were the spectators—a single company of infantry in line, at "parade rest," the butts of the rifles on the ground, the barrels inclining slightly backward against the right shoulder, the hands crossed upon the stock. A lieutenant stood at the right of the line, the point of his sword upon the ground, his left hand resting upon his right. Excepting the group of four at the center of the bridge, not a man moved. The company faced the bridge, staring stonily, motionless. The sentinels, facing the banks of the stream, might have been statues to adorn the bridge. The captain stood with folded arms, silent, observing the work of his subordinates, but making no sign. Death is a dignitary who when he comes announced is to be received with formal manifestations of respect, even by those most familiar with him. In the code of military etiquette silence and fixity are forms of deference.

The man who was engaged in being hanged was apparently about thirty-five years of age. He was a civilian, if one might judge from his habit, which was that of a planter. His features were good—a straight nose, firm mouth, broad forehead, from which his long, dark hair was combed straight back, falling behind his ears to the collar of his well-fitting frock coat. He wore a mustache and pointed beard, but no whiskers; his eyes were large and dark gray, and had a kindly expression which one would hardly have expected in one whose neck was in the hemp. Evidently this was no vulgar assassin. The liberal military code makes provision for hanging many kinds of persons, and gentlemen are not excluded.

The preparations being complete, the two private soldiers stepped aside and each drew away the plank upon which he had been standing. The sergeant turned to the captain, saluted and placed himself immediately behind that officer, who in turn moved apart one pace. These movements left the condemned man and the sergeant standing on the two ends of the same plank, which spanned three of the crossties of the bridge. The end upon which the civilian stood almost, but not quite, reached a fourth. This plank had been held in place by the weight of the captain; it was now held by that of the sergeant. At a signal from the former the latter would step aside, the plank would tilt and the condemned man go down between two ties. The arrangement commended itself to his judgment as simple and effective. His face had not been covered nor his eyes bandaged. He looked a moment at his "unsteadfast footing," then let his gaze wander to the swirling water of the stream racing madly beneath his feet. A piece of dancing driftwood caught his attention and his eyes followed it down the current. How slowly it appeared to move! What a sluggish stream!

He closed his eyes in order to fix his last thoughts upon his wife and children. The water, touched to gold by the early sun, the brooding mists under the banks at some distance down the stream, the fort, the soldiers, the piece of drift—all had distracted him. And now he became conscious of a new disturbance. Striking through the thought of his dear ones was a sound which he could neither ignore nor understand, a sharp, distinct, metallic percussion like the stroke of a blacksmith's hammer upon the anvil; it had the same ringing quality. He wondered what it was, and whether immeasurably distant or near by—it seemed both. Its recurrence was regular, but as slow as the tolling of a death knell. He awaited each stroke with impatience and—he knew not why—apprehension. The intervals of silence grew progressively longer; the delays became maddening. With their greater infrequency the sounds increased in strength and sharpness. They hurt his ear like the thrust of a knife; he feared he would shriek. What he heard was the ticking of his watch.

He unclosed his eyes and saw again the water below him. "If I could free my hands," he thought, "I might throw off the noose and spring into the stream. By diving I could evade the bullets and, swimming vigorously, reach the bank, take to the woods and get away home. My home, thank God, is as yet outside their lines; my wife and little ones are still beyond the invader's farthest advance."

As these thoughts, which have here to be set down in words, were flashed into the doomed man's brain rather than evolved from it the captain nodded to the sergeant. The sergeant stepped aside.

II

Peyton Farquhar was a well-to-do planter, of an old and highly respected Alabama family. Being a slave owner and like other slave owners a politician, he was naturally an original secessionist and ardently devoted to the Southern cause. Circumstances of an imperious nature, which it is unnecessary to relate here, had prevented him from taking service with the gallant army that had fought the disastrous campaigns ending with the fall of Corinth, and he chafed under the inglorious restraint, longing for the release of his energies, the larger life of the soldier, the opportunity for distinction. That opportunity, he felt, would come, as it comes to all in war time. Meanwhile he did what he could. No service was too humble for him to perform in aid of the South, no adventure too perilous for him to undertake if consistent with the character of a civilian who was at heart a soldier, and who in good faith and without too much qualification assented to at least a part of the frankly villainous dictum that all is fair in love and war.

One evening while Farquhar and his wife were sitting on a rustic bench near the entrance to his grounds, a gray-clad soldier rode up to the gate and asked for a drink of water. Mrs. Farquhar was only too happy to serve him with her own white hands. While she was fetching the water her husband approached the dusty horseman and inquired eagerly for news from the front.

"The Yanks are repairing the railroads," said the man, "and are getting ready for another advance. They have reached the Owl Creek bridge, put it in order and built a stockade on the north bank. The commandant has issued an order, which is posted everywhere, declaring that any civilian caught interfering with the railroad, its bridges, tunnels or trains will be summarily hanged. I saw the order."

"How far is it to the Owl Creek bridge?" Farquhar asked.

"About thirty miles."

"Is there no force on this side of the creek?"

"Only a picket post half a mile out, on the railroad, and a single sentinel at this end of the bridge."

"Suppose a man—a civilian and student of hanging—should elude the picket post and perhaps get the better of the sentinel," said Farquhar, smiling, "what could he accomplish?"

The soldier reflected. "I was there a month ago," he replied. "I observed that the flood of last winter had lodged a great quantity of driftwood against the wooden pier at this end of the bridge. It is now dry and would burn like tow."

The lady had now brought the water, which the soldier drank. He thanked her ceremoniously, bowed to her husband and rode away. An hour later, after nightfall, he re-passed the plantation, going northward in the direction from which he had come. He was a Federal scout.

III

As Peyton Farquhar fell straight downward through the bridge he lost consciousness and was as one already dead. From this state he was awakened—ages later, it seemed to him—by the pain of a sharp pressure up his throat, followed by a sense of suffocation. Keen, poignant agonies seemed to shoot from his neck downward through every fiber of his body and limbs. These pains appeared to flash along well-defined lines of ramification and to beat with an inconceivably rapid periodicity. They seemed like streams of pulsating fire heating him to an intolerable temperature. As to his head, he was conscious of nothing but a feeling of fullness—of congestion. These sensations were unaccompanied by thought. The intellectual part of his nature was already effaced; he had power only to feel, and feeling was torment. He was conscious of motion. Encompassed in a luminous cloud, of which he was now merely the fiery heart, without material substance, he swung through unthinkable arcs

ORDER

ANY CIVILIAN

caught interfering with
the railroad bridges,
tunnels or trains will be

SUMMARILY HANGED

The 4° of April 1862

An Occurrence at Owl Creek Bridge (1962) The sign is a form of verbal exposition. Very economically, it substitutes for all of Section II in the short story. *Still shot reproduced courtesy of Contemporary/McGraw-Hill Films.*

of oscillation, like a vast pendulum. Then all at once, with terrible suddenness, the light about him shot upward with the noise of a loud
splash; a frightful roaring was in his ears, and all was cold and dark. The
power of thought was restored; he knew that the rope had broken and
he had fallen into the stream. There was no additional strangulation; the
noose about his neck was already suffocating him and kept the water
from his lungs. To die of hanging at the bottom of a river!—the idea
seemed to him ludicrous. He opened his eyes in the darkness and saw
above him a gleam of light, but how distant, how inaccessible! He was
still sinking, for the light became fainter and fainter until it was a mere
glimmer. Then it began to grow and brighten, and he knew that he was
rising toward the surface—knew it with reluctance, for he was now very
comfortable. "To be hanged and drowned," he thought, "that is not so
bad; but I do not wish to be shot. No; I will not be shot; that is not fair."

He was not conscious of an effort, but a sharp pain in his wrist
apprised him that he was trying to free his hands. He gave the struggle
his attention, as an idler might observe the feat of a juggler, without
interest in the outcome. What splendid effort! What magnificent, what
superhuman strength! Ah, that was a fine endeavor! Bravo! The cord fell
away; his arms parted and floated upward, the hands dimly seen on each
side in the growing light. He watched them with a new interest as first
one and then the other pounced upon the noose at his neck. They tore it
away and thrust it fiercely aside, its undulations resembling those of a
water snake. "Put it back, put it back!" He thought he shouted these
words to his hands, for the undoing of the noose had been succeeded by
the direst pang that he had yet experienced. His neck ached horribly;
his brain was on fire; his heart, which had been fluttering faintly, gave
a great leap, trying to force itself out at his mouth. His whole body was
racked and wrenched with an insupportable anguish! But his disobedient
hands gave no heed to the command. They beat the water vigorously
with quick, downward strokes, forcing him to the surface. He felt his
head emerge; his eyes were blinded by the sunlight; his chest expanded
convulsively, and with a supreme and crowning agony his lungs engulfed
a great draught of air, which instantly he expelled in a shriek!

He was now in full possession of his physical senses. They were,
indeed, preternaturally keen and alert. Something in the awful disturbance of his organic system had so exalted and refined them that they
made record of things never before perceived. He felt the ripples upon
his face and heard their separate sounds as they struck. He looked at the
forest on the bank of the stream, saw the individual trees, the leaves and
the veining of each leaf—saw the very insects upon them: the locusts,
the brilliant-bodied flies, the gray spiders stretching their webs from twig
to twig. He noted the prismatic colors in all the dew-drops upon a mil-

lion blades of grass. The humming of the gnats that danced above the eddies of the stream, the beating of the dragonflies' wings, the strokes of the water spiders' legs, like oars which had lifted their boat—all these made audible music. A fish slid along beneath his eyes and he heard the rush of its body parting the water.

He had come to the surface facing down the stream; in a moment the visible world seemed to wheel slowly round, himself the pivotal point, and he saw the bridge, the fort, the soldiers upon the bridge, the captain, the sergeant, the two privates, his executioners. They were in silhouette against the blue sky. They shouted and gesticulated, pointing at him. The captain had drawn his pistol, but did not fire; the others were unarmed. Their movements were grotesque and horrible, their forms gigantic.

Suddenly he heard a sharp report and something struck the water smartly within a few inches of his head, spattering his face with spray. He heard a second report, and saw one of the sentinels with his rifle at his shoulder, a light cloud of blue smoke rising from the muzzle. The man in the water saw the eye of the man on the bridge gazing into his own through the sights of the rifle. He observed that it was a gray eye and remembered having read that gray eyes were keenest, and that all famous marksmen had them. Nevertheless, this one had missed.

A counter-swirl had caught Farquhar and turned him half round; he was again looking into the forest on the bank opposite the fort. The sound of a clear, high voice in a monotonous singsong now rang out behind him and came across the water with a distinctness that pierced and subdued all other sounds, even the beating of the ripples in his ears. Although no soldier, he had frequented camps enough to know the dread significance of that deliberate, drawling, aspirated chant; the lieutenant on shore was taking a part in the morning's work. How coldly and piti-lessly—with what an even, calm intonation, presaging, and enforcing tranquility in the men—with what accurately measured intervals fell those cruel words:

"Attention, company! . . . Shoulder arms! . . . Ready! . . . Aim! . . . Fire!"

Farquhar dived—dived as deeply as he could. The water roared in his ears like the voice of Niagara, yet he heard the dulled thunder of the volley and, rising again toward the surface, met shining bits of metal, singularly flattened, oscillating slowly downward. Some of them touched him on the face and hands, then fell away, continuing their descent. One lodged between his collar and neck; it was uncomfortably warm and he snatched it out.

As he rose to the surface, gasping for breath, he saw that he had been a long time under water; he was perceptibly farther down stream—

An Occurrence at Owl Creek Bridge (1962) The viewer "sees" Peyton Farquhar *escape* from the water's depths. Therefore, he accepts the reality of his
own observation. As a medium, film encourages credibility. To see is to
believe. *Still shot reproduced courtesy of Contemporary/McGraw-Hill Films.*

nearer to safety. The soldiers had almost finished reloading; the metal
ramrods flashed all at once in the sunshine as they were drawn fom the
barrels, turned in the air, and thrust into their sockets. The two sentinels
fired again, independently and ineffectually.

The hunted man saw all this over his shoulder; he was now swimming vigorously with the current. His brain was as energetic as his arms
and legs; he thought with the rapidity of lightning.

"The officer," he reasoned, "will not make that martinet's error a
second time. It is as easy to dodge a volley as a single shot. He has
probably already given the command to fire at will. God help me, I cannot dodge them all!"

An appalling splash within two yards of him was followed by a
loud, rushing sound, *diminuendo,* which seemed to travel back through
the air to the fort and died in an explosion which stirred the very river
to its deeps! A rising sheet of water curved over him, fell down upon
him, blinded him, strangled him! The cannon had taken a hand in
the game. As he shook his head free from the commotion of the smitten
water he heard the deflected shot humming through the air ahead, and

in an instant it was cracking and smashing the branches in the forest beyond.

"They will not do that again," he thought; "the next time they will use a charge of grape. I must keep my eye upon the gun; the smoke will apprise me—the report arrives too late; it lags behind the missile. That is a good gun."

Suddenly he felt himself whirled round and round—spinning like a top. The water, the banks, the forests, the now distant bridge, fort and men—all were commingled and blurred. Objects were represented by their colors only; circular horizontal streaks of color—that was all he saw. He had been caught in a vortex and was being whirled on with a velocity of advance and gyration that made him giddy and sick. In a few moments he was flung upon the gravel at the foot of the left bank of the stream—the southern bank—and behind a projecting point which concealed him from his enemies. The sudden arrest of his motion, the abrasion of one of his hands on the gravel, restored him, and he wept with delight. He dug his fingers into the sand, threw it over himself in handfuls and audibly blessed it. It looked like diamonds, rubies, emeralds; he could think of nothing beautiful which it did not resemble. The trees upon the bank were giant garden plants; he noted a definite order in their arrangement, inhaled the fragrance of their blooms. A strange, roseate light shone through the spaces among their trunks and the wind made in their branches the music of Aeolian harps. He had no wish to perfect his escape—was content to remain in that enchanting spot until retaken.

A whiz and rattle of grapeshot among the branches high above his head roused him from his dream. The baffled cannoneer had fired him a random farewell. He sprang to his feet, rushed up the sloping bank, and plunged into the forest.

All that day he traveled, laying his course by the rounding sun. The forest seemed interminable; nowhere did he discover a break in it, not even a woodsman's road. He had not known that he lived in so wild a region. There was something uncanny in the revelation.

By nightfall he was fatigued, footsore, famishing. The thought of his wife and children urged him on. At last he found a road which led him in what he knew to be the right direction. It was as wide and straight as a city street, yet it seemed untraveled. No fields bordered it, no dwelling anywhere. Not so much as the barking of a dog suggested human habitation. The black bodies of the trees forced a straight wall on both sides, terminating on the horizon in a point, like a diagram in a lesson in perspective. Overhead, as he looked up through this rift in the wood, shone great golden stars looking unfamiliar and grouped in strange constellations. He was sure they were arranged in some order which had a secret and malign significance. The wood on either side was full of singular noises, among which—once, twice, and again—he distinctly heard whispers in an unknown tongue.

His neck was in pain and lifting his hand to it he found it horribly swollen. He knew that it had a circle of black where the rope had bruised it. His eyes felt congested; he could no longer close them. His tongue was swollen with thirst; he relieved its fever by thrusting it forward from between his teeth into the cold air. How softly the turf had carpeted the untraveled avenue—he could no longer feel the roadway beneath his feet!

Doubtless, despite his suffering, he had fallen asleep while walking, for now he sees another scene—perhaps he has merely recovered from a delirium. He stands at the gate of his own home. All is as he left it, and all bright and beautiful in the morning sunshine. He must have traveled the entire night. As he pushes open the gate and passes up the wide white walk, he sees a flutter of female garments; his wife, looking fresh and cool and sweet, steps down from the veranda to meet him. At the bottom of the steps she stands waiting, with a smile of ineffable joy, an attitude of matchless grace and dignity. Ah, how beautiful she is! He springs forward with extended arms. As he is about to clasp her he feels a stunning blow upon the back of the neck; a blinding white light blazes all about him with a sound like the shock of a cannon—then all is darkness and silence!

Peyton Farquhar was dead; his body, with a broken neck, swung gently from side to side beneath the timbers of the Owl Creek bridge.

THE UNICORN IN THE GARDEN

James Thurber

James Thurber is considered by many to be America's finest humorist of the twentieth century, and his stories, fables, and cartoons continue to be anthologized. Like so much of his work, this fable centers on the eternal battle of the sexes. For Thurber, the protagonists tend to be a dominating wife and her meek, henpecked husband.

In 1953, U. P. A. Productions, under the leadership of Stephen Bosustow, released a seven-minute animated adaptation of Thurber's well-known fable. In visuals of the film, they captured the style and spirit of the original Thurber drawings. While much of Thurber's work has been translated into film, The Unicorn in the Garden *is undoubtedly one of the happiest adaptations of a superb satirist's work.*

Once upon a sunny morning a man who sat in a breakfast nook looked up from his scrambled eggs to see a white unicorn with a gold horn quietly cropping the roses in the garden. The man went up to the bedroom where his wife was still asleep and woke her. "There's a unicorn in the garden," he said. "Eating roses." She opened one unfriendly eye and looked at him. "The unicorn is a mythical beast," she said, and turned her back on him. The man walked slowly downstairs and out into the garden. The unicorn was still there; he was now browsing among the tulips. "Here, unicorn," said the man, and he pulled up a lily and gave it to him. The unicorn ate it gravely. With a high heart, because there was a unicorn in his garden, the man went upstairs and roused his wife again. "The unicorn," he said, "ate a lily." His wife sat up in bed and looked at him coldly. "You are a booby," she said, "and I am going to have you put in the booby hatch." The man, who had never liked the words "booby" and "booby hatch," and who liked them even less on a shining morning when there was a unicorn in the garden, thought for a moment. "We'll see about that," he said. He walked over to the door. "He has a golden horn in the middle of his forehead," he told her. Then he went back to the garden to watch the unicorn, but the unicorn had gone away. The man sat down among the roses and went to sleep.

As soon as the husband had gone out of the house, the wife got up and dressed as fast as she could. She was very excited and there was a gloat in her eye. She telephoned the police and she telephoned a psychiatrist; she told them to hurry to her house and bring a strait jacket. When the police and the psychiatrist arrived, they sat down in chairs and looked at her with great interest. "My husband," she said, "saw a unicorn this morning." The police looked at the psychiatrist and the psychiatrist looked at the police. "He told me it ate a lily," she said. The psychiatrist looked at the police and the police looked at the psychiatrist. "He told me it had a golden horn in the middle of its forehead," she said. At a solemn signal from the psychiatrist, the police leaped from their chairs and seized the wife. They had a hard time subduing her, for she put up a terrific struggle, but they finally subdued her. Just as they got her into the strait jacket, the husband came back into the house.

"Did you tell your wife you saw a unicorn?" asked the police. "Of course not," said the husband. "The unicorn is a mythical beast." "That's all I wanted to know," said the psychiatrist. "Take her away. I'm sorry, sir, but your wife is as crazy as a jay bird." So they took her away, cursing and screaming, and shut her up in an institution. The husband lived happily ever after.

Moral: *Don't count your boobies until they are hatched.*

THE GARDEN PARTY

Katherine Mansfield

In one of her finest short stories, Katherine Mansfield treats a familiar fictional theme, the initiation of a young person into the adult world. Laura encounters death, a stark contrast to her safe, comfortable, insulated, upper-middle-class world.

The story focuses even more directly on the gulf between the young girl's idealism—admittedly melodramatic—and the trivial values of her class-conscious society. Yet Katherine Mansfield scrupulously avoids over-simplified stereotypes. Her quiet tone masks her incisive portrait of a genteel life style.

For the filmmaker, the task of adaptation is formidable. He must convey, through images more than dialogue, perceptions that are not easily articulated. Jack Sholder, who adapted and directed the film, uses his medium expertly to visualize nuances of thought and feeling not readily captured in words.

And after all the weather was ideal. They could not have had a more perfect day for a garden-party if they had ordered it. Windless, warm, the sky without a cloud. Only the blue was veiled with a haze of light gold, as it is sometimes in early summer. The gardener had been up since dawn, mowing the lawns and sweeping them, until the grass and the dark flat rosettes where the daisy plants had been seemed to shine. As for the roses, you could not help feeling they understood that roses are the only flowers that impress people at garden-parties; the only flowers that everybody is certain of knowing. Hundreds, yes, literally hundreds, had come out in a single night; the green bushes bowed down as though they had been visited by archangels.

Breakfast was not yet over before men came to put up the marquee.

"Where do you want the marquee put, mother?"

"My dear child, it's no use asking me. I'm determined to leave everything to you children this year. Forget I am your mother. Treat me as an honoured guest."

But Meg could not possibly go and supervise the men. She had washed her hair before breakfast, and she sat drinking her coffee in a green turban, with a dark wet curl stamped on each cheek. Jose, the butterfly, always came down in a silk petticoat and a kimono jacket.

"You'll have to go, Laura; you're the artistic one."

Away Laura flew, still holding her piece of bread-and-butter. It's so delicious to have an excuse for eating out of doors and besides, she loved to arrange things; she always felt she could do it so much better than anybody else.

Four men in their shirt-sleeves stood grouped together on the garden path. They carried staves covered with rolls of canvas, and they had big tool-bags slung on their backs. They looked impressive. Laura wished now that she had not got the bread-and-butter, but there was nowhere to put it, and she couldn't possibly throw it away. She blushed and tried to look severe and even a little bit short-sighted as she came up to them.

"Good morning," she said, copying her mother's voice. But that sounded so fearfully affected that she was ashamed, and stammered like a little girl, "Oh—er—have you come—is it about the marquee?"

"That's right, miss," said the tallest of the men, a lanky freckled fellow, and he shifted his tool-bag, knocked back his straw hat and smiled down at her. "That's about it."

His smile was so easy, so friendly that Laura recovered. What nice eyes he had, small, but such a dark blue! And now she looked at the others, they were smiling too. "Cheer up, we won't bite," their smile seemed to say. How very nice workmen were! And what a beautiful morning! She mustn't mention the morning; she must be business-like. The marquee.

"Well, what about the lily-lawn? Would that do?"

And she pointed to the lily-lawn with the hand that didn't hold the bread-and-butter. They turned, they stared in the direction. A little fat chap thrust out his under-lip, and the tall fellow frowned.

"I don't fancy it," said he. "Not conspicuous enough. You see, with a thing like a marquee," and he turned to Laura in his easy way, "you want to put it someplace where it'll give you a bang slap in the eye, if you follow me."

Laura's upbringing made her wonder for a moment whether it was quite respectful of a workman to talk to her of bangs slap in the eye. But she did quite follow him.

"A corner of the tennis-court," she suggested. "But the band's going to be in one corner."

"H'm, going to have a band, are you?" said another of the workmen. He was pale. He had a haggard look as his dark eyes scanned the tennis-court. What was he thinking?

"Only a very small band," said Laura gently. Perhaps he wouldn't mind so much if the band was quite small. But the tall fellow interrupted. "Look here, miss, that's the place. Against those trees. Over there. That'll do fine."

Against the karakas. Then the karaka-trees would be hidden. And they were so lovely, with their broad, gleaming leaves and their clusters of yellow fruit. They were like trees you imagined growing on a desert island, proud, solitary, lifting their leaves and fruits to the sun in a kind of silent splendour. Must they be hidden by a marquee?

They must. Already the men had shouldered their staves and were making for the place. Only the tall fellow was left. He bent down, pinched a sprig of lavender, put his thumb and forefinger to his nose and snuffed up the smell. When Laura saw that gesture she forgot all about the karakas in her wonder at him caring for things like that— caring for the smell of lavender. Oh, how extraordinarily nice workmen were, she thought. Why couldn't she have workmen for friends rather than the silly boys she danced with and who came to Sunday night supper? She would get on much better with men like these.

It's all the fault, she decided, as the tall fellow drew something on the back of an envelope, something that was to be looped up or left to hang, of these absurd class distinctions. Well, for her part, she didn't feel them. Not a bit, not an atom. . . . And now there came the chock-chock of wooden hammers. Some one whistled, some one sang out, "Are you right there, matey?" "Matey!" The friendliness of it, the—the— Just to prove how happy she was, just to show the tall fellow how at home she felt, and how she despised stupid conventions, Laura took a big bite of her bread-and-butter as she stared at the little drawing. She felt just like a work-girl.

"Laura, Laura, where are you? Telephone, Laura!" a voice cried from the house.

"Coming!" Away she skimmed, over the lawn, up the path, up the steps, across the veranda, and into the porch. In the hall her father and Laurie were brushing their hats ready to go to the office.

"I say, Laura," said Laurie very fast, "you might just give a squiz at my coat before this afternoon. See if it wants pressing."

"I will," said she. Suddenly she couldn't stop herself. She ran at Laurie and gave him a small, quick squeeze. "Oh, I do love parties, don't you?" gasped Laura.

"Rather," said Laurie's warm boyish voice, and he squeezed his sister too, and gave her a gentle push. "Dash off to the telephone, old girl."

The telephone. "Yes, yes! oh yes. Kitty? Good morning, dear. Come to lunch? Do, dear. Delighted of course. It will only be a very scratch meal—just the sandwich crusts and broken meringue-shells and what's left over. Yes, isn't it a perfect morning? Your white? Oh, I certainly should. One moment—hold the line. Mother's calling." And Laura sat back. "What, mother? Can't hear."

Mrs. Sheridan's voice floated down the stairs. "Tell her to wear that sweet hat she had on last Sunday."

"Mother says you're to wear that *sweet* hat you had on last Sunday. Good. One o'clock. Bye-bye."

Laura put back the receiver, flung her arms over her head, took a deep breath, stretched and let them fall. "Huh," she sighed, and the moment after the sigh she sat up quickly. She was still, listening. All the doors in the house seemed to be open. The house was alive wtih soft, quick steps and running voices. The green baize door that led to the kitchen regions swung open and shut with a muffled thud. And now there came a long, chuckling absurd sound. It was the heavy piano being moved on its stiff castors. But the air! If you stopped to notice, was the air always like this? Little faint winds were playing chase, in at the tops of the windows, out at the doors. And there were two tiny spots of sun, one on the inkpot, one on a silver photograph frame, playing too. Darling little spots. Especially the one on the inkpot lid. It was quite warm. A warm little silver star. She could have kissed it.

The front door bell pealed, and there sounded the rustle of Sadie's print skirt on the stairs. A man's voice murmured; Sadie answered, careless, "I'm sure I don't know. Wait. I'll ask Mrs. Sheridan."

"What is it, Sadie?" Laura came into the hall.

"It's the florist, Miss Laura."

It was, indeed. There, just inside the door, stood a wide, shallow tray full of pots of pink lilies. No other kind. Nothing but lilies—canna lilies, big pink flowers, wide open, radiant, almost frighteningly alive on bright crimson stems.

"O-oh, Sadie!" said Laura, and the sound was like a little moan. She crouched down as if to warm herself at that blaze of lilies; she felt they were in her fingers, on her lips, growing in her breast.

"It's some mistake," she said faintly. "Nobody ever ordered so many. Sadie, go and find mother."

But at that moment Mrs. Sheridan joined them.

"It's quite right," she said calmly. "Yes, I ordered them. Aren't they lovely?" She pressed Laura's arm. "I was passing the shop yesterday, and I saw them in the window. I suddenly thought for once in my life I shall have enough canna lilies. The garden-party will be a good excuse."

"But I thought you said you didn't mean to interfere," said Laura. Sadie had gone. The florist's man was still outside at his van. She put her arm round her mother's neck and gently, very gently, she bit her mother's ear.

"My darling child, you wouldn't like a logical mother, would you? Don't do that. Here's the man."

He carried more lilies still, another whole tray.

"Bank them up, just inside the door, on both sides of the porch, please," said Mrs. Sheridan. "Don't you agree, Laura?"

"Oh, I *do*, mother."

In the drawing-room Meg, Jose and good little Hans had at last succeeded in moving the piano.

"Now, if we put this chesterfield against the wall and move everything out of the room except the chairs, don't you think?"

"Quite."

"Hans, move these tables into the smoking-room, and bring a sweeper to take these marks off the carpet and—one moment, Hans—" Jose loved giving orders to the servants, and they loved obeying her. She always made them feel they were taking part in some drama. "Tell mother and Miss Laura to come here at once."

"Very good, Miss Jose."

She turned to Meg. "I want to hear what the piano sounds like, just in case I'm asked to sing this afternoon. Let's try over 'This Life is Weary.' "

Pom! Ta-ta-ta *Tee*-ta! The piano burst out so passionately that Jose's face changed. She clasped her hands. She looked mournfully and enigmatically at her mother and Laura as they came in.

This Life is *Wee*-ary.
A Tear—a Sigh
A Love that *Chan*-ges,
This Life is *Wee*-ary,
A Tear—a Sigh.
A Love that *Chan*-ges,
And then . . . Goodbye!

But at the word "Good-bye," and although the piano sounded more desperate than ever, her face broke into a brilliant, dreadfully unsympathetic smile.

"Aren't I in good voice, mummy?" she beamed.

This Life is *Wee*-ary.
Hope comes to Die.
A Dream—a *Wa*-kening.

But now Sadie interrupted them. "What is it, Sadie?"

"If you please, m'm, cook says have you got the flags for the sandwiches?"

"The flags for the sandwiches, Sadie?" echoed Mrs. Sheridan

dreamily. And the children knew by her face that she hadn't got them. "Let me see." And she said to Sadie firmly, "Tell cook I'll let her have them in ten minutes."

Sadie went.

"Now, Laura," said her mother quickly. "Come with me into the smoking-room. I've got the names somewhere on the back of an envelope. You'll have to write them out for me. Meg, go upstairs this minute and take that wet thing off your head. Jose, run and finish dressing this instant. Do you hear me, children, or shall I have to tell your father when he comes home to-night? And—and, Jose, pacify cook if you do go into the kitchen, will you? I'm terrified of her this morning."

The envelope was found at last behind the dining-room clock, though how it had got there Mrs. Sheridan could not imagine.

"One of you children must have stolen it out of my bag, because I remember vividly—cream cheese and lemon-curd. Have you done that?"

"Yes."

"Egg and—" Mrs. Sheridan held the envelope away from her. "It looks like mice. It can't be mice, can it?"

"Olive, pet," said Laura, looking over her shoulder.

"Yes, of course, olive. What a horrible combination it sounds. Egg and olive."

They were finished at last, and Laura took them off to the kitchen. She found Jose there pacifying the cook, who did not look at all terrifying.

"I have never seen such exquisite sandwiches," said Jose's rapturous voice. "How many kinds did you say there were, cook? Fifteen?"

"Fifteen, Miss Jose."

"Well, cook, I congratulate you."

Cook swept up crusts with the long sandwich knife, and smiled broadly.

"Godber's has come," announced Sadie, issuing out of the pantry. She had seen the man pass the window.

That meant the cream puffs had come. Godber's were famous for their cream puffs. Nobody ever thought of making them at home.

"Bring them in and put them on the table, my girl," ordered cook.

Sadie brought them in and went back to the door. Of course Laura and Jose were far too grown-up to really care about such things. All the same, they couldn't help agreeing that the puffs looked very attractive. Very. Cook began arranging them, shaking off the extra icing sugar.

"Don't they carry one back to all one's parties?" said Laura.

"I suppose they do," said practical Jose, who never liked to be carried back. "They look beautifully light and feathery, I must say."

"Have one each, my dears," said cook in her comfortable voice. "Yer ma won't know."

Oh, impossible. Fancy cream puffs so soon after breakfast. The very idea made one shudder. All the same, two minutes later Jose and Laura were licking their fingers with that absorbed inward look that comes only from whipped cream.

"Let's go into the garden, out by the back way," suggested Laura. "I want to see how the men are getting on with the marquee. They're such awfully nice men."

But the back door was blocked by cook, Sadie, Godber's man and Hans.

Something had happened.

"Tuk-tuk-tuk," clucked cook like an agitated hen. Sadie had her hand clapped to her cheek as though she had toothache. Hans' face was screwed up in the effort to understand. Only Godber's man seemed to be enjoying himself; it was his story.

"What's the matter? What's happened?"

"There's been a horrible accident," said cook. "A man killed."

"A man killed! Where? How? When?"

But Godber's man wasn't going to have his story snatched from under his very nose.

"Know those little cottages just below here, miss?" Know them? Of course, she knew them. "Well, there's a young chap living there, name of Scott, a carter. His horse shied at a traction-engine, corner of Hawke Street this morning, and he was thrown out on the back of his head. Killed."

"Dead." Laura stared at Godber's man.

"Dead when they picked him up," said Godber's man wtih relish. "They were taking the body home as I come up here." And he said to the cook, "He's left a wife and five little ones."

"Jose, come here." Laura caught hold of her sister's sleeve and dragged her through the kitchen to the other side of the green baize door. There she paused and leaned against it. "Jose!" she said, horrified, "however are we going to stop everything?"

"Stop everything, Laura!" cried Jose in astonishment. "What do you mean?"

"Stop the garden-party, of course." Why did Jose pretend?

But Jose was still more amazed. "Stop the garden-party? My dear Laura, don't be so absurd. Of course we can't do anything of the kind. Nobody expects us to. Don't be so extravagant."

"But we can't possibly have a garden-party with a man dead just outside the front gate."

That really was extravagant, for the little cottages were in a lane to themselves at the very bottom of a steep rise that led up to the house. A broad road ran between. True, they were far too near. They were the greatest possible eyesore, and they had no right to be in that neighbourhood at all. They were little mean dwellings painted a chocolate brown. In the garden patches there was nothing but cabbage stalks, sick hens and tomato cans. The very smoke coming out of their chimneys was poverty-stricken. Little rags and shreds of smoke, so unlike the great silvery plumes that uncurled from the Sheridans' chimneys. Washerwomen lived in the lane and sweeps and a cobbler, and a man whose house-front was studded all over with minute bird-cages. Children swarmed. When the Sheridans were little they were forbidden to set foot there because of the revolting language and of what they might catch. But since they were grown up, Laura and Laurie on the prowls sometimes walked through. It was disgusting and sordid. They came out with a shudder. But still one must go everywhere; one must see everything. So through they went.

"And just think of what the band would sound like to that poor woman," said Laura.

"Oh, Laura!" Jose began to be seriously annoyed. "If you're going to stop a band playing every time some one has an accident, you'll lead a very strenuous life. I'm every bit as sorry about it as you. I feel just as sympathetic." Her eyes hardened. She looked at her sister just as she used to when they were little and fighting together. "You won't bring a drunken workman back to life by being sentimental," she said softly.

"Drunk! Who said he was drunk?" Laura turned furiously on Jose. She said, just as they had used to say on those occasions, "I'm going straight up to tell mother."

"Do, dear," cooed Jose.

"Mother, can I come into your room?" Laura turned the big glass doorknob.

"Of course, child. Why, what's the matter? What's given you such a colour?" And Mrs. Sheridan turned round from her dressing-table. She was trying on a new hat.

"Mother, a man's been killed," began Laura.

"Not in the garden?" interrupted her mother.

"No, no!"

"Oh, what a fright you gave me!" Mrs. Sheridan sighed with relief, and took off the big hat and held it on her knees.

"But listen, mother," said Laura. Breathless, half-choking, she told the dreadful story. "Of course, we can't have our party, can we?" she pleaded. "The band and everybody arriving. They'd hear us, mother; they're nearly neighbours!"

To Laura's astonishment her mother behaved just like Jose; it was harder to bear because she seemed amused. She refused to take Laura seriously.

"But, my dear child, use your common sense. It's only by accident we've heard of it. If some one had died there normally—and I can't understand how they keep alive in those poky little holes—we should still be having our party, shouldn't we?"

Laura had to say "yes" to that, but she felt it was all wrong. She sat down on her mother's sofa and pinched the cushion frill.

"Mother, isn't it really terribly heartless of us?" she asked.

"Darling!" Mrs. Sheridan got up and came over to her, carrying the hat. Before Laura could stop her she had popped it on. "My child!" said her mother, "the hat is yours. It's made for you. It's much too young for me. I have never seen you look such a picture. Look at yourself!" And she held up her hand-mirror.

"But, mother," Laura began again. She couldn't look at herself; she turned aside.

This time Mrs. Sheridan lost patience just as Jose had done.

"You are being very absurd, Laura," she said coldly. "People like that don't expect sacrifices from us. And it's not very sympathetic to spoil everybody's enjoyment as you're doing now."

"I don't understand," said Laura, and she walked quickly out of the room into her own bedroom. There, quite by chance, the first thing she saw was this charming girl in the mirror, in her black hat trimmed with gold daisies, and a long black velvet ribbon. Never had she imagined she could look like that. Is mother right? she thought. And now she hoped her mother was right. Am I being extravagant? Perhaps it was extravagant. Just for a moment she had another glimpse of that poor woman and those little children, and the body, being carried into the house. But it all seemed blurred, unreal, like a picture in the newspaper. I'll remember it again after the party's over, she decided. And somehow that seemed quite the best plan. . . .

Lunch was over by half-past one. By half-past two they were all ready for the fray. The green-coated band had arrived and was established in a corner of the tennis-court.

"My dear!" trilled Kitty Maitland, "aren't they too like frogs for words? You ought to have arranged them round the pond with the conductor in the middle on a leaf."

Laurie arrived and hailed them on his way to dress. At the sight of him Laura remembered the accident again. She wanted to tell him. If Laurie agreed with the others, then it was bound to be all right. And she followed him into the hall.

"Laurie!"

"Hallo!" He was half-way upstairs, but when he turned round

and saw Laura he suddenly pulled out his cheeks and goggled his eyes at her. "My word, Laura! You do look stunning," said Laurie. "What an absolutely topping hat!"

Laura said faintly "Is it?" and smiled up at Laurie, and didn't tell him after all.

Soon after that people began coming in streams. The band struck up; the hired waiters ran from the house to the marquee. Wherever you looked there were couples strolling, bending to the flowers, greeting, moving on over the lawn. They were like bright birds that had alighted in the Sheridans' garden for this one afternoon, on their way to where? Ah, what happiness it is to be with people who all are happy, to press hands, press cheeks, smile into eyes.

"Darling Laura, how well you look!"

"What a becoming hat, child!"

"Laura, you look quite Spanish. I've never seen you look so striking."

And Laura, glowing, answered softly, "Have you had tea? Won't you have an ice? The passion-fruit ices really are rather special." She ran to her father and begged him. "Daddy darling, can't the band have something to drink?"

And the perfect afternoon slowly ripened, slowly faded, slowly its petals closed.

"Never a more delightful garden party . . ." "The greatest success . . ." "Quite the most . . ."

Laura helped her mother with the good-byes. They stood side by side in the porch till it was all over.

"All over, all over, thank heaven," said Mrs. Sheridan. "Round up the others, Laura. Let's go and have some fresh coffee. I'm exhausted. Yes, it's been very successful. But oh, these parties, these parties! Why will you children insist on giving parties!" And they all of them sat down in the deserted marquee.

"Have a sandwich, daddy dear. I wrote the flag."

"Thanks." Mr. Sheridan took a bite and the sandwich was gone. He took another. "I suppose you didn't hear of a beastly accident that happened to day?" he said.

"My dear," said Mrs. Sheridan, holding up her hand, "we did. It nearly ruined the party. Laura insisted we should put it off."

"Oh, mother!" Laura didn't want to be teased about it.

"It was a horrible affair all the same," said Mr. Sheridan. "The chap was married too. Lived just below in the lane, and leaves a wife and half a dozen kiddies, so they say."

An awkward little silence fell. Mrs. Sheridan fidgeted with her cup. Really, it was very tactless of father . . .

Suddenly she looked up. There on the table were all those sand-wiches, cakes, puffs, all uneaten, all going to be wasted. She had one of her brilliant ideas.

"I know," she said. "Let's make up a basket. Let's send that poor creature some of this perfectly good food. At any rate, it will be the greatest treat for the children. Don't you agree? And she's sure to have neighbors calling in and so on. What a point to have it all ready pre-pared. Laura." She jumped up. "Get me the big basket out of the stairs cupboard."

"But, mother, do you really think it's a good idea?" said Laura.

Again, how curious, she seemed to be different from them all. To take scraps from their party. Would the poor woman really like that?

"Of course! What's the matter with you to-day? An hour or two ago you were insisting on us being sympathetic, and now—"

Oh, well! Laura ran for the basket. It was filled, it was heaped by her mother.

"Take it yourself, darling," said she. "Run down just as you are. No. wait, take the arum lilies too. People of that class are so impressed by arum lilies."

"The stems will ruin her lace frock," said practical Jose.

So they would. Just in time. "Only the basket then. And, Laura!"— her mother followed her out of the marquee—"don't on any account—"

"What, mother?"

No, better not put such ideas into the child's head! "Nothing! Run along."

It was just growing dusky as Laura shut their garden gates. A big dog ran by like a shadow. The road gleamed white, and down below in the hollow the little cottages were in deep shade. How quiet it seemed after the afternoon. Here she was going down the hill to somewhere where a man lay dead, and she couldn't realize it. Why couldn't she? She stopped a minute. And it seemed to her that kisses, voices, tinkling, spoons, laughter, the smell of crushed grass were somehow inside her. She had no room for anything else. How strange! She looked up at the pale sky, and all she thought was, "Yes, it was the most successful party."

Now the broad road was crossed. The lane began, smoky and dark. Women in shawls and men's tweed caps hurried by. Men hung over the palings; the children played in the doorways. A low hum came from the mean little cottages. In some of them there was a flicker of light, and a shadow, crab-like, moved across the window. Laura bent her head and hurried on. She wished now she had put on a coat. How her frock shone! And the big hat with the velvet streamer—if only it was another hat! Were the people looking at her? They must be. It was a mistake to have come; she knew all along it was a mistake. Should she go back even now?

No, too late. This was the house. It must be. A dark knot of people stood outside. Beside the gate an old, old woman with a crutch sat in a chair, watching. She had her feet on a newspaper. The voices stopped as Laura drew near. The group parted. It was as though she was expected, as though they had known she was coming here.

Laura was terribly nervous. Tossing the velvet ribbon over her shoulder, she said to a woman standing by, "Is this Mrs. Scott's house?" and the woman, smiling queerly, said, "It is, my lass."

Oh, to be away from this! She actually said, "Help me, God," as she walked up the tiny path and knocked. To be away from those staring eyes, or to be covered up in anything, one of those women's shawls even. I'll just leave the basket and go, she decided. I shan't even wait for it to be emptied.

Then the door opened. A little woman in black showed in the gloom.

Laura said, "Are you Mrs. Scott?" But to her horror the woman answered, "Walk in please, miss," and she was shut in the passage.

"No," said Laura, "I don't want to come in. I only want to leave this basket. Mother sent—"

The little woman in the gloomy passage seemed not to have heard her. "Step this way, please, miss," she said in an oily voice, and Laura followed her.

She found herself in a wretched little low kitchen, lighted by a smoky lamp. There was a woman sitting before the fire.

"Em," said the little creature who had led her in. "Em! It's a young lady." She turned to Laura. She said meaningly, "I'm 'er sister, miss. You'll excuse 'er, won't you?"

"Oh, but of course!" said Laura. "Please, please don't disturb her. I—I only want to leave—"

But at that moment the woman at the fire turned round. Her face, puffed up, red, with swollen eyes and swollen lips, looked terrible. She seemed as though she couldn't understand why Laura was there. What did it mean? Why was this stranger standing in the kitchen with a basket? What was it all about? And the poor face puckered up again.

"All right, my dear," said the other. "I'll thenk the young lady."

And again she began, "You'll excuse her, miss, I'm sure," and her face, swollen too, tried an oily smile.

Laura only wanted to get out, to get away. She was back in the passage. The door opened. She walked straight through into the bedroom, where the dead man was lying.

"You'd like a look at 'im, wouldn't you?" said Em's sister, and she brushed past Laura over to the bed. "Don't be afraid, my lass,—" and now her voice sounded fond and sly, and fondly she drew down the sheet—" 'e looks a picture. There's nothing to show. Come along, my dear."

Laura came.

There lay a young man, fast asleep—sleeping so soundly, so deeply, that he was far, far away from them both. Oh, so remote, so peaceful. He was dreaming. Never wake him up again. His head was sunk in the pillow, his eyes were closed; they were blind under the closed eyelids. He was given up to his dream. What did garden-parties and baskets and lace frocks matter to him? He was far from all those things. He was wonderful, beautiful. While they were laughing and while the band was playing, this marvel had come to the lane. Happy . . . happy. . . . All is well, said that sleeping face. This is just as it should be. I am content.

But all the same you had to cry, and she couldn't go out of the room without saying something to him. Laura gave a loud childish sob.

"Forgive my hat," she said.

And this time she didn't wait for Em's sister. She found her way out of the door, down the path, past all those dark people. At the corner of the lane she met Laurie.

He stepped out of the shadow. "Is that you, Laura?"

"Yes."

"Mother was getting anxious. Was it all right?"

"Yes, quite. Oh, Laurie!" She took his arm, she pressed up against him.

"I say, you're not crying, are you?" asked her brother.

Laura shook her head. She was.

Laurie put his arm round her shoulder. "Don't cry," he said in his warm, loving voice. "Was it awful?"

"No," sobbed Laura. "It was simply marvellous. But, Laurie—" She stopped, she looked at her brother. "Isn't life," she stammered, "isn't life—" But what life was she couldn't explain. No matter. He quite understood.

"*Isn't* it, darling?" said Laurie.

STICKY MY FINGERS, FLEET MY FEET

Gene Williams

On September 11, 1965, Gene Williams' story about the football fantasies of a group of middle-aged men was published in The New Yorker magazine. A sophisticated satire, it leans heavily on verbal allusions and subtle wit. Time-Life Films released the twenty-three minute screen adaptation directed by John Hancock. The film was an Academy Award nominee in 1970.

Hancock's affinity for sports stories is evidenced by his direction of a feature film, Bang the Drums Slowly, based on a novel about baseball by Mark Harris.

Music and sound effects can be an important component of a film. The soundtrack of Sticky My Fingers, Fleet My Feet is especially effective.

"Will you ever mature?" my wife asked.

"I'm a *very* mature pass receiver," I said, lacing my sneakers. "Ask anybody who's tried to cover me."

She groaned and went back to Walter Lippmann. Nobody could want more in a wife; Marian is beautiful, witty, charming, and not a graduate of Sarah Lawrence. But touch football is over her head.

"Baby, exercise is a health-must," I said patiently. "Don't you realize guys die from vegetating?"

"I do the Canadian things and yoga and isometrics, so don't call me pro-vegetation. I'm tired all the time!" She was sort of screaming. Her nerves have really gone downhill since we married. "It's your attitude that bothers me. Play football—fine. Wonderful. But to keep a record of *every* pass you catch, *every* touchdown you score, *every*—"

"Now, you know the notebook is only a joke."

"It's a farce, but it's no joke! My God, if Erich Fromm saw one page of that thing—"

I muffled the rest of her words by putting on my sweatshirt as I went out the door. Outside, it was a clear, bright morning—perfect weather for spectacular pass-snatching. Early practice is very important. Championships that bloom in December are planted in September. Turning into the Park at Seventy-second Street, I trotted through the herds of old people who are pastured on the West Side. They really knock me out, because Allie Sherman and I dig resignation. As my sneakers padded lightly on the walk, pre-game excitement got to my ulcer. (Shofner has one, too.)

We use that shabby open stretch that runs from the high to the low Sixties, and the guys were already there. They'd marked off our field with a pile of sweaters, trash baskets, and an Air France bag. Seeing me, Marv called, "There's the sticky-fingered antelope! You ready to grab a few, Norm?"

"Always ready," I said. Marv works for Port Authority and has a fine arm. We hit for six or seven bombs a week.

I traded insults with the rest of the guys. All of them were veterans of our weekly games, except for one rookie—a scrawny kid of about fifteen, wearing a green sweater. Its cuffs hid his knuckles. George Crimblings, a blocking back from J. Walter Thompson, introduced us. "This is Wesley, my nephew," he said. "I thought we might lose some dilettantes to softball, so I brought him out."

"Glad to know you, sir," Wesley said. I looked at him, but he meant it. Rookies call Mike Ditka "sir," too.

George and I chose up. I took Marv, of course, and George was stuck with Wesley after all the others had been picked. Letting them receive, we all spread out as Marv put the ball on the kicking tee. My ulcer was begging for Maalox, but I didn't even wince, because Ray Berry and I dig pressure. When the going gets rough, the rough get going. Marv raised his arm, brought it down, took two steps toward the ball, stopped, and said, "Hell." A two-year-old boy had wandered onto the field.

"For God's sakes, get him out of here!" I yelled.

"Urry gurry burry," the kid answered, picking the ball off the tee. When we surrounded him, he lay down, hugging the ball, and started to cry. The sound brought his mother.

"Did you hit him?" she demanded.

"Make him give us our ball," I said.

Holding him while we pried the ball loose, she said, "Lester, be nice and return the children's toy."

Finally, we lined up again, and Marv got off the kick. Unfortunately, it went to Harry Gratzwald, who is fat, slow, awkward, and more feared than Jimmy Brown. I touched him, Jacob touched him, Marv touched him, *everybody* touched him, but he kept running. "We got you back here!" I called.

"No, you didn't," Harry answered and went all the way before coming back to argue. He is a lawyer. "You only got me one hand at a time and you have to get me both hands together or it's not a legal touch, and Jacob was offside and Marv was holding and . . ." We kicked again.

The show finally on the road, Marv and I dropped back in our special two-man rolling zone. I'm sensational on defense, even though my real gifts are offensive. Jacob was slapping our linemen on the tail, saying, "Big rush now! Really crash in there. Break their bones." Analysts make great line-backers. On the first play, he red-dogged and nailed them right in the middle of a triple reverse.

"Way to go, Jake baby!" I said. "Be manic."

They gained four inches on an end-around and then threw a buttonhook to Harry, who was wide open. He dropped the ball and yelled, "Interference!"

"Nobody was within ten yards of you," I said.

We gave them the down over, and they tried a flare pass that Jacob intercepted. The ball was ours and glory would be mine. In the huddle, Marv said, "O.K., men. Norm, run a down-and-out to the pile of sweaters; Jack, cut to the Air France bag. On two—*break!*"

I flanked to the left and found George on me. There was fear in his ad man's eyes. I gave him the big inside move and cut to the sweaters. Marv led me nicely, and it was a thirty-yard gain. On the next two plays, we ran sweeps while I lulled George with the same pattern.

"He's ripe," I said.

"Right. Long bomb to the trash basket," Marv said.

I glided out at three-quarter speed, head-faked, and broke deep. George never had a chance. Crossing the goal, I looked toward the Fifth Avenue buildings that rose above the trees. People with binoculars were probably crowding the windows. The team pounded my back. I shrugged and said, "Just lucky."

"Looks like it's your day," Marv said, and it was. Buttonhooks, slant-ins, down-and-outs—I murdered them. Finally, they really got desperate, and I flanked out to find Wesley on me. I gave him a friendly nod to show I'd go easy on him. Real pros win without shaming their opponents; always leave a guy part of his ego or he gets tougher defensively. I faked to the sideline and hooked back.

"Good fake, sir," Wesley said, after knocking the ball down.

In the huddle, Marv said, "He looks tough."

"Forget it, he's playing me much too tight. Anything deep will kill him."

This time, I gave Wesley the works—head fake, full pivot, innocent smile—and streaked downfield. I tagged him the minute he made the interception.

"My fault for not slanting in more," I lied to Marv.

"No, it was mine for not throwing sooner," he said truthfully.

As a reward for this lucky play, they shifted Wesley to tailback.

He waited for the snap from center, hauling at his sleeves to make his hands visible. The play was an easy end sweep and our linemen trapped him on the sideline, but he cut back toward his own goal, and the chase was on. It lasted a long, long time. Eventually, I collapsed beside Jacob, who was kneading a stitch in his side. We watched Wesley skitter. Finally, the whole team was too tired to chase him anymore, and he jogged over the goal unpursued. His teammates pounded his back. Wesley shrugged and said, "Just lucky." If there's anything I hate, it's phony modesty.

That play took the heart (and wind) out of everybody on our team except me. Jacob stood around rationalizing, and Marv's passing became hysterical; everything he threw to me Wesley intercepted or knocked down. We fell behind. I kept my cool, though. As Vince Lombardi says, it's last-quarter teams that win championships. One big play could salvage the game. After Wesley ran back a punt for his sixth touchdown, he made his mistake—leaving me alone on two straight plays while he covered somebody else.

"He's ripe," I said.

"For what—the Hall of Fame?" Marv said. Still, he called my big tide-turner—a delayed bomb to the trash basket.

Hesitating at the line, I studied my nails and faked tying my shoe-lace until Wesley broke toward the middle zone. Then I streaked down-field. Nobody was near me, and the pass was perfect. The pros' pro, old Stickyfingers, was in the clear! But I must have expected the flash of his green sweater in front of me, because the ball somehow ricocheted off my chest. It bounced to a stop about five yards away just as I jack-knifed into the trash basket.

There was laughter from both teams. It didn't surprise me. The world is full of fair-weather hypocrites. I didn't lose my poise, though, even while peeling a Mounds wrapper from my forehead. Unfortunately, it did hurt my credibility as a receiver. Marv started throwing to others and calling clown plays for me, like "O.K., Norm, go deep to the zoo and fall in the sea-lion pool." Also, I'd pulled a muscle in my leg.

The game broke up a while later, and Marv, the treacherous bastard, said to the kid, "Come out next week. I'd like to have you on my squad. We'd make a great combination." He shook his head in admiration. "You must run wild on your high-school team."

"Not hardly, sir," Wesley said. "I'm the manager."

The trip home was a limping retreat from Caporetto—only with fewer laughs. I'm no fool. You don't have to draw me a picture. Football belongs to the young, and I'm only a memory, like Jim Thorpe, Mel Hein, Otto Graham, and the rest. Around me, other old people sat on benches, waiting to die a little deader. A horse galloped along the bridle path on his way into a tube of glue or can of dog food. I knew it was over. Jack Armstrong, fat and getting bald, sat behind a desk waiting for a coronary; the Mounties had retired Sergeant Preston. Britt Reid and Kato, Lamont Cranston and the lovely Margo Lane—gone, all gone. Soon dirt would be shovelled in my face while the choir sang "Have you tried Wheaties?" in dirge tempo.

Climbing the stairs, I rested often, because of my leg and Marian. I was right "Oh God, this is exactly what I need—an immature cripple!" she yelled. "Is anything broken?"

"Nothing that would show on an X-ray. I'm washed up, baby." I picked up my notebook, heavy with touchdowns, yardage, and dreams, and threw it with all my elderly strength. It didn't even break anything.

"*That* was a healthy thing to do," Marian said.

She went into the bathroom, and there was the sound of water flooding into the tub. I sat down and massaged my ruined thigh; they should give Purple Hearts just for living. Then she practically dragged me from the living room and stuffed me into the hot water. I complained.

"Shut up and *soak!* I've about had it with you!" For a while, she just glared at me, with her teeth pretty well gritted. Then she sighed and said, "Nobody is in your class for immaturity. There you sit with your leg and ego crippled because of football—*you*, the best tennis player in the West Seventies."

"That's not true," I said. "You're just cheering me up."

"It *is* true, but you won't admit it. Your ground strokes are unbelievable." Her voice was much softer.

"That's not altogether true."

"Why do I try? You have no sense of proportion. Nobody else would waste that tennis leanness on body contact."

She left me, and I eased lower in the water. Marian was vicious but astute; football *is* immature. It belongs to kids like Wesley and would-be kids like Marv, Harry, and Jacob, who want to hide from adult responsibilities. They can't, though. A man grows up and stays grown; he can't go home again. My leg wasn't hurting quite so much, and I tried a few backhands with the soap. Rosewall uses the Continental grip, too.

chapter 6

Appendices

FILM AWARDS

The Bet (1967)

Golden Leaf Award, Hollywood International Film Festival
Cine Golden Eagle
Edinburgh and Venice Film Festivals

The Garden Party (1974)

American Film Festival Red Ribbon
San Francisco Special Jury Award
Chris Bronze Plaque, Columbus Film Festival
Silver Plaque Award, Chicago International Film Festival

The Lady or the Tiger (1969)

Golden Hugo, Chicago International Film Festival
Chris Statuette, Columbus Film Festival
Red Ribbon, American Film Festival

The Legend of Sleepy Hollow (1972)

Golden Hugo, Chicago International Film Festival
Jack London Award, National Educational Film Festival
Blue Ribbon Award, American Film Festival, EFLA
Bronze Medal, Atlanta Film Festival

The Masque of the Red Death (1970)

Silver Pelican, Mamaia Film Festival
Blue Ribbon Award, American Film Festival

An Occurrence at Owl Creek Bridge (1962)

Grand Prix, Cannes
Academy Award

The Open Window (1972)

Cine Golden Eagle
Gold Medal Special Jury Award, Atlanta Film Festival
Edinburgh Film Festival

Sticky My Fingers, Fleet My Feet (1970)

Academy Award Nominee
Cine Golden Eagle

A Time Out of War (1954)
"Pickets"

Academy Award
Silver Dolphin, Venice International Film Festival
British Film Academy Award
Best Student Film of the Decade Award, Screen Producers Guild

Young Goodman Brown (1972)

Special Jury Award and Gold Medal, Atlanta Film Festival
Cine Golden Eagle
Judges prize, Midwest Film Festival

BASIC DATA ON FILMS ADAPTED FROM STORIES IN THE TEXT

		Year	Length	Cost	Distributor
1. *Bartleby*	color	1969	28m	$359.00	EB
2. *The Bet*	color	1967	24m.	300.00	P
3. *Dr. Heidegger's Experiment*	color	1969	22m.	296.00	EB
4. *The Garden Party*	color	1974	24m.	325.00	ACI
5. *The Lady or the Tiger*	color	1969	16m.	232.50	EB
6. *The Legend of Sleepy Hollow*	color	1972	13m.	180.00	P
7. *The Lottery*	color	1969	18m.	265.00	EB
8. *The Masque of the Red Death*	color	1970	10m.	160.00	C
9. *An Occurrence at Owl Creek Bridge*	b/w	1962	27m.	250.00	C
10. *The Open Window*	color	1972	12m.	160.00	P
11. *Sticky My Fingers, Fleet My Feet*	color	1970	23m.	250.00	TL
12. *A Time Out of War* ("Pickets")	b/w	1954	22m.	200.00	P
13. *The Unicorn in the Garden*	color	1953	7m.	100.00	LCA
14. *The Upturned Face*	color	1973	10m.	150.00	P
15. *Young Goodman Brown*	color	1973	30m.	375.00	P

DISTRIBUTOR CODE

EB   Encyclopaedia Britannica Educational Corporation
P   Pyramid Films
ACI   ACI Films, Inc.
C   McGraw-Hill-Contemporary Films
TL   Time-Life Films, Inc.
LCA   Learning Corporation of America

FILM DISTRIBUTORS

1. ACI Films
(212) 582-1918
35 West 45th Street
New York, N.Y. 10036

2. Stephen Bosustow Productions
(213) 394-0218
1649 Eleventh Street
Santa Monica, Ca. 90404

3. Contemporary/McGraw-Hill
330 West 42nd Street
New York, N.Y. 10036

(609) 448-1700
Princeton Road
Hightstown, N.J. 08520

(312) 869-5010
828 Custer Avenue
Evanston, Illinois 60202

(415) 362-3115   1714 Stockton Street
                                                  San Francisco, Ca. 94133

4. Encyclopaedia Britannica   425 N. Michigan Avenue
   Educational Corporation   Chicago, Illinois 60611

5. Learning Corporation of America   1350 Avenue of the Americas
   (212) 751-4400   New York, N.Y. 10019

6. Pyramid Films   P. O. Box 1048
   (213) 828-7577   Santa Monica, Ca. 90406

7. Time-Life Films   4 West 16th Street
                                        New York, N.Y. 10011

SOME ADDITIONAL SHORT FILMS ADAPTED FROM FICTION— AND DISTRIBUTORS

The Bass Fiddle	Anton Chekhov	Contemporary/McGraw-Hill
Chickamauga (1961)	Ambrose Bierce	Contemporary/McGraw-Hill
The Nose (1963)	Nikolai Gogol	Contemporary/McGraw-Hill
The Crocodile (1973)	Feodor Dostoevsky	Encyclopaedia Britannica
My Old Man (1969)	Ernest Hemingway	Encyclopaedia Britannica
The Secret Sharer (1973)	Joseph Conrad	Encyclopaedia Britannica
The Family That Dwelt Apart	E. B. White	Learning Corp. of America
The Tell-Tale Heart (animated)	Edgar Allan Poe	Learning Corp. of America
Bezhin Meadow (1935)	Ivan Turgenev	Macmillan Audio-Brandon
The Mockingbird (1966)	Ambrose Bierce	34 MacQuesten Pkwy. S.
Silent Snow, Secret Snow (1966)	Conrad Aiken	Mt. Vernon, N. Y. 10550
The Man and the Snake (1972)	Ambrose Bierce	Pyramid Films
The Juggler of Notre Dame (1968, "Our Lady's Juggler")	Anatole France	Pyramid Films
The Lightning-Rod Man (1975)	Herman Melville	Pyramid Films
The Selfish Giant (1972)	Oscar Wilde	Pyramid Films
The Doll's House	Katherine Mansfield	S-L Film Productions 5126 Hartwick St. Los Angeles, Ca. 90041
The Tell-Tale Heart (live action, 1973)	Edgar Allan Poe	Time-Life Films

A Glossary of
Film Terms

ADAPTATION: the process by which a literary work such as a novel, play, poem, or short story is made into a motion picture.

ALTERNATION OF SHOTS: a cinematic technique whereby two or more lines of plot development are juxtaposed in an alternating pattern of shots. For example, a director could show the heroine tied to the railroad tracks followed by a shot of the approaching train. Then, he could cut to the hero riding to her rescue and then cut back to shots of the struggling heroine and the approaching train. This technique is also known as cross-cutting or parallel editing. In the early days of film history, D. W. Griffith created what came to be known as "Griffith chases" in order to heighten the dramatic impact of the events. See CROSS CUTTING.

ANIMATION: the process of arranging drawings or objects so that they can be filmed one frame at a time. When projected, they produce the illusion of movement. An animator can work directly on the film instead of photographing each frame. Norman McLaren of the National Film Board of Canada has experimented with "camera-less" animation.

AUTEUR THEORY: a film theory that places a central controlling intelligence, usually the director's, at the core of a body of films. Critics using such a theory seek out cinematic characteristics common to the entire canon of a director's work.

433

BACKLIGHTING: a method of lighting designed to produce a soft romantic effect. Backlighting an actress' hair produces a halo effect.

CAMERA EYE SHOT: the most conventional method of shooting a film, in which the camera appears to record objective reality. The camera is like a neutral, third-person observer, the counterpart of the omniscient author in fiction.

CINEMA-VERITE: a style of filmmaking which de-emphasizes technical equipment and concentrates on the spontaneous use of a hand-held 16mm camera in order to suggest unrehearsed reality.

CLOSE SHOT: a distance shot that focuses on a limited space such as the head and shoulders of a performer.

CLOSE-UP: a distance shot that emphasizes a small area such as the head of an actor.

CONTINUITY: editors will match sequential shots to insure a smooth transition from image to image.

CONTINUITY EDITING: a style of editing that emphasizes a sequential pattern of development in time and place. See also DYNAMIC EDITING, and MONTAGE (RELATIONAL EDITING).

CONVENTIONS: tacit understandings between filmmakers and film viewers which establish the usual limitations of the medium. In early silent films, filmgoers expected to see eye-level shots of actors; they did not expect to see a close-up of a head cut off by the limits of the frame. Modern audiences accept an off-screen voice and infer the presence of a speaker. Sophisticated contemporary audiences accept the jarring discontinuity of space or time in the jump cut. For example, in *The Graduate,* Ben turns over on his pool float and the director cuts to Ben rolling over onto Mrs. Robinson in their hotel room. Originally, a fade or dissolve was the transition to a flashback or dream sequence; today, directors cut directly to a flashback, dream, or other interpolated sequence. In cinematic history, today's innovations are tomorrow's conventions.

CRANE: a mechanical device holding the cameraman and his equipment. It can move flexibly in many directions, allowing the camera to follow the action. It permits a director to add the external movement of the camera to any internal movement within the shot.

CROSS CUTTING: an editing technique that juxtaposes more than one line of film action. See ALTERNATION OF SHOTS.

CUT: the basic transition between two separate shots. One screen image is instantaneously replaced by another image.

DEEP FOCUS: a camera technique that simultaneously makes people and objects in the background of a shot as clearly focused as people or objects in the foreground of the shot. The most famous example occurs in *Citizen Kane.*

DISSOLVE: a technique in which one screen image slowly fades from the screen while simultaneously a new image appears and finally takes over the screen. For a brief time, both images co-exist. The dissolve is a transition that suggests a relationship between the two images. Also, see SUPERIMPOSED SHOT.

DOLLY: a wheeled vehicle that permits the camera to move with the action being photographed. Originally, a dolly moved on tracks to insure a smooth and steady shot.

DYNAMIC EDITING: a method of editing in which shots and sequences are juxtaposed for effects other than story continuity. The unities of time and space become subservient to a more complex mosaic of shots. The film viewer must supply the connections linking the discontinuous screen images. For contrast, see CONTINUITY EDITING.

EDITING: the basic skill of filmmaking: pulling together into a meaningful order the multipicity of disparate individual shots that make up a motion picture. Editorial functions include decisions on length of shots, order of shots, optical effects, soundtracks, etc. In the majority of films discussed in this book, the editorial function was closely linked to the directorial function.

ESTABLISHING SHOT: an extremely long shot that usually comes at the beginning of a sequence; it is designed to establish the context and geographical locale for the shots to follow.

EXTREME CLOSE-UP: a detailed shot focusing on a very small area. In *The Lottery,* there are extreme close-ups of Bill Hutchinson's eye and of clenched fingers gripping slips of paper. The shot is often used to underline the significance of a particular detail.

EXTREME LONG SHOT: often a panoramic shot, it shows relationship between an actor and his social or geographical context.

EYE LEVEL SHOT: the height from which the camera conventionally photographs the action (5–6 feet).

FADE-IN: an optical technique in which the screen gradually goes from dark to light and the image becomes clear.

FADE-OUT: an optical technique in which the image on screen gradually goes from light to dark until the image disappears. The director can control the speed of a fade-in or fade-out.

An Occurrence at Owl Creek Bridge (1962) Spatial editing implies a hierarchy of importance. In the vastness of nature, man's bridges and man himself are trivialized by the filmmaker's extreme long shot. In contrast, Bierce's short story opens with the focus on Peyton Farquhar. *Still shot reproduced courtesy of Contemporary/McGraw-Hill Films.*

FAST MOTION: an acceleration of the images which is achieved by photographing the action at a slower speed than normal and projecting it at a normal rate. This technique is often used for comic effect. In the early days of film, it was popularized by the Keystone Cops.

FILM CONTINUITY: the process of matching successive shots so each sequential image seems to be a logical continuation in space and time of the preceding shot.

FILM TRANSITIONS: the various means by which a shot may be linked to the preceding and succeeding shots. Basic film transitions include cuts, fades, and dissolves.

FLASHBACK: a shot or sequence that takes place at a time period earlier than the surrounding shots and sequences. While the film medium necessarily shows flashbacks in the present tense, they are understood by the audience to represent past action.

FLASH CUTS: an editing technique for minimizing the length of time a shot is on screen. The technique is used in *The Bet* when brief shots of the girl and the boat appear and disappear rapidly near the end of the film. In this instance, they are clues to the protagonist's thought processes.

FLASH FORWARD: the opposite of a flashback. The shot represents future action despite the fact it is occurring on screen in the present tense. A flash forward is often a subjective shot as perceived by a character imagining the future.

FRAME: the smallest fixed unit of film. Motion pictures are projected at a rate of 24 frames per second in standard projection. A frame in film can be compared to a word in language. Like the word in a sentence, a frame in a shot takes its meaning from its context.

FREEZE: a single, unmoving image. See FREEZE FRAME.

FREEZE FRAME: when a single frame of film is photographed and repeated again and again at the standard rate of projection, the image seems to be frozen in place, like a still photograph. A freeze frame is frequently used at the end of a movie, allowing the image to remain on screen while the final credits are shown. Examples of freeze frames occur in *The Open Window, An Occurrence at Owl Creek Bridge,* and *The Lottery.*

FULL SHOT: a shot that includes the entire figure of a person within the limits of the screen.

GRIFFITH CHASE: a series of alternating shots designed to intensify the dramatic impact of the film. See ALTERNATION OF SHOTS.

HIGH-ANGLE SHOT: a shot in which the camera is located above the height of the actor and shoots downward. The effect is to diminish the stature of the person being photographed.

HIGH-KEY LIGHTING: a lighting technique that produces very bright illumination. It is often used for light comedy.

IRIS-IN: an optical method in which an image begins to appear on screen as a tiny circle of light which quickly enlarges until the entire picture is visible.

IRIS-OUT: an optical method of removing an image from the screen. The image is seen through a circular opening which quickly gets smaller and smaller until the picture is entirely obliterated.

JUMP CUT: a cut that results in the viewer being disoriented because the film's continuity has been abruptly shattered, usually by an unex-

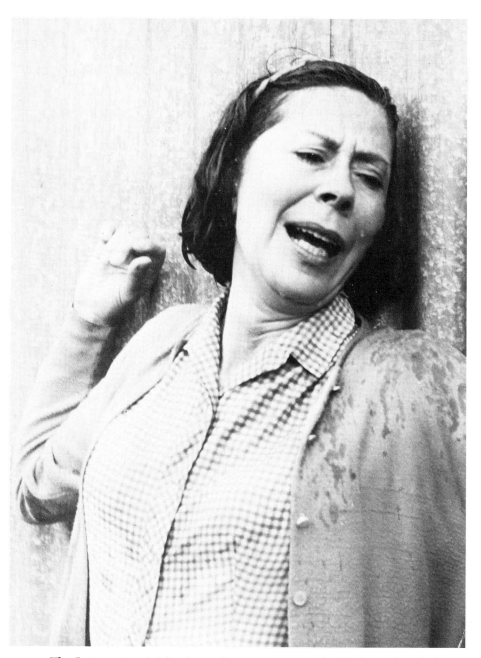

The Lottery (1969) The freeze frame serves as a kind of visual underlining. It accentuates the importance of the final shot. In "The Lottery," the short story concludes, ". . . and then they were upon her." The film freeze captures the horror by freezing on Tessie's fear-filled face. *Still shot reproduced courtesy of Encyclopaedia Britannica Educational Corporation.*

Bartleby (1969) A long shot includes "not only the character or characters being photographed but much of their immediate setting as well." In this way, the filmmaker establishes relationships. *Still shot reproduced courtesy of Encyclopaedia Britannica Educational Corporation.*

pected shift in time or place. The two screen images separated by a jump cut seem to be unrelated to each other and the abrupt transition gives the viewer little time to regain his equilibrium.

LONG SHOT: a distance shot that includes not only the character or characters being photographed but much of their immediate setting as well.

LOW-ANGLE SHOT: a shot taken with the camera below the height of the person, object, or action being photographed and shooting upward. This technique makes a character seem larger, more dominant, and sometimes more menacing. A slight low-angle shot of the "hero" makes him seem worthy of respect.

LOW-KEY LIGHTING: a technique of lighting that results in less illumination and produces more shadows; it is often used in scenes of dramatic tension.

MEDIUM SHOT: a distance shot showing a person from about the waist up.

MONTAGE: (1) the juxtaposing of disparate shots which creates an impression different from the effect of any one shot alone. In the opening sequence of Charlie Chaplin's *Modern Times,* the shots of sheep are followed by shots of workers behaving much like the sheep. (2) an editing technique of combining a rapid series of shots to establish a mood or tone. In *An Occurrence at Owl Creek Bridge,* the director cuts to a series of shots focusing on one leaf on a branch, a black centipede crawling across the leaf, a blade of grass with gem-like droplets of dew on it, and a highlighted image of a spider creating a web. Cumulatively, the shots delineate the marvelously detailed world of nature, a world not normally observed, but very carefully noted by someone whose zest for living stems from his nearness to death. (3) an editing technique using superimposed shots to convey an idea or a concept. For example, in *The Masque of the Red Death,* the swinging pendulum symbolizing death is superimposed over the devastated countryside in one scene and over the figure of Prospero later in the film.

OBJECTIVE SHOT: an apparently realistic shot as seen from the point of view of a detached and neutral observer. See CAMERA EYE SHOT.

OMNISCIENT POINT OF VIEW: a literary term denoting the ability of a "voice" or "persona" in a story to tell readers what every character thinks, sees, feels, and does. Sometimes, the term "omniscient author" is used, implying that the "persona" speaking in the story represents the author himself. The film equivalent would be the omniscient camera or CAMERA EYE SHOT.

OPTICALS: a technical term to refer to cinematic effects such as fades, dissolves, iris shots, etc.

OVER-THE-SHOULDER SHOT: a shot often used to photograph two characters engaged in conversation. The camera photographs one person from behind or over the shoulder of the other. The audience sees the character facing the camera as he speaks or reacts to the words of the other character.

PAN: the side to side, horizontal movement of the camera as it rotates approximately parallel to the ground.

PARALLEL EDITING: an editing technique for alternating two or more plot lines occurring in the same time period but at different places by juxtaposing shots and scenes. See also GRIFFITH CHASE.

PERSISTENCE OF VISION: a physiological phenomenon that permits the eye to retain an image for a fractional part of a second after the source of the image has disappeared. When a film unreels at twenty-four frames per second, the dark space between frames is not seen by the eye because the image from frame one persists until it is replaced by the image from frame two, etc. Thus, the discrete frames of a shot seem to produce a moving picture. If the film were projected at a slower speed, the images would begin to flicker.

POINT OF VIEW: a literary and cinematic term to denote the specific way in which a reader or viewer receives information. In fiction, a story may be told by a first person narrator within the story or a third person outside the story. In film, an audience sees images subjectively as they are perceived by a character in the film, or objectively as perceived by a presumably neutral camera.

REACTION SHOT: a shot depicting the effect of a screen image or sound upon a character in the film. A common directorial technique which stimulates the curiosity of the viewer is to show a character's reaction before cutting to the stimulus provoking the response. An alternative technique allows the audience to experience the stimulus first and then observe the reaction of the character. Film has been described as less a medium of action than a medium of reaction.

RELATIONAL EDITING: See MONTAGE.

SCENARIO: the plot of a film organized in scenes and sequences. It is usually more detailed than a treatment but less specific than a shooting script.

SCENE: a short segment of a film usually composed of several shots linked together by a common action, setting, or dramatic situation. It is analogous to a paragraph in fiction. The word has different meanings when applied to a play.

SCREENPLAY: a written blueprint for a film containing descriptions of the actions and setting as well as the dialogue in the sequential order intended in the final film. It may be the work of a writer or the joint product of a writer and director.

SEQUENCE: an organized segment of a film; it contains a group of scenes linked by significant dramatic unity. If compared to a play, it is roughly analogous to an act; if compared to a novel, it is analogous to a chapter.

SHOOTING SCRIPT: the final written description of the film prior to the actual shooting. It includes everything in the screenplay, and in addition, the individual shots are described in detail and the transitions between shots noted. Even though a shooting script is more detailed than a screenplay, the two terms are sometimes used interchangeably.

SHOT: the uninterrupted length of film from the moment the camera begins to run until it stops. Shots may range from less than a second in length to much longer units of time. *An Occurrence at Owl Creek Bridge*, which runs for 27 minutes, has slightly less than one hundred fifty shots. A shot is roughly analogous to a sentence in fiction.

SHOT ANALYSIS: a detailed, written analysis of each shot in the final form of the released film. It comes as close as a verbal description can to recreating the visual experience.

SILENT FILM SPEED: silent films were photographed and projected at a rate of sixteen frames per second. See STANDARD FILM SPEED.

SLOW MOTION: by photographing the action at a more rapid speed than normal and projecting it at a normal rate, the effect on screen is a slowing down of the action. Slow motion has frequently been used to suggest a "poetic" mood, as evidenced by its use in TV commercials. In *The Open Window*, an imaginative director uses slow motion for slapstick comedy. In contrast, note the functions of slow motion in *An Occurrence at Owl Creek Bridge* and *Sticky My Fingers, Fleet My Feet*.

SOFT FOCUS: the technique of using a slightly out-of-focus camera, or shooting through vaseline, to produce a hazy effect. For older actors or actresses, the technique can be flattering.

SOUND TRACK: the band along the side of the film; it carries the music, dialogue, and sound effects that accompany the visual images.

STANDARD FILM SPEED: the rate at which sound films are photographed and projected: twenty-four frames per second.

STILL: (1) a photograph of a single frame from a movie. (2) a picture taken on the set by a still photographer and usually used for publicity purposes.

STORYBOARD: a sequence of drawings or sketches, usually with captions, which shows both the visual and audio continuity of film. See, for example, the storyboard of *The Legend of Sleepy Hollow* which presents the visuals and the voice-over narration.

SUBJECTIVE POINT OF VIEW: a shot as seen through the eyes of one of the film's characters. Compare with OBJECTIVE SHOT.

SUPERIMPOSED SHOT (SUPER): an optical technique for showing two images on screen at the same time. See DISSOLVE.

SWISH PAN: a rapid horizontal camera movement that produces a blurred image because of the speed of the camera's movement.

THREE-SHOT: a shot that shows three actors at once. In distance, it is usually a medium shot.

TILT: a vertical or diagonal movement of the camera.

TRACKING SHOT: a shot in which the camera moves to the action. In early studios, the dolly holding the camera was mounted on tracks to insure steady movement. See also DOLLY.

TREATMENT: a preliminary verbal description, usually rather short, of a forthcoming film. See the treatments for *The Legend of Sleepy Hollow*.

TWO-SHOT: a shot that shows two actors at once. In distance, it usually ranges from a close to a medium shot.

UNDER-LIGHTING: a method of lighting from below that produces shadows and usually creates a sinister effect.

VOICE-OVER: an off-screen voice that accompanies the film visuals.

ZOOM SHOT: a technique by which the cameraman can shift distances, i.e. from long shot to close-up, by means of a lens adjustment rather than moving the camera.

Selected Bibliography

AGEE, JAMES. *Agee on Film: Five Film Scripts.* Boston: Beacon Press, 1964.

ARNHEIM, RUDOLPH. *Art and Visual Perception.* Berkeley: University of California Press, 1954.

———. *Film As Art.* Berkeley: University of California Press, 1957.

BALÁZS, BÉLA. *Theory of the Film.* New York: Roy Publishers, 1953.

BARRETT, GERALD R. and ERSKINE, THOMAS L. *From Fiction to Film: Conrad Aiken's "Silent Snow, Secret Snow."* Encino: Dickenson Pub. Co., 1972.

———. *From Fiction to Film: Ambrose Bierce's "An Occurrence at Owl Creek Bridge."* Encino: Dickenson Pub. Co., 1973.

———. *From Fiction to Film: D. H. Lawrence's "The Rocking-Horse Winner."* Encino: Dickenson Pub. Co., 1974.

BAZIN, ANDRÉ. *What is Cinema?* Berkeley: University of California Press, 1967.

BENOÎT-LEVY, JEAN. *The Art of the Motion Picture.* New York: Coward-McCann and Geoghegan, 1946.

BLUESTONE, GEORGE. *Novels Into Film.* Berkeley: University of California Press, 1957.

BOBKER, LEE. *Elements of Film.* New York: Harcourt Brace Jovanovich, 1969.

CASTY, ALAN HOWARD. *The Dramatic Art of Film,* New York: Harper & Row, 1970.

CLAIR, RENÉ. *Reflections on the Cinema.* London: Kimber, 1953.

COSTELLO, DONALD P. *The Serpent's Eye.* South Bend: Notre Dame Press, 1967.

DAVY, CHARLES. *Footnotes to the Film.* New York: Oxford University Press, 1937.

DURGNAT, RAYMOND. *Films and Feelings.* London: Faber and Faber, 1967.

EISENSTEIN, SERGEI M. *Film Form and the Film Sense.* New York: Meridian Books, 1957.

FISCHER, EDWARD. *Screen Arts.* New York: Sheed and Ward, 1960.

FULTON, ALBERT R. *Motion Pictures.* Norman: University of Oklahoma Press, 1960.

GESSNER, ROBERT. *The Moving Image.* New York: E. P. Dutton & Co., 1970.

HALL, STUART. *Film Teaching.* London: British Film Institute, 1964.

HARRINGTON, JOHN. *The Rhetoric of Film.* New York: Holt, Rinehart & Winston, 1973.

HODGKINSON, ANTHONY W. *Screen Education: Teaching a Critical Approach to Cinema and Television.* Paris: UNESCO Publications, 1964.

HUSS, ROY, and SILVERSTEIN, NORMAN. *The Film Experience.* New York: Harper & Row, 1968.

JACOBS, LEWIS. *Introduction to the Art of the Movies.* New York: Farrar, Straus and Giroux, 1960.

———. *The Movies As Medium.* New York: Farrar, Straus & Giroux, 1970.

JINKS, WILLIAM. *The Celluloid Literature.* Beverly Hills: Glencoe Press, 1971.

KATZ, JOHN STUART. *Perspectives on the Study of Film.* Boston: Little, Brown and Co., 1971.

KRACAUER, SIEGFRIED. *Theory of Film.* New York: Oxford University Press, 1960.

KUHNS, WILLIAM and STANLEY, ROBERT. *Exploring the Film.* Dayton: George A. Pflaum, 1968.

LAWSON, JOHN HOWARD. *Film: The Creative Process.* New York: Hill and Wang, 1964.

LINDEN, GEORGE W. *Reflections on the Screen.* Belmont: Wadsworth Pub. Co., 1970.

LINDGREN, ERNEST. *The Art of the Film.* New York: Macmillan Co., 1963.

LINDSAY, VACHEL. *The Art of the Moving Picture.* New York: Macmillan Co., 1922.

MacCANN, RICHARD DYER. *Film: A Montage of Theories.* New York: E. P. Dutton & Co., 1966.

MADDOX, RACHEL et. al. *Fiction Into Film.* New York: Delta Books, 1972.

MALLERY, DAVID. *School and the Art of Motion Pictures.* Boston: National Association of Independent Schools, 1966.

MARCUS, FRED H. *Film and Literature: Contrasts in Media.* Scranton: Intext Educational Publishers, 1971.

MAYNARD, RICHARD A. *The Celluloid Curriculum.* New York: Hayden Book Co., 1971.

McLUHAN, MARSHALL. *Understanding Media: The Extensions of Man.* New York: McGraw-Hill, 1964.

NICHOLS, DUDLEY. "The Writer and the Film." *Twenty Best Film Plays,* edited by John Gassner and Dudley Nichols. New York: Crown Publishers, 1943.

NICOLL, ALLARDYCE. *Film and Theatre.* New York: Crowell Co., 1936.

PETERS, J. M. L. *Teaching About the Film.* Paris: UNESCO Publications, 1961.

POTEET, G. HOWARD. *The Compleat Guide to Film Study.* Urbana: National Council of Teachers of English, 1971.

PUDOVKIN, V. I. *Film Technique and Film Acting.* New York: Crown Pubs., 1949.

REISZ, KAREL. *The Technique of Film Editing.* New York: Hastings House Pubs., 1968.

RICHARDSON, ROBERT. *Literature and Film.* Bloomington: Indiana University Press, 1969.

ROBINSON, W. R., and GARRETT, GEORGE. *Man and the Movies.* Baton Rouge: Louisiana State University Press, 1961.

SCHILLACI, ANTHONY, and CULKIN, JOHN. *Films Deliver.* New York: Citation Press, 1970.

SHERIDAN, MARION C. et al. *The Motion Picture and the Teaching of English.* New York: Appleton-Century-Crofts, 1965.

SOLOMON, STANLEY J. *The Film Idea.* New York: Harcourt Brace Jovanovich, 1972.

SPOTTISWOODE, RAYMOND. *Film and Its Technique.* Berkeley: University of California Press, 1966.

———. *A Grammar of the Film.* Berkeley: University of California Press, 1962.

STEPHENSON, RAPLH, and DEBRIX, J. R. *Cinema As Art.* Baltimore: Penguin Books, 1965.

STEWART, DAVID C. *Film Study in Higher Education.* Washington: American Council on Education, 1966.

SULLIVAN, SISTER BEDE. *Movies: The Universal Language.* South Bend: Fides Pub., 1967.

TALBOT, DANIEL. *Film: An Anthology.* Berkeley: University of California Press, 1966.

WARSHOW, ROBERT. *The Immediate Experience.* New York: Doubleday & Co., 1964.

WHATTON, W. VICTOR. *The Uses of Film in the Teaching of English.* Toronto: The Ontario Institute for Studies in Education, 1971.

WHITAKER, ROD. *The Language of Film.* Englewood Cliffs: Prentice-Hall, 1970.

WOLLEN, PETER. *Signs and Meaning in the Cinema.* Bloomington: Indiana University Press, 1969.

YOUNGBLOOD, GENE. *Expanded Cinema.* New York: E. P. Dutton & Co., 1970.